COWLES FOUNDATION
FOR RESEARCH IN ECONOMICS
AT YALE UNIVERSITY

MONOGRAPH 22

COWLES FOUNDATION

For Research in Economics at Yale University

The Cowles Foundation for Research in Economics at Yale University, established as an activity of the Department of Economics in 1955, has as its purpose the conduct and encouragement of research in economics, finance, commerce, industry, and technology, including problems of the organization of these activities. The Cowles Foundation seeks to foster the development of logical, mathematical, and statistical methods of analysis for application in economics and related social sciences. The professional research staff are, as a rule, faculty members with appointments and teaching responsibilities in the Department of Economics and other departments.

The Cowles Foundation continues the work of the Cowles Commission for Research in Economics founded in 1932 by Alfred Cowles at Colorado Springs, Colorado. The Commission moved to Chicago in 1939 and was affiliated with the University of Chicago until 1955. In 1955 the professional research staff of the Commission accepted appointments at Yale and, along with other members of the Yale Department of Economics, formed the research staff of the newly established Cowles Foundation.

A list of Cowles Foundation Monographs appears at the end of this volume.

Economic Theory of Teams

Jacob Marschak and Roy Radner

New Haven and London, Yale University Press

Designed by John O. C. McCrillis
and set in Times Roman type.
Printed in the United States of America by
The Murray Printing Co., Westford, Massachusetts.

Published in Great Britain, Europe, Africa, and Asia (except Japan)
by Yale University Press, Ltd., London.
Distributed in Latin America by Kaiman & Polon, Inc., New York City;
in Australia and New Zealand by Book & Film Services,
Artarmon, N.S.W., Australia; in Japan by John Weatherhill, Inc., Tokyo.

Contents

Preface

Actions performed in an organization differ, in general, from those of a single person in two respects.

First, the kind of information on the basis of which each member of an organization decides about his actions may differ from one member to another. Thus the production manager and the personnel manager of a company do not completely share information, nor do the commanders of two divisions of the same army.

Second, the interests and beliefs of each member of an organization may differ from the interests and beliefs of his fellow members.

A team is defined as an organization in which the first but not the second characteristic is present. The authors feel that the study of this intermediate case is useful as a step toward a fuller and more complex economic theory of organization.

The members of a team have the same interests and beliefs but do not share the same information. We can also regard the team problem as that facing an organizer. How should the tasks of inquiring, communicating, and deciding be allocated among the members of an organization so as to achieve results that would be best from the point of view of their common interests and beliefs, or of those of the organizer?

Accordingly, the bulk of the present book is concerned with economic, that is, optimal, efficient ways of providing information and of allocating it among the decision-makers who constitute a team: optimal, that is, with respect to common interests and beliefs. This is preceded by a Prologue dealing with the still simpler problem, that of a single person's optimal choice of information. An Epilogue points to a fuller theory of organization, in which the concept of optimality is appropriately revised.

The book was started while both authors were on the staff of the Cowles Commission for Research in Economics at the University of Chicago (later Cowles Foundation at Yale University). Some of the earlier ideas were discussed in various Papers (reprints) and mimeographed Discussion Papers of that organization, both by the authors and by their colleagues, notably Martin Beckmann, Donald Bratton, Karl Faxen, C. B. McGuire, Leo Tornqvist, A. Tritter, and Daniel

Waterman. At a later stage, individual chapters of the book were read and commented upon by John Harsanyi, Thomas Marschak, Kenneth MacCrimmon, C. B. McGuire, Sandra Schwartz, and Lloyd Shapley; Truman Bewley and Reinhard Selten did the same for the entire manuscript. We acknowledge our debt to them, and also to Leo Hurwicz, Koichi Miyasawa, L. J. Savage, and Herbert Simon for many fruitful discussions.

At various times, the authors were able to use the facilities of the Cowles Commission (Foundation) at Chicago and Yale, and of the Center for Research in Management Science and the Western Management Science Institute on the Berkeley and the Los Angeles campuses, respectively, of the University of California. The support provided by the Office of Naval Research, the Ford Foundation, and the National Science Foundation is gratefully acknowledged.

Finally, our thanks to Miss Barbara Ellis for her editorial contributions, and to Mrs. Julia Rubalcava for her customarily beautiful job of typing the manuscript.

J.M.
R.R.

ECONOMIC THEORY OF TEAMS

Introduction

Economics is concerned with efficient ("best," "optimal") use of limited resources. A decision is "economical" if, among available decisions, it is the most desirable one. During the last two or three decades, explicitly economic thinking has been extended beyond its traditional domain, that of the production and distribution of marketable goods. The same general principles that are used to determine efficient sites and production plans for factories and farms, to explain the prices agreed upon by presumably efficient buyers and sellers, or to outline plans for the material development of a country have been applied to broader fields of human decisions and of interactions between men.

The economic concern, the interest in optimal choices, has of course characterized practical arts such as engineering, military planning, and medicine from their very inception. In our generation, this concern has become articulate. Under names such as operations research, cost-efficiency analysis, systems analysis, mathematical programming—clumsy, casual names suggesting their origin in practice rather than in philosophy—complex decision problems are being stated explicitly as such. That is to say, both the constraints of feasibility (limited resources, set of available actions) and the criteria of desirability (ordering of preferences, goals, values) are stated, opening the way to a systematic solution of some maximization problem.

Parallel with these practical developments, economic thinking has also penetrated the very foundations of empirical science. The current logic of inductive inference developed by logicians and mathematicians—notably F. P. Ramsey (1931), B. de Finetti (1937), R. Carnap (1962), and L. J. Savage (1954)—has related a man's "beliefs" about the "probabilities" of uncertain events to his choices between actions that have uncertain outcomes and are viewed as "bets." Moreover, the decision-maker's beliefs will vary depending on his access to information, and his choice of action can be improved by changing his instrument of information. For example, suppose that the results of each possible experiment (or a sampling, a survey) will be used to choose the best possible action; which is then the best possible experiment? Such problems have occupied

3

workers in statistics—beginning with J. Neyman and E. S. Pearson (1928 to 1938) and A. Wald (1950)—and in "adaptive control processes," so called by R. Bellman (1961). In essence, decision theory can be called the "economics of information."

The economic approach has been applied not only to efficient choices of a single person, but also to joint actions of several men. In the theory of games of von Neumann and Morgenstern (1943), further developed by other mathematicians and economists, two or more persons follow generally different desirability criteria ("interests," "preferences"), and are constrained by different feasibility conditions ("rules of the game") or at least attach to them different probabilities; but each player is efficient in a well-defined sense. The problem is to find which arrangements exist (if any) that would be supported by each player's self-interest as he sees it, because no change that he might be able to enforce would better him. Such arrangements, if attained, would be maintained. They are called viable. In this sense, viability can be regarded as a generalization of the optimality requirement, extended from decision-making by a single person to the case of several persons. Corresponding to the choice of the best information instrument, and of the best action based on the information it provides, the viable arrangement between players of a game is implemented by allocating to each certain activities, possibly including the tasks of gathering or communicating specified kinds of information. Viewed in this way, the problem of viable arrangements in games can be conveniently called a theory of efficient organizations. The problem of the optimal information instrument and the optimal decision for a single person can then be regarded as a special (though by no means trivial) case.

The economic theory of teams attacks a middle ground. We study the case in which several persons perform various tasks including those of gathering and communicating information and of making decisions; but they have common, not divergent, interests and beliefs. Hence the optimality requirement is easily defined, just as in the case of a single person. But the single person's problem of optimizing his information instrument and its use is replaced by that of optimizing the allocation of tasks among the members of the team.

We have equated *economical* and *efficient* to denote an arrangement that is most desirable (or, in the general case of organization, one that is viable), under given feasibility constraints. These constraints include the limitations of human capacities for communication and good decision-making (and analogous limitations of inanimate instruments). While our concern is a practical, purposive, prescriptive one, the general solutions we discuss would depend, when applied to any concrete case, on data supplied by workers in descriptive fields—the names of R. Cyert, J. March, and H. Simon come to mind![1]—psychological or sociological data along with those of natural technology. On the other hand, our results may prove of some value to descriptive theorists of human organization by pointing to those data, quantitative and otherwise, that would be of most importance if one wanted to increase the efficiency of a given organization.

Part One of this book, the Prologue, prepares the ground for the theory of teams by discussing the case in which the team consists of one man. Chapter 1 defines his tastes and beliefs, under the condition that he is consistent in the sense of obeying the rules of logic and certain plausible, quasi-logical postulates of decision behavior.

These conditions imply the "expected utility theorem," which is then used throughout the book. Chapter 2 outlines what we have called above the economics of information: the problem of choosing an optimal information instrument. Chapter 3 provides simple illustrations.

In the central Part Two of the book, the team problem is first simplified into the problem of optimal *information structure*: we ask "who should know what?", without inquiring how this allocation of information is achieved. We proceed from some simple illustrative examples in Chapter 4 to the problem, treated in Chapter 5, of finding optimal decision rules for the team members when the information structure is given. In Chapter 6, various important information structures are compared as to the maximum expected payoffs that they can yield. In most of the cases studied in the book, a "static" environment is assumed, but Chapter 7 outlines an approach to the case in which the environment is a process over time, and in which delays intervening between information and decision may, under certain conditions, result in losses.

A given information structure can be generated by a variety of "networks." Each element of a network is characterized by a "task function" transforming the element's inputs into its outputs. The task may be one of observing the environment, of making a decision, of communicating messages about the environment or the decisions, or of performing "final actions" that impinge upon the environment and thus affect the payoff to the team. A network is "implemented" by associating a set of its elements with a physically defined "instrument"—possibly a team member— thus allocating tasks among individuals. Chapter 8 defines the study of networks and analyzes a few simple examples of phenomena that are usually denoted by terms such as coordination, subordination, and so forth. The usual vocabulary is, however, less rich than the variety

1. See, for example, Cyert and March 1963 and March and Simon 1958.

of possible network configurations. The authors regret not having been able to pursue a systematic study of such configurations, to compare the (gross) payoffs they can yield under given payoff and environment conditions, and to attempt, whenever possible, an intuitive interpretation of such results. This is somewhat foreshadowed by the examples given in Chapter 8. It is followed, in Chapter 9, by a rather informal outline of the problems of costs and constraints that must be taken into account when choosing among networks, and thus allocating tasks, optimally. This choice is in itself a complex decision problem; we suppose that it is being solved by an "organizer," a fictitious construct possibly implemented in a physically identifiable "leader" or a leading group of team members. The logic of solving complex problems involves difficult paradoxes, which we meet in an empirical fashion, showing that it may be economical to ignore some information and to treat logical alternatives as if they were so many states of the physical environment. This chapter applies certain previously developed concepts—such as delegation, specialization, and postponement of decision—to the task of organizing.

In Part Three, the Epilogue, we take up again the theme of this Introduction: to specify the place of the economic theory of teams within the general perspective of the problem of efficient organization, and its relation to descriptive theories.

PART ONE
PROLOGUE: SINGLE-PERSON
DECISION PROBLEMS

CHAPTER 1

Decision under Uncertainty

1. TEAMS

We define an *organization* as a group of persons whose actions (decisions) agree with certain rules that further their common interests. We define a *team* as an organization the members of which have only common interests. We are going to discuss an *economic* theory of teams.

We have just used such terms as "interests," "rules," and "economic" but have not yet defined them. If we first confine our attention to a simple case, the one-man team (that is, a *single decision-maker*), we shall be able not only to present convenient definitions of those terms, but also to introduce some other important aspects of the economic theory of teams. Most of the complications that arise from the presence of several persons in a team will be postponed until Part Two of the book.

2. ECONOMIC BEHAVIOR

It is usual to define economic behavior as the *best use of limited alternatives*. In practice, economists confine their study more particularly to the use of limited alternatives in producing and consuming so-called commodities, or goods and services, assumed to be divisible into small physical units. Yet the best use of limited alternatives is also the subject of disciplines such as military and political science. We use the adjective *economic* in the title of our book in its more general sense, and some of our results should be applicable outside the economics of commodities.

It so happens, however, that our concern with the best use of available alternatives (resources) finds its clearest expression when we are dealing with divisible commodities. This divisibility permits the extensive use of continuous real variables; under certain conditions prevailing in our culture (and some others), market prices of goods and services can be

9

used to express the complex results of many actions in the form of a single continuous quantity such as monetary profit. Accordingly, our general ideas will often be most simply illustrated by examples taken from the special domain of commodities and money. The business firm will often furnish the most convenient example of a team concerned with the best use of its alternatives. However, the reader should remain aware that, even in a business firm, decisions on indivisible things (site of plant, appointment of executives, methods of financing) play an important role.

3. CONSISTENT TASTES UNDER CERTAINTY

If the criterion of what the individual considers "good" were not in some sense fixed, making his decisions "consistent," it would not be ascertainable whether a good use is or is not made of available alternatives, and the word *economic* would therefore be meaningless. Consistency of decisions can be defined operationally and can be ascertained from the chooser's actions, not merely from his verbal statements, in the following convenient way.

First, we shall say that a given decision-maker desires the alternative *a* more than *b* (and *b* less than *a*)—or *prefers a to b*—if he never chooses *b* when *a* is available; second, we shall say that he desires *a* and *b* equally— or is *indifferent between a* and *b*—if from sets of alternatives containing both *a* and *b* he sometimes chooses *a*, sometimes *b*. It follows that his preferences are complete: he is either indifferent between any *a* and *b* or he prefers one of them. Finally, we say he is *consistent under certainty* if his preferences are transitive; that is, if, whenever he desires *a* not less than *b*, and *b* not less than *c*, he desires *a* not less than *c*.

It follows that it is possible to rank all alternatives that can ever face a given consistent man in a unique order of desirabilities (also called order of utilities, or preference order), with the understanding that equally desirable alternatives have equal rank (a tie). We can describe a given consistent man's *interests* (or tastes) by his particular ordering of alternatives.[1]

1. Our definition of preference is based on observing actions ("he has chosen *a* when *b* was available"), rather than on recording verbal statements ("he has said, 'I prefer *a* to *b*' "). It can be presumed that future choices are better predicted from actual past choices than from past verbal statements using an undefined term ("I prefer").

Moreover, our definition is based on a person's "multiple choices," i.e., on choices made from any number—not necessarily a pair—of alternatives. If we wanted to predict a multiple choice from our knowledge of a person's past choices from pairs only, we should need an additional, independent assumption, such as Arrow's (1963) principle of "independence of irrelevant alternatives." With our definitions, this principle need not be assumed independently. If a consistent man prefers *a* to *b* in our sense, he will never choose *b* when *a* is available, regardless of whether a third alternative, *c*, is or is not available.

4. DESCRIPTION VS. NORM

If taken literally, the above definition of consistency is no doubt too strong to describe real men. The word "never" in the definition of desirability should be replaced by "very seldom," lest the majority of people be classified either as indifferent among almost all alternatives or as inconsistent. Accordingly, and in agreement with some practices of empirical psychology, a more general approach has been offered. This describes a man's choice in terms of the probability that, when offered a given set of alternatives, he will choose a particular one; so that, for example, "indifference between a and b" is defined as a 50-50 chance of choosing a out of the pair (a, b).[2] We shall not pursue this approach here. Instead we shall assume that departures from consistency, as defined, are not serious enough to make consistency useless as an approximate description of some people and as an attainable norm for all. Following Ramsey (1931), one can regard the theory of consistent choice as a branch of logic, a normative discipline. The theory of consistent choice may be related to actual choices as is ordinary logic—the logic of thought—to the psychology of thought.[3] But just as the logic of thought is a guide and first approximation to the psychology of thought, so is the logic of choice a guide to the study of actual decision.

This twofold use of theory, as an approximate description and as a system of prescriptions or norms, is quite common to all disciplines bearing on practice. Economics offers theories descriptive of human responses (to price changes, for example), as well as policies for statesmen and businessmen. Military science has produced war histories as well as army manuals. Medicine describes sick men and has the ideal of a healthy man. Consistency of choice is a possible norm of human behavior, and it is *the* economic norm; but because it also serves as an approximate description of reality, this norm is not completely inapplicable. As we proceed to develop the consistency concept, the reader should keep in mind this double orientation of our book.[4] The team concept itself will be seen to play this double role: to say that a firm is a team of executives is not only to approximate reality; it also establishes a useful norm, desired by the organizer.

2. Luce 1959; J. Marschak 1960; Luce and Suppes 1965. In a more recent alternative approach (Fishburn 1970), the indifference relation is not assumed transitive.

3. Abelson and Rosenberg (1958) have shown how logical rules can be replaced by those of a "psycho-logic." See also Bruner, Goodnow, and Austin 1956.

4. With respect to the subject matter of the present chapter, this double orientation is well represented in Edwards and Tversky 1967.

5. Actions and Outcomes

So far we have considered only one kind of action: choosing among available alternatives. Here the action and its result coincide: each can be identified with the alternative chosen. In a more general case, it is useful to distinguish between an action a and its result (outcome), $r = \rho(a)$, and to call ρ the outcome function.[5] Thus a_1 and a_2 (two values of the variable a) may be two methods of production, and $r_1 = \rho(a_1), r_2 = \rho(a_2)$ the respective money profits. There is a preference ordering on sums of money: if r_1 and r_2 were available directly, the larger one would be chosen. But it is the actions, not the sums of money, that are available for choice. In subsequent sections, it will prove useful to define preference ordering on outcomes as a special case of preference ordering on actions.

We shall use interchangeably the words *decision* and *action*, and the words *result* and *outcome*, sometimes called *consequence*.

6. Environment and Uncertainty

The same action can result in different outcomes, depending on factors not controlled by the decision-makers. These factors can be denoted by a variable, x, called *nature*, *environment*, or *the external world*. We have thus to rewrite the outcome function: $r = \rho(x, a)$. In general, the value of x is not known to the decision-maker in advance, and therefore the result r of the action a is not known even if the outcome function ρ is known. We say that there is uncertainty about the variable x, and therefore also about the variable r, given a.

For example, suppose that a firm producing for a competitive market is about to set the level of production for the coming month, but is uncertain about the price that will prevail during that month. If a denotes the amount produced, x the price, and $\kappa(a)$ the cost of producing an amount a, then the resulting profit to the firm is given by the outcome function

$$\rho(x, a) = xa - \kappa(a).$$

Here the action variable is the quantity a, and the state of the environment is described by the price x.

What if there is uncertainty about the outcome function itself, as well as about the state of the environment? This difficulty can always be overcome by describing the possible states of the environment in sufficiently great detail. With reference again to the production example, the firm may not know which of several cost functions will actually apply—

5. As far as possible, we shall use Greek letters for functions and the corresponding Latin letter for the values of the functions.

for example, because of the possibility of technological improvements. If we denote the various possible alternative cost functions by κ_1, κ_2, and so forth, then we can describe the state of the environment by the price p *and* the number n corresponding to the true cost function. The appropriate outcome function is now

$$\rho(p, n; a) = pa - \kappa_n(a);$$

the form of the function is once again certain, although the variables p and n describing the state of the environment are not. The environment variable x is now a vector: $x = (p, n)$.

Let us denote by X the set of all possible states of the environment, and let R be the set of results. Every action a determines a function, say $\mathbf{f}_a$, from X to R, namely,

(6.1a) $$\mathbf{f}_a(x) \equiv \rho(x, a).$$

Conversely, every function $\mathbf{f}$ from X to R can be thought of as being generated by an "action," say $a_\mathbf{f}$, with the outcome function defined by

(6.1b) $$\rho(x, a_\mathbf{f}) = \mathbf{f}(x).$$

From an abstract point of view, the function $\mathbf{f}_a$ tells us all we need to know about the action a; if two actions, say a and b, determine the same outcome in each state of the environment, then we have no real need to distinguish them. Thus, for our theory, two actions are essentially equivalent if

(6.2) $$\rho(x, a) = \rho(x, b) \qquad \text{for all } x \text{ in } X,$$

or, in the notation of (6.1a), if

(6.3) $$\mathbf{f}_a(x) = \mathbf{f}_b(x) \qquad \text{for all } x \text{ in } X.$$

Following Savage (1954), we shall call a function $\mathbf{f}$ from X to R an *act*. Dealing with *acts*, rather than with *actions* and an *outcome function*, has the advantages of conceptual economy and of focusing attention on the important point that the essential thing to know about an action is not its "name," but its consequences under alternative states of the environment. Nevertheless, in this book we shall retain the concepts of "action" and "outcome function" as we have introduced them above, since they correspond more closely to the everyday connotations of the words.

The concept of *act* does help us to define what we mean by *the set of all conceivable actions*; by this last we shall mean either the set of all acts (i.e., the set of all functions from X to R), or some suitable index set for the set of all acts. This set will be denoted by A.

In any given decision situation, typically not all *conceivable* actions will be feasible. Therefore a *feasible subset* of A will have to be indicated.

Up to this point, then, our decision problem is characterized by a set X of alternative states (of the environment) x, a set R of alternative outcomes r, the set A of conceivable actions a, and an outcome function ρ from $X \times A$ to R, which specifies the outcome resulting from each state-action pair,

$$(6.4) \qquad\qquad\qquad r = \rho(x, a).$$

7. CONSISTENT BELIEFS AND TASTES UNDER UNCERTAINTY

Formally, one might maintain the original definition of consistency—even after introducing uncertainty. One might simply say that a consistent man has a preference ordering on his actions, and not inquire into the reasons underlying this ordering, just as the economist does not inquire into the reasons for a man's preferring pickles to olives. This approach, taken, for example, by Debreu (1959), will not suffice for the purposes of this book.

To study concrete problems of decision under uncertainty, it will prove useful to define not only consistent interests ("tastes"), but also consistent "beliefs." A decision-maker is said to have consistent tastes if he can rank the alternative choices confronting him in accordance with his *preferences*. Under uncertainty, each of these alternatives is an action resulting in several possible outcomes depending on the environment. A decision-maker is said to have consistent beliefs if he can rank future alternative events (sets of states of environment) according to his views of their comparative *probabilities*. Moreover, we require a consistent decision-maker to be free of both "wishful thinking" and "persecution mania"; that is, his ranking of the probabilities of events should not depend on whether a given event will result in a more or a less desirable outcome of a given action.

We shall also require that the decision-maker's preferences among actions under uncertainty and his preferences among outcomes under certainty be consistent. Roughly speaking, let a and b be two actions such that the outcome $\rho(x, a)$ is preferred to the outcome $\rho(x, b)$ for every state x; then we shall require that action a be preferred to action b. This requirement, together with those assumptions needed to give it a precise meaning, goes a long way toward structuring the decision-maker's preferences among actions.

Finally, we shall require that our decision-maker obey the rules of logic.

We shall show in outline that, under fairly general conditions, these properties of a consistent decision-maker imply that he "maximizes expected utility," in the following sense.[6] The preference ranks that he assigns to alternative outcomes can be replaced by numbers called utilities; and the probability ranks that he assigns to alternative events can be replaced by numbers called subjective probabilities. These numbers retain the same respective orderings as the ranks they have replaced; but, unlike mere ranks, utilities and subjective probabilities can be meaningfully added and multiplied. Moreover, subjective probabilities obey the usual rules of the probability calculus. The expected utility of an action under uncertainty is defined to be the average of the utilities of its several possible outcomes, each weighted by the probability of the event under which that outcome will obtain. The expected utility of an action under certainty is then, of course, identical with the utility of its (unique) outcome. The ordering of actions by expected utilities will be shown to be identical to their ordering by preference. Therefore, since the action chosen is that with the highest preference rank, it will also be the one with the highest expected utility.

The given preferences among actions will be denoted by the symbol $\precsim_A$, so that

$$a \precsim_A b$$

is to be read "action a is not preferred to action b."

By an *event* we shall mean any set of states, that is, any subset of X. Suppose that the set R of alternative outcomes is finite, so that R consists of the N alternative outcomes $r_1, \ldots, r_N$. For any action a, let $Z_i(a)$ denote the set of states x such that

$$\rho(x, a) = r_i;$$

in other words, $Z_i(a)$ is the event "action a has outcome r_i."

In the remainder of this chapter, we shall discuss the representation of the preference ordering $\precsim_A$ of actions by means of two "auxiliary" numerical functions: a function π on the events, called the *subjective probability function*, and a function v on R, called the utility function. The *expected utility* $\Omega(a)$ for a given action a is defined by

$$(7.1) \qquad\qquad \Omega(a) = \sum_{i=1}^{N} v(r_i)\pi[Z_i(a)].$$

6. See also Luce and Suppes 1965; J. Marschak 1968; and numerous references given in Fishburn 1968.

The expected utility function Ω is said to *represent* the preference ordering $\underset{A}{\precsim}$ if for all actions a and b in A

(7.2) $a \underset{A}{\precsim} b$ if and only if $\Omega(a) \leq \Omega(b)$.

Our concern will be to show that, under certain plausible conditions, a preference ordering can thus be represented, and to explain how the probability and utility functions can be measured in any particular case. Although our discussion will fall short of being completely rigorous, we shall go into some detail to expose the logical structure of the problem.

We have already mentioned that we shall require the consistent decision-maker to display a certain independence between his tastes and his beliefs. One can distinguish three aspects of this independence. They can be associated, respectively, with the possibility of defining:

1. Conditional preferences among actions, given events,
2. An ordering of outcomes according to preference, independent of the states in which they occur,
3. An ordering of states according to probability, independent of the outcomes with which they are associated.

PREFERENCES AMONG ACTIONS

Consider a given event Z, and consider any two actions, a' and b', that result in the same consequences outside Z (i.e., when Z does not happen). That is,

(7.3) $\rho(x, a') = \rho(x, b')$ for x not in Z.

This is illustrated by the first two rows of Table 1.1a, where the four states $x_1, \ldots, x_4$ are divided into two disjoint events Z and $\bar{Z}$, and the entries in the body of the table indicate the outcomes. Thus, for example, $\rho(x_2, b') = s_2'$. To fix the ideas still further, the entries in Table 1.1b are dollar amounts, the state x_i is *candidate i will be elected*, and the actions are bets.

The first independence condition states that the preference ordering of two such actions should be independent of their (common) outcomes outside Z. Formally, let a'' and b'' (as in Table 1.1) be two other actions such that

(7.4) $\left.\begin{array}{l} \rho(x, a'') = \rho(x, a') \\ \rho(x, b'') = \rho(x, b') \end{array}\right\}$ for $x \in Z$,

$\rho(x, a'') = \rho(x, b'')$ for $x \notin Z$.

TABLE 1.1a

Events States	Z		$\bar{Z}$	
	x_1	x_2	x_3	x_4
Actions				
a'	r'_1	r'_2	r'_3	r'_4
b'	s'_1	s'_2	r'_3	r'_4
a''	r'_1	r'_2	r''_1	r''_2
b''	s'_1	s'_2	r''_1	r''_2

TABLE 1.1b

	Z		$\bar{Z}$	
	x_1	x_2	x_3	x_4
a'	-3	8	-5	7
b'	-1	6	-5	7
a''	-3	8	4	-9
b''	-1	6	4	-9

The pairs (a', b') and (a'', b'') will now be considered separately, each as a different feasible subset of the set A of all conceivable actions.

INDEPENDENCE CONDITION 1: CONDITIONAL PREFERENCES IN ONE EVENT ARE INDEPENDENT OF CONSEQUENCES IN OTHER EVENTS. *For a', a'', b', and b'', satisfying (7.3) and (7.4),*

$$a' \precsim_A b' \quad \text{if and only if} \quad a'' \precsim_A b''.$$

Notice that a'' and b'' can be thought of as obtained from a' and b' by modifying their common outcomes outside Z. Independence Condition 1 states that, as long as these outcomes remain common to both actions, such modifications should not affect the choice between actions.

Independence Condition 1 makes it possible to define conditional preferences among actions. Consider any two actions, a and b, and any event Z; construct two other actions a' and b' such that (as in Table 1.2), if Z happens, then a' has the same outcomes as a, and b' has the same outcomes as b; but, if Z does not happen, then a' and b' have common outcomes:

(7.5)
$$\left. \begin{array}{l} \rho(x, a) = \rho(x, a') \\ \rho(x, b) = \rho(x, b') \end{array} \right\} \quad \text{for } x \in Z,$$

$$\rho(x, a') = \rho(x, b') \quad \text{for } x \notin Z.$$

We define

$$a \precsim_A b \quad \text{given } Z$$

to mean

$$a' \precsim_A b'.$$

The situation described by (7.5) is illustrated by Table 1.2. Independence Condition 1 guarantees that, for fixed a and b, the ordering of any pair a' and b' will be the same, provided that a' and b' satisfy (7.5). In other words, Independence Condition 1 guarantees that the definition of conditional preference just given does not depend upon the particular choice of a' and b' that satisfies (7.5).

TABLE 1.2a

Events States	Z		$\bar{Z}$	
Actions	x_1 x_2		x_3 x_4	
a	r_1	r_2	r_3	r_4
b	s_1	s_2	s_3	s_4
a'	r_1	r_2	t_3	t_4
b'	s_1	s_2	t_3	t_4

TABLE 1.2b

	Z		$\bar{Z}$	
	x_1 x_2		x_3 x_4	
a	-3	8	-5	7
b	-1	6	4	-9
a'	-3	8	1	-2
b'	-1	6	1	-2

An important consequence of Independence Condition 1 is what we shall call the Sure-Thing Theorem for Conditional Preferences.[7] Before proceeding to a discussion of this principle, we make a few definitions.

First, in the realm of notation, we define

$$\text{``}a \sim b\text{'' to mean ``}a \precsim b \text{ and } b \precsim a\text{''}$$

$$\text{``}a \prec b\text{'' to mean ``}a \precsim b \text{ but not } b \precsim a.\text{''}$$

The first is to be read "a is equivalent to b," and the second, "b is strictly preferred to a." The second could also be written "$b \succ a$."

Second, by a *partition* of X we shall mean a collection of events $Z_1, \ldots, Z_n$ such that

every state x is in some event Z_j; and

no state x is in two *different* events Z_j and Z_k.

We are now in a position to state the following theorem:

SURE-THING THEOREM FOR CONDITIONAL PREFERENCES. *Let* $\{Z_i\}$, $i = 1, \ldots, n$ *be a partition of* X, *and let* a *and* b *be two actions.*

(i) *If, for every* i, $a \underset{A}{\precsim} b$ *given* Z_i, *then* $a \underset{A}{\precsim} b$.

(ii) *If, further,* $a \underset{A}{\prec} b$ *given* Z_j *for some* j, *then* $a \prec b$.

An immediate consequence of condition (i) is:

(iii) *If, for every* i, $a \underset{A}{\sim} b$ *given* Z_i, *then* $a \underset{A}{\sim} b$.

---

7. The term *sure-thing principle* was introduced by Savage (1954). We elaborate somewhat on Savage's presentation by formally distinguishing two theorems, as will be seen shortly.

We shall not give a complete proof that this proposition follows from complete ordering of actions and Independence Condition 1, but only illustrate the proof by an example. The extension to a general proof will, we hope, be obvious. Consider the situation described by Table 1.3, with four states, and a partition of the states into two events.

		TABLE 1.3a			
Events		Z_1		Z_2	
States		x_1 x_2		x_3 x_4	
Actions					
	a	r_1 r_2		r_3 r_4	
	b	s_1 s_2		s_3 s_4	

	TABLE 1.3b			
	Z_1		Z_2	
	x_1 x_2		x_3 x_4	
a	-3 8		-5 7	
b	-1 6		4 -9	

Suppose that [as in condition (i) above], $a \underset{A}{\precsim} b$ given Z_1, and $a \underset{A}{\precsim} b$ given Z_2. To show that $a \underset{A}{\precsim} b$, we construct a third action, c, which we can show to be between a and b, with respect to preference, as displayed in Table 1.4.

	TABLE 1.4a			
	Z_1		Z_2	
	x_1 x_2	x_3	x_4	
a	r_1 r_2	r_3	r_4	
c	s_1 s_2	r_3	r_4	
b	s_1 s_2	s_3	s_4	

	TABLE 1.4b			
	Z_1		Z_2	
	x_1 x_2	x_3	x_4	
a	-3 8	-5	7	
c	-1 6	-5	7	
b	-1 6	4	-9	

By the definition of conditional preference, $a \underset{A}{\precsim} c$, since $a \underset{A}{\precsim} b$ given Z_1. Similarly, $c \underset{A}{\precsim} b$, since $a \underset{A}{\precsim} b$ given Z_2. Hence, by the transitivity of preferences, $a \underset{A}{\precsim} b$.

Independence Condition 1, together with certain continuity assumptions, already implies the possibility of representing the preference ordering $\underset{A}{\precsim}$ by a numerical function of a rather special form,[8] namely,

$$\Omega^*(a) = \sum_x v^*[x, \rho(x, a)].$$

The two additional independence conditions to be discussed have the further implication that v^* can be expressed in the form

$$v^*(x, r) = \phi(x)v(r).$$

8. Apply Theorem 3 of Debreu 1960. In addition to certain regularity conditions, the application of this theorem requires that X be finite and have at least three states.

PREFERENCES AMONG OUTCOMES

We shall now consider the case in which an event Z consists of a single state x. Thus $Z = \{x\}$. The conditional ordering of actions given the event $\{x\}$ defines a conditional ordering of outcomes r given the event $\{x\}$, since an action (a function from the set of states to the set of outcomes) results in a unique outcome for any given state. We can express the conditional ordering of outcomes r and s given $\{x\}$ by writing

$$r \underset{R}{\precsim} s \quad \text{given } \{x\}$$

whenever $r = \rho(x, a)$, $s = \rho(x, b)$ and

$$a \underset{A}{\precsim} b \quad \text{given } \{x\}.$$

The second independence condition states that these conditional orderings of outcomes should be identical.[9]

INDEPENDENCE CONDITION 2: TASTES ARE INDEPENDENT OF BELIEFS. *The conditional ordering of outcomes given $\{x\}$ is independent of x.*

By virtue of this second independence condition, the ordering $\underset{A}{\precsim}$ of actions induces a unique ordering of outcomes, which we shall denote by $\underset{R}{\precsim}$. The ordering may be interpreted as the ordering of outcomes under certainty.

An immediate consequence of Independence Condition 2 and the Sure-Thing Theorem for Conditional Preferences is the following:

SURE-THING THEOREM FOR OUTCOMES. *If for every state x in X*

$$\rho(x, a) \underset{R}{\precsim} \rho(x, b),$$

then $a \underset{A}{\precsim} b.$

Another interpretation of "preferences among outcomes under certainty" arises from the consideration of "constant actions," that is, actions that have the same outcome for all states. If actions a and b are such that

$$\rho(x, a) = r \qquad \text{for all } x$$

$$\rho(x, b) = s \qquad \text{for all } x,$$

and if $a \underset{A}{\precsim} b$, then it seems reasonable to say that outcome r is not preferred to outcome s (under certainty). The Second Independence Condition

---

9. The statement given here is actually a little simpler than is desirable; see the fine print at the end of this section.

(and the Sure-Thing Theorem for Outcomes) tell us, in effect, that this latter ordering of outcomes is identical with the ordering given by conditional preferences.

The third independence condition will be introduced in connection with the concept of subjective probability.

There may be events Z such that the decision-maker is (conditionally) indifferent among *all* actions given Z; this would be the case if he regarded the event Z as impossible. Such an event would have the property that modifying the consequence of any action for states in Z would not affect the preference ordering of the action. Of course, we could assume that there are no such events for the decision-maker in question; if there were, the corresponding states could be eliminated from the description of X. However, for technical reasons it is sometimes convenient to allow such events in the theory.

Formally, we define an event Z to be *null* if for all actions a and b,

$$a \underset{A}{\sim} b \qquad \text{given } Z;$$

a state x is said to be null if the event $\{x\}$ is null. Independence Condition 2 should now be modified by adding the phrase "for all nonnull x."

If X is infinite but not denumerable, then a slightly more general statement is required, in which one defines conditional orderings of outcomes given (any) events; the Second Independence Condition then would read: The conditional ordering of outcomes given Z is independent of Z, for all nonnull events Z.

8. SUBJECTIVE PROBABILITY ORDERINGS

To give an idea of the reasoning that establishes the existence of numerical subjective probabilities, we consider first a farmer who must choose between two actions. Action a consists in planting a crop that thrives only in a wet summer (event W); action a^* is to plant another crop, which requires low humidity (event non-W, denoted by $\overline{W}$). Suppose the success of either crop is equally desirable: for example, let success mean in both cases the same large money gain. Similarly, let the desirability of failure of either crop be the same, failure consisting in both cases of a certain small money gain, or a loss, as in Table 1.5.

TABLE 1.5

Events Actions	W	$\overline{W}$
a	$1000	−$ 200
a^*	−$ 200	$1000

It is consistent with ordinary usage to say that the farmer's comparison of probabilities of the two events is revealed by his preference ordering of the two actions. For, if he prefers to plant the wet crop (action *a*), we usually say that he believes a wet summer (event *W*) to be more probable than a dry summer (event $\overline{W}$). More generally, in Table 1.6a, let *Y* and $\overline{Y}$

TABLE 1.6a

	W	$\overline{W}$		*Y*	$\overline{Y}$		*Z*	$\overline{Z}$
a	$1000	−$200	*b*	$1000	−$200	*c*	$1000	−$200

be another pair of exhaustive and mutually exclusive events. For example, *Y* may be: "a certain presidential candidate is elected." Let *b* denote an action (a bet) that will yield $1000 if *Y* occurs, and −$200 otherwise. Similarly, let *c* be still another bet, with the same outcomes ($1000 and −$200), but this bet depends on whether the event *Z* occurs. For example, *Z* may be: "the next card drawn from this deck will be a spade." When the decision-maker prefers action *a* to action *b* (i.e., he bets, with the same amounts at stake, on event *W* rather than on event *Y*), it is usual to say that, to him, *W* seems to be more probable than *Y*. Now if he prefers *a* to *b* and *b* to *c*, and is consistent, he will prefer *a* to *c*. Hence, if, to a consistent man, *W* seems more probable than *Y*, and *Y* than *Z*; then, to him, *W* seems more probable than *Z*—the ordering of the probabilities of these events having been defined, so far, with respect to a particular pair ($1000, −$200) of outcomes. Thus the transitivity of preferences among actions has induced the transitivity of probabilities of events with respect to the particular pair of outcomes.

It has been pointed out (Drèze 1960 and 1961) that the choices between bets such as those in Table 1.6a do not always make a comparison between probabilities of the corresponding events possible. For example, let *Y* = "your favorite candidate is elected" and *Z* = "the next card is a spade." Then the payoffs entered for *Y* and $\overline{Y}$ should be not "$1000" and "−$200," respectively, but rather "$1000 and the victory of your candidate" (which is better than $1000) and "−$200 and the defeat of your candidate" (which is worse than just the loss of $200). In the language of F. P. Ramsey (1931), event *Y* is "ethically non-neutral." The payoffs of bet *b*, as entered in Table 1.6, are, then, not the same as those of bet *c*; and your preference between *b* and *c* does not reveal whether you judge *Y* more probable or less probable than event *Z*. However (as suggested by T. Marschak), you can correct the entries in Table 1.6 so as to make such a comparison possible. Ask yourself whether "$1000 and victory" is preferable to $1100, 1200, ..., 2000, ... to find that you are indifferent between "$1000 and victory" and "1500," say. Enter, then "$1500" (instead of $1000) as your payoff in case bet *c* succeeds (i.e., if the next card is a spade). Similarly, if your cash equivalent of "−$200 and defeat" is "−$800", enter this amount as the payoff of bet *c* if event $\overline{Z}$ takes place. If you now prefer bet *b* to the (modified) bet *c*, you have judged event *Y* to be more probable than event *Z*. Note that we have modified the payoffs, not the events. But to modify the payoffs we have implicitly used a continuity assumption: if an outcome is preferred to x_1 dollars but is not preferred to x_2 dollars, then there exists a dollar amount x_0 (where $x_1 < x_0 < x_2$) such that you are indifferent between the outcome and x_0.

So far, only one characteristic of consistency has been used: the existence of a preference ordering among actions. From this, an ordering of the probabilities of events has followed, the ordering having been defined in accordance with ordinary language, but with only one pair of possible outcomes considered. We now introduce, as a further characteristic of the consistent man, the independence of tastes and beliefs. The same man who bets on *W* rather than *Y*, and on *Y* rather than *Z* when the pair of outcomes is ($1000, $-$200) will, if he is consistent, preserve the same ordering among the bets when the pair of outcomes is (*s*, *f*), where *s* ("success") is something, anything, that he prefers to *f* ("failure"). (The outcomes *s* and *f* may, or may not, be money amounts.) Thus in Table 1.6b, if he prefers *a* to *b* to *c*, he should prefer *a'* to *b'* to *c'* if he is consistent; his judgment about comparative probabilities of events should not depend on what rewards or punishments they entail.

TABLE 1.6b

	W	$\overline{W}$		Y	$\overline{Y}$		Z	$\overline{Z}$
a	$1000	$-$200	*b*	$1000	$-$200	*c*	$1000	$-$200
a'	*s*	*f*	*b'*	*s*	*f*	*c'*	*s*	*f*

More formally, we have the following condition.

INDEPENDENCE CONDITION 3: BELIEFS ARE INDEPENDENT OF TASTES. *Let f, s, f', s' be outcomes such that*

$$f \underset{R}{<} s, \qquad f' \underset{R}{<} s'.$$

Let W and Z be two events, and define actions a, b, a', b' by

$$\rho(x, a) = \begin{cases} s & \text{if } x \text{ in } W \\ f & \text{if } x \text{ not in } W \end{cases}$$

$$\rho(x, b) = \begin{cases} s & \text{if } x \text{ in } Z \\ f & \text{if } x \text{ not in } Z \end{cases}$$

(8.1)

$$\rho(x, a') = \begin{cases} s' & \text{if } x \text{ in } W \\ f' & \text{if } x \text{ not in } W \end{cases}$$

$$\rho(x, b') = \begin{cases} s' & \text{if } x \text{ in } Z \\ f' & \text{if } x \text{ not in } Z; \end{cases}$$

then

$$a \precsim_A b \qquad \text{if and only if} \qquad a' \precsim_A b'.$$

The situation described by (8.1) is depicted in Table 1.7.

TABLE 1.7

	W	$\overline{W}$		Z	$\overline{Z}$
a	s	f	b	s	f
a'	s'	f'	b'	s'	f'

The independence of tastes and beliefs permits us to order events by probability without reference to the particular outcomes considered. If, in the situation of (8.1), $a \precsim_A b$, then we shall say that *event W is not more probable than event Z*, and write

$$W \precsim_X Z.$$

It follows that, if $a \sim_A b$, then $W \sim_X Z$ (*W* and *Z* are equally probable). The ordering $\precsim_X$ will be called the *subjective probability ordering of events*. The word *subjective* emphasizes that the ordering is valid for the particular decision-maker in question, and that two different persons may (but need not) have different probability orderings of events.

9. NUMERICAL SUBJECTIVE PROBABILITIES

We can now indicate how the consistency requirement leads logically to the existence of numerical subjective probabilities that obey the usual laws of the probability calculus. For a while, let us distinguish just two possible outcomes, s and f, of which s ("success") is preferable to f ("failure"); and let there be n mutually exclusive and exhaustive events W_i. Consider, to begin with, n actions $a_1, \ldots, a_n$ such that a_i succeeds *only* if W_i happens, and fails otherwise, as in the upper part of Table 1.8. The first n rows of this table are merely an extension of Table 1.5 from 2 to n events. Again, if a_1 is preferred to a_2, a_2 to $a_3, \ldots, a_{n-1}$ to a_n, then it is usual to say that the decision-maker ranks the subjective probabilities thus:

$$W_1 \succ_X W_2 \succ_X \ldots \succ_X W_n.$$

Now let us suppose we can define the n events W_i and n actions a_i in such a way that the decision-maker is indifferent among all actions

TABLE 1.8

	W_1	W_2	W_3	$\ldots$	W_{n-2}	W_{n-1}	W_n
a_1	s	f	f	$\ldots$	f	f	f
a_2	f	s	f	$\ldots$	f	f	f
.	.	.	.	$\ldots$			.
a_{n-1}	f	f	f	$\ldots$	f	s	f
a_n	f	f	f	$\ldots$	f	f	s
b_1	s	f	f	$\ldots$	f	f	s
b_2	f	s	f	$\ldots$	f	f	s
.	.	.	.	$\ldots$	.	.	.
b_{n-1}	f	f	f	$\ldots$	f	s	s
c_1	s	f	f	$\ldots$	f	s	s
c_2	f	s	f	$\ldots$	f	s	s
.	.	.	.	$\ldots$	.	.	.
c_{n-2}	f	f	f	$\ldots$	s	s	s

$a_1, \ldots, a_n$. Thus in our example of the farmer, we can adjust, up and down, the humidity degrees that define the boundaries between pairs of adjacent events ("very dry summer," "moderately dry," etc.), until indifference between correspondingly defined actions is achieved.[10] As in the case $n = 2$ considered before, it will then again accord with ordinary language to say that the decision-maker regards all the n events $W_1, \ldots, W_n$ as equally probable.

With the n events $W_1, \ldots, W_n$ and n actions $a_1, \ldots, a_n$ of Table 1.8 thus redefined, let us consider, in the same table, a new set of $(n - 1)$ actions $b_1, \ldots, b_{n-1}$ such that b_i is successful if and only if the compounded event "W_i or W_n" happens. Now we compare b_1 with a_1. These two actions result in the same outcome if the event "non-W_n" happens; but the result (s) of b_1 is preferable to the result (f) of a_1 when W_n happens. Hence, by the Sure-Thing Theorem for Outcomes, b_1 is preferred to a_1; we conclude that, for the decision-maker, the event "W_1 or W_n" is subjectively more probable than "W_1" and also than "W_n." Clearly, a corresponding conclusion is reached if we replace W_1 by any W_i ($i \neq n$),

$$(W_i \text{ or } W_n) \underset{X}{\succ} W_i \qquad i = 1, \ldots, n - 1,$$

(thus, a larger subjective probability is assigned to a larger set of states). Moreover, indifference between a_1 and a_2 implies indifference between

10. We have made here, in fact, a continuity assumption.

b_1 and b_2, by Independence Condition 1, so that replacing W_1, W_2 by any W_i, W_j (i, j distinct from n) gives

$$(W_i \text{ or } W_n) \underset{X}{\sim} (W_j \text{ or } W_n) \underset{X}{\succ} W_i \underset{X}{\sim} W_j \underset{X}{\sim} W_n.$$

Since, instead of replacing failures by successes in the nth column, we could do the same thing in any column, we have, for any column k,

$$(W_i \text{ or } W_k) \underset{X}{\sim} (W_j \text{ or } W_k) \qquad (i, j \text{ distinct from } k).$$

We have similarly $(W_k \text{ or } W_i) \underset{X}{\sim} (W_h \text{ or } W_i)$ (h, k distinct from i); and, since "W_k or W_i" is logically the same event as "W_i or W_k," then by transitivity

$$(9.1) \quad (W_j \text{ or } W_k) \underset{X}{\sim} (W_h \text{ or } W_i) \underset{X}{\succ} W_h \underset{X}{\sim} W_j$$

$$(h \text{ and } i \text{ distinct}, j \text{ and } k \text{ distinct}).$$

Further, we can define, in Table 1.8, a set of actions c_i ($i = 1, \ldots, n - 2$), each succeeding in three cases and failing in all others. Reasoning as before, we can show that indifference between $b_1, \ldots, b_{n-1}$ implies that all actions c_i are equally desirable and each is preferable to any of the actions $b_1, \ldots, b_{n-1}$. By similar reasoning, all actions that succeed exactly in m ($\leq n$) cases are equally desirable, and are better than any action that succeeds in m' ($< m$) cases. Therefore (9.1) can be generalized thus:

$$(9.2) \qquad (W_{i_1} \text{ or } W_{i_2} \text{ or } \ldots W_{i_m}) \underset{X}{\succsim} (W_{j_1} \text{ or } W_{j_2} \text{ or } \ldots W_{j_{m'}})$$

if the W's are equiprobable, all the i's are distinct, all the j's are distinct, and $m \geq m'$.

We can now represent the ordering $\underset{X}{\precsim}$ of events according to subjective probability by a numerical function π in such a way that the numbers $\pi(W_i)$, $\pi(W_i \text{ or } W_j)$, and so forth, obey the laws of the probability calculus. We introduce, without loss of generality, the convention

$$(9.3) \qquad \sum_{i=1}^{n} \pi(W_i) = 1,$$

for any n-tuple of exhaustive and mutually exclusive events W_i (i.e., any partition of X). In the particular case considered, indifference among all actions a_i implies that all $\pi(W_i)$ are equal, and hence $\pi(W_i) = 1/n$ for all i. Moreover, the implication (9.2) is not contradicted if we put

$$(9.4) \qquad \pi(W_{i_1} \text{ or } W_{i_2} \text{ or } \ldots W_{i_m}) = m/n \qquad \text{all } i \text{ distinct}.$$

Let $Z = (W_{i_1} \text{ or } W_{i_2} \text{ or } \dots W_{i_m})$, $Z' = (W_{j_1} \text{ or } W_{j_2} \text{ or } \dots W_{j_{m'}})$, $m \leq n, m' \leq n$, where $i_1, \dots, i_m$ are distinct, $j_1, \dots, j_{m'}$ are distinct, and some i's are identical with some j's. That is, there is an overlap, "Z and Z'" being constituted of those mutually exclusive events that are common to Z and Z'. If there are r such common events, then the event "Z or Z'" consists of $m + m' - r$ mutually exclusive events. Hence by (9.4),

$$\pi(Z \text{ or } Z') = (m + m' - r)/n,$$

and, since $(m + m' - r)/n = (m/n) + (m'/n) - (r/n)$,

(9.5) $$\pi(Z \text{ or } Z') = \pi(Z) + \pi(Z') - \pi(Z \text{ and } Z');$$

thus numerical subjective probabilities obey the *addition rule* of the probability calculus.

Let us summarize our progress thus far. For a given positive integer n we have partitioned X into n equiprobable events $W_1, \dots, W_n$. Let $\mathscr{W}'$ denote the class of all events (sets) of the form

(9.6) $$(W_{i_1} \text{ or } W_{i_2} \text{ or } \dots \text{ or } W_{i_m}),$$

where $i_1, i_2, \dots, i_m$ are distinct integers between 1 and n. (Note that X is in $\mathscr{W}'$.) Each event W of the form (9.6) has been assigned the numerical *subjective probability* $\pi(W) = m/n$. This function π represents the ordering of events in $\mathscr{W}'$ according to subjective probability, in the sense that for W, W' in $\mathscr{W}'$,

(9.7) $$W \underset{X}{\precsim} W' \qquad \text{if and only if } \pi(W) \leq \pi(W').$$

Finally, the function π satisfies the following properties:

(i) $\pi(W) \geq 0$, for all W in $\mathscr{W}'$

(9.8) (ii) $\pi(X) = 1$

(iii) $\pi(W \text{ or } W') = \pi(W) + \pi(W')$, for all disjoint W and W' in $\mathscr{W}'$.

Thus by (9.8), the function π has all the properties of a probability measure for those events belonging to $\mathscr{W}'$.

Suppose, now, that for arbitrarily large integers n we can partition X into n equiprobable events. To be precise, suppose that such a partition can be constructed for each number n_i in some increasing, unbounded sequence n_1, n_2, and so forth, of positive integers. Then, for each n_i, we can construct a class $\mathscr{W}_i$ of events and a probability measure π_i, satisfying (9.7) to (9.8).

Suppose, further, that if $n_i \geq n_j$, then $\mathscr{W}_i$ contains $\mathscr{W}_j$, that is every event in $\mathscr{W}_j$ is also in $\mathscr{W}_i$. This could be accomplished, in particular, if the partitions in question could be constructed by a process of successive subdivisions, for example, by dividing each event in any one partition into two equally probable events, to yield the succeeding partition. (In the example of the farmer, this could be done by exploiting the continuity of the variable "humidity.") In this case, the sequence of numbers n_i would be 2, 4, 8, and so on.

If each class $\mathscr{W}_i$ includes the preceding one, as in the above construction, then it is obvious that all the probability measures π_i agree, in the sense that, if an event W belongs to both $\mathscr{W}_i$ and $\mathscr{W}_j$, then

$$(9.9) \qquad\qquad\qquad \pi_i(W) = \pi_j(W).$$

By virtue of (9.9) we are justified in dropping the subscript i on the measures π_i.

Let us pause again for a summary. We have now arrived at a numerical representation π of the subjective probability ordering $\underset{X}{\precsim}$ for a large class of events, namely, the class $\mathscr{W}$ of all events W that are in class $\mathscr{W}_i$ for some i. For this class $\mathscr{W}$, π has the properties (9.7) and (9.8), with $\mathscr{W}'$ replaced by $\mathscr{W}$. Let $\mathscr{R}$ be the set of rational numbers of the form (m/n_i), $0 \leq m \leq n_i$; then π has the property:

(9.10)
    (i) for every event W in $\mathscr{W}$, $\pi(W)$ is a rational number in $\mathscr{R}$

    (ii) for every rational number m/n in $\mathscr{R}$, there is an event W in $\mathscr{W}$ such that $\pi(W) = m/n$.

By virtue of (9.10) we can assign to every rational number k in $\mathscr{R}$ an event W_k with probability k. We shall use these events W_k as "bench marks" to measure the probabilities of other events.

Our final task in this section is to extend the measurement of subjective probability to events outside the class $\mathscr{W}$. Using the bench mark events W_k just derived, we can measure the probability of any event Z to any desired degree of accuracy. If for some rational number k in $\mathscr{R}$,

$$Z \underset{X}{\sim} W_k,$$

then we define

$$(9.11a) \qquad\qquad\qquad \pi(Z) = k.$$

More generally, we employ a method of successive approximation. Note that every number between 0 and 1 can be approximated as well as one pleases by a number in $\mathscr{R}$. For example, suppose that $\mathscr{R}$ is the set of all rational numbers of the form $(m/2^p)$, $p \geq 1$, $0 \leq m \leq 2^p$. We may first ask whether

$$Z \underset{X}{\precsim} W_{1/2};$$

if the answer is "yes," then we ask whether

$$Z \underset{X}{\prec} W_{1/4};$$

if the answer is "no," then we ask whether

$$Z \underset{X}{\precsim} W_{3/8};$$

and so forth. In this way we construct a sequence of approximations, so that after N steps we can make a statement of the form

$$W_{\frac{M_N}{2^N}} \underset{X}{\precsim} Z \precsim W_{\frac{M_N+1}{2^N}} \qquad 0 \leq M_N < 2^N;$$

furthermore, by construction, the sequence $(M_N/2^N)$ is nondecreasing, and the sequence $(M_N + 1)/2^N$ is nonincreasing [in our example above, the sequence $(M_N/2^N)$ might start out $0, 1/4, 1/4$, and the sequence $(M_N + 1)/2^N$ might start out $1/2, 1/2, 3/8$]. We define the subjective probability of Z to be

$$(9.11b) \qquad \pi(Z) \equiv \lim_{N \to \infty} \frac{M_N}{2^N}.$$

The definition (9.11b) includes (9.11a) as a special case, since all real numbers between 0 and 1, rational or otherwise, can be approximated to any desired degree of accuracy by numbers of the form $(M/2^N)$, with $0 \leq M \leq 2^N$.

That the probability measure, π, as extended by (9.11b), possesses properties (9.7) and (9.8) for *all* events is, we hope, plausible in view of the method of measurement, since these properties are satisfied for events in $\mathcal{W}$. We omit a proof, however, because of the mathematical technicalities involved. We should mention here that, in typical developments of the mathematical theory of probability, one does not suppose that all events have a probability measure, but only those belonging to some suitably restricted class (see remarks at the end of this section). For our purpose, it will suffice to suppose that π has been extended to some class, say $\mathcal{X}$, with the following properties:

    (i) X is in $\mathcal{X}$

(9.12) (ii) if Z is in $\mathcal{X}$, then (not-Z) is in $\mathcal{X}$

    (iii) if Z and Z' are in $\mathcal{X}$, then (Z and Z') and (Z or Z') are in $\mathcal{X}$.

For events in the class $\mathscr{X}$, we can summarize the required properties of the subjective probability measure π, rewriting (9.7) and (9.8) as follows: for every Z and Z' in $\mathscr{X}$,

(9.13)

(i) $\pi(Z) \geq 0$

(ii) $\pi(X) = 1$

(iii) $\pi(Z \text{ or } Z') = \pi(Z) + \pi(Z')$, if Z and Z' are disjoint (mutually exclusive)

(iv) $Z \underset{X}{\precsim} Z'$ if and only if $\pi(Z) \leq \pi(Z')$.

From (9.12) and (9.13), the usual theory of probability follows, including the development of the concepts of conditional probability, independence, and so forth (see, however, the remarks at the end of this section).

In particular, the conditional probability of Z given Z' is defined by

(9.13a) $$\text{Prob}[Z|Z'] \equiv \frac{\pi(Z \text{ and } Z')}{\pi(Z')},$$

provided that $\pi(Z') > 0$. The sets Z and Z' are said to be independent if

(9.13b) $$\pi(Z \text{ and } Z') = \pi(Z)\pi(Z').$$

This implies

(9.13c) $$\text{Prob}[Z|Z'] = \pi(Z)$$

if Z and Z' are independent.

In extending π to some class $\mathscr{X}$ of measurable events, it is natural to suppose that $\mathscr{X}$ is sufficiently rich so that the following extension of property (ii) of (9.10) holds: For any event Z in $\mathscr{X}$, and any real number k between 0 and 1, there is a partition of Z into two (disjoint) events Z' and Z'' such that

(9.14)
$$\pi(Z') = k\pi(Z)$$
$$\pi(Z'') = (1 - k)\pi(Z).$$

In particular, for any k between 0 and 1, we can find an event W_k in $\mathscr{X}$ such that $\pi(W_k) = k$. In other words, the family $\{W_k\}$ of bench mark events can be extended from k in $\mathscr{R}$ to all real k. These bench mark events will be used in measuring utility.

In the sections on utility (Sections 11 and 12), it will be useful to have property (iv) of (9.13) restated in terms of actions. Consider two actions, a and a' whose outcomes are restricted to the pair (s, f) where $f \underset{R}{\prec} s$.

Let Z be the set of states x for which $\rho(x, a) = s$, and similarly for Z' and a'; that is,

(9.15)
$$\rho(x, a) = \begin{cases} s & \text{for } x \text{ in } Z \\ f & \text{for } x \text{ not in } Z \end{cases}$$

$$\rho(x, a') = \begin{cases} s & \text{for } x \text{ in } Z' \\ f & \text{for } x \text{ not in } Z'. \end{cases}$$

By the definition of the probability ordering $\underset{X}{\precsim}$,

$$a \underset{A}{\precsim} a' \qquad \text{if and only if } Z \underset{X}{\precsim} Z'.$$

Hence, by property (iv) of (9.13)

(9.16) $\qquad a \underset{A}{\precsim} a' \qquad$ if and only if $\pi(Z) \leq \pi(Z')$.

Condition (9.16) can be paraphrased as follows: "If each of two actions can result in either success or failure, then the preferred action is the one with the highest *probability of success.*"

The general method described here for deriving subjective probabilities from orderings on actions is due to Ramsey 1931, de Finetti 1937, and Savage 1954. Raiffa (1968) gives a vivid elementary presentation, and Winkler (1967) reports some interesting experiments. In particular, the third independence condition is due to Ramsey; it also corresponds to Savage's postulate P4. Independence Condition 1 is Savage's postulate P2, and Independence Condition 2 corresponds to, but is not the same as, Savage's P3. It should be noted that, although our statement of Independence Condition 3 has a clear intuitive meaning, it would not be convenient for a rigorous mathematical discussion, since in a formulation with an infinite number of states every single state might well have probability zero, and therefore constitute a null event (recall that an event Z is *null* if, for every pair of actions a and b, $a \sim b$ given Z).

Some readers may have noticed that we have required that the class $\mathscr{X}$ of measurable events be just a ring, and not necessarily a σ-ring, and that the probability measure π be finitely additive, but not necessarily countably additive (see, for example, Halmos 1950 for definitions of these concepts). This was done to simplify the exposition, but in subsequent parts of this book we shall not hesitate to perform probability calculations that are based on countable additivity. This is related to the problem of restricting the class of events that are considered measurable. For a discussion of these and related matters, see Savage (1954, Chapter 3, Section 4).

10. Subjective and Objective Probabilities

We have not inquired why a given consistent decision-maker makes particular choices that reveal particular subjective probabilities of given events. Note that he can bet on repeatable events (weather, or the suit of a card) as well as nonrepeatable ones. Our discussion can apply, for example, to betting that men will first land on Mars between the years 2000 and 2010; or to betting that the specific weight of a metal not yet available in one's laboratory will be such and such.

We have seen that it is possible to calibrate subjective probabilities using as bench marks a set of mutually exclusive and exhaustive events (i.e., a partition of X) such that the subject is indifferent among bets on any of them, as is the case, in Table 1.8 for the bets $a_1, a_2, \ldots, a_n$ on the events $W_1, W_2, \ldots, W_n$, respectively. In this way one may calibrate a person's subjective probabilities of events that are nonrepeatable such as the alternative values of an unknown datum of physics or history or, for that matter, mathematics.[11] Now, we can assume that different subjects will display such indifferences among bets when they have reason (pending further information) to regard the corresponding events as interchangeable, in the sense illustrated by the following examples:

The subject believes that a certain die is almost "well made," and the events considered are the following six: the upper face of the die shows $1, 2, \ldots, 6$ dots.

The subject has no information about the 5th and subsequent digits of $\sqrt{2}$, and the events considered are the following ten: the 100th digit of $\sqrt{2}$ is $0, 1, \ldots, 9$.

If it is granted that all reasonable persons are indifferent among all the six bets of the first example, and among all the ten bets of the second example, their behavior will reveal the same subjective probabilities: 1/6 for each of the events of the first example, and 1/10 for each of the events of the second example. Because of this intersubjective agreement about preferences among bets, the above subjective probabilities will also be objective. The almost "well made" (or almost "ideal") die is quite analogous to the almost "ideal" straight edge or solid body, in the sense that people agree about certain properties of it. (See also de Finetti 1968.)

In an important case, (1) there exists intersubjective agreement that certain ("repeatable") events are interchangeable; and (2) it is possible to observe some (a "sample") of these events. For example, suppose there is no reason to assume that any change in the structure of a not necessarily well-made die or in its environment occurs from one throw to the next, and hence no reason to prefer betting on the ace in one rather than another throw. Or suppose there is no reason for an insurance company to prefer betting on the survival, over the period of one year, of one rather than another native-born white male of a given age and occupation. Let a sequence of throws of that die, or let a sample of those males, be observed.

11. See, however, Chapter 9, Section 6, with regard to the logical difficulty in applying subjective probabilities to the outcomes of logical or mathematical operations.

Such observations are called "repeated and independent," and these properties will be defined more precisely in Chapter 2, Section 10. Let the relative frequency of the occurrence of aces or of survivors, respectively, be honestly recorded. There is then no intersubjective disagreement about these recorded numbers for the particular samples observed. Nor is there (as already remarked) disagreement about the indifference among bets on the first, second, or any successive throw resulting in an ace; nor about the indifference among bets on the survival of any of the appropriately specified males. To this extent, the probabilities estimated from observed frequencies would have the feature of "objectivity."

Would a man be well advised to behave as if his subjective probabilities were equal to corresponding (and "objective") relative frequencies? In a certain sense the answer is "yes." It corresponds to common sense to say that, if a man with consistent tastes has a belief in the probability of an event, which was originally formed without repeatedly observing the occurrence or nonoccurrence of the event, then he will reveal, by a revised decision, a revised probability belief after being able to make such observations. The more numerous the observations, the more drastic may be this revision; the subjective probability of an event will approach more and more the observed relative frequency of its occurrence, and will depend less and less on the original "uninformed" belief. We cannot give here a completely rigorous formulation and proof, which combines Thomas Bayes's (1763) old idea of "a posteriori probabilities" with some properties of consistent behavior discussed here.[12] However, we do provide some further discussion of this topic in Chapter 2, Sections 9 to 11.

11. Expected Utility: Case of Two Outcomes

We begin our discussion of the measurement of the utility of outcomes and the representation of preferences among actions with the case in which the set R consists of only two outcomes. We do this, first, because the case of two outcomes is extremely simple, and second, because it can be used as a first step in the discussion of the general case.

Let the two outcomes in R be denoted by s (success) and f (failure), with

(11.1) $$f \underset{R}{\prec} s.$$

---

12. See Savage 1954 and Marschak 1970b. Economic thought and terminology have been much influenced by F. Knight (1921) who emphasized the prevalence of nonrepeatable events in practical life and reserved the word "uncertainty" for the case of nonrepeatable events, using the term "risk" for the case of repeatable events. He took a resigned stand as to the possibility of an economic analysis of behavior under "uncertainty" thus defined. For an excellent survey, see Arrow 1951.

For any action a, let $Z(a)$ denote (for the purposes of this section only) the set of states for which a results in success, that is,

(11.2)
$$\rho(x, a) = \begin{cases} s & \text{for } x \text{ in } Z(a) \\ f & \text{for } x \text{ not in } Z(a). \end{cases}$$

Our task will be to find two numbers $v(s)$ and $v(f)$, called the utilities of s and f, respectively, such that for any two actions a and b,

(11.3) $a \underset{A}{\precsim} b$ if and only if $\Omega(a) \leq \Omega(b)$,

where for any action a,

(11.4) $\Omega(a) \equiv v(s)\pi(Z[a]) + v(f)[1 - \pi(Z[a])].$

[This is the special form taken by (7.1) in the case of two outcomes, in view of (9.3)]. The number $\Omega(a)$ is called the *expected utility* of the action a.

We shall show that, for $v(s)$ and $v(f)$, one may take any two numbers v_1 and v_0 such that $v_0 < v_1$. In particular, one may take

(11.5)
$$v(s) = 1$$
$$v(f) = 0.$$

Indeed, with this last assignment of utilities, the expected utility (11.4) of an action is equal to the probability of success. We have already noted at the end of Section 9 that, for two-outcome actions, the preference ordering is the same as the ordering by probability of success. Hence the preference ordering $\underset{A}{\precsim}$ can be represented by expected utility [in the sense of (7.2)] if the utilities of success and failure are 1 and 0, respectively.

More generally, we rewrite (11.4) as

(11.6) $\Omega(a) = [v(s) - v(f)]\pi[Z(a)] + v(f).$

It is clear that the function Ω orders actions a in the same order as the probability of success $\pi[Z(a)]$ if and only if

(11.7) $v(s) - v(f) > 0.$

Hence any assignment of utilities satisfying (11.7) will yield an expected utility function Ω that represents the preference ordering $\underset{A}{\precsim}$.

12. Expected Utility: General Case

Suppose now that the set R of alternative outcomes is finite;[13] we may label the outcomes $r_1, \ldots, r_N$ in R in such a way that, for all r_i in R,

(12.1) $$r_1 \underset{R}{\precsim} r_i \underset{R}{\precsim} r_N.$$

To avoid an uninteresting degenerate case, we suppose that r_N is strictly preferred to r_1:

(12.2) $$r_1 \underset{R}{\prec} r_N.$$

For any action a, let $Z_i(a)$ be the event[14] "a has the outcome r_i":

(12.3) $$\rho(x, a) = r_i \qquad \text{for } x \text{ in } Z_i(a),$$

a generalization of (11.2). Notice that, for each action a, the events $Z_1(a), \ldots, Z_N(a)$ form a partition of X.

Recall that our goal is to find a function v on R, the *utility function*, such that the *expected utility function*

(12.4) $$\Omega(a) \equiv \sum_{i=1}^{N} v(r_i)\pi[Z_i(a)]$$

represents the preference ordering $\underset{A}{\precsim}$ of actions [see (7.1) and (7.2)]. We shall first show how to measure a utility function v, and then show that the corresponding expected utility function Ω does represent the preference ordering $\underset{A}{\precsim}$.

Following an approach suggested by the two-outcome case, first define the utilities of the worst and best outcomes in R to be 0 and 1, respectively,

(12.5)
$$v(r_1) \equiv 0,$$
$$v(r_N) \equiv 1.$$

To measure the utilities of the other outcomes in R, we construct a class of *bench-mark actions*. By (9.14) we can, for each number k between 0 and 1, find an event W_k such that $\pi(W_k) = k$. Define the action a_k by

(12.6) $$\rho(x, a_k) = \begin{cases} r_N & \text{for } x \text{ in } W_k \\ r_1 & \text{for } x \text{ not in } W_k. \end{cases}$$

---

13. For the case of an infinite R, see Savage 1954, Chapter 5, Section 4.

14. It is assumed that, for all actions a in A, the events $Z_i(a)$ are measurable, i.e. are in the class $\mathscr{X}$ [see (9.12) to (9.14)].

The expected utility of the bench-mark action a_k is immediately seen to be k:

(12.7) $\Omega(a_k) = k.$

Now consider any outcome r_i in R. Since

$$r_1 \underset{R}{\lesssim} r_i \underset{R}{\lesssim} r_N,$$

we may write, applying definition (12.6) with $k = 0$ or 1,

(12.8) $a_0 \lesssim r_i \lesssim a_1$

(this comparison between actions and outcomes is meaningful by virtue of Independence Condition 2 and the Sure-Thing Theorem for Outcomes; henceforth we shall often omit the letters R and A under the $\lesssim$ symbol without risk of ambiguity).

It follows from (12.8) that there is some number k such that $r_i \sim a_k$; we define that number k to be the utility of r_i. To measure k, one can use the same type of process of successive approximation that was used to measure the subjective probability of an event. To summarize, the utility $v(r_i)$ of an outcome r_i in R is defined by

(12.9) $r_i \sim a_{v(r_i)}.$

It remains to show that the determination (12.9) of the utility function v yields an expected utility function Ω that represents the preference ordering $\underset{A}{\lesssim}$ such that for any two actions a and b,

(12.10) $a \lesssim b$ if and only if $\Omega(a) \leq \Omega(b)$.

First note that in Section 11 (the two-outcome case) it was demonstrated in essence that (12.10) is satisfied for all actions a and b that result in the outcomes r_1 and r_N only (this includes, of course, the bench-mark actions). Our method of proving that (12.10) holds for all actions will be to show that any action is equivalent in preference to some action with the same expected utility, but resulting in the outcomes r_1 and r_N only; (12.10) will then follow by the transitivity of preferences.

We first prove the following auxiliary proposition.

LEMMA. Suppose that
  (i) *r is an outcome, with utility* $u \equiv v(r)$;
  (ii) *W is an event, with probability* $p \equiv \pi(W)$;
  (iii) *c is an action such that* $\rho(x, c) = r$ *for x in W*;

(iv) *b is a two-outcome action such that*

$$\pi[Z_N(b)] = u$$

$$\pi[Z_N(b) \text{ and } W] = up$$

$$\pi[Z_1(b)] = 1 - u;$$

then

$$c \sim b \text{ given } W.$$

Proof. By the use of (12.5), one notes that the expected utility of action b is u, and hence $r \sim b$. Also, in the language of probability theory, W and $Z_N(b)$ are independent events. It will suffice to consider the case in which p is a rational number (m/n), the irrational case following by approximation. By repeated application of (9.14) one can partition X into $W_{1N}, W_{11}, \ldots, W_{mN}, W_{m1}, \ldots, W_{nN}, W_{n1}$ such that

$$\pi(W_{jN}) = \frac{u}{n}$$
$$j = 1, \ldots, n,$$
$$\pi(W_{j1}) = \frac{1 - u}{n}$$

(12.11)
$$W = (W_{1N} \text{ or } W_{11} \text{ or} \ldots \text{or } W_{mN} \text{ or } W_{m1}),$$

$$Z_N(b) = (W_{1N} \text{ or} \ldots \text{or } W_{nN}),$$

$$Z_1(b) = (W_{11} \text{ or} \ldots \text{or } W_{n1}).$$

For each $j = 1, \ldots, n$, define actions c_j and b_j by

$$\rho(x, c_j) = \begin{cases} r & \text{for } x \text{ in } W_{jN} \text{ or } W_{j1} \\ r_1 & \text{otherwise} \end{cases}$$

(12.12)

$$\rho(x, b_j) = \begin{cases} r_N & \text{for } x \text{ in } W_{jN} \\ r_1 & \text{otherwise.} \end{cases}$$

Define c by

(12.13)
$$\rho(x, c) = r \qquad \text{for all } x;$$

then $c \sim b$.

The situation defined by (12.11) to (12.13) is illustrated in Table 1.9. All the c_j are equivalent (as to preference) and all the b_j are also equivalent, since all the W_{jN} are equiprobable and all the W_{j1} are equiprobable.

Suppose that $b \prec c$ given (W_{iN} or W_{i1}) for some i. Then $b_i \prec c_i$; hence $b_j \prec c_j$ for all $j = 1, \ldots, n$ and $b \prec c$ given (W_{jN} or W_{j1}) for all j. Then, by the Sure-Thing Theorem for Conditional Preferences, $b \prec c$. Similarly, if $c \prec b$ given (W_{iN} or W_{i1}) for some i, then $c \prec b$. Hence $c \sim b$ implies that $c \sim b$ given (W_{iN} or W_{i1}) for all i.

By repeated application of Independence Condition 1, we can easily show that $c \sim b$ given W, which completes the proof of the lemma.

TABLE 1.9

Actions \ Events	W						non-W	
	W_{1N}	W_{11}	...	W_{mN}	W_{m1}	...	W_{nN}	W_{n1}
c	r	r		r	r	...	r	r
b	r_N	r_1		r_N	r_1	...	r_N	r_1
c_1	r	r		r_1	r_1	...	r_1	r_1
b_1	r_N	r_1		r_1	r_1	...	r_1	r_1
.	.	.		.	.		.	.
.	.	.		.	.		.	.
.	.	.		.	.		.	.
c_m	r_1	r_1		r	r	...	r_1	r_1
b_m	r_1	r_1		r_N	r_1	...	r_1	r_1

Now consider any action a. By application of (9.14) one can partition each event $Z_i(a)$ into two events, Z_{iN} and Z_{i1} such that

$$\pi(Z_{iN}) = [v(r_i)]\pi[Z_i(a)]$$

$$\pi(Z_{i1}) = [1 - v(r_i)]\pi(Z_i(a)).$$

Define an action b by

$$(12.14) \qquad \rho(x, b) = \begin{cases} r_N & \text{if } x \text{ in } Z_{iN} \quad \text{for any } i \\ r_1 & \text{if } x \text{ in } Z_{i1} \quad \text{for any } i. \end{cases}$$

By construction

$$Z_N(b) = (Z_{1N} \text{ or} \dots \text{or } Z_{nN})$$

$$Z_1(b) = (Z_{11} \text{ or} \dots \text{or } Z_{n1});$$

hence

$$\pi[Z_N(b)] = \sum_{i=1}^{n} [v(r_i)]\pi[Z_i(a)]$$

$$(12.15) \qquad\qquad \Omega(b) = \Omega(a).$$

We shall now show that $b \sim a$. For each i, the preceding lemma applies, so that $b \sim a$ given $Z_i(a)$. Hence, by the Sure-Thing Theorem for Conditional Preferences, $b \sim a$. We have thus concluded the demonstration that, with the utility function determined by (12.9), the expected utility function (12.4) does represent the preference ordering $\underset{A}{\precsim}$.

THE UTILITY FUNCTION DETERMINED UP TO
ORIGIN AND SCALE

The question arises whether there are other functions beside the function v determined by (12.9) that can serve as utility functions in our present sense. It can be shown that any utility function v^* must have the form

(12.16a)
$$v^*(r) = (u_1 - u_0)v(r) + u_0$$
$$= u_1 v(r) + u_0[1 - v(r)],$$

where v is the function determined by (12.9), and u_1 and u_0 are any numbers such that

(12.16b) $u_1 > u_0.$

Notice that, with v^* given by (12.16a),

(12.17)
$$v^*(r_N) = u_1,$$
$$v^*(r_1) = u_0.$$

In other words, the utility function is determined up to an arbitrary choice of origin and scale.

To prove that a v^* of the form (12.16a) and (12.16b) is a utility function is an easy exercise, which we leave to the reader. To prove the converse is more difficult; see, for example, Savage 1954, Section 5.3, Theorem 3.

The treatment of utility just presented is due essentially to von Neumann and Morgenstern (1953), except that their development of the concept is not tied to any particular concept of probability. Ramsey (1931) had earlier developed the expected utility concept from preferences among actions, in connection with his work on subjective probability. Our treatment of utility, as of subjective probability, follows the more complete one of Savage (1954), who also provides extended historical and critical comments. Other references are J. Marschak 1950, Herstein and Milnor 1953, and Debreu 1960.

Two important consequences of the representation of preferences among actions by expected utility have not been brought out explicitly in the course of our abbreviated treatment. These propositions are often stated as postulates in those treatments of the subject that are not tied to a concept of subjective probability. To state these propositions, we need the concept of a *prospect*. Consider a given action a, and let p_i be the probability that a results in the outcome r_i, that is

$$p_i \equiv \pi[Z_i(a)].$$

The n-tuple

$$\mathbf{p}(a) \equiv (p_1, \ldots, p_n)$$

will be called the *prospect*[15] *associated with the action a.*

15. Savage (1954) uses the term "gamble."

It is an immediate consequence of the representability of $\precsim_A$ by expected utility that any two actions with the same associated prospect are equivalent with respect to preference. Developments of utility that start with probability as a primitive concept take as a point of departure a preference ordering among prospects.

If $\mathbf{p} = (p_1, \ldots, p_n)$ is a prospect, then

$$p_i \geqq 0, \qquad i = 1, \ldots, n,$$

$$\sum_{i=1}^{n} p_i = 1.$$

We may suppose that for every n-tuple $\mathbf{p}$ satisfying these last two conditions, there is an action for which $\mathbf{p}$ is the corresponding prospect. It follows that if $\mathbf{p}$ and $\mathbf{q}$ are prospects, and k is a number between 0 and 1, then

$$k\mathbf{p} + (1 - k)\mathbf{q} \equiv [kp_1 + (1 - k)q_1, \ldots, kp_n + (1 - k)q_n]$$

is also a prospect. This "mixture" of $\mathbf{p}$ and $\mathbf{q}$ may be thought of as being concretely represented by a lottery in which the "prizes" are themselves prospects.

A special kind of mixture may be interpreted as resulting from the "substitution" of a prospect $\mathbf{p}$ for a given outcome r_j in another prospect $\mathbf{q}$, to yield a prospect $\mathbf{q}^*$ defined by

$$q_i^* = \begin{cases} q_i + q_j p_i & i \neq j, \\ q_j p_j & i = j. \end{cases}$$

A simple calculation shows that, if $\Omega(\mathbf{p}) = v(r_j)$, then $\Omega(\mathbf{q}^*) = \Omega(\mathbf{q})$, or, in terms of preference orderings,

$$\text{if } \mathbf{p} \sim r_j, \text{ then } \mathbf{q}^* \sim \mathbf{q}.$$

This last form of the proposition, which may be called the *substitution principle*, was essentially proved for a special case in the lemma of this section, and has been taken as a postulate in alternative treatments of utility.

Confusion sometimes arises between the concept of a utility function as developed here, and another concept of utility function as simply a numerical representation of preferences among *outcomes*. It is true that any utility function v satisfying (7.1) and (7.2) will, in particular, have the property that

(12.18) $r_i \precsim_R r_j$ if and only if $v(r_1) \leqq v(r_j)$,

for all outcomes r_i and r_j. However, it was pointed out that the class of utility functions satisfying (7.1) and (7.2) is determined up to the choice of origin and scale, that is, up to a strictly increasing *linear* transformation, whereas the class of functions satisfying (12.18) is determined only up to a strictly increasing transformation. One may say that the utility function of (7.1) and (7.2) represents not only preferences among outcomes, but also the decision-maker's attitude towards risk. For example, if the outcome variable r is numerical-valued (or vector-valued), then a decision-maker with a *concave* utility function (diminishing marginal utility) would be called *averse to risk*. For further remarks on this point, see the next section.

13. GENERALITY OF THE EXPECTED UTILITY PRINCIPLE

In the last six sections, we have shown how certain consistency requirements constrain a decision-maker to choose an action that maximizes expected utility on the set of feasible actions, with suitable definitions of the probabilities of events and of the utilities of outcomes. These consistency requirements fall primarily into two groups:

1. The complete ordering of actions according to preference.
2. The independence of tastes and beliefs.

The independence of tastes and beliefs is expressed in three independence conditions; the first two lead, respectively, to the definition of conditional preferences among actions, given events, and to the definition of preferences among outcomes (Section 7). The third condition leads to the definition of an ordering of events by (subjective) probability.

In a third category are the essentially technical conditions: (1) there are at least two actions that are not equivalent with respect to preference, (2) the set X of all states can be partitioned into arbitrarily many equiprobable events, and (3) the set R of alternative outcomes is finite.

Although all these conditions place some restriction on an individual's preferences with respect to actions, they still leave room for a wide variety of preference orderings. Thus both *risk aversion* (leading a person to a diversification of his investments, taking out insurance, etc.) and *risk preference* (leading him to speculation, participation in lotteries, etc.) are possible modes of behavior under these conditions, and can be related to the shape of the function (called the utility function of money) assigning numerical utilities to varying levels of monetary wealth.[16] On the other hand, the independence of tastes and beliefs, and hence the expected utility principle, is incompatible with "love of danger," that is, a preference for some actions in spite of their lower success probability.[17]

16. See Friedman and Savage 1948, Radner 1964, Pratt 1964, and Arrow 1971 (Chap. 3). Risk aversion and risk preference require the utility function of money to be nonlinear.

17. "Love of danger in this sense may very well be present in what are usually considered economic decisions. The danger of loss, including ruin, though probably shunned in the conservative code or cant of business, has quite possibly added to the zest and desirability of many an historically important venture, in the careers of the leaders of mercenary armies, in the financing of great geographic discoveries, or, closer to our time, in the financing of inventions and theater plays, and in stock and commodity speculation." J. Marschak (1950). Alternatively, one can preserve the expected utility principle by redefining each outcome as represented, not only by an amount of money but, additionally, by aspects of the outcome that are related to ambition, curiosity, etc. But with this interpretation the prospects chosen by a "lover of danger" will still fail to reveal the utility function of money, unless one finds a way to keep the nonmonetary aspects of outcomes constant.

In many practical instances, the utility function on the set of outcomes has been given a sinple form. In the business of large companies, it suffices for many purposes to identify utility with money profit (thus neglecting both risk preference and aversion), at least as long as bankruptcy is not considered possible. Fruitful results have been obtained from the simple assumption that the company is interested in maximizing the mathematical expectation of its profit, or in minimizing the mathematical expectation of its cost (the sales value being given). Examples of such results are rules for the control of inventories and of production under uncertainty (see, for example, Arrow, Karlin, and Scarf 1958). For still more special purposes, there are useful implications of minimizing the mathematical expectation of waiting time, as in the analysis of queues (Cox and Smith 1961), or of some other physical quantities relevant to a particular aspect of business. This is also true of industrial quality control and other applications of statistics. Modern statistics led by A. Wald (1950) has found in the minimization of "expected loss" a principle for selecting among alternative procedures of getting and processing observational data. This has been often exemplified by assuming that losses increase as the estimation error increases.

When replacing utility by some handy monetary or physical variable, one should not be too light-hearted. The wise physician will not completely identify his patient's health with his state of nutrition, or identify good nutrition with the intake of numerous calories. While the technocrats' identification of public welfare with the amount of energy leads to absurdities, a cautious use of the "national income" figure yields fruitful results. If, as pointed out by Hitch (1953), one forgets that the goal of transatlantic convoys of the two World Wars was to increase Europe's supplies, and maximizes instead the more easily computed ratio of U-boats sunk to Allied ships sunk, one ends up with the ridiculous recommendation that Allied destroyers accompany no merchant ships at all.

An even more drastically simple approximation to utility is obtained if one classifies all outcomes into "bad" and "good" ones. In this case, maximizing expected utility is equivalent to maximizing the probability of a "good" outcome (see Section 11).

Not all authors have found it necessary, or even desirable, to accept the expected utility principle (see references in Arrow 1951 and in J. Marschak 1950). In the case of actions that result in numerical outcomes, such as money income, the most common alternative is the suggestion that an action be evaluated in terms of the mean and variance of the corresponding probability distribution (see, e.g., Markowitz 1959). In general, such an evaluation will generate a preference ordering that violates the conditions of the expected utility principle, though there are special cases in which no conflict arises. Other parameters of the probability distribution have also been suggested as being relevant. We shall not follow up the implications of such suggestions here; they are merely mentioned to place the expected utility principle in the proper perspective.

14. EXPECTED PAYOFF OF AN ACTION

It will be recalled that each outcome r is the result of an action a in a given state x of the environment. Thus $r = \rho(x, a)$, where ρ is the outcome function. If, as before, $Z_i(a)$ denotes the event "action a results in outcome r_i," then the expected utility for action a is

$$(14.1) \qquad \Omega(a; \rho, \pi, \upsilon) \equiv \sum_{i=1}^{n} \upsilon(r_i)\pi[Z_i(a)],$$

where π is the subjective probability function and υ is the utility function. The expression on the left-hand side of (14.1) emphasizes that the expected utility depends on the decision-maker's action only, given the functions ρ, π, and υ. These functions summarize the factors beyond his control: his beliefs π, his tastes υ, and his idea of the "physical" relation ρ that states how outcomes are determined by himself and by the environment. His action a, on the other hand, is under his control. He chooses an action with the greatest expected utility.

Since $r = \rho(x, a)$, and the utility of r is $\upsilon(r)$, we can express the utility of outcome directly as a function of x and a:

$$(14.2) \qquad \upsilon(r) = \upsilon[\rho(x, a)] \equiv \omega(x, a).$$

Here ω will be called the *payoff function*; it is equivalent to the successive application of the outcome function and the utility function. It is thus a combined expression of a person's tastes and of his explanation of the outcome as determined by his action and the environment.

To simplify the notation, suppose that the set X of alternative states of the environment is finite, and write $\phi(x)$ for the probability of the state[18] x,

$$(14.3) \qquad \phi(x) \equiv \pi(\{x\}).$$

---

18. Strictly speaking, we should say "probability of the set consisting of the single element x," which we have denoted by $\{x\}$.

The function ϕ is usually called a *probability density function*. We can now rewrite the expected utility of an action in the simpler form

$$(14.4) \qquad \Omega(a; \omega, \phi) \equiv E\omega(x, a) \equiv \sum_x \omega(x, a)\phi(x)$$

$$\equiv \sum v[\rho(x, a)]\phi(x).$$

We call this quantity the *expected payoff* of the action a. Again, the symbols ω and ϕ summarize the noncontrolled conditions.[19]

To sum up, we shall say that a person is consistent under uncertainty if his behavior agrees with the expected utility principle. That is, for a consistent man, there exist a probability distribution ϕ on the set of the states of environment, an outcome function ρ by which he explains the outcome as a joint result of his and nature's actions, and a utility function v on the set of outcomes, with the following property: the action chosen is one that makes the expression $\sum_x v[\rho(x, a)]\phi(x) = \sum_x \omega(x, a)\phi(x)$ as large as possible.

19. Even if X is denumerably infinite, the notation of (14.3) and (14.4) need not be modified. More generally, ϕ may be a density function with respect to some underlying measure, in which case the sum in (14.4) would be replaced by an integral. In general, (14.4) would be a generalized integral with respect to the probability measure π (see any standard text on measure and integration).

CHAPTER 2

Organizational Form: Information and Decision Functions

1. RULE OF ACTION

So far we have discussed the consistency of decisions and emerged with the concept of the expected payoff as our primary tool for the evaluation of actions under uncertainty. Given the (subjective) probability distribution of the states of the environment, the best action is the one with the highest expected payoff. Choice under certainty is a special case, with probability 1 assigned to one particular state of the environment.

We now modify—and, in a sense, generalize—the problem in the following way: the individual chooses, not among actions, but among *rules of action*. A rule of action (also called a *decision rule*, a *strategy*, or a *decision function*) is a schedule that determines in advance, for each possible future information signal, the action that will be taken in response to it. Rules of action (sometimes called "roles") for the individual members of an organization are essential for the very concept of organization as we have defined it. The search for the best rules of action is essential to the economic theory of teams, as we shall show. It is also essential for a realistic theory of single-person decisions, since one often has to decide in advance how to respond to each of possible future contingencies. This will be shown in various examples in the present and the next chapters. As emphasized by Wald (1950) and by von Neumann and Morgenstern (1943), this introduction of the possibility of using new information will not alter the basic features of the decision problem. Formally, the rules of action will now play the same role as did the actions themselves in the previous chapter.

The "future" information that enters in the decision rule is to be distinguished from "prior" information. The prior information consists of the description of the set X of possible states x of the environment,[1] the probability distribution π on X, the set A of alternative actions a, and the payoff function ω. In what follows, information will always mean future information. This will be defined more precisely in Section 2, but we shall use a familiar example to illustrate the meaning of our concepts.

Consider a firm producing a single commodity for a market in which the price is set by the government at the beginning of each year, at which time the firm sets its production for the coming year. If the goal of the firm is to maximize profits for the coming year then, under the usual assumptions of increasing marginal costs, and so forth, one derives the familiar rule: "Choose the level of production that will make marginal cost equal to price." This rule defines implicitly a functional relation between the action (the quantity a produced) and the information (the price y set by the government),

$$a = \alpha(y).$$

Thus α is the decision function prescribed by economic theory.

One can, of course, imagine other decision functions for this firm, say the one implied by the rule: "Choose a level of production such that average cost is 90 percent of price." (This decision function typically will not maximize profits, however.) Another decision function, although a somewhat "degenerate" one, is the *constant function*, namely, the rule that fixes the same level of production year after year, whatever the price happens to be.

In general, let Y be the set of possible alternative information signals; then a *decision function* α is a function from Y to the set A of feasible actions.[2] (In the example of the firm just given, Y is the set of possible prices, and A is the set of alternative possible levels of production.) An action a depends on the information y; thus $a = \alpha(y)$. The set of alternative decision functions is, in principle, the set of all functions from Y to A. However, in actual decision problems, there may be some restrictions. It may not be feasible to compute certain decision functions; for example, if a and y are numerical, the computation of nonlinear functions α may be physically infeasible with given equipment within available time.

1. To avoid certain technical mathematical complications, we shall assume that the set X is finite, except in some special applications, in which cases the reader will be warned. For convenience, we shall also assume, except where noted, that X does not contain any states that have zero probability.

2. Note that A will denote the set of *feasible* actions, not the (generally larger) set of *conceivable* actions. See Chapter 1, Section 6.

We can now rewrite the payoff $\omega(x, a)$ as $\omega[x, \alpha(y)]$, where x is the generic element of X and y is the generic element of Y. If y_1 and y_2 are elements of Y, we shall also say that they are two alternative information signals or two values of the information variable y. We shall show presently the relation between X and Y.

2. Information

Typically, information will give only a partial description of the state of the world; this description can have varying degrees of completeness. For example, instead of getting a complete list of today's closing prices on the New York Stock Exchange, one may get information only about all the oil stock prices; or only about the average of all stock prices; or only about the average oil stock price. Each of these types of information specifies some set of states of the environment within which the true state lies. This set is, of course, the set of all states that have in common the partial description given by the information. Thus, to be told that the average closing stock price was 55 is to be told that the list of prices is in the set of all those lists that have an average of 55.

Thus each information signal y (an element of Y) is identified with a particular subset of X, the set of states. To take another example, the information relevant to a motorist's decision in traffic may be a signal, green, or red. In this case, the set Y consists of two elements. The set X of all possible traffic situations is thus partitioned in two subsets; if traffic is in one subset, the signal is green; otherwise it is red. This partitioning defines η, the *information structure*; given η, certain signals (symbols) are assigned to certain subsets of X.

Sometimes a decision is to be based on information that reflects aspects of the environment that, in fact, do not influence the payoff. For example, in choosing the parts of a country in which a campaign against infantile diseases is most urgent, one may have to base the decision, in the absence of better data, on mortality figures not broken down by age groups. The decision is then based on what is sometimes called "incorrect" or, in the language of communication engineers, "noisy" information. There is, in principle, no need for a special concept of incorrect information. Every item of information is correct with respect to some aspect of the state of the environment, although that aspect may be irrelevant to the payoff. For example, instead of saying that the results of a market survey are "incorrect," we can say that those results reflect not only the responses of the people interviewed, but also the characteristics of the interviewer, the method of recording the data, and so forth; and that, if one ignores this nature of the particular information, he can make poor decisions.

Thus, if two states of the environment are identical in all respects except that a given signal-producing instrument behaves differently in the two states, we consider the two states as distinct elements of the set X.

To give another example, suppose that an urn is known to contain two balls, of which each may be either red or black. A single ball is drawn from the urn; its color (but not the identity of the ball) is observed. Thus the color is the information signal. There are $2^2 = 4$ possible original compositions of the urn, and two possible outcomes of the sampling experiment; hence, there might be said to be $2 \times 4 = 8$ alternative states. Of these, two would be considered impossible, since one could not draw a red ball if the urn contained only black balls, and vice versa. The six remaining states are listed in Table 2.1. We must regard states x_2 and x_3 as distinct, even though the composition of the urn is the same in both, because the signals (the colors of the ball drawn) are different. The same is true of x_4 and x_5.

TABLE 2.1   STATES

State	Urn		Sample
	Ball 1	Ball 2	Ball drawn
x_1	B	B	B
x_2	R	B	R
x_3	R	B	B
x_4	B	R	R
x_5	B	R	B
x_6	R	R	R

In summary, then, an information signal represents a subset of the states of the environment; in the formulation of a decision problem, the states of the environment must be described in sufficient detail to cover not only those aspects relevant to the payoff function, but also those aspects relevant to the type of information on which the decisions may be based.

3. INFORMATION STRUCTURE; ORGANIZATIONAL FORM

Information can be regarded as the outcome of *information-gathering*. A given method of information-gathering applied to the true state of environment x results in a particular signal. As before, let Y denote the set of alternative possible information signals y. To each x in X will correspond a signal y. Thus, to a given information-gathering method is associated a function, say η, from X to Y. We shall call such a function an *information function* or an *information structure*. Thus,

$$y = \eta(x).$$

For a fixed information structure η, each signal y is identified in a natural way with a subset of X, namely, the set of states x for which $\eta(x) = y$. It follows that every information structure induces a *partition* of X into an exhaustive family of mutually exclusive subsets, each subset identified with a particular information signal. We shall denote this partition by $\mathscr{Y}$.

Without danger of ambiguity, we shall sometimes denote by the same letter y both the physical signal (an element of Y) and the corresponding element of $\mathscr{Y}$, that is, a subset of X.

For the purposes of this book, it will be convenient to give to the pair (η, α)—the combination of an information structure with a decision rule possible under this structure—a special name: the *organizational form*.

Any partition of the set X (for example, an information structure) can be regarded as a method of description of states of the environment, typically in an incomplete fashion. Descriptions of the environment specially related to the payoff function will be discussed in Section 7.

4. EXPECTED PAYOFF REFORMULATED

Given the information structure η and the true state of environment x, the information signal y is determined by $y = \eta(x)$; we can therefore rewrite the payoff again, as follows:

$$\omega(x, a) = \omega[x, \alpha(y)] = \omega[x, \alpha(\eta[x])].$$

Hence, given the true state of environment, the payoff is determined by the information structure, the decision function, and the payoff function. Using now the probability density function, ϕ, we can write the expected payoff U thus:

(4.1) $$U = \sum_x \omega[x, \alpha(\eta[x])]\phi(x) \equiv \Omega(\eta, \alpha; \omega, \phi).$$

This quantity depends on the noncontrolled conditions ω, ϕ; and on the decision function α and the information structure η. In general, these two latter functions are under the control of the decision-maker. He has at his disposal more than one pair (η, α), and he will choose that pair which makes the expected payoff U a maximum. This justifies our previous assertion that the problem of choosing the best decision function (and we may now add, the best information structure) is formally the same as the simpler one of choosing the best action.

We shall often be able to simplify the discussion by assuming η as given, thus leaving only α to the individual's choice. The expected payoff yielded by the best decision function, given the information structure η, will be denoted by

$$(4.2) \qquad\qquad \hat{\Omega}(\eta; \omega, \phi) = \max_{\alpha} \Omega(\alpha, \eta; \omega, \phi).$$

Consider the example of a firm (see Section 1 above), but now introduce an additional factor into the description of the states of the environment, namely, the price of an important raw material. Denote by x_1 the price of product, and by x_2 the price of raw material. Suppose that, at the time the decision about the level of production is to be made, x_1 is known but not x_2; that is, it is not known what price will have to be paid for the raw material during the coming year. Thus the information variable y is not identical with the state of environment x. The latter is described by the pair

$$x = (x_1, x_2);$$

the information y consists of the price x_1 alone. The information structure is given by

$$\eta(x) = x_1.$$

Let us assume this to be the only information structure available. Suppose that the cost of producing a quantity a, for given x_2, is $\kappa(x_2, a)$; and that the firm takes as its measure of utility the net profit; then the payoff function is

$$(4.3) \qquad\qquad \omega(x_1, x_2, a) = x_1 a - \kappa(x_2, a).$$

If the firm decides upon a rule that tells it to produce the quantity $a = \alpha(x_1)$, when it learns that the price of the product is to be x_1 (regardless of x_2), then the payoff for any state (x_1, x_2) is

$$u = \omega(x_1, x_2, a) = x_1 \alpha(x_1) - \kappa[x_2, \alpha(x_1)].$$

The prices x_1 and x_2 will have some joint probability distribution $\phi(x_1, x_2)$, and the decision function α will be evaluated by the expected value of the payoff u just given.

5. MAXIMIZING CONDITIONAL EXPECTATION

A decision function is best if it results in the largest possible expected payoff, that is, the largest possible value of $E\omega(x, a)$. We shall now show that the nature of $E\omega(x, a)$ enables one to give a more detailed characterization of a best decision function, for a fixed information structure η.

First, consider the situation in which the decision-maker finds himself after he has received the information signal $\eta(x) = y$. He is about to take an action, $\alpha(y)$, and the consequence of this action is (typically) uncertain, since he knows only that the true state of the environment is one of the (typically) many that could have resulted in the particular information signal y.

We shall show that, given the information signal y, the best action $a = \alpha(y)$ is the one that maximizes the *conditional* expectation of the payoff, given that the true state x is in y (considered as a subset of X). The probability that the signal y is received is

$$(5.1) \qquad \pi(y) = \sum_{x \in y} \phi(x);$$

Since x is contained in y, the joint probability of x and y is $\phi(x)$. Hence the conditional probability of x, given that x is in y, is

$$(5.2) \qquad \phi(x|y) = \frac{\phi(x)}{\pi(y)},$$

provided, of course, that $\pi(y) \neq 0$ [see (9.13a) of Chapter 1]. It will be seen that these conditional probabilities naturally arise in the course of determining a best decision function.

To prove the above characterization of a best decision function, consider again the expression (4.1) for the expected payoff for a given decision function:

$$(5.3) \qquad U = \sum_x \omega[x, \alpha(\eta[x])]\phi(x).$$

If we group the states x according to the corresponding signals $y = \eta(x)$, then the expected payoff (5.3) can be rewritten

$$(5.4) \qquad U = \sum_y \sum_{x \in y} \omega[x, \alpha(y)]\phi(x).$$

Choosing a decision function α that maximizes (5.4) is equivalent to choosing, for each signal y for which $\pi(y) > 0$, an action $\alpha(y)$ that maximizes the term

$$(5.5) \qquad \sum_{x \in y} \omega[x, \alpha(y)]\phi(x) = \sum_{x \in y} \omega[x, \alpha(y)]\phi(x|y)\pi(y)$$

$$= \pi(y) \sum_{x \in y} \omega[x, \alpha(y)]\phi(x|y)$$

[see (5.2)]. This last is equivalent to maximizing

$$(5.6) \qquad \sum_{x \in y} \omega[x, \alpha(y)]\phi(x|y).$$

The reader will easily recognize (5.6) as the conditional expected payoff for the action $\alpha(y)$, given that x is in y.

Using (5.2) to (5.6), we may rewrite the expected utility of a decision function α as

$$(5.7) \qquad\qquad U = \sum_y \pi(y) \sum_{x \in y} \omega[x, \alpha(y)]\phi(x|y).$$

We have proved the following theorem:

For α to be a best decision function, it is necessary and sufficient that, for every y with positive probability, $\alpha(y)$ be an action that maximizes the conditional expected payoff given $\eta(x) = y$.

To illustrate, consider the last example of the production decision problem (Section 4). Here $x = (x_1, x_2)$, $y = \eta(x) = x_1$. For any level of production a, the expected net profit, given output price x_1, is

$$(5.8) \qquad\qquad E[\omega(x, a)|x_1] = x_1 a - E[\kappa(x_2, a)|x_1]$$

[see (4.3)]. Setting the derivative, with respect to a, of this last expression equal to zero, we find that the best value of a, given x, must satisfy[3]

$$(5.9) \qquad\qquad E\left[\frac{\partial}{\partial a}\kappa(x_2, a)|x_1\right] = x_1.$$

In other words, "conditional expected marginal cost must equal price."

The conditional distribution $\phi(x|y)$ is sometimes called the *posterior probability* distribution, relative to a given information signal y, because it is the distribution that is relevant to action "after" the signal y has been received. Similarly, the unconditional distribution $\phi(x)$ is sometimes called the *prior* distribution. We shall return to a more detailed consideration of the posterior distribution in Section 7.

In our definition of a best decision function we have thus far ignored one important factor, the *costs* of using a decision function.[4] The mere calculation of the action prescribed by a complicated decision function for given information may be a costly procedure. Beyond this, some decision functions may be more difficult to explain, to remember, or to apply, and thus may involve greater "administrative" expense than others. Some of the decision costs are fixed once the decision function α is chosen. Others depend on the state of the world x (in particular, they might depend on the information y) and are therefore themselves variables. Unfortunately,

3. It is assumed, of course, that the various conditions necessary for this "marginal analysis" to be valid are satisfied.

4. However, the case of nonfeasible and thus infinitely costly decision functions was mentioned at the end of Section 1.

there has been very little theoretical analysis of costs of decision that we are aware of, and aside from this brief acknowledgment of the importance of these costs, they shall play no role in our formal theory.[5]

6. COMPARISON OF INFORMATION STRUCTURES: FINENESS

Once a best decision function has been chosen, given the information structure, nothing more can be achieved in the way of increasing the expected payoff without changing the information structure itself. A different information structure would, of course, typically require a different best decision function, and might possibly result also in a higher expected payoff. Thus one is led to a natural comparison between two information structures in terms of the maximum expected payoffs that can be achieved through their use.

We shall say of two information structures, η_1 and η_2, that η_1 is not more valuable than η_2, relative to a payoff function ω and a probability distribution ϕ, if

(6.1) $$\Omega(\eta_1; \omega, \phi) \leq \Omega(\eta_2; \omega, \phi),$$

where $\Omega(\eta; \omega, \phi)$ is the maximum expected payoff

(6.2) $$\max_\alpha \sum_x \omega[x, \alpha(\eta[x])]\phi(x),$$

as in (4.1) and (4.2). This comparison does not take into account the cost of information (let alone the cost of decision; see Section 5), and therefore might be called a *gross* comparison. A reformulation including the cost of information is given in Section 12.

Is it possible for one information structure to be more valuable than another, or at least not less valuable, whatever the payoff function ω and the probability distribution ϕ? The answer is "yes," and the characterization of such a relationship is provided by the concept of fineness.

In the remainder of this section, we shall consider an information structure to be a partition of X, as indicated in Section 3; that is, we shall regard two information structures as identical if they induce the same partition (regardless of physical differences in the signals used). We shall say of two given information structures, η_1 and η_2, that η_1 is *as fine as* η_2 if η_1 is a subpartition of η_2; that is, if every set in η_1 is contained in some set in η_2. (Thus η_1 tells us all that η_2 can tell, and possibly more besides.)[6] If η_1 and η_2 are distinct, and η_1 is as fine as η_2, then we shall say that η_1 is *finer than* η_2.

---

5. See, however, Chapter 9 for an informal discussion.
6. In another terminology, η_1 is an extension of η_2, and η_2 a contraction of η_1.

For example, if X is the set of all numbers between 0 and 1, and η_1 partitions X into 10 equal intervals, while η_2 partitions X into 100 equal intervals, then η_2 is finer than η_1 (η_2 has one digit more). If X is the set of all pairs (x_1, x_2) of integers, and under η_1 each pair constitutes a subset, while under η_2 all pairs with the same value of x_1 constitute a subset, η_1 is finer than η_2.

Clearly, it cannot be said of every pair η_1, $\eta_2(\eta_1 \neq \eta_2)$ that one of them is finer than the other. For example, let X be the set of all numbers between 0 and 1; let η_1 be the partition of X into two sets: "elements of X larger than 1/2," and "elements of X not larger than 1/2"; and let η_2 partition X into three sets: "elements of X larger than 2/3," "elements of X smaller than 1/3" and "other elements of X." Then η_2 is not finer than η_1 in the sense defined, nor is η_1 finer than η_2. In such a case, we say that η_1 and η_2 are noncomparable with respect to fineness. (Thus the relation "as fine as" induces only a partial, not a complete, ordering of partitions of X.)

The finest possible information structure is *complete information*, defined by

(6.3) $\eta(x) = \{x\}$ for all x in X.

In this partition, each set consists of a single state.

On the other hand, the least fine (or "coarsest") information structure is the partition consisting of the set X itself. It is clear that this information structure gives no information at all that has not already been incorporated into the formulation of the decision problem. We call this structure *no information*.

A decision function based upon no information is constant, that is, the same action is taken for all states x.

The significance, for the present question, of the concept of fineness lies in the following theorem.

THEOREM. *Let η_1 and η_2 be distinct information structures; if η_1 is as fine as η_2, then, and only then, η_1 is at least as valuable as η_2 for every probability density and every payoff function, that is,*

$$\hat{\Omega}(\eta_1; \omega, \phi) \geqq \hat{\Omega}(\eta_2; \omega, \phi) \qquad \textit{for all } \omega \textit{ and } \phi.$$

The "then" part of this theorem is fairly obvious, for the set of decision functions available to a person using η_1 includes essentially all of the decision functions available to a person using η_2, and possibly more, so that the first person cannot do worse than the second.

The "only then" part of the theorem is perhaps not quite so obvious. Suppose that η_1 and η_2 are noncomparable with respect to fineness. Let ϕ be a strictly positive density function on X. We shall show that, for some payoff function, η_1 is more valuable than η_2, and for some other payoff function, η_1 is less valuable than η_2.

Since η_1 and η_2 are not comparable (and are distinct), η_1 is not finer than η_2, and therefore there are two distinct states, say x_1 and x_2, such that

(6.4)
$$\eta_1(x_1) = \eta_1(x_2),$$
$$\eta_2(x_1) \neq \eta_2(x_2).$$

Similarly, since η_2 is not finer than η_1, there are two distinct states, say x_3 and x_4, such that

(6.5)
$$\eta_1(x_3) \neq \eta_1(x_4),$$
$$\eta_2(x_3) = \eta_2(x_4).$$

The pairs $\{x_1, x_2\}$ and $\{x_3, x_4\}$ may have no state in common or one state in common (but not both states in common). Consider the two cases separately.

Case 1: $x_1, x_2, x_3,$ and x_4 are distinct.

Figure 2.1 represents the properties (6.4) and (6.5) of the two information structures for this case. Only the states x_1, x_2, x_3, and x_4 are shown in the figure; η_1 is indicated by the solid-line curves, and η_2 by the dashed-line curves.

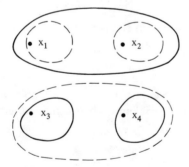

FIGURE 2.1. Non-comparable information structures: Case I. η_1———. η_2————.

We shall construct two decision problems, (i) and (ii). In problem (i), the payoff function is such that it is important for the decision-maker to distinguish between x_3 and x_4, but not between x_1 and x_2 (for this problem

η_1 would be the more valuable structure). In problem (ii) the reverse is true.

To define decision problem (i), let there be two alternative actions, a_1 and a_2, and let the payoff function be

(6.6)
$$\omega(x_3, a_1) = 1$$
$$\omega(x, a_1) = 0 \qquad \text{for all } x \neq x_3$$
$$\omega(x_4, a_2) = 1$$
$$\omega(x, a_2) = 0 \qquad \text{for all } x \neq x_4.$$

The payoff function (6.6) is given in Table 2.2. (Notice, incidentally, that a_1 and a_2 are actions one might use for the measurement of the probabilities of the states x_3 and x_4, respectively; see Chapter 1, Sections 8 and 9.)

TABLE 2.2

Actions	States						
	x_1	x_2	x_3	x_4	x_5	x_6	...
a_1	0	0	1	0	0	0	...
a_2	0	0	0	1	0	0	...

It is easily verified that, with the information structure η_1, the maximum expected payoff is

$$\phi(x_3) + \phi(x_4);$$

whereas with the information structure η_2, the maximum expected payoff is

$$\max\{\phi(x_3), \phi(x_4)\}.$$

Hence for decision problem (i), η_1 is more valuable than η_2.

Now define decision problem (ii) by changing the payoff function (6.6) to

$$\omega(x_1, a_1) = 1$$
$$\omega(x, a_1) = 0 \qquad \text{for all } x \neq x_1$$
$$\omega(x_2, a_2) = 1$$
$$\omega(x, a_2) = 0 \qquad \text{for all } x \neq x_2.$$

This payoff function is given in Table 2.3. For problem (ii) one easily

TABLE 2.3

Actions \ States	x_1	x_2	x_3	x_4	x_5	x_6	...
a_1	1	0	0	0	0	0	...
a_2	0	1	0	0	0	0	...

verifies that the maximum expected payoff for information structure η_1 is

$$\max\{\phi(x_1),\ \phi(x_2)\},$$

whereas for η_2 it is

$$\phi(x_1) + \phi(x_2).$$

Hence, in problem (ii), η_2 is more valuable than η_1.

Case 2: the pairs (x_1, x_2) and (x_3, x_4) have a state in common.

Without loss of generality, we may suppose that $x_1 = x_4$. This case is illustrated by Figure 2.2.

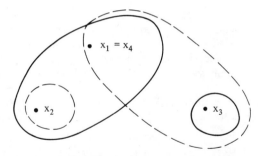

FIGURE 2.2. Non-comparable information structures:
Case II. η_1———. η_2————.

The construction of two decision problems corresponding to problems (i) and (ii) of case 1, which would complete the proof, is left as an exercise.

One interesting corollary of this theorem is that it is impossible to define a single measure of the "amount" of information (without regard to the payoff function) such that, if one information structure adds a greater amount of information than another, the first will be more valuable than the second, for every payoff function. A measure of the amount of information independent of the payoff function and depending only on the probabilities of the alternative signals y, was proposed by C. Shannon (Shannon and Weaver 1949). In the simple case in which the signals are finite in number and equiprobable, Shannon's measure is an increasing function (the logarithm) of the number of signals. For example, if x is uniformly distributed over an interval X, which is divided into n equal subintervals, and if the information $y = \eta(x)$ consists of stating the subinterval in which the number x falls, then Shannon's measure is the larger, the larger n. Yet this ranking of information structures according to the number of subintervals need not coincide with the ranking of the values of those information structures. In our Example 3B, the payoff function is such that the value of information is highest when the number of subintervals is two or any even number; so that it is more valuable to use two equal subintervals than to use one hundred and one!

We give here, for future reference, a useful formula for the "iteration" of expectations conditional on partitions of increasing fineness. Let partition $\mathscr{Y}_1$ be as fine as the partition $\mathscr{Y}_2$, let ϕ be a probability density function on X, and let f be any real-valued function defined on the partition $\mathscr{Y}_1$. For any y_2 in $\mathscr{Y}_2$, define the conditional expectation

(6.7)
$$E[f|y_2] \equiv \sum_{\substack{y_1 \in \mathscr{Y}_1 \\ y_1 \subset y_2}} f(y_1)\pi(y_1|y_2),$$

where $\pi(y_1|y_2)$ denotes the conditional probability of y_1 given y_2 [see 9.13a of Chapter 1]. In particular, $\mathscr{Y}_1$ could be the finest possible partition of X (i.e., the partition of X into one-element subsets), in which case (6.7) would define the conditional expectation of a function of x. Notice that $E[f|y_2]$ depends upon y_2, that is, $E[f|y_2]$ is a function on the partition $\mathscr{Y}_2$. We shall denote this function by the symbol $E[f|\mathscr{Y}_2]$.

Now consider *three* partitions of X, $\mathscr{Y}_1$, $\mathscr{Y}_2$, and $\mathscr{Y}_3$, such that $\mathscr{Y}_1$ is as fine as $\mathscr{Y}_2$, and $\mathscr{Y}_2$ is in turn as fine as $\mathscr{Y}_3$. Let f again be a real-valued function defined on $\mathscr{Y}_1$. We shall show that

(6.8)
$$E(f|\mathscr{Y}_3) = E[E(f|\mathscr{Y}_2)|\mathscr{Y}_3].$$

The formula (6.8) is equivalent to asserting that for every y_3 in $\mathscr{Y}_3$,

(6.9)
$$\sum_{\substack{y_1 \subset y_3 \\ y_1 \in \mathscr{Y}_1}} f(y_1)\pi(y_1|y_3) = \sum_{\substack{y_2 \subset y_3 \\ y_2 \in \mathscr{Y}_2}} \sum_{\substack{y_1 \subset y_2 \\ y_1 \in \mathscr{Y}_1}} f(y_1)\pi(y_1|y_2)\pi(y_2|y_3).$$

From (9.13a) of Chapter 1,

$$\pi(y_1|y_2) = \frac{\pi(y_1)}{\pi(y_2)}, \qquad \pi(y_2|y_3) = \frac{\pi(y_2)}{\pi(y_3)},$$

and hence

$$\pi(y_1|y_2)\pi(y_2|y_3) = \frac{\pi(y_1)}{\pi(y_3)} = \pi(y_1|y_3)$$

(recall that we are concerned with the case $y_1 \subset y_2 \subset y_3$). Hence the right side of (6.9) equals

$$(6.10) \qquad \sum_{\substack{y_2 \subset y_3 \\ y_2 \in \mathscr{Y}_2}} \sum_{\substack{y_1 \subset y_2 \\ y_1 \in \mathscr{Y}_1}} f(y_1)\pi(y_1|y_3).$$

The set of y_1's over which the sum (6.10) is taken is the set of all y_1 in $\mathscr{Y}_1$ such that for some y_2 in $\mathscr{Y}_2$,

$$y_1 \subset y_2 \subset y_3,$$

but since $\mathscr{Y}_1$ is as fine as $\mathscr{Y}_2$ and $\mathscr{Y}_2$ is as fine as $\mathscr{Y}_3$, this set is simply the set of all y_1 in $\mathscr{Y}_1$ such that $y_1 \subset y_3$. Hence (6.10) is equal to the left-hand side of (6.9), which completes the proof of (6.8).

In the course of proving the Theorem of this section, we have actually demonstrated a stronger result: Let ϕ^0 be a strictly positive probability density function on X, and let η_1 and η_2 be distinct information structures; then η_1 is as fine as η_2 if and only if η_1 is as valuable as η_2 for ϕ^0 and every payoff function ω. One can also prove an analogous result in which the payoff function is fixed. Call a payoff function *sensitive* if for every state x there is an action a_x such that, when the state is x, the payoff for action a_x is one, and the payoff for any other action is zero. One can prove the following theorem: Let ω^0 be a sensitive payoff function, and let η_1 and η_2 be two distinct information structures; then η_1 is as fine as η_2 if and only if η_1 is as valuable as η_2 for ω^0 and every probability density function ϕ.

7. Payoff-Adequate Description, Noisy Information, Bayes's Theorem

In Section 2, the term *noisy* was used heuristically in introducing the concept of information. In Section 5, we showed that a best decision must be based on the posterior probability distribution, conditional upon the information signal. In this section, we give a precise definition of *noisy information* and derive Bayes's theorem,[7] a particular representation of posterior probability distributions based upon noisy information.

A partition $\mathscr{Z}$ of the set X of states is called *payoff-adequate* if it is sufficiently fine, with respect to the payoff function ω, in the following sense: for every set z (event) in the partition,[8] every pair x_1, x_2 of states in z, and every action a,

$$(7.1) \qquad \omega(x_1, a) = \omega(x_2, a).$$

It is clear that, if an information structure induces a payoff-adequate partition of X, then it is as valuable as complete information. (The converse, however, is not true.)

7. Named after Thomas Bayes (1763).
8. Warning: we depart here somewhat from the notation used in Chapter 1, where subsets of X were denoted by capital letters, Z, W, etc. Recall that y, too, is a subset of X.

Let $\mathscr{Z}$ be a given payoff-adequate partition of X, and let η be an information structure inducing a partition $\mathscr{Y}$ (not necessarily the same as $\mathscr{Z}$).

Clearly, for these partitions, the probability distribution π on X determines the joint probabilities $\pi(z \cap y)$, and therefore the conditional probabilities

$$\pi(y|z) \equiv \text{Prob}\{x \in y | x \in z\} \equiv \frac{\pi(z \cap y)}{\pi(z)},$$

(7.2a)

$$\pi(z|y) \equiv \text{Prob}\{x \in z | x \in y\} \equiv \frac{\pi(z \cap y)}{\pi(y)}$$

[see (9.13a) of Chapter 1].[9] Corresponding to $\pi(\cdot|z)$ and $\pi(\cdot|y)$ we have the conditional probability density functions,

$$\phi(x|z) = \begin{cases} \dfrac{\phi(x)}{\pi(z)} & \text{for } x \in z \\ 0 & \text{for } x \notin z \end{cases}$$

(7.2b)

$$\phi(x|y) = \begin{cases} \dfrac{\phi(x)}{\pi(y)} & \text{for } x \in y \\ 0 & \text{for } x \notin y. \end{cases}$$

The information structure η is said to be *noiseless* (with respect to $\mathscr{Z}$) if, for each z in $\mathscr{Z}$, the conditional probability distribution $\pi(\cdot|z)$ assigns probability *one* to some signal; otherwise η is said to be *noisy*. In Section 2, the average stock price was an example of a noiseless information structure, whereas the market survey would, in most instances, turn out to be noisy.

Many decision problems are naturally, or conventionally, described in terms of a payoff-adequate partition, and the conditional distribution $\pi(\cdot|z)$. Indeed, this is the standard form for a problem of statistical inference. We shall illustrate this form with the "classical" random sampling problem already introduced at the end of Section 2. An urn is known to contain two balls, of which each one may be either red or black. A single ball is drawn from the urn; on the basis of observing the color of this ball, it is desired to estimate the original number (0, 1, or 2) of red balls in the urn. The set of states is given in Table 2.1.

---

9. We shall freely use the usual symbols $\cap$ and $\cup$ for the words *and* and *or*, respectively, of Chapter 1.

State	Urn		Sample
	Ball 1	Ball 2	Ball drawn
x_1	B	B	B
x_2	R	B	R
x_3	R	B	B
x_4	B	R	R
x_5	B	R	B
x_6	R	R	R

The alternative actions are the three alternative estimates of the number of red balls, namely 0, 1, and 2. Consider the payoff function that yields a payoff of 1 for a correct estimate, and 0 for an incorrect estimate (see Table 2.4).

TABLE 2.4. PAYOFF FUNCTION

Actions	States					
	x_1	x_2	x_3	x_4	x_5	x_6
0	1	0	0	0	0	0
1	0	1	1	1	1	0
2	0	0	0	0	0	1

A payoff-adequate partition $\mathscr{Z}$ of X is

$$(7.3) \quad \begin{aligned} z' &= \{x_1\}, \\ z'' &= \{x_2, x_3, x_4, x_5\}, \\ z''' &= \{x_6\}; \end{aligned}$$

this partitions X according to the initial number of red balls. (In fact, $\mathscr{Z}$ is the coarsest possible payoff-adequate partition.)[10]

An information structure representing the sampling of one ball is

$$(7.4) \quad \eta(x) = \begin{cases} B & \text{if } x = x_1, x_3, x_5 \\ R & \text{if } x = x_2, x_4, x_6. \end{cases}$$

This information structure induces the twofold partition,

$$(7.5) \quad \mathscr{Y} = [\{x_1, x_3, x_5\}, \{x_2, x_4, x_6\}].$$

The two partitions $\mathscr{Z}$ and $\mathscr{Y}$ are represented in Figure 2.3.

10. The partition $\mathscr{Z}$ is payoff-relevant in the sense of J. Marschak 1963.

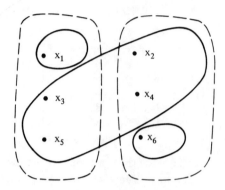

FIGURE 2.3. Partition $\mathscr{X}$____.   Partition $\mathscr{Y}$___ .

The probability distribution $\pi(z)$ will, of course, depend upon the decision-maker in question. However, many people who would not agree on a probability distribution $\pi(z)$ *would* agree on assigning conditional probabilities, as follows. Given that the urn contains only black balls, they would be indifferent between betting a dollar on the event "the drawn ball is black" and receiving a dollar whatever the color of the drawn ball. (A similar statement would apply if there were only red balls.) On the other hand, given that the urn contains one red and one black ball, most people would be indifferent between betting on red and betting on black. These preferences would imply the following conditional (subjective) probabilities:

$$\pi(B|z') = 1 \qquad \pi(R|z') = 0$$

(7.6) $$\pi(B|z'') = 1/2 \qquad \pi(R|z'') = 1/2$$

$$\pi(B|z''') = 0 \qquad \pi(R|z''') = 1.$$

[In (7.6) the symbol B denotes the event "$\eta(x) = B$," i.e., the set $\{x_1, x_3, x_5\}$, etc., and similarly for R.] Because of the second line of (7.6), the information structure η is noisy.

MAXIMIZING CONDITIONAL EXPECTED PAYOFF; BAYES'S THEOREM

Returning to a general discussion of payoff-adequate partitions, we now derive a particular form that will be obtained by the condition of maximizing conditional expected payoff, which characterizes best decision functions (Section 5).

Let η be a given information function, and let $\hat{\alpha}$ be an optimal decision function (for η). For a given signal y, the best action $\hat{\alpha}(y)$ maximizes the conditional expected payoff

(7.7) $$\sum_{x \in y} \omega(x, a)\phi(x|y).$$

If $\mathscr{Z}$ is payoff-adequate, we may define a payoff function $\tilde{\omega}$ in terms of the sets z in $\mathscr{Z}$:

(7.8) $$\tilde{\omega}(z, a) \equiv \omega(x, a) \qquad \text{if } x \in z, z \in \mathscr{Z}.$$

In terms of $\tilde{\omega}$, we may rewrite the conditional expected payoff (7.7) as

(7.9) $$\sum_{z \in \mathscr{Z}} \tilde{\omega}(z, a) \sum_{x \in y \cap z} \phi(x|y) = \sum_{z \in \mathscr{Z}} \tilde{\omega}(z, a)\pi(z|y),$$

and the maximum total expected payoff as

(7.10) $$\hat{\Omega}(\mathscr{Y}; \omega, \pi) = \sum_{y \in \mathscr{Y}} \pi(y) \max_a \sum_{z \in \mathscr{Z}} \tilde{\omega}(z, a)\pi(z|y)$$
$$= \sum_{y \in \mathscr{Y}} \pi(y) \sum_{z \in \mathscr{Z}} \tilde{\omega}[z, \hat{\alpha}(y)]\pi(z|y).$$

As in the terminology introduced in Section 5, the unconditional probabilities $\pi(z)$ are called the *prior probabilities* of the sets z, and the conditional probabilities $\pi(z|y)$ are called their *posterior probabilities*.

A simple formula, known as *Bayes's theorem*, relates the prior and posterior probabilities, and the conditional probabilities $\pi(y|z)$: for any two sets z and z' in $\mathscr{Z}$,

(7.11) $$\frac{\pi(z|y)}{\pi(z'|y)} = \frac{\pi(y|z)\pi(z)}{\pi(y|z')\pi(z')}.$$

For, from the second line of (7.2a),

(7.12) $$\frac{\pi(z|y)}{\pi(z'|y)} = \frac{\pi(z \cap y)}{\pi(z' \cap y)}.$$

From the first line of (7.2a),

(7.13) $$\pi(z \cap y) = \pi(y|z)\pi(z),$$
$$\pi(z' \cap y) = \pi(y|z')\pi(z').$$

Substituting (7.13) in (7.12), we obtain (7.11).

Bayes's theorem (7.11) can also be written in another form:

(7.14) $$\pi(z|y) = \frac{\pi(y|z)\pi(z)}{\displaystyle\sum_{z' \in \mathscr{Z}} \pi(y|z')\pi(z')}.$$

For example, in the case of the sampling from an urn described above, if the prior probabilities are all equal $[\pi(z_i) = 1/3]$, then the posterior probabilities are, from (7.14),

$$\pi(z'|B) = 2/3 \qquad \pi(z'|R) = 0$$

(7.15)
$$\pi(z''|B) = 1/3 \qquad \pi(z''|R) = 1/3$$

$$\pi(z'''|B) = 0 \qquad \pi(z'''|R) = 2/3.$$

8. Comparison of Information Structures: Garbling

If, in a decision problem, the payoff-adequate partition $\mathscr{Z}$ is fixed, then one can obtain a sharper condition for comparing the values of information structures than the fineness condition of Section 6. Let $\Omega_{\mathscr{Z}}$ denote the set of all payoff functions ω for which $\mathscr{Z}$ is payoff-adequate. For any two information structures, with respective partitions $\mathscr{Y}$ and $\mathscr{Y}'$, we shall say that $\mathscr{Y}$ is at least as valuable as $\mathscr{Y}'$, given $\mathscr{Z}$, if

(8.1) $\hat{\Omega}(\mathscr{Y}; \omega, \pi) \geqq \hat{\Omega}(\mathscr{Y}'; \omega, \pi)$ for all ω in $\Omega_{\mathscr{Z}}$ and π on $\mathscr{Z}$.

Recall that, if $\mathscr{Y}$ is as fine as $\mathscr{Y}'$, then it is at least as valuable as $\mathscr{Y}'$ (Section 6); in this case any signal y in $\mathscr{Y}$ determines a signal y' in $\mathscr{Y}'$, in the sense that, for any y in $\mathscr{Y}$, there is exactly one y' in $\mathscr{Y}'$ that contains y. Thus $\mathscr{Y}'$ can be related to $\mathscr{Y}$ by a function:

(8.2) $f(y) = $ that y' in $\mathscr{Y}'$ for which $y \subset y'$;

the corresponding information functions, η and η' are then related by

(8.3) $\eta'(x) = f[\eta(x)].$

In the case of a noisy information structure $\mathscr{Y}$ (noisy relative to the given payoff-adequate partition $\mathscr{Z}$), there corresponds to the information function η the family of conditional probability distributions $\pi(y|z)$. This suggests generalizing the condition "as fine as" to one in which the deterministic function f is replaced by a possibly "noisy" determination of the signal y' given the signal y. One could imagine that given z the signal y is determined by a conditional probability distribution $\pi(y|z)$; and thereupon the signal y' is determined by a conditional probability distribution, say $p(y'|y)$, *that is independent of z*. This latter condition expresses the condition that y' is determined solely by y, but possibly with the intervention of "noise." We are thus led to the following condition on the joint probabilities of z, y, and y':

(8.4) $\pi(y'|z \cap y)$ is independent of z,

for all $z \in \mathscr{Z}$, $y \in \mathscr{Y}$, $y' \in \mathscr{Y}'$.

In this case, we shall say that $\mathscr{Y}'$ *is a garbling of* $\mathscr{Y}$.

Note that if, for every z and y, $\pi(y'|z \cap y)$ is equal to 1 for some y', then the garbling condition reduces to the fineness condition.

We shall show that a sufficient condition for $\mathscr{Y}$ to be as valuable as $\mathscr{Y}'$, given $\mathscr{Z}$, is that $\mathscr{Y}'$ be a garbling of $\mathscr{Y}$. However, garbling is not a necessary condition; a condition that is both necessary and sufficient is given in the following theorem, due to Blackwell (see Blackwell and Girshick (1954), Theorem 12.2.2).

THEOREM. $\mathscr{Y}$ *is at least as valuable as* $\mathscr{Y}'$, *given* $\mathscr{Z}$, *if and only if there are nonnegative numbers* $\beta_{y'y}$ *such that*

(8.5) $\pi(y'|z) = \sum_{y \in \mathscr{Y}} \beta_{y'y} \pi(y|z)$ *for every* $z \in \mathscr{Z}$, $y' \in \mathscr{Y}'$;

(8.6) $\sum_{y' \in \mathscr{Y}'} \beta_{y'y} = 1$ *for every* $y \in \mathscr{Y}$.

COROLLARY. *If* $\mathscr{Y}'$ *is a garbling of* $\mathscr{Y}$, *given* $\mathscr{Z}$, *then* $\mathscr{Y}$ *is at least as valuable as* $\mathscr{Y}'$, *given* $\mathscr{Z}$.

For further discussion of this topic, see J. Marschak and Miyasawa 1968, J. Marschak 1971, with some differences in terminology.

For an intuitive interpretation of the theorem and of its relation to the corollary, we can imagine that the decision-maker, upon receiving signal y in $\mathscr{Y}$, uses a random device that chooses signal y' in $\mathscr{Y}'$ with probability $\beta_{yy'}$, thus satisfying condition (8.5), (8.6). A decision is taken that is optimal for signal y' (i.e., maximizes conditional expected payoff, given y'). It will not necessarily be optimal for the original signal y. *A fortiori*, the *expected* payoff cannot be larger than if decisions optimal for the original signals y were used. This is what the sufficiency part of the theorem asserts. Note that the signal y' in $\mathscr{Y}'$ chosen by the random device need not coincide with the actual signal that is produced by an information system $\mathscr{Y}'$ when event z occurs and when system $\mathscr{Y}$ produces signal y. That is, the conditional probability $\beta_{y'y}$, characterizing the random device, is not necessarily equal to the conditional probability $\pi(y'|y)$ characterizing the information system $\mathscr{Y}$. In the corollary, such a coincidence is indeed assumed. Therefore, the corollary follows from the theorem, but not conversely.

To prove the corollary from the theorem, first note that, by (8.4),

$$\pi(y'|z \cap y) = \pi(y'|y),$$

and hence

$$\pi(y'|z) = \sum_{y\in\mathscr{Y}} \pi(y'|z \cap y) \cdot \pi(y|z) = \sum_{y\in\mathscr{Y}} \pi(y'|y) \cdot \pi(y|z).$$

Hence the hypothesis of the theorem is satisfied by taking $\beta_{y'y} \equiv \pi(y'|y)$.

Concerning the theorem itself, we give here only a proof of the sufficiency of (8.5) and (8.6); for a proof of the necessity, see Blackwell and Girschick (1954, Theorem 12.2.2). Let α and α' denote, respectively, best decision rules for the information structures $\mathscr{Y}$ and $\mathscr{Y}'$. The value of $\mathscr{Y}'$ is, from (7.10),

$$(8.7) \qquad \hat{\Omega}(\mathscr{Y}';\omega,\pi) = \sum_{y'\in\mathscr{Y}'} \pi(y') \sum_{z\in\mathscr{Z}} \tilde{\omega}[z, \alpha'(y')]\pi(z|y'),$$

where α' is the optimal function from $\mathscr{Y}'$ to A. From the definition of conditional probability [see 9.13a of Chapter 1], and the hypothesis (8.5) of the theorem,

$$\pi(y')\pi(z|y') = \pi(y' \cap z) = \pi(z)\pi(y'|z)$$

$$= \pi(z) \sum_{y\in\mathscr{Y}} \beta_{y'y}\pi(y|z)$$

$$= \sum_{y\in\mathscr{Y}} \beta_{y'y}\pi(y \cap z)$$

$$= \sum_{y\in\mathscr{Y}} \beta_{y'y}\pi(z|y)\pi(y).$$

Hence (8.7) can be rewritten:

$$\hat{\Omega}(\mathscr{Y}';\omega,\pi) = \sum_{\substack{y\in\mathscr{Y}\\y'\in\mathscr{Y}'\\z\in\mathscr{Z}}} \tilde{\omega}[z, \alpha'(y')]\beta_{y'y}\pi(z|y)\pi(y).$$

$$= \sum_{y\in\mathscr{Y}} \pi(y) \sum_{y'\in\mathscr{Y}'} \beta_{y'y} \sum_{z\in\mathscr{Z}} \tilde{\omega}[z, \alpha'(y')]\pi(z|y).$$

By (7.10), since α is an optimal decision rule for $\mathscr{Y}$,

$$\sum_{z\in\mathscr{Z}} \tilde{\omega}[z, \alpha'(y')]\pi(z|y) \leq \sum_{z\in\mathscr{Z}} \tilde{\omega}[z, \alpha(y)]\pi(z|y),$$

so that [making use of (8.6)]

$$\hat{\Omega}(\mathscr{Y}';\omega,\pi) \leq \sum_{y\in\mathscr{Y}} \pi(y) \sum_{z\in\mathscr{Z}} \tilde{\omega}[z, \alpha(y)]\pi(z|y)$$

$$= \hat{\Omega}(\mathscr{Y};\omega,\pi).$$

This completes the proof of the sufficiency of (8.5) and (8.6).

The following example shows that garbling is not itself a necessary condition for $\mathscr{Y}$ to be as valuable as $\mathscr{Y}'$ given $\mathscr{Z}$. Let us suppose that $\mathscr{Z}$, $\mathscr{Y}$, and $\mathscr{Y}'$ each have two elements, that $\pi(z_1) = \pi(z_2) = 1/2$, and that the conditional probabilities $\pi(y \cap y'|z)$

are as follows

$$\pi(y \cap y'|z_1) \qquad\qquad \pi(y \cap y'|z_2)$$

	y_1	y_2
y_1'	19/32	1/32
y_2'	5/32	7/32

	y_1	y_2
y_1'	5/32	7/32
y_2'	3/32	17/32

We leave it as an exercise to verify that this distribution satisfies the hypothesis of the theorem, but that $\mathcal{Y}'$ is not a garbling of $\mathcal{Y}$.

One can easily verify that condition (8.4), garbling, is equivalent to each of the following conditions:

(8.8) $$\pi(z|y \cap y') \text{ is independent of } y'.$$

(8.9) $$\pi(y \cap y'|z) = \pi(y|z)\pi(y'|y).$$

9. ADAPTATION TO INCREASING INFORMATION

Suppose that a decision-maker is faced with a sequence of decision problems, identical except with respect to information structure. Suppose further that in the sequence each information structure is finer than its predecessor and independent of previous actions. How will the corresponding sequence of optimal decision functions, and the actual actions taken, look?

We shall call such a situation one of increasing information. In principle, one should analyze such a situation as a *single* decision problem, in which

1. The action variable a is itself a sequence $(a_1, a_2, \ldots, a_T)$ of variables.
2. The decision concerning the tth component, a_t, is based upon an information function η_t.
3. For $t = 1, \ldots, T - 1$, η_{t+1} is finer than η_t.
4. There is a single over-all payoff function ω, and the payoff u for a given state x and a given action (sequence) $a = (a_1, \ldots, a_T)$ is

(9.1) $$u = \omega(x, a_1, \ldots, a_T).$$

To fix the idea that the decision-maker faces a "sequence of identical decision problems" (except for the changing information), we shall assume that the components a_t can all take on the same set of alternative values, and that the overall payoff function ω in (9.1) has the form[11]

(9.2) $$\omega(x, a_1, \ldots, a_T) = \sum_{t=1}^{T} \bar{\omega}(x, a_t).$$

(This approach to a dynamic decision problem will be explored further, in a more general setting, in Chapter 7.) For example, a firm might maximize the expectation of the sum (but not, for example, the expectation of the product) of (nondiscounted) profits made in T successive years, the profit of each year being related to the action of that year only by a function $\bar{\omega}$ that does not vary over time.

The special form (9.2) of the over-all payoff function makes possible a determination of the optimal sequence of decision functions "component by component." For any given sequence $(\alpha_1, \ldots, \alpha_T)$ of component decision functions, the expected payoff is, from (9.2),

(9.3) $$E\omega\{x, a_1[\eta_1(x)], \ldots, \alpha_T[\eta_T(x)]\} = \sum_{t=1}^{T} E\bar{\omega}\{x, \alpha_t[\eta_t(x)]\}.$$

Hence the tth component of the optimal sequence of decision functions is the optimal decision function for a decision problem that one may call the "tth component decision problem," defined as follows:

1. The state variable is x.
2. The action variable is a_t.
3. The payoff function is $\bar{\omega}$.
4. The information function is η_t.

For example, suppose that a hotel cook must prepare an egg for each of two guests every day, and each egg may be either hard-boiled or soft-boiled. Each of the two diners has a definite preference for hard or soft-boiled eggs, the same for all days, and we shall say that the cook's action is "correct" on any day if he boils the right type of egg for each diner. Unfortunately, on the first day the cook does not know the diners' preferences; he learns the first one's preference after the first day, and the second one's preference after the second day.

The cook's decision problem might be formulated as follows. The state x is the state of the two diners; that is, it can take on one of the four values,

(9.4) $HH, HS, SH, SS,$

11. For a discussion of preferences that are additively "decomposable" in time, see Koopmans 1960.

where, for example, "$x = HS$" means that the first person's egg should be hard and the second person's egg should be soft. The action variable for any one day is also a pair, which can take on any of the four values (9.4). The payoff function for any one day is

(9.5)
$$\bar{\omega}(x, a_t) = \begin{cases} 1 & \text{if } a_t = x \text{ (correct)} \\ 0 & \text{if } a_t \neq x \text{ (incorrect).} \end{cases}$$

Then the expected payoff is the expected number of days on which the cook prepared the correct pair of eggs.

If there are three days, the three information structures induce the following partitions of X:

(9.6)
$$\begin{aligned} \mathcal{Y}_1 &: \{HH, HS, SH, SS\}, \\ \mathcal{Y}_2 &: \{HH, HS\}, \{SH, SS\}, \\ \mathcal{Y}_3 &: \{HH\}, \{HS\}, \{SH\}, \{SS\}. \end{aligned}$$

The example just given brings out the fact that, if the set X of alternative states is finite, then a sequence of information structures strictly increasing in fineness cannot be indefinitely long. (Thus, in the example, the cook can learn nothing new about the state of the world after the third day.) If X is finite, then a sufficiently long sequence of information structures with *strictly increasing* fineness will eventually reach *complete* information.

REVISION OF POSTERIOR PROBABILITIES

If $\eta_1, \eta_2, \ldots$ is a sequence of increasingly fine information structures, then the corresponding posterior probabilities can be obtained by a process of successive revision. It will be seen that the posterior probabilities based upon the information y_{t+1} can be calculated, using a modification of Bayes's theorem (Section 7) in which the role of the prior probabilities is played by the posterior probabilities based on the information y_t.

More precisely, we shall show that, for any z and z' in $\mathscr{Z}$, the ratio of the new posterior probabilities is obtained by multiplying the old ratio by a correction factor reflecting the new information, as follows:

(9.7)
$$\frac{\pi(z|y_{t+1})}{\pi(z'|y_{t+1})} = \frac{\pi(z|y_t)}{\pi(z'|y_t)} \cdot \frac{\pi(y_{t+1}|z \cap y_t)}{\pi(y_{t+1}|z' \cap y_t)}$$

Equation 9.7 is a formal expression of the decision-maker's "learning process."

To prove (9.7), first observe that, since η_{t+1} is finer than η_t,

(9.8)
$$\eta_{t+1}(x) \subset \eta_t(x) \qquad \text{for all } x \text{ in } X.$$

Consider then $y_t \in \mathcal{Y}_t$ and $y_{t+1} \in \mathcal{Y}_{t+1}$, with $y_{t+1} \subset y_t$; for such sets,

(9.9)
$$y_{t+1} = y_{t+1} \cap y_t.$$

By (7.2a),

$$\pi(z|y_{t+1}) = \frac{\pi(y_{t+1} \cap z)}{\pi(y_{t+1})}.$$

Again by (7.2a), with (9.9),

$$\pi(y_{t+1} \cap z) = \pi(y_{t+1} \cap y_t \cap z)$$
$$= \pi(y_{t+1}|y_t \cap z)\pi(y_t \cap z)$$
$$= \pi(y_{t+1}|y_t \cap z)\pi(z|y_t)\pi(y_t),$$

so that

(9.10)
$$\pi(z|y_{t+1}) = \pi(y_{t+1}|y_t \cap z)\pi(z|y_t)\left[\frac{\pi(y_t)}{\pi(y_{t+1})}\right].$$

Dividing (9.10) by the corresponding expression for $\pi(z'|y_{t+1})$ gives the desired formula (9.7).

10. Conditionally Independent Partitions

The most intensively studied type of sequence of increasingly fine information structures is that associated with what are commonly called *repeated, independent observations*. Random sampling with replacement, and independent replications of experiments, are examples of such sequences. In this type of situation one deals with a given payoff-adequate partition, say $\mathscr{Z}$, and a sequence of information structures η_t of increasing fineness, but such that no η_t is as fine as $\mathscr{Z}$ (i.e., induces a partition that is as fine as $\mathscr{Z}$). This last condition expresses the impossibility of "direct observation" of $\mathscr{Z}$. We shall show, nevertheless, that *under certain conditions one can obtain an information structure η_t as close as one likes to being as fine as $\mathscr{Z}$* (in a sense to be defined), *by taking t sufficiently large*. This result may be interpreted as saying that, even if one cannot observe directly in which set z in $\mathscr{Z}$ the true state x lies, by making sufficiently many (suitable) independent observations, one can come as close to certainty as one likes about the set z in which the true x lies, and therefore as close as one likes to the maximum possible payoff.

An Example

Before presenting a general formulation, we shall first study in some detail an example of random sampling with replacement. Consider an urn with a fixed number of balls, say N, which is known to the decision-maker. Each ball may be red or black; let i denote the number of red balls. The information structure η_t will be generated by a random sample, with replacement, of t balls from the urn; any particular random sample of t balls will be denoted by $(b_1, \ldots, b_t)$, where for $s = 1, \ldots, t$,

$$(10.1) \qquad b_s = \begin{cases} 1 \\ 0 \end{cases} \quad \text{means the } s\text{th ball sampled is} \begin{cases} \text{red} \\ \text{black.} \end{cases}$$

Suppose that for any single t, the decision-maker must estimate the number of red balls in the urn, on the basis of the random sample of t balls. If there is an upper limit, say T, to the sample size, then one can represent a typical state of nature as

$$(10.2) \qquad x = (i, b_1, \ldots, b_T).$$

If the sample size is unlimited, then one must in principle describe a typical state as an infinite sequence

$$(10.3) \qquad x = (i, b_1, b_2, \ldots,).$$

Therefore in this case X is infinite. In either case, the sampling is represented by the information function

$$(10.4) \qquad y_t = \eta_t(x) = (b_1, \ldots, b_t).$$

For any t, the action taken is an estimate of i, that is, some one of the numbers $0, 1, \ldots, N$. To be definite, let us assume the single-period payoff function $\bar{\omega}$ of (9.2) is

$$(10.5) \qquad \bar{\omega}(x, a_t) = \begin{cases} 1 & \text{if } a_t = i \\ 0 & \text{if } a_t \neq i. \end{cases}$$

For this payoff function, the partition $\mathscr{Y}$ of X according to the values of i is payoff-adequate. Notice that it is not possible to determine the value of i exactly from any finite sample, that is, no η_t is as fine as $\mathscr{Y}$.

To express precisely the concept of random sampling with replacement, for each s we denote by $\beta_s(x)$ the value of b_s (sth ball sampled), and suppose that the decision-maker assumes that, for each t,

$$\text{(a) } \operatorname{Prob}\{\beta_t(x) = 1 | i\} = \frac{i}{N} = p_i,$$

$$(10.6) \qquad \text{(b) } \operatorname{Prob}\{\beta_t(x) = 0 | i\} = \frac{N - i}{N} = 1 - p_i,$$

$$\text{(c) } \beta_1(x), \ldots, \beta_t(x) \text{ are statistically independent, given } i.$$

Using (9.13b) of Chapter 1, it follows from the independence assumption
(c) that

(10.7) $\mathrm{Prob}\{\eta_t(x) = (b_1, \ldots, b_t)|i\} = p_i^{\Sigma^t_1 b_s} \cdot (1 - p_i)^{t - \Sigma^t_1 b_s} \equiv \pi(y_t|i)$

For each number $j = 0, \ldots, N, \pi(j)$ denotes the prior probability
that there are j red balls in the urn; and $\pi(j|y_t)$ denotes the posterior
(conditional) probability that there are j red balls in the urn given that
$\eta_t(x) = y_t$.

We shall show that, if t is sufficiently large, then, *given i*, the decision-
maker is very sure that the posterior probability $\pi(j|\eta_t[x])$ will be close to
zero for all $j \neq i$, and close to *one* for $j = i$. To be precise, we shall show that,
for any $\varepsilon > 0$,

(10.8)

$$\lim_{t \to \infty} \mathrm{Prob}\{\pi(j|\eta_t[x]) \leq \varepsilon|i\} = 1 \qquad \text{for } j \neq i;$$

$$\lim_{t \to \infty} \mathrm{Prob}\{\pi(i|\eta_t[x]) \geq 1 - \varepsilon|i\} = 1.$$

[In (10.8), both probabilities ("Prob" and "π") are, of course, subjective
and thus reflected in the choice of action, as in (9.16) of Chapter 1.]

Before proceeding to sketch the proof of (10.8), we note an important
corollary. If information were complete, the best action would be $a = i$,
and the expected (one-period) payoff would be 1. It is easy to verify, using
the rule of maximizing conditional expected payoff (Sections 5 and 7)
that the best decision a_t for each y_t is

(10.9) $a_t = \hat{a}_t(y_t) =$ that j for which $\pi(j|y_t)$ is maximum.

Hence the assertion (10.8) about the posterior probabilities implies that,
*for t sufficiently large, the expected payoff using $\hat{a}_t$ is close to 1, the maximum
possible.*

To sketch the proof of assertion (10.8) about the posterior probabilities,
we use Bayes's theorem (7.11), to calculate the ratios of the posterior
probabilities for a given t and a given sample $y_t = (b_1, \ldots, b_t)$: by (10.7),

(10.10)

$$\frac{\pi(j|y_t)}{\pi(k|y_t)} = \left(\frac{p_j}{p_k}\right)^{\Sigma^t_1 b_s} \left(\frac{1 - p_j}{1 - p_k}\right)^{t - \Sigma^t_1 b_s} \left[\frac{\pi(j)}{\pi(k)}\right]$$

$$= (\bar{L}_{jk})^t \cdot \left[\frac{\pi(j)}{\pi(k)}\right],$$

where

(10.11)
$$\bar{L}_{jk} \equiv \left(\frac{p_j}{p_k}\right)^{\bar{b}_t} \left(\frac{1 - p_j}{1 - p_k}\right)^{1 - \bar{b}_t} ,$$

$$\bar{b}_t \equiv \frac{1}{t} \sum_1^t b_s .$$

By the law of large numbers,[12] for large t the decision-maker is very sure that $\bar{b}_t$ is close to p_i, given that the urn has i red balls; hence he is very sure that, given i, $\bar{L}_{jk}$ is close to

(10.12)
$$\left(\frac{p_j}{p_k}\right)^{p_i} \left(\frac{1 - p_j}{1 - p_k}\right)^{1 - p_i} .$$

In particular, for large t, he is very sure that $\bar{L}_{ji}$ is close to

(10.13)
$$\tilde{L}_{ji} \equiv \left(\frac{p_j}{p_i}\right)^{p_i} \left(\frac{1 - p_j}{1 - p_i}\right)^{1 - p_i} .$$

Now note that $\tilde{L}_{ii} = 1$; whereas if $j \neq i$, then (by the strict concavity of the logarithmic function)

$$\log \tilde{L}_{ji} = p_i \log \left(\frac{p_j}{p_i}\right) + (1 - p_i) \log \left(\frac{1 - p_j}{1 - p_i}\right)$$

$$< \log \left[p_i \left(\frac{p_j}{p_i}\right) + (1 - p_i) \left(\frac{1 - p_j}{1 - p_i}\right) \right]$$

$$= \log 1$$

$$= 0,$$

so that

(10.14)
$$\tilde{L}_{ji} < 1.$$

Hence for large t, $(\tilde{L}_{ji})^t$ is close to zero, for $j \neq i$; and hence, given i red balls in the urn, if $j \neq i$, then the ratio of posterior probabilities

$$\frac{\pi(j|y_t)}{\pi(i|y_t)}$$

is very sure to be close to zero.[13] It follows that, *given i red balls in the urn, the posterior probability* $\pi(j|y_t)$ *is very sure to be close to zero for* $j \neq i$, *and close to one for* $j = i$, *for large t.*

---

12. This sketch of a proof is only heuristic. For a detailed proof, see the end of this section. For the law of large numbers, see Chapter 10 of Feller 1968.

13. A separate argument must be made if i or j is 0 or N.

Note that this last is a conditional probability statement about the values of the posterior probabilities, and an expression of the decision-maker's probability judgments. Nevertheless, the convergence of the posterior probabilities, and the resulting convergence of the expected payoff to the maximum possible, take place whatever the numerical values of the prior probabilities $\pi(j)$, provided only that they are all positive. Thus two different decision-makers facing the same problem, who agree on the conditional probability statements (10.6) but who disagree on the prior probabilities $\pi(j)$, will nevertheless agree closely on the posterior probabilities $\pi(j|y_t)$ if they have both been exposed to the same information signal y_t, if t is sufficiently large, and if all the prior probabilities are positive for both decision-makers.

GENERAL CASE

We turn now to a more general treatment of the convergence of posterior probabilities and the approach to the maximum possible expected payoff. Consider again a decision problem with a sequence of increasingly fine information structures η_t, as described in Section 9, and let $\mathscr{Z}$ be a finite payoff-adequate partition of X. To formalize the idea of independent repeated observations, let B be some finite set (the set of alternative values of the "variable" that is observed), and for each $s = 1, 2, \ldots$, let β_s be a function from X to B. For each $t = 1, 2, \ldots$, define the information structure η_t by

$$(10.15) \qquad \eta_t(x) = [\beta_1(x), \ldots, \beta_t(x)].$$

Let π be a probability measure on X. The functions $\beta_1, \ldots, \beta_t$ are said to be *statistically independent* with respect to the given probability measure if, for any t elements $b_1, \ldots, b_t$ in B (not necessarily distinct),

$$(10.16) \quad \mathrm{Prob}\{\beta_1(x) = b_1, \ldots, \beta_t(x) = b_t\} = \prod_{s=1}^{t} \mathrm{Prob}\{\beta_s(x) = b_s\}.$$

Similarly, $\beta_1, \ldots, \beta_t$ are (conditionally) statistically independent *given the partition $\mathscr{Z}$* if, for every set z in $\mathscr{Z}$ and every t elements $b_1, \ldots, b_t$ in B,

$$(10.17) \qquad \mathrm{Prob}\{\beta_1(x) = b_1, \ldots, \beta_t(x) = b_t | x \in z\}$$

$$= \prod_{s=1}^{t} \mathrm{Prob}\{\beta_s(x) = b_s | x \in z\}.$$

First, we shall assume that, for $s = 1, 2, \ldots$ and for every z in $\mathscr{Z}$ and every b in B,

$$(10.18) \qquad \text{Prob}\{\beta_s(x) = b | x \in z\} = p(b|z).$$

Note that the probability (10.18) *is the same for all s*. This corresponds to conditions (10.6a) and (10.6b) in the example of random sampling and expresses the *repetition* of the observations. (To avoid trivial situations, we shall assume that, if $z \neq z'$, then the two distributions $p(b|z)$ and $p(b|z')$ are different.)

Second, we shall assume that, for $t = 1, 2, \ldots$, the functions $\beta_1, \ldots, \beta_t$ are statistically independent given $\mathscr{Z}$. This corresponds to condition (10.6c).

For the above assumptions to be satisfied for an infinite sequence of observations, it is necessary that X be infinite.

The posterior probability of a set z, given that $\eta_t(x) = y_t$, is denoted by $\pi(z|y_t)$. We shall prove that the posterior probabilities converge, in a sense to be made precise. The expression

$$(10.19) \qquad \pi(z|\eta_t(x))$$

indicates that the posterior probabilities that are actually realized in the course of observation depend upon the true state x, so that for any set z, and any t, the probability measure π on X implies certain probabilities of the different values of (10.19). For example, it is meaningful to talk about the conditional probability

$$(10.20) \qquad \text{Prob}\{\pi(z|\eta_t[x]) > 1 - \varepsilon | x \in z\}.$$

This is the conditional probability that the posterior probability of a set z will turn out to be within ε of 1, given that the true state is actually in z. We shall show that for fixed z and ε, this probability (10.20) converges to 1 as t increases without limit.[14]

THEOREM. *If z is in $\mathscr{Z}$, then for any $\varepsilon > 0$,*

$$(10.21) \qquad \lim_{t \to \infty} \text{Prob}\{\pi(z|\eta_t[x]) > 1 - \varepsilon | x \in z\} = 1.$$

Before proving this theorem, we discuss some of its consequences. An immediate consequence is that, for any $z' \neq z$ in $\mathscr{Z}$,

$$(10.22) \qquad \lim_{t \to \infty} \text{Prob}\{\pi(z'|\eta_t[x]) < \varepsilon | x \in z\} = 1.$$

---

14. In the language of probability theory, $\pi(z|\eta_t(x))$ "converges in probability" to 1, given that x is in z, as t increases without limit. We are assuming, as usual, that $\pi(z) > 0$ for all z in $\mathscr{Z}$.

A further consequence concerns the maximum expected payoff in period t that can be obtained through the use of the information structure η_t; this expected payoff converges to the maximum possible payoff obtainable under complete information, as stated in the following corollary.

COROLLARY. *For every t, let $\hat{\alpha}_t$ denote the best (component) decision function for period t, using the information structure η_t; then*

(10.23)
$$\lim_{t \to \infty} E\bar{\omega}(x, \hat{\alpha}_t[\eta_t(x)]) = E \max_a \bar{\omega}(x, a).$$

By (10.17) and (10.18), the conditional probability of an information signal $y_t = (b_1, \cdots, b_t)$, given that the true state is in z, is

(10.24)
$$\text{Prob}\{\eta_t(x) = (b_1, \ldots, b_t) | x \in z\} = \prod_{s=1}^{t} p(b_s | z).$$

For simplicity, consider only the case in which $p(b|z) > 0$ for all b in B. (For the case in which $p(b|z) = 0$ for some b, the proof must be slightly modified.) By Bayes's theorem, (7.11), the ratio of posterior probabilities of z' and z, given $\eta_t(x) = y_t \equiv (b_1, \ldots, b_t)$, is

(10.25)
$$\frac{\pi(z'|y_t)}{\pi(z|y_t)} = \frac{\prod_{s=1}^{t} p(b_s|z')}{\prod_{s=1}^{t} p(b_s|z)} \cdot \frac{\pi(z')}{\pi(z)};$$

or

(10.26)
$$L(z', z; y_t) = \left[\prod_{s=1}^{t} \lambda(b_s; z', z) \right] \cdot \frac{\pi(z')}{\pi(z)},$$

where

(10.27)
$$\lambda(b; z', z) \equiv \frac{p(b|z')}{p(b|z)},$$

(10.28)
$$L(z', z; y_t) \equiv \frac{\pi(z'|y_t)}{\pi(z|y_t)}.$$

Taking the logarithm of both sides of (10.26), we obtain

(10.29)
$$\log L(z', z; y_t) = \sum_{s=1}^{t} \log \lambda(b_s; z', z) + \log \left[\frac{\pi(z')}{\pi(z)} \right].$$

In (10.29), if we substitute $\eta_t(x)$ for y_t, and $\beta_s(x)$ for b_s, we get

(10.30)
$$\log L(z', z; \eta_t(x)) = t\bar{L}_t(x; z', z) + \log \frac{\pi(z')}{\pi(z)},$$

where

(10.31) $$\bar{L}_t(x; z', z) \equiv \frac{1}{t} \sum_{s=1}^{t} \log \lambda[\beta_s(x); z', z].$$

By (10.18), the *conditional* probability distribution of $\log \lambda[\beta_s(x); z', z]$, given that x is in z, is the same for all s. The mean of this distribution is

(10.32) $$\tilde{L}(z', z) \equiv \sum_{b \in B} \log \lambda(b; z', z)p(b|z).$$

If $z' \neq z$, then the numbers $\lambda(b; z', z)$ are not all equal. Hence, since the logarithm is a strictly concave function,

(10.33) $$\tilde{L}(z', z) < \log\left[\sum_{b \in B} \lambda(b; z', z)p(b|z) \right] = \log 1 = 0.$$

By Chebyshev's inequality (see, e.g., Feller 1968, Chapter 9, Section 6), for any number $k > 0$,

(10.34) $$\text{Prob}\{|\bar{L}_t(x; z', z) - \tilde{L}(z', z)| \geq k | x \in z\} \leq \frac{\sigma^2}{tk^2},$$

where σ^2 is the conditional variance of $\log \lambda[\beta(x); z', z]$, given $x \in z$, and hence (σ^2/t) is the conditional variance of $\bar{L}_t(x; z', z)$, given $x \in z$.

By (10.33), $\tilde{L}(z', z)$ is strictly negative. Taking

(10.35) $$k = -\frac{\tilde{L}(z', z)}{2},$$

inequality (10.34) implies

$$\text{Prob}\left\{ t\bar{L}_t(x; z', z) \leq \frac{t\tilde{L}(z', z)}{2} \middle| x \in z \right\} \geq 1 - \frac{4\sigma^2}{t[\tilde{L}(z', z)]^2}$$

which in turn implies

(10.36) $$\text{Prob}\{e^{t\bar{L}_t(x; z', z)} \leq e^{[t\tilde{L}(z', z)]/2} | x \in z\} \geq 1 - \frac{4\sigma^2}{t[\tilde{L}(z', z)]^2}.$$

For any $\varepsilon > 0$, letting t increase without limit in (10.36) implies

(10.37) $$\lim_{t \to \infty} \text{Prob}\{e^{t\bar{L}_t(x; z', z)} \leq \varepsilon | x \in z\} = 1,$$

since $\tilde{L}(z', z)$ is strictly negative, by (10.33).

Comparison of (10.37) with (10.30) shows that, for any $\varepsilon > 0$,

(10.38) $$\lim_{t \to \infty} \text{Prob}\{L(z', z; \eta_t(x)) \leq \varepsilon | x \in z\} = 1.$$

From this, and the definition (10.28) of L, the conclusion of the theorem follows immediately.

11. CONDITIONAL PROBABILITIES CONVERGE TO OBSERVED FREQUENCIES

We continue our analysis of repeated independent observations and now pose the question: After large samples, what is the decision-maker's conditional subjective probability that the *next* observation will take on a particular value, say b, given that in t previous observations the relative frequency of the value b has been f. Denoting this subjective conditional probability by $P_t(f)$, we shall show, roughly speaking, that for t sufficiently large, $P_t(f)$ is close to f, provided the prior distribution satisfies certain conditions.

To simplify the discussion, we shall deal only with the case in which each observation can take only one of two alternative values, that is $b = 0$ or 1. In the notation of Section 10, the set B has two elements. This would correspond to the example of sampling from an urn with red and black balls (beginning of Section 10), were it not for the fact that we shall assume that the payoff-adequate partition $\mathcal{Z}$ of X is *infinite*, and furthermore that the conditional probability

$$p(b|z) \equiv \mathrm{Prob}\{\beta_s(x) = b|x \in z\}$$

[see (10.18)] takes on *all* values between 0 and 1 as z varies in $\mathcal{Z}$. It will be seen below that this assumption is crucial for the above-mentioned convergence.

Since we are dealing with a two-element set B,

$$p(0|z) = 1 - p(1|z),$$

for every z in $\mathcal{Z}$, and so we can index the partition $\mathcal{Z}$ by the values of $p(1|z)$, and represent $\mathcal{Z}$ by the closed interval $[0, 1]$. Writing

$$p = p(1|z),$$

(10.17) and (10.18), defining the process of observation, imply

(11.1) $\mathrm{Prob}\{\beta_1(x) = b_1, \ldots, \beta_t(x) = b_t|z = p\} = p^{tf_t}(1 - p)^{t(1 - f_t)},$

where

(11.2) $$f_t \equiv \frac{1}{t} \sum_{s=1}^{t} b_s$$

is the relative frequency of 1's in the sample $b_1, \ldots, b_t$. This corresponds to (10.7) in the example of sampling from an urn.

Suppose that the prior probability distribution can be represented by a probability density function, ϕ, on the closed interval $[0, 1]$ (the formal meaning of this statement is given below). We wish to analyze the conditional probability

(11.3) $\text{Prob}\{\beta_{t+1}(x) = 1 | \beta_1(x) = b_1, \ldots, \beta_t(x) = b_t\}$

that the $(t + 1)$st observation is a 1, given that the first t observations were $b_1, \ldots, b_t$.

We shall show first that the conditional probability (11.3) is equal to

(11.4) $$P_t(f_t) \equiv \frac{\displaystyle\int_0^1 p^{tf_t+1}(1 - p)^{t(1-f_t)}\phi(p)\,dp}{\displaystyle\int_0^1 p^{tf_t}(1 - p)^{t(1-f_t)}\phi(p)\,dp},$$

where, again, f_t is the relative frequency of 1's in the sample $b_1, \ldots, b_t$, as in (11.2). Second, we shall show that, if the prior density $\phi(p)$ is positive for all p in $[0, 1]$, and if its first derivative $\phi'(p)$ is bounded on $[0, 1]$, then there is a number $K > 0$ such that for all t and f (with $t \geq 1$ and $0 \leq f \leq 1$),

(11.5) $$|P_t(f) - f| \leq \frac{K}{t}.$$

Note that the number K depends upon the prior density function ϕ but not on the observed relative frequency f.

If some assumption like the one that the prior distribution of p has a positive density is not made, then one cannot expect to get convergence of $|P_t(f) - f|$ to zero. For example, if the partition $\mathscr{Z}$ is *finite*, so that the prior distribution is concentrated on a finite set of values $p(1|z)$, then for large t, $P_t(f)$ will be close to that value $p(1|z)$ which is, roughly speaking, closest to f. Thus, if $\mathscr{Z}$ were a four-fold partition, with $p(1|z)$ taking values, say, 0, 1/3, 2/3, or 1, and if $f = 1/4$, then for very large t, $P_t(1/4)$ would be approximately equal to 1/3.

Before turning to the proof of (11.4) and (11.5), we make precise the meaning of the density function ϕ. For any interval $[a, b]$ contained in the unit interval $[0, 1]$ we define, for the moment,

$$\xi(a, b) \equiv \cup \{z : z \in \mathscr{Z} \text{ and } a \leq p(1|z) \leq b\}.$$

We assume that the subjective probability measure π on X satisfies

$$\pi[\xi(a, b)] = \int_a^b \phi(p)\,dp,$$

where ϕ is a probability density function on $[0, 1]$, that is $\phi \geq 0$ and $\int_0^1 \phi(p)\,dp = 1$.

By the definition of conditional probability [see (9.13a) of Chapter 1],

(11.6) $\text{Prob}\{\beta_{t+1}(x) = 1 | \beta_1(x) = b_1, \ldots, \beta_t(x) = b_t\}$

$$= \frac{\text{Prob}\{\beta_1(x) = b_1, \ldots, \beta_t(x) = b_t, \beta_{t+1}(x) = 1\}}{\text{Prob}\{\beta_1(x) = b_1, \ldots, \beta_t(x) = b_t\}}.$$

Averaging (11.1) over p, weighted by the density ϕ, gives

(11.7) $\text{Prob}\{\beta_1(x) = b_1, \ldots, \beta_t(x) = b_t\} = \int_0^1 p^{tf}(1 - p)^{t(1 - f)}\phi(p)\,dp.$

Similarly,

(11.8) $\text{Prob}\{\beta_1(x) = b_1, \ldots, \beta_t(x) = b_t, \beta_{t+1}(x) = 1\}$

$$= \int_0^1 p^{tf + 1}(1 - p)^{t(1 - f)}\phi(p)\,dp.$$

Division of (11.8) by (11.7) yields (11.4).

It is of some interest to note that $P_t(f)$ is equal to the mean of the posterior (conditional) distribution of p given the sample $b_1, \cdots, b_t$. Let $\phi_t(p | b_1, \ldots, b_t)$ denote the density function of this posterior distribution. The extension of Bayes's theorem [in the form of (7.14)] to the case of continuous distributions yields for this problem

(11.9) $\phi_t(p | b_1, \ldots, b_t) = \dfrac{p^{tf}(1 - p)^{t(1 - f)}\phi(p)}{D_t(f)},$

where

(11.10) $D_t(f) \equiv \int_0^1 p^{tf}(1 - p)^{t(1 - f)}\phi(p)\,dp.$

Hence (11.4) can be rewritten

(11.11) $P_t(f) = \int_0^1 p\phi_t(p | b_1, \cdots, b_t)\,dp.$

To prove (11.5), we use (11.4) and (11.10) to write

(11.12) $P_t(f) - f = \dfrac{\int_0^1 p^{tf + 1}(1 - p)^{t(1 - f)}\phi(p)\,dp - fD_t(f)}{D_t(f)}$

$$= \frac{\int_0^1 (p - f)p^{tf}(1 - p)^{t(1 - f)}\phi(p)\,dp}{D_t(f)}.$$

At this point we must make more precise our definition of the integrand in (11.10) and (11.12). Define, for $0 \le p \le 1$,

(11.13)
$$g(p,f) = \begin{cases} 1 - p & f = 0, \\ p^f(1 - p)^{1-f} & 0 < f < 1, \\ p & f = 1. \end{cases}$$

In terms of (11.13), (11.12) can be written

(11.14)
$$P_t(f) - f = \frac{N_t(f)}{D_t(f)},$$

where

(11.15a)
$$N_t(f) \equiv \int_0^1 (p - f)[g(p,f)]^t \phi(p) \, dp,$$

and by (11.10),

(11.15b)
$$D_t(f) \equiv \int_0^1 [g(p,f)]^t \phi(p) \, dp.$$

One routinely verifies that

(11.16)
$$\frac{\partial}{\partial p}\{p(1 - p)\phi(p)[g(p, t)]^t\} = t(f - p)[g(p,f)]^t \phi(p)$$
$$+ [(1 - 2p)\phi(p) + p(1 - p)\phi'(p)][g(p,f)]^t.$$

Integration of (11.16) from 0 to 1 gives

$$0 = - tN_t(f) + \int_0^1 [(1 - 2p)\phi(p) + p(1 - p)\phi'(p)][g(p,f)]^t \, dp,$$

or

(11.17)
$$N_t(f) = \frac{1}{t}[D_t(f) - 2N_{1t}(f) + N_{2t}(f)]$$

where

$$N_{1t}(f) \equiv \int_0^1 p[g(p,f)]^t \phi(p) \, dp,$$

$$N_{2t}(f) \equiv \int_0^1 p(1 - p)[g(p,f)]^t \phi'(p) \, dp.$$

Since by hypothesis ϕ' is bounded on $[0, 1]$, and ϕ is positive and continuous on $[0, 1]$, there are numbers M and m such that,[15] for all p in $[0, 1]$,

$$(11.18) \qquad |\phi'(p)| \leq M, \qquad 0 < m \leq \phi(p).$$

Hence, noting that $0 \leq p \leq 1$ and $0 \leq p(1 - p) \leq 1$, we write

$$N_{1t}(f) \leq \int_0^1 [g(p,f)]^t \phi(p) \, dp = D_t(f),$$

$$(11.19) \qquad |N_{2t}(f)| \leq M \int_0^1 [g(p,f)]^t \, dp,$$

$$D_t(f) \geq m \int_0^1 [g(p,f)]^t \, dp.$$

From (11.14) and (11.17), we have

$$(11.20) \qquad P_t(f) - f = \frac{1}{t} \left[1 - \frac{2N_{1t}(f)}{D_t(f)} + \frac{N_{2t}(f)}{D_t(f)} \right].$$

The inequalities (11.19) imply

$$\frac{N_{1t}(f)}{D_t(f)} \leq 1,$$

$$(11.21)$$

$$\frac{|N_{2t}(f)|}{D_t(f)} \leq \frac{M}{m}.$$

Applying these inequalities to (11.20), one gets

$$(11.22) \qquad |P_t(f) - f| \leq \frac{1}{t} \left(3 + \frac{M}{m} \right),$$

which proves (11.5).

12. COST AND VALUE OF INFORMATION

Information, like decision, usually costs something. The information structure that results in the highest expected payoff may involve costs of decision and of information that are so high as to make some other information structure preferable.

One part of the information cost may be fixed once the information structure is chosen. For example, one may choose to base his future decisions on the outcome of a sample of a fixed size, or on the information of a forecaster who charges a fixed fee regardless of the outcome of each forecast. Another part of the information cost may be a random variable whose

15. Since ϕ is continuous on $[0, 1]$, it attains a minimum on $[0, 1]$, and since ϕ is positive on $[0, 1]$, its minimum is positive.

value depends on the actual state of the world. For example, instead of fixing the sample size in advance, one may make the decision whether to continue or stop sampling dependent on the outcome of observations already made (sequential sampling). One may arrange with the forecaster to pay him larger sums for those forecasts that prove to be more successful. One may also arrange to pay him a fixed overhead sum plus a success bonus. Thus, in general, total information cost will be a random variable.

As is the case for decision cost, little is known about the cost of information. It is important to note that, unlike the value of information, the cost of information typically does not depend in a direct way on the payoff function. Like Shannon's (1949) amount of information, the cost of information does depend on mathematical properties of the set Y of signals, and on the probability distribution over this set. This, in turn, depends on the information structure η and on the probability distribution π over the set X of states of nature. However, two systems of signals with the same probability distributions may involve different costs. The cost in time that it takes a decision-maker to get information on his own, or the money cost that is charged in the market of purchaseable information services, depends on additional factors. The fees for information services depend, for example, on the relative bargaining positions of sellers and buyers of such services, so that, ultimately, the values of a given information structure—for other users of this kind of information as well as for the particular decision-maker—do influence the cost of information. This subject matter has been opened up by Good (1952) and McCarthy (1956) but we shall not pursue it here.

In general, taking account of the costs of information and decision will require a fairly drastic reformulation of the decision problem as we have presented it. The outcome will depend generally on the state of nature, x, on the decision function, α, and on the information structure, η, thus:

$$(12.1) \qquad\qquad r^* = \rho^*(x, \alpha, \eta).$$

The decision-maker would choose, from some set of feasible pairs, a pair (α, η) that maximizes the expected utility of (12.1) with respect to his probability distribution π on X. Note that a particular pair (α, η) may not be feasible, even though action $\alpha(y)$ is feasible for each y.

One might call ρ^* the *net outcome function*, to emphasize that, for any state x, the outcome depends upon α and η, and not just on the particular action $a = \alpha[\eta(x)]$ that is taken. Corresponding to the net outcome function we define the *net payoff function*,

(12.2) $\omega^*(x, \alpha, \eta) \equiv \upsilon[\rho^*(x, \alpha, \eta)]$,

where, as before, υ denotes the utility function on the set of outcomes.

It does not appear that much of interest can be said at this level of generality. A special case of interest is the one in which the outcome variable is vector-valued (or, in particular, numerical), and the net outcome (12.1) is a *difference* between a term that depends only on x and a—the *gross outcome*—and a term that depends upon x, α, and η—the *cost*. Thus

(12.3) $\rho^*(x, \alpha, \eta) = \rho(x, \alpha[\eta(x)]) - \gamma(x, \alpha, \eta)$,

where ρ is the *gross outcome function*, and γ is to be interpreted as the *cost function*.[16]

If the utility function υ is a *linear* function of outcome, then, by an appropriate choice of the origin from which utility is measured, one can take υ to be homogeneous as well. (Recall that the utility function is defined only up to an increasing linear transformation; see Chapter 1, Section 12.) In this case, the net payoff function takes the form

(12.4) $\omega^*(x, \alpha, \eta) = \upsilon[\rho(x, \alpha[\eta(x)])] - \upsilon[\gamma(x, \alpha, \eta)]$

$$= \omega(x, \alpha[\eta(x)]) - \tilde{\gamma}(x, \alpha, \eta),$$

where, as before (Chapter 1, Section 14),

(12.5) $\omega(x, a) \equiv \upsilon[\rho(x, a)]$,

and further,

(12.6) $\tilde{\gamma}(x, \alpha, \eta) \equiv \upsilon[\gamma(x, \alpha, \eta)]$.

The function ω is the *gross payoff function*, and $\tilde{\gamma}$ is the *cost function* in terms of utility.

From the point of view of general utility theory as discussed in Chapter 1, the separation, and subtraction, of "costs" from "gross payoff" is not permissible except in special cases. The decision-maker assigns a utility to each outcome of his decisions and the state of the world. If he has to sacrifice time or other factors in order to achieve certain desirable results, then the "outcome" is the combination of the sacrifices and the achievements. The utility assigned to this combination is not, in general, repre-

---

16. Of course, in a formal sense (12.3) is no less general than (12.1), as can be seen by taking $\rho(x, a) \equiv 0$, and $\gamma = -\rho^*$. The formulation (12.3) becomes interesting when one can attribute special properties to the functions ρ and γ.

sentable as a *difference* between some "utility of things achieved" and "utility of things sacrificed." However, because of its simplicity, the assumption that such separation of achievements from sacrifices is possible has great methodological advantages, at least as an approximation. For example, insofar as the cost of information has entered into the analysis of statistical problems, this assumption has typically been made (see Savage 1954, pp. 116–19 and Wald 1950, pp. 8–10). In particular, in the analysis of problems with repeated observations (sequential or not), it is usually assumed, if only implicitly, that the cost of sampling in terms of utility is a linear function of the number of observations (see Wald 1950, pp. 10, 103).

The problem of decision-making, especially in its applications to several-person organizations, is so full of subtle complications that it seems worthwhile to make the assumption of separable achievements and sacrifices in order to throw some light on the problem.

VALUE OF INFORMATION

Suppose that
  (i) The outcome variable is numerical (e.g., profit).
  (ii) The net outcome function can be decomposed into a difference between gross outcome and cost, as in (12.3).
  (iii) The cost $\gamma(x, \alpha, \eta)$ is actually independent of x and α, that is, is a (nonstochastic) number that depends only on the information structure.
  (iv) The utility function v of (12.2) is continuous and strictly increasing (but not necessarily linear).

In this situation one can define a simple and useful concept of the value of an information structure, namely, that cost which would equate the maximum net expected utility for the given information structure to the maximum net expected utility obtained with no information.

If the cost is C for a given information structure η, then the maximum net expected utility that can be obtained using η is

(12.7) $$\max_{\alpha} E\{v[\rho(x, \alpha[\eta(x)]) - C]\}.$$

We may suppose, without loss of generality, that the cost of no information is zero;[17] then the maximum net expected utility with no information is

(12.8) $$\max_{a} Ev[\rho(x, a)].$$

---

17. This can be achieved by a suitable choice of origin for the measurement of outcomes.

The *value* of η, denoted by $V(\eta)$, is defined to be that value of C that makes (12.7) equal to (12.8), that is, the solution of the equation

(12.9) $\max\limits_{\alpha} E\{v[\rho(x, \alpha[\eta(x)]) - V(\eta)]\} = \max\limits_{a} Ev[\rho(x, a)].$

It will be shown below that, under assumptions (i) to (iv), (12.9) does indeed have a unique solution.

The concept of value of information just defined is related to, but not the same as, the concept implicit in the relation "not more valuable than" that was defined in Section 6, namely,

(12.10) $\max\limits_{\alpha} Ev\{\rho(x, \alpha[\eta(x)])\} - \max\limits_{a} Ev[\rho(x, a)].$

In the next section, we shall give an example in which two information structures are ranked in one order if the value of information is measured according to (12.9), and in the opposite order according to (12.10).

However, the basic theorem of Section 6, relating fineness of information to value of information, remains true with the definition (12.9) of value.

There is one important special case in which (12.9) and (12.10) give the same measure of value, namely, the case of a *linear* utility function v. We shall restrict our analysis to this special case throughout the greater part of this book.[18]

To prove that (12.9) has a unique solution, let η be a given information structure, and define, for the purpose of this proof only, the functions f and g by

(12.11)

$$f(C, \alpha) \equiv Ev\{\rho(x, \alpha[\eta(x)]) - C\}$$

$$g(C) \equiv \max\limits_{\alpha} f(C, \alpha).$$

Since v is strictly increasing, $f(C, \alpha)$ is strictly decreasing in C for each α. Therefore g is strictly decreasing. Now every information structure is as fine as no information; hence

(12.12) $g(0) \geqq \max\limits_{a} Ev[\rho(x, a)].$

On the other hand, for C sufficiently large, $g(C)$ can be made not to exceed the right-hand side of (12.12). The continuity of v implies the continuity[19] of g; hence there is a solution to

(12.13) $g(C) = \max\limits_{a} Ev[\rho(x, a)],$

and by the strict monotonicity of g, it is unique.

18. G. Debreu suggested the present extension of the definition of value of information to the case of a nonlinear utility function.

19. We assume here that X is finite; if not, then some further regularity conditions are needed. We also implicitly assume that $g(C)$ is well defined for all C and all η.

13. AN EXAMPLE

A simple example will serve to illustrate the concept of value of information and to show that the two definitions of value, (12.9) and (12.10), need not lead to the same ranking of information structures.

Let there be *four equally likely states* and *five actions*, with a numerical outcome function as shown in Table 2.5.

TABLE 2.5. OUTCOME FUNCTION

Actions	States (equally likely)			
	1	2	3	4
1	1	0	-100	-100
2	-100	-100	1	0
3	0.4	-100	0.4	-100
4	-100	0.4	-100	0.4
5	0	0	0	0

We shall consider three information structures, η_0, η_1, and η_2.

(13.1) $$\eta_0(x) = 0 \qquad \text{for all } x.$$

(13.2) $$\eta_1(1) = \eta_1(2) = 0,$$
$$\eta_1(3) = \eta_1(4) = 1.$$

(13.3) $$\eta_2(1) = \eta_2(3) = 0,$$
$$\eta_2(2) = \eta_2(4) = 1.$$

The first is "no information"; the second partitions X into the two sets $\{1, 2\}$ and $\{3, 4\}$; and the third partitions X into the two sets $\{1, 3\}$ and $\{2, 4\}$. The partitions corresponding to η_1 and η_2 are shown in Figure 2.4. Note that η_1 and η_2 are not comparable with respect to fineness.

Suppose that the utility function is

(13.4) $$v(r) = \begin{cases} r & \text{for } r \leq 1/2 \\ 1/2 + (0.2)[r - (1/2)] & \text{for } r \geq 1/2. \end{cases}$$

Figure 2.5 shows a graph of this (nonlinear) utility function.

It is easily verified that the best action (constant decision function) under no information (η_0) is $a_0 = 5$, and the expected utility for this action (assuming the cost of no information to be zero) is *zero*, that is,

(13.5) $$\max_a Ev[\rho(x, a)] = 0$$

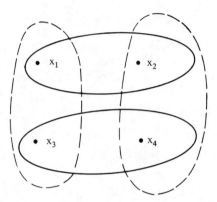

FIGURE 2.4. Information structures.
η_1———. η_2– – –.

Suppose now, for the time being, that the information structure η_1 also has zero cost. We shall show that the best decision function for η_1 is

(13.6) $\alpha_1(0) \equiv 1, \qquad \alpha_1(1) \equiv 2.$

We apply the theorem on maximizing conditional expectations (Section 5). Given that $\eta_1(x) = 0$, we find that the states 1 and 2 each have conditional probability 1/2. The conditional expected payoff for each of the five actions is given in Table 2.6. Note that if one applies (13.4) in the calculation of Table 2.6, $v(r) = r$ for all of the outcomes involved except $r = 1; v(1) = 0.6$.

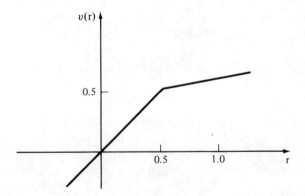

FIGURE 2.5. Utility function.

TABLE 2.6. CONDITIONAL EXPECTED UTILITY

Action a	$E\{v[\rho(x, a)]\|\eta_1(x) = 0\}$
1	$(1/2)(0.6) + (1/2)(0) = 0.3$
2	$(1/2)(-100) + (1/2)(-100) = -100$
3	$(1/2)(0.4) + (1/2)(-100) = -49.8$
4	$(1/2)(-100) + (1/2)(0.4) = -49.8$
5	$(1/2)(0) + (1/2)(0) = 0$

From Table 2.6 it is clear that action 1 is best when $\eta_1(x) = 0$; that is, $\alpha_1(0) = 1$. A similar argument shows that $\alpha_1(1) = 2$. The details are left to the reader.

In the same way, one can show that the best decision function for η_2 is

(13.7) $$\alpha_2(0) = 3, \qquad \alpha_2(1) = 4.$$

Table 2.7 shows the gross outcomes and the gross payoffs (utility of gross outcome) that result from using each of the decision functions α_1 and α_2. Recalling that the four states are equally likely, one calculates from Table 2.7 the expected gross payoffs for α_1 and α_2:

(13.8)
$$Ev\{\rho(x, \alpha_1[\eta_1(x)])\} = 0.3,$$
$$Ev[\rho(x, \alpha_2[\eta_2(x)])] = 0.4.$$

(For example, the expected gross payoff for α_1 is

$$(1/4)(0.6) + (1/4)(0) + (1/4)(0.6) + (1/4)(0) = .3).$$

Since the expected payoff for no information is zero, (13.8) also gives the value of information for η_1 and η_2 when calculated according to (12.10).

TABLE 2.7. GROSS PAYOFFS AND OUTCOMES FOR α_1 AND α_2

State	Gross Outcome α_1	α_2	Gross Payoff α_1	α_2
1	1	0.4	0.6	0.4
2	0	0.4	0	0.4
3	1	0.4	0.6	0.4
4	0	0.4	0	0.4

Consider now the value of information determined by (12.9). We shall verify that the values of η_1 and η_2 are

(13.9) $$V(\eta_1) = 0.5, \qquad V(\eta_2) = 0.4.$$

Indeed if one takes the cost of η_1 to be 0.5 and the cost of η_2 to be 0.4, then it is easy to verify that α_1 and α_2 are still the best decision functions for η_1 and η_2, respectively. The net outcomes for (η_1, α_1) and (η_2, α_2) are shown in Table 2.8. Since none of the net outcomes in Table 2.8 exceeds $1/2$, the utility of outcome equals the outcome for all of them, and it is immediately found that the expected net payoff is zero for both α_1 and α_2. Hence the values 0.5 and 0.4 do solve (12.9) for η_1 and η_2, respectively.

TABLE 2.8. NET OUTCOMES

State	Net Outcome (η_1, α_1)	(η_2, α_2)
1	0.5	0
2	−0.5	0
3	0.5	0
4	−0.5	0

Thus, if value is calculated according to (12.9), η_1 is more valuable than η_2, but, if value is calculated according to (12.10), the ranking is reversed. In this case, the reason is that the decision function α_1 results in a more "risky" distribution of outcomes than does α_2, and the (nonlinear) utility function v of (13.4) expresses *risk aversion*. On the other hand, the expected *outcome* for α_1 is higher than that for α_2. The subtraction of the costs brings all the net outcomes down into a range in which v is linear (i.e., a range of "neutrality toward risk"), which in this example is sufficient to reverse the ranking of the two information structures.

14. SUMMARY OF CONCEPTS

Our brief sketch of the single-person organization problem is complete, and this seems to be a good place for a list of the concepts, and the symbols denoting them, that will be used in the following chapters. The reader will notice that not all the concepts that have been introduced in this chapter are included in the list. Some of them, such as "bench-mark event," have already fulfilled their roles as introductory or intermediary ideas. Others, such as "sequence of independent repeated observations," will be used only rarely, if at all, in the remainder of the book.

Symbol	Concept
X	The set of (mutually exclusive) states, x, of the environment. The uncertainty about x is expressed by a probability distribution on X.
R	The set of alternative possible outcomes of action.

A	The set of all *conceivable* actions, a, equivalent to the set of all functions from X to R. It is larger than the set of *feasible* actions, but the latter will also be denoted by A if the meaning is clear from the context.
ρ	The outcome function. If the decision-maker takes action a, and the true state of the environment is x, then the outcome is $r = \rho(x, a)$.
π	Probability measure on X. The probability of an event W (a subset of X) is $\pi(W)$.
ϕ	Probability density function on X; for example, if X is finite, $\pi(W) = \Sigma_{x \in W} \, \phi(x)$.
υ	Utility function; a real-valued function on R. The utility to the decision-maker of the outcome r is $\upsilon(r)$.
ω	Gross payoff function; for any state x and action a,

$$\omega(x, a) \equiv \upsilon[\rho(x, a)].$$

Here $\omega(x, a)$ is the payoff, in utility, to the decision-maker when he takes action a, and x is the true state of the environment, provided costs of information and decision are disregarded.

$\mathscr{Z}$	Payoff-adequate partition of X.

$$\omega(x_1, a) = \omega(x_2, a)$$

for all z in $\mathscr{Z}$, all x_1, x_2 in z, and all a in the set of feasible actions.

Y	A set of possible alternative information signals, y.
η	An information function (or structure): a function from X to Y. The symbol $\eta(x)$ denotes the information signal when x is the true state of the environment.
α	A decision function (or decision rule): a function from Y to A. The symbol $\alpha(y)$ denotes the action prescribed by the decision function α when signal y is received.
(η, α)	An organizational form.
$\Omega(\eta, \alpha; \omega, \pi)$	The expected gross payoff resulting from the use of the information structure η and the decision function α;

$$\Omega(\eta, \alpha; \omega, \pi) = E\omega(x, \alpha[\eta(x)]).$$

If ω and π are clearly identified by the context, this may be abbreviated to $\Omega(\eta, \alpha)$.

$\hat{\Omega}(\eta; \omega, \pi)$	Maximum expected gross payoff for a given information structure η, sometimes abbreviated to $\hat{\Omega}(\eta)$.
$\gamma(x, \eta)$	Cost of information.
$\tilde{\gamma}(x, \eta)$	Cost of information in units of utility;

$$\tilde{\gamma}(x, \eta) = \upsilon[\gamma(x, \eta)].$$

ω^* Net payoff function.

$$\omega^*(x, \alpha, \eta) = v[\rho(x, a) - \gamma(x, \eta)].$$

Notice that we have restricted ourselves to the special case in which outcomes and costs are numbers, or possibly vectors, and cost can be subtracted from gross outcome.

$\Omega^*(\eta, \alpha; \rho, \gamma, \pi, v)$ Expected net payoff. May be abbreviated to $\Omega^*(\eta, \alpha)$.

$V(\eta)$ Net value of the information structure η, defined as the solution for C of the equation

$$\max_{\alpha} \Omega^*(\eta, \alpha; \rho, C, \pi, v) = \max_{a} E\omega(x, a),$$

where outcome and C are numerical. In the case of a linear utility function one has[20]

$$V(\eta) = \max_{\alpha} \Omega(\eta, \alpha) - \max_{a} E\omega(x, a).$$

We shall characterize the single-person decision problem as: given $X, R, A, \rho, \gamma, \pi$, and v, choose an organizational form (η, α) so as to maximize the expected net payoff $\Omega^*(\eta, \alpha)$, which in the case of vector outcomes can be written

(14.1) $\Omega^*(\eta, \alpha; \rho, \gamma, \pi, v) = Ev[\rho(x, \alpha^\lceil \eta(x)\rceil) - \gamma(x, \eta)].$

In the special case of a linear utility function, the expected net payoff (14.1) may be rewritten

(14.2) $\Omega^*(\eta, \alpha) = \Omega(\eta, \alpha) - Ev[\gamma(x, \eta)]$

$$= E\omega(x, \alpha[\eta(x)]) - E\tilde{\gamma}(x, \eta).$$

Note that in both expressions we ignore the cost of decision.

---

20. One is also justified in using this as a definition of value of information if the outcome is vector-valued and v is linear.

CHAPTER 3

Some Special Models

1.Introduction 2.Assumed probability distributions 3.Assumed payoff functions 4.Example 3A: Buying faultless market information 5.Example 3B: The speculator 6.Example 3C: Production with constant returns 7.Example 3D: Decreasing returns: output a quadratic function of a single input 8.Example 3E: Output a quadratic function of two inputs

1. INTRODUCTION

In expression (14.2) for the expected net payoff at the end of the last chapter,

$$\Omega^*(\eta, \alpha) = E\omega(x, \alpha[\eta(x)]) - E\tilde{\gamma}(x, \eta),$$

the state variable x is a *dummy variable*: the net payoff is averaged over all values of x; its expectation depends only on the functions

$$\alpha, \eta; \omega, \pi, \tilde{\gamma}.$$

The functions α, η are chosen, or controlled, by the decision-maker. But he cannot control the payoff function ω, the probability distribution π, and the cost function $\tilde{\gamma}$. These functions are the *givens* of the problem, while α and η are the *unknowns*.[1]

We shall propose in this chapter some restrictions on the givens of the problem and shall specify the restrictions still further in a series of examples. Some of the restrictions, duly modified, will be carried over to the multi-person team problem of Part Two.

We shall restrict the probability distributions, the payoff functions, and (to an even more drastic extent) the organizational cost functions in such a way as to bring out some essentials of the problem, while maintaining the greatest possible mathematical simplicity. The properties of most of the distribution functions and payoff functions we are going to use are

1. One might think that the utility and probability functions, representing as they do the tastes and beliefs of the decision-maker, would be under his own control. The norm represented by our theory prohibits this. Of course, beliefs may change in the sense that posterior (conditional) probabilities represent revisions of prior probabilities in the light of information received.

thoroughly familiar to students of statistics and economics, respectively. But it seems worthwhile to repeat the familiar in order to show how those properties are related to our problem of optimal decision functions and information structures.

Each of the simple functions used will involve only a few parameters, mostly amenable to intuitive interpretation. This is customary scientific strategy. Many theories start with the assumption of linearity, or even strict proportionality, using the coefficients to define some basic concepts: mass, resistance, or, in economics, the velocity of circulation, the marginal propensity to consume, and so forth. Many propositions of theoretical and descriptive economics are discussed in terms of "elasticities" (logarithmic derivatives) assumed constant in the first approximation; that is, the relevant relationship is assumed linear in the logarithms of the dependent and the independent variables. In applied statistics certain distributions (normal, uniform, Poisson, etc.) are tried as approximations, mostly because of their simplicity. In addition to serving as approximations, subject to revision and refinement in the light of experience, the simple functions fulfill the important task of clarifying the logical nature of a problem. They help "to fix the ideas."

2. ASSUMED PROBABILITY DISTRIBUTIONS

THE CASE OF DISCRETE STATES

In some of our examples, we shall assign arbitrary probabilities to each of the finite number of alternative states x. Even the case of just two alternative states, with respective probabilities ϕ and $(1 - \phi)$ (or the still simpler case of two equiprobable alternatives) is sometimes instructive. The distribution parameter $- \Sigma_x \phi(x) \log \phi(x)$ has sometimes been proposed as the measure of "uncertainty" in the discrete case.

THE STATES AS VALUES OF A SINGLE NUMERICAL VARIABLE

When it is meaningful to consider the state x as a numerical variable (whether discrete or continuous), it becomes useful to employ parameters such as

$$\text{the mean} = m = Ex,$$

$$\text{the variance} = s^2 = E(x - m)^2.$$

The variance (or sometimes the "range"—the difference between the maximum and minimum value of x) is often taken to gauge "uncertainty."

CONTINUOUS UNIVARIATE DISTRIBUTIONS: UNIFORM; NORMAL

When x is a continuous variable, it will be convenient to use a uniform distribution if x is confined to an interval, or a normal distribution if x runs over all real numbers (from $-\infty$ to $+\infty$). In both cases, the distribution is fully described by its mean and variance. In the uniform distribution, m coincides with the midpoint of the interval over which x varies, and the standard deviation s (the square root of the variance) is proportional to the range.

MULTIVARIATE DISTRIBUTIONS; STATISTICAL INTERDEPENDENCE

When each state of the world is represented by a vector, $x = (x_1, \ldots, x_K)$, a new feature of the distribution becomes important: the degree of statistical interdependence between the variables. To what extent does the occurrence of a particular value of one variable affect the probability distribution of another? It is intuitively plausible that this should influence the choice of information structure. If the probabilities attached to the various values of the variable x_2 depend on the value actually taken by x_1, then the knowledge of this value of x_1 will diminish the uncertainty about x_2: one can "estimate" x_2 better when x_1 is known that when it is unknown. Statistical interdependence may even make it superfluous to observe the second variable if the cost of such observations is large. If two local newspapers are likely to contain the same news, I shall subscribe to only one of them!

In the case in which $x_1, \ldots, x_K$ are numerical variables, statistical interdependence is often conveniently measured, for each pair x_i, x_k of distinct variables, by the correlation coefficient $r_{ik} = r_{ki}$. It indicates the degree to which the two variables tend, on the average, to move together or to move in opposite directions, and is defined thus:

$$r_{ik} = E(x_i - m_i)(x_k - m_k)/s_i s_k \qquad i \neq k.$$

If each variable is measured from its mean, so that $m_k = m_i = 0$, the formula is simplified to:

$$r_{ik} = E x_i x_k / s_i s_k \qquad i \neq k.$$

Further simplification is obtained by choosing units such that $s_k = s_i = 1$; then $r_{ik} = E x_i x_k$; $i \neq k$.

MULTIVARIATE NORMAL DISTRIBUTION

In particular, if the joint distribution of the K variables is normal, it is fully described by the K means, K variances, and $K(K-1)/2$ correlation coefficients. Thus if $K = 2$ (in which case we shall simply write $r_{12} = r$), a normal distribution is fully described by the five parameters m_1, m_2, s_1, s_2, r.

It will be recalled (Chapter 2, Section 5) that, under uncertainty, the decision-maker has to maximize the *conditional* expectation of the payoff, given the information. For an important class of payoff functions, this involves computing conditional expectations of some state variables given others; and in particular, expressing $E(x_k|x_i)$ $(i \neq k)$ as a function of x_i (called *regression function of x_k on x_i*). It is a convenient property of the normal distribution that this function is linear:

(2.1) $$E[(x_k - m_k)|(x_i - m_i)] = r_{ik} \cdot (s_k/s_i) \cdot (x_i - m_i)$$

$(r_{ik}s_k/s_i$ is the *regression coefficient of x_k on x_i*); or when $m_i = 0 = m_k$,

(2.1a) $$E(x_k|x_i) = r_{ik} \cdot (s_k/s_i) \cdot x_i.$$

A SIMPLE JOINT DISTRIBUTION OF TWO-VALUED VARIABLES

It will simplify some of our illustrations if we assume that each variable x_k, $k = 1, \ldots, K$, is capable of taking just two numerical values, each with probability $1/2$. This multivariate extension of the case in which a single variable takes two equiprobable values turns out to be very convenient, for it yields the same linear regression equations, (2.1) or (2.1a), as the normal distribution. Because of its simplicity, the suggested discrete distribution provides direct insight into the logic of the problem by enabling the reader to proceed step by step instead of relying on ready-made results from textbooks.

The two equiprobable values of x_k can be expressed in terms of its mean and its standard deviation: as $m_k + s_k$ and $m_k - s_k$ $(s_k > 0)$. To verify this, compute

$$E(x_k) = (1/2)(m_k + s_k) + (1/2)(m_k - s_k) = m_k,$$
$$E(x_k - m_k)^2 = (1/2)s_k^2 + (1/2)(-s_k)^2 = s_k^2.$$

It will often be convenient to measure each variable from its mean, that is, to take the mean as the origin. Then x_k takes the values $+s_k$ and $-s_k$ with equal probabilities; it has zero mean and variance s_k^2. For every pair x_i, x_k, the correlation coefficient can be computed as follows: If we write

$p = \mathrm{Prob}(x_i = s_i$ and $x_k = s_k)$, then the joint distribution becomes

(2.2)

	$x_k = s_k$	$x_k = -s_k$
$x_i = s_i$	p	$(1/2) - p$
$x_i = -s_i$	$(1/2) - p$	p

Hence $r_{ik} = E(x_i x_k)/s_i s_k = 4p - 1$; therefore $p = (1 + r_{ik})/4$, and the above joint distribution of x_i and x_k can be rewritten as

(2.3)

	$x_k = s_k$	$x_k = -s_k$
$x_i = s_i$	$(1 + r_{ik})/4$	$(1 - r_{ik})/4$
$x_i = -s_i$	$(1 - r_{ik})/4$	$(1 + r_{ik})/4$

(If $K = 2$, this matrix fully describes the distribution.) We can now evaluate the conditional probabilities

$$\mathrm{Prob}(x_k = +s_k | x_i = +s_i) = \mathrm{Prob}(x_k = -s_k | x_i = -s_i) = (1 + r_{ik})/2,$$

$$\mathrm{Prob}(x_k = -s_k | x_i = +s_i) = \mathrm{Prob}(x_k = +s_k | x_i = -s_i) = (1 - r_{ik})/2,$$

and the conditional expectations $E(x_k | x_i)$:

$$E(x_k|x_i) = \begin{cases} s_k \cdot \mathrm{Pr}(x_k = s_k|x_i = s_i) + (-s_k)\cdot\mathrm{Pr}(x_k = -s_k|x_i = s_i), \\ \qquad\qquad\qquad\qquad\qquad\qquad\qquad\qquad \text{if } x_i = s_i \\ s_k \cdot \mathrm{Pr}(x_k = s_k|x_i = -s_i) + (-s_k) \cdot \mathrm{Pr}(x_k = -s_k|x_i = -s_i), \\ \qquad\qquad\qquad\qquad\qquad\qquad\qquad\qquad \text{if } x_i = -s_i \end{cases}$$

$$= \begin{cases} r_{ik}s_k & \text{if } x_i = s_i \\ -r_{ik}s_k & \text{if } x_i = -s_i; \end{cases}$$

or

(2.4) $$E(x_k|x_i) = r_{ik} \cdot (s_k/s_i) \cdot x_i.$$

Thus (2.1a), or using the original variables, (2.1), is valid not only for a joint normal distribution but also for a joint distribution in which each variable takes two equiprobable values. When there are only two variables, the distribution (2.2) will be called a "*simple* 2×2 *distribution*."

3. ASSUMED PAYOFF FUNCTIONS
RELATION TO GAME THEORY AND OPERATIONS RESEARCH

The set A of feasible actions a may be discrete (e.g., buy, sell, do nothing). If the set X of states x is also discrete (e.g., market price high, medium, low), the payoff function can be represented by a matrix with a finite number of rows and columns such as one encounters in the elementary theory of two-person games: one player (the decision-maker) has at his disposal the set A of (pure) strategies, the other player (nature) has a set X of (pure) strategies; so that a given probability distribution π on X represents one of nature's mixed strategies. Since π is known to the decision-maker, he will not find it advantageous to use mixed instead of pure strategies. For the expected payoff of a mixed strategy is an average of expected payoffs of pure strategies, and an average cannot exceed each of its components.

This relation to game theory carries over to cases in which X or A or both are continuous, with the action a a real number or a real vector.

The single-person decision problem, under the assumption of known probability distribution π, is a trivial one from the point of view of game theory. Yet, if the payoff function is not too simple, the problem is identical with many difficult problems of firm management and of military science, now often identified as "operations research." Particularly important difficulties arise in the case of "dynamic programming": here X is the set of possible time sequences of states, and the payoff function depends on this sequence and on the time sequence of actions. We shall return to this in Chapter 7.

NONSMOOTH PAYOFF FUNCTIONS

Often a nonsmooth or even noncontinuous payoff function of real action variables is essential to describe a decision situation. For example, the inventory control problem under uncertainty, even in its simplest, nondynamic form, gives rise to a discontinuous function. If a is the amount chosen to be held in stock, and x is the unknown demand, the profit is a certain smooth (i.e., differentiable) function of a and x when $a - x \geqq 0$; and another smooth function of a and x when $a - x < 0$: for if the firm is out of stock it suffers a "depletion penalty," through the necessity of placing a costly emergency order or through the loss of goodwill. Another nonsmooth case (which, in a modified form, will later be extended to a multi-person case in Chapter 4, Section 8) is of the form

$$(3.1) \qquad\qquad \text{profit } u = \min(a, x) - ca,$$

where a is the output (in dollars) of a nonstorable commodity, c its unit cost, and x the amount demanded (in dollars); so that the sales value is equal to a or x, whichever is smaller.

LINEAR PAYOFF FUNCTIONS: BOUNDED ACTION VARIABLES

Among smooth payoff functions, our examples will make use of both linear and nonlinear functions of numerical action variables, each bringing out some essential features of the general problem. Let the payoff be linear in a:

$$u = \mu(x) \cdot a + v(x),$$

where μ and v are numerical functions on X. If a can take all values from $-\infty$ to $+\infty$, the payoff, at a given value of x, will not achieve a maximum at any finite value of a. On the other hand, if a has a maximum (minimum) value and $\mu(x)$ is positive (negative), maximum payoff will be at the maximum (minimum) value of a. It follows that, in the case of a linear payoff function, only the two extremal values of a have to be considered. The problem becomes identical with one in which the action variable is two-valued. Thus in Example 3C below, the only decisions to consider are production at full capacity or no production at all. This accounts for some peculiarities of the linear case, which (as the reader will find) may outweigh its simplicity in other respects.

The expectation of the linear payoff is itself a linear function of the action variable. Therefore our problem is, in effect, one of *linear programming* (see Chapter 5, Section 4): to maximize a linear form subject to linear inequalities.

SMOOTH NONLINEAR PAYOFF FUNCTIONS: THE CONCAVITY CONDITION

In general, a nonlinear payoff function yields a problem in nonlinear programming: to maximize a nonlinear form, subject to constraints. Whenever we shall find it useful, in our simpler examples, to introduce smooth payoff functions not linear in the action variable, we shall assume that the optimal value of the action variable is in the interior of the set of possible values and not at a boundary. Hence we shall be able to make use of the usual first-order conditions of the differential calculus—the marginal conditions, in the economists' language—in characterizing an optimum. In applying the second-order conditions, an important role is played by the assumption of strict concavity of the payoff function. This is implied, for example, in the "law of diminishing returns" of traditional economics. The concavity condition is expressed, in the case of a smooth function of a single numerical action variable, by the negativity of the second derivative $\partial^2 u / \partial a^2$.

CONCAVE SMOOTH MULTIVARIATE PAYOFF FUNCTIONS

When the decision-maker can vary simultaneously several numerical variables, so that action a can be thought of as an M-tuple of numbers, $a = (a_1, \ldots, a_M)$, the strict concavity of a smooth payoff function is expressed by the condition that the matrix $[\partial^2 u/\partial a_i \partial a_m]$ $(i, m = 1, \ldots, M)$ of second derivatives must be negative definite. Consider, for example, the case of a quadratic payoff function of two variables. We shall find it convenient to write it in the form

(3.2) $u = -a_1{}^2 - a_2{}^2 + 2qa_1a_2 + 2\mu_1(x)a_1 + 2\mu_2(x)a_2 + \lambda(x).$

We have $\partial^2 u/\partial a_1{}^2 = \partial^2 u/\partial a_2{}^2 = -2, \partial^2 u/\partial a_1 \partial a_2 = 2q$, so that the concavity condition

(3.3) $\dfrac{\partial^2 u}{\partial a_1{}^2} < 0,$ $\begin{vmatrix} \dfrac{\partial^2 u}{\partial a_1{}^2} & \dfrac{\partial^2 u}{\partial a_1 \partial a_2} \\[2mm] \dfrac{\partial^2 u}{\partial a_1 \partial a_2} & \dfrac{\partial^2 u}{\partial a_2{}^2} \end{vmatrix} > 0,$

is satisfied when $|q| < 1$. This result will be used in Example 3E.

ADDITIVE AND NONADDITIVE PAYOFF FUNCTIONS; INTERACTION

When, as in the case just discussed, the action variable is an M-tuple, $a = (a_1, \ldots, a_M)$, where a_i may or may not be a number, an important distinction arises between additive and nonadditive payoff functions. The payoff function ω is said to be *additive* if and only if it can be represented as a sum

(3.4) $\omega(x, a_1, \ldots, a_M) = \omega_1(x, a_1) + \ldots + \omega_M(x, a_M).$

Clearly, if ω is additive, if $a_1, \ldots, a_M$ are real numbers, and h is an increment of, say, a_1, then the corresponding increment of payoff is

$\omega(x, a_1 + h, a_2, \ldots, a_M) - \omega(x, a_1, a_2, \ldots, a_M)$

$$= \omega_1(x, a_1 + h) - \omega_1(x, a_1);$$

that is, a change in the action variable a_1 (from a_1 to $a_1 + h$) results in a change of payoff by an amount that does not depend on the other action variables, $a_2, a_3, \ldots, a_m$.

The linear payoff function

$$\omega(x, a) = (a_1 + a_2)(x_1 + x_2)$$

is clearly additive. So is the quadratic payoff function (3.2), *provided that q is zero*. In fact, we can use the absolute value $|q|$ as a measure of non-additivity in the quadratic two-variable case. We also say that q measures the interaction between the action variables a_1, a_2. In general, if the function is twice differentiable in $a_1, \ldots, a_M$, then the second derivative

$$\frac{\partial^2 \omega}{\partial a_i \partial a_j}$$

may be used to gauge the *interaction* between action i and action j, that is, the degree to which a change in a_j influences the effect of a change in a_i on the payoff, for given values of the other action variables and of x. In general, this interaction depends upon the values of x and all the action variables. In the special case (3.2), it is a constant. This parameter of the payoff function ω will be shown to affect the optimal decisions and the values of information structures, just as they are affected by the parameters (e.g., variances, correlation coefficients) of the distribution π.

COMPLEMENTARITY IN TEAMS

The concepts of a nonadditive payoff function and of interaction, while playing a role in the analysis of the decision-making of a single person, will acquire a new and still more important interpretation when, in Part Two, we shall investigate multi-person teams. A team consists of M persons, each acting on the basis of information $y_m (m = 1, \ldots, M)$ that, in general, differs from person to person. We shall define the team action a as an M-tuple of actions of the team members, $a = (a_1, \ldots, a_M)$. Each a_m $(m = 1, \ldots, M)$ may, in turn, consist of M_m components: $a_m = (a_{m1}, a_{m2}, \ldots, a_{mM_m})$; but the decision about each of these components is always based on the *same* information y_m. It is intuitively plausible that, if the actions a_1, a_2 of the members 1 and 2 interact in the sense defined, the team will benefit from communication between these two members, provided that communication is not too costly.

4. EXAMPLE 3A: BUYING FAULTLESS MARKET INFORMATION

A firm suffers a loss if it either underestimates or overestimates the demand for its product. Assume this loss to be proportional to the absolute value of the error:

$$\text{loss} = k \cdot |x - a|,$$

$k > 0$, where x is the true demand and a is the amount (called supply) that the firm brings to the market, equal to its estimate of demand. The firm knows the probability distribution of demand: x can be small (1), medium (2), or large (3), with probabilities .1, .3, and .6, respectively. The firm is faced with the following alternatives:

1. To determine the supply on the basis of its own knowledge of the probabilities of demand.
2. To pay a market research agency, which we shall suppose faultless, and which, for different fees, can tell whether the demand will be
   2′: small or not small;
   2″: large or not large; or
   2‴: medium or not medium.
3. To pay the market research agency for information on whether the demand will be small, medium, or large.

Problem: What are the minimum expected losses under each of the five alternatives (1, 2′, 2″, 2‴, 3), not counting the research fees? How much should the firm be willing to pay, at most, for each of the four research services, if it tries to maximize its expected profit, or in other words, to minimize its expected losses? (We thus assume a linear utility function of money.)

Since the main purpose of the example is to illustrate certain abstract concepts, let us perform a translation. The five cases are identified with five different information structures, which can be numbered in the same way. Thus $\eta = 1, 2', 2'', 2'''$, or 3. To each of the five values of η corresponds a different set $\mathscr{Y}$ of subsets of X (a different partition of X), which we represent, by enclosing each relevant subset of X (i.e., each element of $\mathscr{Y}$) in braces:

$$\eta = 1 : \mathscr{Y} = (\{1, 2, 3\}); \text{(one subset of } X)$$

$$\eta = 2' : \mathscr{Y} = (\{1\}, \{2, 3\}); \text{(two subsets of } X)$$

$$\eta = 2'' : \mathscr{Y} = (\{1, 2\}, \{3\}); \text{(two subsets of } X)$$

$$\eta = 2''' : \mathscr{Y} = (\{1, 3\}, \{2\}); \text{(two subsets of } X)$$

$$\eta = 3 : \mathscr{Y} = (\{1\}, \{2\}, \{3\}); \text{(three subsets of } X).$$

We can compute and compare the minimal expected losses, $\hat{\Omega}(\eta)$,[2] for each of the five information structures. First let us conveniently tabulate our *loss* function (instead of the payoff function), $\omega(x, a)$, and the probabilities $\phi(x)$ of the states of nature (see Table 3.1). The quantities x and a are expressed in units chosen so that $k = 1$; then $|x - a| = $ loss.

_____

2. In our list of concepts (Chapter 2, Section 14), the maximum expected payoff was denoted by $\hat{\Omega}(\eta)$; here we minimize loss instead of maximizing payoff.

TABLE 3.1

Demand (x)

Supply (a)	1	2	3
1	0	1	2
2	1	0	1
3	2	1	0
Probabilities	.1	.3	.6

In case 1, the expected losses $E\omega(x, a)$ for each of the three actions are:

$$E\omega(x, 1) = (0)(.1) + (1)(.3) + (2)(.6) = 1.5$$
$$E\omega(x, 2) = (1)(.1) + (0)(.3) + (1)(.6) = \;\;.7$$
$$E\omega(x, 3) = (2)(.1) + (1)(.3) + (0)(.6) = \;\;.5.$$

The best (constant) decision is $a = 3$, resulting in an average loss of .5. Thus the minimum expected loss $\hat{\Omega}(\eta)$ is equal to .5 when $\eta = 1$. We write $\hat{\Omega}(1) = .5$.

For case $2'$, first compute the minimum expected losses conditional upon each of the two possible communications obtained: $x = 1$ and $x \neq 1$. Then compute the weighted average of the two conditional expectations. When $x = 1$, the optimal action is $a = 1$, and the minimum loss $= 0$. When $x \neq 1$, the optimal a is the one that gives the smallest of the following expected losses (use columns 2 and 3 of Table 3.1):

$$(1) \cdot (3/9) + (2) \cdot (6/9) = 5/3 \text{ (when } a = 1),$$
$$(0) \cdot (3/9) + (1) \cdot (6/9) = 2/3 \text{ (when } a = 2),$$
$$(1) \cdot (3/9) + (0) \cdot (6/9) = 1/3 \text{ (when } a = 3).$$

Hence the best a is equal to 3, yielding the minimum conditional expected loss 1/3. Since $x = 1$ occurs with probability .1, and $x \neq 1$ with probability .9, we have

$$\hat{\Omega}(2') = (0)(.1) + (1/3)(.9) = .3.$$

By similar operations we find:

$$\hat{\Omega}(2'') = (0)(.6) + \min(3/4, 1/4, 5/4) \cdot (.4) = .1$$
$$\hat{\Omega}(2''') = (0)(.3) + \min(12/7, 1, 2/7) \cdot (.7) = .2$$

Finally, if the research agency identifies the demand precisely, then the optimal decision function is $\alpha(x) = x$, and hence $\hat{\Omega}(3) = 0$. We summarize our results in Table 3.2, remembering that a linear utility function of money was used.

TABLE 3.2

Information Structure η	Minimum Expected Loss $\hat{\Omega}(\eta)$	Value of Information Structure $\hat{\Omega}(1) - \hat{\Omega}(\eta)$
1	.5	.0
2′	.3	.2
2″	.1	.4
2‴	.2	.3
3	.0	.5

The ranking of the figures in the second column agrees with the statements made in Chapter 2, Section 6. Information structure $\eta = 3$ is finer than any of the structures 2′, 2″, 2‴, and, accordingly, is not less profitable than any one of these. No comparison of fineness can be made among 2′, 2″, and 2‴; the ranking of their expected loss will vary with the parameters of the problem.

The lowest profit (highest loss) being, under all conditions, associated with the information structure $\eta = 1$, the values of the information structures in column 3 of Table 3.2 are as defined in (12.10) of Chapter 2. The column gives the upper bounds on the research fees that the firm should be willing to pay for each kind of service.

5. EXAMPLE 3B: THE SPECULATOR

Suppose a speculator cannot sell short or buy more than one share of a stock. Let x be the difference between future and present price and suppose x is distributed uniformly over the interval $[-1, +1]$. Our problem again is to compare the maximum expected payoffs possible under several alternative information structures. This time, each will be characterized by a different number n of subintervals of equal length into which the whole interval $[-1, +1]$ is partitioned. Each of these information structures can be unambiguously labelled as $n = 1, 2, \ldots$. We have to evaluate $\hat{\Omega}(n)$ for various integers n.

Denote by a the amount bought (if $a \geq 0$) or sold (if $a < 0$). Then $-1 \leq a \leq 1$, and the payoff function is

$$u = \omega(x, a) = ax.$$

Let $n = 1$; that is, the speculator is not informed about the amount or direction of the price change. Since $Eax = aEx$ and he knows that $Ex = 0$ (in fact, this is the only relevant *a priori* information, in this case), all decisions a based on this information yield the same expected payoff— zero—and are therefore equally good. Hence $\hat{\Omega}(1) = 0$.

Let $n = 2$; since the speculator knows whether the price will rise or fall, he will buy or sell, accordingly. In fact, if $x \geq 0$, optimal decision is $a = 1$; if $x < 0$, $a = -1$. The payoff yielded by this decision rule is $u = |x|$; the conditional expected payoff is equal to $1/2$ (midvalue between 0 and 1) whether the price rises or falls, and, since each of these two cases is equally probable, the expected payoff is $\hat{\Omega}(2) = 1/2$.

Let $n = 4$; that is, the speculator is informed not only whether the price will rise or fall, but also whether it will change by more or less than $1/2$. Clearly this additional information will not change the best decision rule: to buy (sell) one unit when the price is going to rise (fall); at each x the payoff will be $u = |x|$; and the expected payoff $\hat{\Omega}(4) = \hat{\Omega}(2) = 1/2$. This will remain so, no matter in how many subintervals the positive and the negative parts of the interval $[-1, +1]$ are partitioned. Hence $\hat{\Omega}(2k) = 1/2$ for any positive integer k. It is also clear that, if x is always exactly known to the decision-maker, this will not change the decision rule just given nor add to the expected payoff of $1/2$. We can say that $\hat{\Omega}(\infty) = 1/2$.

But now let $n = 3$. Although the problem remains simple, we shall explicitly introduce here the information signal y to illustrate our system of concepts more fully. The signal y will now have three possible values, which we can denote thus:

$$y = \begin{cases} y_- \\ y_0 \\ y_+ \end{cases} \quad \text{if } x \text{ is in the interval} \begin{cases} [-1, -1/3) \\ [-1/3, 1/3], \\ (1/3, 1]. \end{cases}$$

Clearly if $y = y_+$ or y_- the best actions are $\hat{a}(y) = 1$ or -1, respectively, and $u = |x|$; the conditional expected payoffs are in each of these two cases equal to $2/3$ (midvalue between $1/3$ and 1). But, if $y = y_0$, any action yields the same conditional expected payoff 0 (analogous to the case $n = 1$ above); thus

$$E\{\omega(x, \hat{a}[y])|\eta(x) = y\} = \begin{cases} 2/3 \\ 0 \\ 2/3 \end{cases} \quad \text{if } y = \begin{cases} y_+ \\ y_0 \\ y_-. \end{cases}$$

$\hat{\Omega}(3)$ is the weighted average of these three quantities (with equal weights $1/3$); hence $\Omega(3) = 4/9$.

The fact that $\hat{\Omega}(1) < \hat{\Omega}(2) = \hat{\Omega}(4) = \hat{\Omega}(2k) = \hat{\Omega}(\infty)$ (with k any positive integer) agrees with the "then" part of the theorem in Chapter 2, Section 6: with any payoff function, making the information structure finer (in the sense defined) never decreases, but may possibly increase, the expected payoff. Moreover, our payoff function happens to be such that $\hat{\Omega}(3) < \hat{\Omega}(2)$. This is in agreement with the "only then" part of the statement. For, in the sense defined, neither of the structures 2 or 3 is finer than the other (although the latter carries a larger "amount of information" in Shannon's sense; see Shannon and Weaver 1949). Our payoff conditions make it more important to distinguish between, say, $x = 1/5$ and $x = -1/5$ (which, with information structure 3 result in the same signal y_0 but with 2 result in different signals) than to distinguish between 1/5 and 2/5 (which is possible with 3 but impossible with 2). In fact, dividing the interval $[-1, 1]$ into any odd number, however large, of equal subintervals will always be less valuable to our decision-maker than dividing it into just two subintervals, the positive and the nonpositive. This is due to the fact that, when the number of subintervals is odd, the knowledge that x has fallen into the middle subinterval is of no value to the speculator, who needs to know whether x is positive or negative.

6. EXAMPLE 3C: PRODUCTION WITH CONSTANT RETURNS

Suppose that a firm operates under constant returns to scale with fixed capacity. Denote the input by a, and choose the units of measurement so that output equals input and total capacity equals 1; thus

(6.1) $$0 \le a \le 1.$$

Denote by $m_1 + x_1$ the unit price of output, and by $-(m_2 + x_2)$ the unit price of input, where x_1 and x_2 are random variables with zero means. The expected profit at full capacity production is equal to

$$E(m_1 + x_1 + m_2 + x_2) \cdot 1 = m_1 + m_2,$$

a constant. We shall measure profits as deviations from this constant. This will simplify the algebra without affecting the difference between the

TABLE 3.3

	x_1	
x_2	$-s_1$	$+s_1$
$-s_2$	$(1 + r)/4$	$(1 - r)/4$
$+s_2$	$(1 - r)/4$	$(1 + r)/4$

expected profits yielded by any two different decision rules. Accordingly, we put $m_1 + m_2 = 0$. Then the profit is

(6.2) $u = (x_1 + x_2) \cdot a.$

We shall assume the price variables x_1, x_2 to have the simple 2×2 distribution[3] defined in (2.3). See the table of joint probabilities, Table 3.3.

If the correlation coefficient r is positive, a high price x_1 of output is more likely to be accompanied by a low than by a high price $(-x_2)$ of input; if r is negative, both prices are more likely to move in the same direction. We shall assume $s_1 \geq s_2$; the results can easily be applied to the case $s_1 \leq s_2$ by interchanging 1 and 2 (since x_1 and x_2 enter the payoff function, as well as the distribution, symmetrically).

The only free parameters of our problem are the distribution parameters s_1, s_2, r. We want to inquire how they influence the expected payoffs of the four possible information structures:

$$\eta = [00]: \text{neither } x_1 \text{ nor } x_2 \text{ is known}$$

$$[10]: x_1 \text{ but not } x_2 \text{ is known}$$

$$[01]: x_2 \text{ but not } x_1 \text{ is known,}$$

$$[11]: x_1 \text{ and } x_2 \text{ are both known.}$$

As before, we denote the maximum expected payoff for η by $\hat{\Omega}(\eta)$.

Let $\eta = [00]$. Then $Eu = 0$ for any a. Therefore $\hat{\Omega}(00) = 0$.

Let $\eta = [11]$. Then the sum $(x_1 + x_2)$ is known exactly, and a good decision rule (comparable to that of the case "$\eta = \infty$" of Example 3B) is

$$a = 1 \text{ if } x_1 + x_2 > 0; \qquad a = 0 \text{ otherwise.}$$

But since $s_1 \geq s_2 > 0$, the sum $(x_1 + x_2)$ is positive if and only if $x_1 = +s_1$. Hence, if one knows x_1, information on x_2 is useless. Therefore $\hat{\Omega}(11) = \hat{\Omega}(10)$.

To evaluate $\hat{\Omega}(10)$, and also $\hat{\Omega}(01)$, we shall first compute

$$E(u|x_i) = E\{a(x_1 + x_2)|x_i\} = a[x_i + E(x_k|x_i)] \qquad k \neq i;$$

3. If the joint distribution of x_1, x_2 were normal with means zero, variances $s_1{}^2$ and $s_2{}^2$, and correlation coefficient r, the results would be similar in many respects. (See Footnote 4.) We have chosen distribution (2.3) to enable the reader to compute the conditional expected payoff without relying on any classical theorems. This gives a better insight into the essence of the problem at the present introductory stage of our argument.

but we have seen in Section 1 that, in the case of a simple 2×2 distribution (as in the case of a normal distribution)

(6.3) $E(x_k|x_i) = r \cdot (s_k/s_i) \cdot x_i$ for $i \neq k$;

hence

$$E(u|x_i) = ax_i + ax_i r \frac{s_k}{s_i} = \frac{x_i}{s_i} \cdot a(s_i + rs_k) = \begin{cases} a(s_i + rs_k) & \text{if } x_i = +s_i, \\ \\ -a(s_i + rs_k) & \text{if } x_i = -s_i. \end{cases}$$

Suppose $s_i + rs_k \geqq 0$. Then clearly a good decision rule is

$$a = \alpha(x_i) = 1 \quad \text{when } x_i = +s_i; \qquad a = 0 \text{ otherwise.}$$

Since $\text{Prob}(x_i = s_i) = 1/2 = \text{Prob}(x_i = -s_i)$, the expected profit yielded by this rule is:

$$(1/2) \cdot (s_i + rs_k) + (1/2) \cdot 0 = (s_i + rs_k)/2.$$

If, on the other hand, $s_i + rs_k < 0$, a good decision rule is

$$a = 1 \text{ when } x_i = -s_i; \qquad a = 0 \text{ otherwise.}$$

This yields an expected profit $-(s_i + rs_k)/2$.

In summary, the expected profit obtained under a good decision rule, when only the variable x_i is observed, is

$$\max_{\alpha} E\{\alpha(x_i) \cdot (x_1 + x_2)|x_i\} = |s_i + rs_k|/2,$$

a nonnegative number. We thus have the following maximum expected profits:[4]

(6.4)

$$\hat{\Omega}(00) = 0,$$

$$\hat{\Omega}(01) = |s_2 + rs_1|/2 \geqq \hat{\Omega}(00),$$

$$\hat{\Omega}(11) = \hat{\Omega}(10) = (s_1 + rs_2)/2 \geqq \hat{\Omega}(01);$$

the last line follows from our assumption $s_1 \geqq s_2$. These results can be

4. If the prices were continuous variables, instead of each having just two possible levels, and if x_1, x_2, the deviations from their means, had a joint normal distribution with standard deviations s_1, s_2 and with correlation r (see footnote 3): then, apart from a scale factor, the results for $\hat{\Omega}(00)$, $\hat{\Omega}(10)$, and $\hat{\Omega}(01)$ would be exactly the same as in our example. But $\hat{\Omega}(11)$ would become proportional to $(s_1^2 + s_2^2 + 2rs_1s_2)^{1/2}$ (this quantity is the standard deviation of the sum $x_1 + x_2$); and we would have $\hat{\Omega}(11) \geqq \hat{\Omega}(10)$ (with equality holding at $|r| = 1$).

interpreted as follows. Consider first the symmetrical case, $s_1 = s_2 = s$. Then $\hat{\Omega}(01) = \hat{\Omega}(10) = \hat{\Omega}(11) = s(1 + r)/2$; so that, since $\hat{\Omega}(00) = 0$, the value of getting informed on at least one variable increases with the degree of uncertainty measured by s. Moreover, this information value increases with the correlation coefficient. This is as it should be, for the expected profit from plant operation (with optimal $a > 0$) is lowest when the correlation is perfect between the output price, $m_1 + x_1$, and the input price, $-(m_2 + x_2)$, that is, when $r = -1$; and is highest in the opposite case.

Consider now the case $s_1 > s_2$. Then the relation $\Omega(10) \geq \hat{\Omega}(01)$ is still true but the equality holds only when $|r| = 1$. Thus, it is, on the average, more profitable to know the more uncertain of the two variables (i.e., x_1), except when perfect correlation (positive or negative) makes each variable exactly predictable from the other. The maximum profit, $\hat{\Omega}(01)$, from observing the less uncertain of the two variables (x_2) reaches its minimum, zero; and the advantage $[\hat{\Omega}(10) - \hat{\Omega}(01)]$ of observing, instead, the more uncertain variable (x_1) reaches its maximum, $(s_1{}^2 - s_2{}^2)/2s_1$, when the correlation coefficient $r = -s_2/s_1 < 0$. In this critical case, by (6.3), the estimate of x_1 from x_2, $E(x_1|x_2) = -x_2$, so that the estimated profit $E(u|x_2) = a[x_2 + E(x_1|x_2)] = 0$ (measured from $m_1 + m_2$) regardless of a, the scale of operations.

Because of information cost, the equality of $\hat{\Omega}(11)$ and $\hat{\Omega}(10)$ under our assumption of two-valued price variables rules out the information structure [11]; for it requires observing both x_1 and x_2, while [10] requires observing only x_1. One can easily find the observation costs at which [10], [01], or [00] is the best information structure.

To conclude, note that the information amounts (Shannon measures), say $I(\eta)$, of the considered structures obey the following relation;

$$I(11) > I(10) = I(01) > I(00).$$

On the other hand, the payoffs were shown—for $s_1 > s_2$—to obey the relations

$$\hat{\Omega}(11) = \hat{\Omega}(10) > \hat{\Omega}(01) > \hat{\Omega}(00).$$

Finally, the relations of fineness were:

> [11] is finer than both [10] and [01];
> both [10] and [01] are finer than [00];
> [10] and [01] are not comparable in fineness.

This confirms again the statements of Chapter 2, Section 6.

7. Example 3D: Decreasing Returns:
Output a Quadratic Function of a Single Input

This model is adapted from those of traditional economists, who with good instinct exploited the simple mathematical properties of the case in which the marginal productivity of an input smoothly diminishes as the amount of input increases ("law of diminishing returns"). We make the case more specific by using a quadratic approximation. Denote by b the single input (or, more generally, a bundle of inputs that can be applied only in constant proportions), and assume output $\psi(b)$ to be quadratic in b, with a negative second derivative (this is implied by diminishing marginal productivity). Then it is possible to choose input units so as to make the coefficient of the quadratic term in $\psi(b)$ equal to -1; thus

$$\psi(b) = -b^2 + gb + h.$$

Let the output have a constant unit price. An appropriate choice of output units will make this price equal to unity. Denote by m the mean of input unit price, and by $(m + x)$ the current input unit price (hence, $Ex = 0$). Then the profit is quadratic in b:

(7.1)
$$u = \psi(b) \cdot 1 - (m + x)b$$
$$u = -b^2 + (g - m)b + h - bx.$$

This can be further simplified without loss of generality by measuring input from an appropriate origin, as follows. Replace b by a new action variable $a = b - b^*$, the deviation of input from a certain constant, $b^* = (g - m)/2$ (the economic meaning of this constant will become apparent presently). Then $b = a + b^*$, and by substituting into (7.1), the profit can be rewritten as

(7.2)
$$u = \omega(x, a) = -a^2 - ax + u^* - b^*x$$

where u^* is another constant. Clearly, if $x = 0$, then the profit u has a unique maximum at $a = 0$; that is, when the input b is equal to b^*. Thus the constant b^*, the new origin we have chosen, is the input that is optimal when the input price is at its mean level; and the constant u^* is the maximum profit that is then obtained. The payoff function ω depends on the environment variable x (input price measured from its mean level) and the action variable a (input measured from that level which is the best one at the mean input price).

The term $(u^* - b^*x)$ in (7.2) is of little interest, since it does not depend on the decision variable a. The same value of a that maximizes the profit u also maximizes the profit measured as a deviation from $(u^* - bx)$. We can therefore redefine the origin from which profits are measured and express the profit thus measured (thereby changing the meaning of the symbols u and ω in a trivial way and making maximum profit at mean price equal to zero) as

(7.3) $$u = \omega(x, a) = -a^2 - ax.$$

Our problem is to derive the best decision functions and measure the resulting expected profits under various alternative information structures. We shall consider two information structures:

(7.4)
    (1) $\eta(x) = x$, i.e., the producer is kept informed of the price;

    (2) $\eta(x) = X$, i.e., the producer is not so informed (the set X comprises all nonnegative numbers).

As in Example 3B, we may call the first information structure "∞" and the second "1." We shall denote the maximum expected profits by $\hat{\Omega}(\infty)$ and $\hat{\Omega}(1)$, respectively.

If $\eta = \infty$, the producer will, upon learning the value of x, choose the input $\hat{a}(x)$ that maximizes u for that value of x. Setting the derivative of (7.3), $(-2a - x)$, equal to zero (thus "equating the marginal product to the price of input"), we obtain the optimal decision

(7.5) $$\hat{a}(x) = -x/2.$$

The second derivative is negative (-2). The maximum profit is $\hat{u} = x^2/4$. Since the expectation of x is zero, the maximum expected payoff

(7.6) $$\hat{\Omega}(\infty) = Ex^2/4 = s^2/4,$$

where s^2 is the variance of x.

On the other hand, if $\eta = 1$, so that the producer does not know x, the best action will be some constant independent of x. It is obtained by maximizing, with respect to a, the expected profit

$$Eu = -a^2 - aEx;$$

hence the optimal output $\hat{a}$ must satisfy the condition

(7.7) $$0 = -2\hat{a} - Ex, \qquad \hat{a} = -Ex/2 = 0.$$

We note here certain important properties of the quadratic payoff function. This will simplify our presentation in all future examples where such payoff functions are used. If we denote by $\hat{a}$ the optimum decision function in the case of certainty (i.e., if, for every x, $\hat{a}(x)$ is best), and by $\hat{a}$ the (constant) optimum action in the case of no information, the comparison of (7.5) and (7.7) yields two properties, both due to the linearity of $\hat{a}$:

(7.8) $\hat{a} = \hat{a}(Ex),$

and

(7.9) $\hat{a} = E\hat{a}(x).$

Property (7.8) is sometimes described by saying that, when ω is quadratic, then Ex is the "certainty equivalent" of the random variable x; in the face of uncertainty the decision-maker does well to behave as if he were certain that x takes its value equal to its mean.[5] Property (7.9) states that the best action under uncertainty is an average of the best actions that would be taken under certainty. (Other payoff functions do not, in general, have this property. For example, it is not true that, if we do not know which of two events will happen, our best decision must be a compromise between two decisions each of which is best for one of the events: If I do not know whether I shall be invited to a formal dinner or to a beach party, I shall be ill-advised to combine bathing trunks with a white tie.) For the case of no information ($\eta = 1$), we have obtained the optimal output $\hat{a} = 0$. This yields the maximum expected profit, zero (measured from the appropriate origin, as stated above).

The advantage of the information structure "∞" over "1," that is the advantage of being kept informed about the current price of input, is

(7.10) $\hat{\Omega}(\infty) - \hat{\Omega}(1) = s^2/4.$

In terms of Chapter 2, expression (12.10), this is the value of the information structure "∞," that is, the value of getting exact information about x.

The result (7.10) seems to agree with common sense: the advantage of knowing the value of a variable should be the larger, the less "certain" or "predictable" it is, or the larger is "variability." However, variance is not the only possible measure of the vague property, variability; variance happens to be relevant in our particular case: that of a quadratic payoff function.[6]

5. In Chapter 7, Section 2, this is extended to a "dynamic" case.

6. One might use a different economic illustration of a quadratic payoff function, also adapted from ancient mathematical economics (Cournot). A monopolist chooses a price a of his product so as to maximize the profit $u = a\psi(a) - c$ where $\psi(a)$ is the quantity demanded at price a, and c is the total cost, assumed constant. Assume the demand function linear. Then (using appropriate units of measurement) $\psi(a) = -a + m + x$ where $Ex = 0$. x measures the random "shift" in the public's desire for the product. If x is known, the best decision rule is $\hat{a}(x) = (m + x)/2$; if x is not known, the best action is $\hat{a} = m/2$. The value of information about x is again proportional to the variance of x.

It is also worthy of note that the example given in the text extends to the case of imperfect markets. Suppose the price of input is a linear function, $m + x + kb$, where x is a random "shift" with zero mean. Then (7.1) still applies, with the coefficients properly reinterpreted.

8. EXAMPLE 3E: OUTPUT A QUADRATIC FUNCTION OF TWO INPUTS

We shall generalize Example 3D to the case in which two inputs have to be used, and the producer can freely vary their quantities. This will bring out the role of an important characteristic of the payoff function, the *complementarity* between various actions. The distinction between payoff functions with and without complementarity will prove of great importance in the theory of teams but is already present in the case of single-person decisions. Moreover, the example will throw additional light on the role of correlation between states of the world, already discussed in Example 3C.

Let x_i $(i = 1, 2)$ denote the price of the ith input, measured from the mean level of that price. Suppose as before that the output price is constant; set it equal to 1 by a proper choice of the units in which the output is measured. Suppose the output is a quadratic function of the two inputs. It is possible to measure inputs in such units, and from such origins, as would enable us to express the profit thus:

$$(8.1) \qquad u = \omega(x, a) = \omega(x_1, x_2, a_1, a_2)$$
$$= -a_1{}^2 - a_2{}^2 + 2qa_1a_2 - a_1x_1 - a_2x_2 + u^* - b_1^*x_1 - b_2^*x_2.$$

This profit function is analogous to that of (7.2), Example 3D, with the single-action variable a replaced by the vector (a_1, a_2). The input units being fixed (so as to make the coefficients of both $a_1{}^2$ and $a_2{}^2$ equal to -1), the price variables are measured in units depending on the chosen money unit; and they are measured from their respective means. The constant q measures the degree of interaction, as defined in Section 3. In the present economic example, and using a term of older economics, q measures the complementarity (and $-q$ the substitutability) between the two inputs.[7] (On notation, see Note, Table 4.14, p. 151.)

To guarantee that maximum profit is achieved at input levels other than the boundaries, the absolute value $|q|$ must be bounded: $|q| < 1$, as was shown in Section 3. Larger complementarity (whether positive or negative) has the same effect as increasing returns: It drives the optimal inputs to their highest or lowest possible levels.

---

7. Following J. R. Hicks (1946), the term *complementarity* has become attached to a property of the production function (or of the utility function) that is mathematically somewhat more complicated. For our purposes, the older use of the word is more convenient. Also, "interference" might be a better term than "substitutability," in our context.

As in Example 3D, if both prices are at their mean levels, $x_1 = x_2 = 0$, then the maximum profit (equal then to u^*) is attained at $a_1 = a_2 = 0$.[8] This is the economic interpretation of the term u^* and of the origins from which the inputs are measured. Moreover, as in (7.3) of Example 3D, it is convenient to measure the profit itself from an origin chosen so as to get rid of the terms that are not affected by the actions variables a_1 and a_2. With this new definition of u (and u^*),

$$(8.2) \quad u = \omega(x, a_1, a_2) = -a_1{}^2 - a_2{}^2 + 2qa_1a_2 - a_1x_1 - a_2x_2.$$

As in Example 3C, the state of nature is described by two variables (x_1, x_2), giving rise to the same four information structures [00], [10], [01], and [11]; but the action that was described by a single variable in Example 3C will now have two dimensions a_1 and a_2.

We now proceed to find the optimal decision rules and the resulting expected payoffs under each of the four information structures considered.

If $\eta = [00]$, that is, no information about prices is gathered and actions are "routine," the expected profit is equal to

$$(8.3) \qquad\qquad Eu = -a_1{}^2 - a_2{}^2 + 2qa_1a_2 + 0 + 0,$$

which is to be maximized with respect to a_1 and a_2. The optimal actions are constant,

$$(8.4) \qquad\qquad \hat{a}_1 = \hat{a}_2 = 0,$$

and the maximum expected profit is

$$(8.5) \qquad\qquad \hat{\Omega}(00) = 0.$$

Because of (8.5), the value $\hat{\Omega}(\eta) - \hat{\Omega}(00)$ of any information structure η [in the sense of (12.10) of Chapter 2] will simply be equal to the expected payoff $\hat{\Omega}(\eta)$.

If $\eta = [11]$, that is, both prices are known before the decision is made, the optimal inputs for given x_1 and x_2 are obtained by differentiating the profit $\omega(x_1, x_2, a_1, a_2)$ in (8.2), separately with respect to a_1 and with

8. For, if $x_1 = x_2 = 0$, then (8.1) can be rewritten thus:

$$u = u^* - (a_1{}^2 - 2qa_1a_2 + q^2a_2{}^2) + q^2a_2{}^2 - a_2{}^2$$
$$= u^* - (a_1 - qa_2)^2 - a_2{}^2(1 - q^2).$$

The term $-(a_1 - qa_2)^2$ is largest $(=0)$ when $a_1 = qa_2$; and the term $-a_2{}^2(1 - q^2)$ is largest when $a_2 = 0$, since we have assumed $q^2 < 1$. Hence when $a_1 = a_2 = 0$, the profit attains its maximum value, u^*. Thus the condition $-1 < q < 1$ guarantees that the "profit surface" has a "summit." A more general discussion is given in Chapter 5.

respect to a_2, and equating each partial derivative to 0. This will result in a maximum (and not a minimum) profit because of the condition $-1 < q < 1$, as shown in footnote 8.

We obtain two equations:

(8.6)
$$-2a_1 + 2qa_2 = x_1$$
$$2qa_1 - 2a_2 = x_2,$$

that is, the "marginal product of each input should equal its price." This result is, of course, well known from the economics of certainty. Solving (8.6) for a_1, a_2 we obtain two decision functions, each linear in x_1 and x_2:

(8.7)
$$\frac{-1}{2(1-q^2)}x_1 + \frac{-q}{2(1-q^2)}x_2 = \hat{a}_1(x_1, x_2)$$

$$\frac{-q}{2(1-q^2)}x_1 + \frac{-1}{2(1-q^2)}x_2 = \hat{a}_2(x_1, x_2).$$

Thus (remembering that $q^2 < 1$) the optimal quantity of an input falls as its price rises, and it falls (rises) when the price of the other input rises if q is positive (negative). If $q = 0$, each optimal input depends on its own price only (in fact, we obtain again the result of Example 3D). Comparing (8.4) and (8.7), we see once more the convenient property of the quadratic payoff function that has already been discussed in the single-input case of Example 3D [(7.8) and (7.9)]:

(8.8)
$$\hat{a}_i = \hat{a}_i(Ey) = E\hat{a}_i(y),$$

where $\hat{a}_i$ is the best ith input under no information ($\eta = [00]$); and $\hat{a}_i$ is the best decision function for the ith input under complete information [$\eta = [11]$; $y = (x_1, x_2)$].

Substituting (8.7) into (8.2), we obtain for given x_1, x_2 the maximum profit

(8.9)
$$\omega(x_1, x_2, \hat{a}_1, \hat{a}_2) = \frac{x_1{}^2 + 2qx_1x_2 + x_2{}^2}{4(1-q^2)}.$$

The expected maximum profit is therefore

(8.10)
$$\hat{\Omega}(11) = \frac{s_1{}^2 + 2qrs_1s_2 + s_2{}^2}{4(1-q^2)},$$

where as before, $s_i{}^2$ is the variance of x_i and r is the correlation coefficient.

The quantity $[\Omega(11) - \Omega(00)] = \Omega(11)$ measures the advantage of decisions taken in full knowledge of both prices over mere "routine" actions. Equation (8.10) shows that this advantage depends not only on the variances of the prices—compare the result of Example 3D—but also on their correlation, provided that there is interaction. This advantage is larger, the larger the product (qr) of the coefficients of interaction and correlation. Hence, if correlation is positive but complementarity is negative, then the advantage of using information about both prices (as against using information on none) is smaller than if interaction and correlation are both positive or both negative.

To compare the value of knowing both prices with the value of knowing only one, and to compare the value of knowing only x_1 with that of knowing only x_2, we must consider the remaining information structures [10] and [01].

Consider the case $\eta = [10]: x_1$, but not x_2, is known when the decision is made. We have to maximize, with respect to a_1 and a_2, the conditional expected profit

$$(8.11) \qquad E(u|x_1) = -a_1{}^2 - a_2{}^2 + 2qa_1a_2 - a_1x_1 - a_2E(x_2|x_1).$$

Equating the partial derivatives of this expression to zero with respect to a_1 and a_2, we obtain

$$-2a_1 + 2qa_2 = x_1$$

$$(8.12)$$

$$2qa_1 - 2a_2 = E(x_2|x_1)$$

that is, "The marginal product of each input should equal the conditional expectation of its price," a statement more general than the one we used after (8.6).

System (8.12) can be obtained from (8.6) by replacing x_2 by $E(x_2|x_1)$, a quantity that can be regarded as the estimate of x_2 on the basis of x_1. Accordingly, the solution of (8.12) is obtained by substituting $E(x_2|x_1)$ for x_2 in (8.7):

$$a_1 = -(1/2) \cdot \frac{x_1 + qE(x_2|x_1)}{1 - q^2}$$

$$(8.13)$$

$$a_2 = -(1/2) \cdot \frac{qx_1 + E(x_2|x_1)}{1 - q^2}.$$

Subtracting the expression for each a_i in (8.13) from the corresponding expression in (8.7), we see that the inputs that are optimal when x_2 is not known differ from the inputs that are optimal under complete information by amounts proportional to the "estimation error," $E(x_2|x_1) - x_2$.

At this point, it is useful to specify the assumed distribution of (x_1, x_2) in order to evaluate $E(x_2|x_1)$ explicitly. If we assume the simple 2×2 distribution (and also if we assume a joint normal distribution), we have the regression equation

$$E(x_2|x_1) = r \cdot (s_2/s_1) \cdot x_1.$$

Substituting into (8.13), we obtain two decision functions, each linear in x_1, the one price that is known to the decision-maker:

(8.14)
$$\hat{a}_1(x_1) = \frac{-x_1}{2(1 - q^2)} \cdot \left(1 + qr \frac{s_2}{s_1}\right)$$

$$\hat{a}_2(x_1) = \frac{-x_1}{2(1 - q^2)} \cdot \left(q + r \frac{s_2}{s_1}\right).$$

We note that the decision about a_2 is simply the routine decision, $\hat{a}_2 = 0$ (that is, the knowledge of x_1 remains unused in determining a_2) if there is neither correlation between x_1 and x_2 nor interaction between a_1 and a_2, that is, if $q = r = 0$. This clearly makes sense. It also makes sense that, if $q = 0$ but $r \neq 0$, then $\hat{a}_2$ does depend on x_1. For, although the profit can then be decomposed into two independent subprofits $u_i = -a_i^2 - a_i x_i$ due to each of the two inputs separately, as in (3.4), and although each subprofit depends only on the corresponding price, information about x_1 does help to increase u_2 because that knowledge contains some information about the correlated variable x_2. The coefficient of x_1 in each of the equations (8.14) is best understood by comparing (8.14) with equations (8.7), remembering that x_2 is now replaced by its estimate. Thus, in the second of the equations (8.14), the coefficient $[q + r(s_2/s_1)]$ consists of two parts: q expresses the effect of the change in the price of the first input upon the best second input, due to complementarity; $r(s_2/s_1)$ expresses the effect upon the second input of its estimated price. This latter effect is the larger, the larger the correlation.

Inserting (8.14) into (8.11), we find the best conditional expected payoff, given x_1. Taking the expected value (with respect to x_1) of the resulting expression, we obtain after collecting terms

(8.15)
$$\hat{\Omega}(10) = \frac{s_1^2 + s_2^2 r^2 + 2qrs_1 s_2}{4(1 - q^2)}.$$

As for the information structure $\eta = [01]$, we obtain a_1, a_2 (this time as functions of x_2 only) by interchanging the subscripts 1 and 2 in (8.14); and by a similar interchange of subscripts in (8.15), we get the expected payoff

(8.16)
$$\hat{\Omega}(01) = \frac{s_2^2 + s_1^2 r^2 + 2qrs_1 s_2}{4(1 - q^2)}.$$

It is interesting to compare $\hat{\Omega}(10)$ and $\hat{\Omega}(01)$. Subtracting, we obtain

$$(8.17) \qquad \hat{\Omega}(10) - \hat{\Omega}(01) = \frac{(s_1{}^2 - s_2{}^2)(1 - r^2)}{4(1 - q^2)}.$$

Suppose that (with measurement units chosen as they were, namely, so as to make the coefficients of $a_1{}^2$ and $a_2{}^2$ in the payoff function both equal to -1), the two prices have equal variances. Then it is equally useful to know only x_1 or only x_2. The formula (8.17) also shows that, if the two prices are strongly correlated, either positively or negatively (so that the one can be estimated from the other without a large error), it does not matter much which of the two prices is known. On the other hand, the advantage of knowing the more volatile, rather than the more constant price, is greater the stronger is the (positive or negative) interaction.

What is the advantage of knowing both prices over that of knowing only one, say x_1? From (8.10) and (8.15),

$$(8.18) \qquad \hat{\Omega}(11) - \hat{\Omega}(10) = \frac{s_2{}^2(1 - r^2)}{4(1 - q^2)}.$$

Hence, adding information about x_2 to that about x_1 is the more advantageous the stronger the interaction q (positive or negative) between the two action variables $\hat{a}_1$ and $\hat{a}_2$, the smaller the correlation (positive or negative) between the state variables x_1, x_2, and the larger the variance of x_2. This advantage is, in fact, proportional to $s_2{}^2(1 - r^2) = E[E(x_2|x_1) - x_2]^2$, the square of the so-called "standard error of estimating x_2 from x_1."

A more complete discussion becomes possible if the costs of information are known and, as before, linear utility of money is assumed. Let c be the cost of getting information about either x_1 or x_2; and let $2c$ be the cost of getting information on both. Since

$$(8.19) \qquad \hat{\Omega}(11) \geq \max[\hat{\Omega}(10), \hat{\Omega}(01)] \geq \hat{\Omega}(00),$$

the best information structure is [11] when $c = 0$ and [00] when c is very large. One may ask whether, for some intermediate c, either the information structure [10] or [01] (depending on whether s_1 or s_2 is larger) is best, so that

$$(8.20) \qquad \max[\hat{\Omega}(10) - c, \hat{\Omega}(01) - c] \geq \max[\hat{\Omega}(00), \hat{\Omega}(11) - 2c].$$

Let $s_1 \geq s_2$ (without loss of generality); then $\hat{\Omega}(10) \geq \hat{\Omega}(01)$, and (8.20) requires that

$$\hat{\Omega}(11) - \hat{\Omega}(10) \leq c \leq \hat{\Omega}(10) - \hat{\Omega}(00).$$

Thus a necessary condition for the optimality of observing just one variable is that "nonincreasing returns to information" prevail, in the sense that

$$(8.21) \qquad \hat{\Omega}(11) - \hat{\Omega}(10) \leq \hat{\Omega}(10) - \hat{\Omega}(00).$$

Substituting from (8.18), (8.15), and (8.5), and recalling that $q^2 < 1$, we obtain the condition

$$(8.22) \qquad s_1{}^2 + s_2{}^2(2r^2 - 1) \geq -2qrs_1s_2.$$

Since $s_1 \geq s_2 > 0$, this condition is always satisfied when there is no interaction ($q = 0$) or no correlation ($r = 0$), or if q and r have the same signs. In the symmetry case $s_1 = s_2$ we obtain, moreover,

$$(8.23) \qquad r(r + q) \geq 0.$$

If (8.22) or, in the symmetry case, (8.23) does not hold, then either both variables or neither have to be observed, depending on the cost c of observing each variable.

PART TWO

TEAM ORGANIZATION PROBLEMS

CHAPTER 4

The Problem and Some Examples

1. MULTI-PERSON TEAMS

At the beginning of this book, an organization was defined to be a group of persons whose actions agree with certain rules that further their common interests. When they have only common interests, these persons are said to form a team.

In a trivial sense, a single decision-maker is a team: a one-person team. Optimality problems essential to the more general theory already arise in this special, simple case. They were treated in Part One. The proper, multi-person team differs from the one-person team mainly in the extended meaning that must be given to the term *rules*. Each individual member of a team decides about a different action variable, and each member's decision is based, in general, on different information. Accordingly, the concepts of decision rule and information structure developed in Part One for the single-person case must be reinterpreted. If there are n members, the team's information structure and decision rule will consist, respectively, of n information structures and n decision rules. The problem is to choose the pair of n-tuples that best serves the well-defined interests of the team.

We must now define *interests* more precisely. They are usually identified with goals, or, better, the hierarchy of goals; these are other expressions for the preference ordering among outcomes of actions ("tastes"), which we analyzed in Chapter 1 in the case of a single consistent decision-maker. However, in our context it is useful to let the term *interests* embrace both tastes *and* beliefs. We have seen that the ordering of the consistent man's actions (as to which of any two actions is better) and his ordering of non-controlled events (as to which of any two events is more probable) can be represented by numerical utilities and probabilities, respectively, in such a way that, of any two actions, the one with greater expected utility will be chosen. If, then, the consistent decision-maker can choose among various information structures and, for each information structure, among various decision rules, then his choice should maximize expected utility, taking account of the cost of information and decision.

Similarly, the joint outcome of any combination of actions of team members will be associated with a utility common to all members and hence justifiably called *utility to the team*; any event not influenced by their actions will be associated with a probability "from the point of view of the team," the same for all its members. The team problem is to choose simultaneously the team information structure and the team decision rule that will yield the highest expected utility, taking account of information and decision costs. The information and the decision rule of the team taken together can be called its *organizational form*.

As an example, in the pre-computer age, airline companies had a number of ticket agents who were authorized to sell reservations on future flights with only partial (if any) information about what reservations had been booked by other agents. One can study the best rules for these agents to use under such circumstances, taking account of the joint probability distribution of demands for reservations at the several offices, the losses due to selling too many or too few reservations in total, and so forth. M. Beckmann (1958) analyzed an airline's reservation problem along these lines; and C. B. McGuire (1961) has studied certain other models of sales organization, also from a team theoretic point of view.

As a second example, the decision-maker might be an individual making different decisions in successive time periods, the payoff being a function of all the decisions made over the total time period. In such a case, if the decision-maker does not "forget" anything from one time period to the next, then the problem is a typical sequential or dynamic programming problem. However, the keeping of records might be so costly that it would be worthwhile to forget some things, in which case new problems emerge: see Chapter 7.

2. Teams and Organizations

The assumption of identical interests of its members makes the team simpler than a general organization. However, the team problem is sufficiently complex to justify our attacking it separately, instead of introducing at once the additional difficulty of conflicting interests.

Some thoughts on the relation of the team problem to those arising in a full-fledged, conflict-ridden organization, and in particular to the problem of a nonzero sum game, will be found at the end of the book. Here we may add that formally equivalent to the team problem is that of the *organizer* — for example, a management consultant or the author of an army manual. Given the interests of the organization as stated to him by his client, the organizer's task is to draft the information and decision rules that best serve these interests, assuming that the rules will be obeyed. To be sure, this assumption is seldom fully valid, although the problem of organizing a system of automata does have both practical importance and theoretical value. Accordingly, the organizer will modify the information and decision rules by introducing *incentives*, such that each member will serve his own interests best (i.e. will maximize the expected utility *to him*) by acting in a manner that will serve the interests of the organization. However, we shall neglect the problem of incentives. In a general analysis like the present one, there is a virtue in taking up the difficulties one at a time. See, however, Groves (1970).

Instead of an "organizer" we can think of a "foundation." The interests of a foundation are, in general, different from those of its staff members. But the staff members' task is to serve these interests. We can judge the performance of a church, an army, or a business firm according to set standards and proclaim the organization more or less efficient according to those standards.

The student of organizations can also apply a variety of standards of his own and thus go beyond the case of "foundations." He can ask whether a certain set of rules has been efficient according to some given standards (e.g., in making both management and labor prosperous) or according to some other standards (e.g., in achieving the prosperity of management). In particular he can, like the student of evolutionary biology, ask whether a particular organizational form does or does not have good chances of survival and longevity in a given environment. This is equivalent to setting utility equal to 1 for survival to a certain date, and equal to 0 for nonsurvival, or, more generally, utility can be associated with the number of years of survival. Viability is thus a particular case of efficiency (see J. Marschak, 1959).

To judge an organization's efficiency by its expected utility presupposes a consistent system of tastes and beliefs. This may seem artificial and unrealistic, since in real organizations the interests vary from member to member; even the organizer himself, as a real person, will lack perfect consistency. And yet it will prove useful to compare the advantages of various organizational forms under various assumptions about the payoff conditions and the cost of information and decision, from the point of view of rational team efficiency. The reader who follows our development of the theory of efficient teams will, again and again, recognize important features of actual organizations. Considerations of efficiency seem indeed to have shaped many characteristics of actual organizations, either because of deliberate efforts of organizers, or because of the weeding out of inefficient or nonviable organizational forms in a gradual process of adaptation and selection.

3. TEAM PAYOFF AND ACTION

In a single-person team, such as those considered in Chapter 3, the decision-maker chooses an action a from the set A of feasible actions. In a multi-person or general team, there are n members. Member i $(i = 1, \ldots, n)$ chooses an action a_i from some set A_i of all the actions that he can perform. The gross payoff function

$$(3.1) \qquad\qquad u = \omega(x, a_1, a_2, \ldots),$$

which was introduced in Part One for a single person controlling several variables $a_1, a_2, \ldots$, can be retained, with the symbol u now denoting the utility to the team (and to each of its members). The symbol x stands as before for the state of the world; it is an element of the set X on which a subjective probability measure is defined, denoted as before by π and now characterizing the beliefs of the team. The symbol a_i will now stand for the action variable controlled by the ith member, so that any particular value of a_i is an element of the feasible set A_i assigned to the ith member. Note that a_i itself may be an m-tuple of several physically distinct variables, all controlled by the same member i.

We can now reinterpret and reapply the concepts of additive and nonadditive payoff functions introduced in Chapter 3, Section 3. If ω is additive, then there exist n "subpayoff" functions ω_i $(i = 1, \ldots, n)$ such that, with $a \equiv (a_1, \ldots, a_n)$

$$(3.2) \qquad\qquad \omega(x, a) = \sum_i \omega_i(x, a_i).$$

We then say that there is no interaction. Whenever a_i and a_j are real numbers and the cross derivative,

$$(3.3) \qquad\qquad q_{ij} = \frac{\partial \omega(x, a)}{\partial a_i \, \partial a_j},$$

exists, q_{ij} can be taken as the measure of interaction. This quantity is, in general, not constant but depends on a_i and a_j as well as on x.

For brevity, we shall speak of a team as additive, quadratic, and so forth, whenever its payoff function has these properties as a function of $a_1, \ldots, a_n$, for each x.

4. DECISION AND INFORMATION FUNCTIONS IN A TEAM

In a single-person team, the action a is related to the information y of the decision-maker by the decision function (decision rule) α; thus $a = \alpha(y)$. Similarly, the ith member of a general team takes his action a_i on the basis of *his* information, y_i. Accordingly, there are n decision functions $\alpha_1, \ldots, \alpha_n$; and $a_i = \alpha_i(y_i)$. The n-tuple of decision functions can then be denoted by $\alpha = (\alpha_1, \ldots, \alpha_n)$ and called the *decision rule of the team*. If we write $a = (a_1, \ldots, a_n)$ for the (joint) action of the team members and $y = (y_1, \ldots, y_n)$ for their information, then the equation

$$a = \alpha(y),$$

which was set up in Chapter 2 for the single-person team, can continue to be used, properly interpreted for the general team.

It will also be recalled that, in the single-person team, the information variable y is related to the true state of the world x by a function η, which we called the information function or information structure. Thus $y = \eta(x)$, $a = \alpha[\eta(x)]$. Correspondingly, the information variable y_i of the ith member of a general team is related to the state of the world x by a function η_i; that is, if the world is in state x, then member i will have information $y_i = \eta_i(x)$. The n-tuple $\eta = (\eta_1, \ldots, \eta_n)$ may be called the *information function (structure) of the team*. Again in condensed notation,

$$y = \eta(x), a = \alpha(y) = \alpha[\eta(x)],$$

thus reinterpreting the equations of Chapter 2. In particular, the gross payoff (3.1) of a team can be written as

$$(4.1) \qquad u = \omega(x, a) \equiv \omega(x, \alpha[\eta(x)])$$

$$\equiv \omega(x, \alpha_1[\eta_1(x)], \ldots, \alpha_n[\eta_n(x)]) ;$$

the gross expected payoff of a team is

$$(4.2) \qquad Eu = \Omega(\eta, \alpha) = E\omega(x, \alpha[\eta(x)]).$$

The maximal gross expected payoff of a team, given its information structure $\eta = (\eta_1, \ldots, \eta_n)$, is the gross expected payoff maximized with respect to α:

$$(4.3) \qquad \hat{\Omega}(\eta) = \max_{\alpha} \Omega(\eta, \alpha)$$

$$= \max_{\alpha_1, \ldots, \alpha_n} E\omega(x, \alpha_1[\eta_1(x)], \ldots, \alpha_n[\eta_n(x)]).$$

It was shown in Chapter 2 that every information structure η for a single decision-maker can be identified with some partition of the set X of all states of the world into subsets. For example, if X is the set of all cards that can happen to be at the top of a deck of cards, η may be the partition of X into two colors (red and black), or into four suits, or into 13 values (ace, 2, 3, ..., jack, etc.). The same applies to the information structure η_i of the ith member of a general team. Thus member i may learn about the color of the top card, member j may learn about the suit, and member k about its value. The extensions to the "noisy" case (Chapter 2, Section 8) is obvious.

We shall often consider cases in which the information structure of a team is fully described by a statement as to "who knows what." It is then convenient to represent the information structure as a matrix, $\eta = [\eta_{ik}]$ $(i = 1, \ldots, n; k = 1, \ldots, K)$, such that

$$(4.4) \qquad \eta_{ik} = \begin{cases} 0 & \text{if } a_i \text{ does not depend on } x_k \\ 1 & \text{if } a_i \text{ does depend on } x_k. \end{cases}$$

This case does not exhaust all possible information structures. For example, the notation just suggested would fail to state "who knows what with what precision." The notation applies only if the relevant set X of the states of the world can be represented by points in a finite-dimensional space of variables—so that each state of the world is described by the values of a K-tuple $x = (x_1, \ldots, x_K)$—and if the set X is partitioned only according to the values of some or all of these variables. Such was the case with the single-person information structures [00], [10], [01], and [11], of Example 3D; they could be regarded as single-row matrices $[n_{ij}]$.

5. CAN ONE-PERSON SOLUTIONS BE APPLIED TO TEAMS?

It is instructive to point out some obvious, but very special, cases in which solutions of one-person problems can be directly applied to an n-person problem.

One such case is that of fully shared information. Suppose that each team member learns, directly or through some clearing agency, all the information available to the other members; then let

$$(5.1) \qquad \eta_i = \eta^* \qquad i = 1, \ldots, n.$$

Referring to (4.3), we see that, in this case, the maximal gross payoff of the team can be regarded as the maximal gross payoff of a single person controlling n variables.

Another case will be given in Section 10.

6. Specialization, Organizational Cost, Net Expected Payoff

It is intuitively evident that, by adding to a team member's knowledge the knowledge of some or all of his partners, the (gross) expected payoff of the team cannot be decreased, and may be increased. This is an extension of the results of Chapter 2; after noiseless communication with other members, a team member has a finer information structure than before. If communication were costless, it would indeed be worthwhile to have all team members share their information fully, as in the case (5.1) of the preceding section.

We said in previous chapters that the cost of information might lead a single decision-maker not to obtain complete information. For the same reason, it will not, in general, be worthwhile to have every member of a team informed about the same events, and in the same detail. In a business corporation, the executive in charge of finance and the one in charge of personnel will share some information (on the general business conditions and the broad problems of the firm, for example) but will also "specialize," that is, will keep informed of things that are particularly relevant to financial decisions or to decisions on personnel, respectively.

The information cost considered in the chapters that dealt with a single-person team was the cost of gathering information *from outside*; we shall call it the *cost of observation*. We should now add the cost of *communication among the members of the team*. The capacity of men to transmit and receive information is limited even when enlarged by mechanical communication devices. People and devices with high capacity are in rare supply (and therefore expensive), or just do not exist at all, so that certain information structures are not feasible (or can be said to be infinitely costly).

The information cost, consisting of costs of observation and of communication, may thus justify a *specialization of information* in the sense that the information structures η_i and η_j of any two members may be different.

There is also *specialization of action* in the sense that the distinct sets A_i and A_j are physically dissimilar—they are, of course, never identical formally). This is partly a consequence of specialization of information; it is cheaper to assign the hiring of personnel to the man who receives information on personnel. But even if team members shared the same knowledge (information cost being assumed negligible for a moment), it might pay to specialize their actions. This is due to the *cost of decision*, the study of which we shall not pursue here. It would lead us, in fact, into the economics (and the underlying psychology or physiology) of the division of labor, and the advantages and penalties of specialization of any work. We shall use the term *organizational cost* to include the decision as well as the information cost, and we shall give some further elaboration in Chapter 9.

We shall say that a team has centralized or decentralized information or, more briefly, is a *centralized* or *decentralized team*, depending on whether all its members have or do not have the same information structure. If it were not for the organizational cost, the problem of a centralized team would be identical with that of a *single-person team* and, accordingly, all nontrivial problems arising in a *several-person* (or *proper*) team would be those of a decentralized team. Organization cost (and noise) will be neglected in our Chapters 5, 6, and 7, but will be taken up explicitly in Chapter 8, on Networks.

It will be remembered from Chapter 2, Section 12, that the concept of a net payoff to the single decision-maker as a difference between the gross payoff and the cost of information and decision is applicable, with payoffs and costs expressed in money, when the person's utility function of money is linear. The same clearly applies to the general team. If the organizer can assume the team's utility function of outcome to be linear, his task is to maximize, with respect to α and η, the net expected payoff

$$E\omega(x, \alpha[\eta(x)]) - E\gamma(x, \alpha, \eta),$$

where $\gamma(x, \alpha, \eta)$ is the team's cost of information and decision when the environment is in state x. If the assumption of a linear utility function is dropped, the problem becomes more complex, as shown in Chapter 2. One then has to specify the function relating expected utility to each feasible combination (η, α). At present too little is known about the nature of such functions. More is known about monetary gross payoff functions, and some few (too few!) statements can be made about monetary organizational cost. We therefore choose, rather than speculate on the implications of various utility functions, to confine ourselves to the special case in which maximization of the net expected monetary payoff is indicated.

7. Cospecialization of Action and Observation

Suppose that there is a one-to-one correspondence between the action variables a_i $(i = 1, \ldots, n)$ and the state variables x_k $(k = 1, 2, \ldots, n)$ in the following sense: The cost c_{ik} of having the kth variable *observed* by the ith member is prohibitively large when $i \neq k$, but is not when $i = k$. Then the ith member can be said to be a specialist (and the only one) on the ith variable. Any other member can obtain information about that variable only by communicating with the ith member, directly or indirectly.

In this case, which we shall call *cospecialization* (*of action and observation*), many information structures can at once be excluded from consideration as being definitely less profitable than some other information structure. For example, if we apply the matrix notation suggested in (4.4), to a two-person team with two appropriately indexed state variables, we could have in general $4 \times 4 = 16$ information structures, since the first row can be either [00], [10], [01], or [11], and similarly for the second row. Cospecialization eliminates all those matrices in which $\eta_{ii} = 0$ (i.e., member i does not observe x_i) but $\eta_{ji} = 1$ (i.e., member j knows x_i), where $j \neq i$. The 16 information structures are shown in the following 4×4 table, Table 4.1. A dash means that the corresponding matrix is not eligible when there is cospecialization. When a matrix is eligible, the symbols entered show the "network" that *can* generate it.[1] An arrow ($\rightarrow$) indicates the direction of communication; a cross ($\times$) on the left-hand (or right-hand) side means, respectively, that member 1 (or 2) does observe variable 1 (or 2) in which he is a specialist; the hollow square ($\square$) on the left-hand (or right-hand) side means, similarly, that the member in question does not observe "his" variable. There are altogether nine eligible networks, and $16 - 9 = 7$ ineligible networks. Moreover, the total cost of observation plus communication is entered in parentheses, assuming for illustrative purposes that the cost of observation is the same for all variables, $c_{ii} = c$; that the cost of one-way communication, c', is always the same; and that the cost of two-way communication is $2c'$ (e.g., an exchange of letters, not a conference).

TABLE 4.1   NETWORKS AND ASSUMED INFORMATION COSTS IN A TWO-PERSON TEAM
WITH COSPECIALIZATION

η_2 \ η_1	00	10	01	11
00	$\square$ $\square$ (0)	$\times$ $\square$ (c)	—	—
01	$\square$ $\times$ (c)	$\times$ $\times$ ($2c$)	$\square \leftarrow \times$ ($c + c'$)	$\times \leftarrow \times$ ($2c + c'$)
10	—	$\times \rightarrow \square$ ($c + c'$)	—	—
11	—	$\times \rightarrow \times$ ($2c + c'$)	—	$\times \leftrightarrow \times$ ($2c + 2c'$)

1. The network concept will be treated more generally in Chapter 8.

8. Example 4A: a Two-Person Team with Nonadditive, Nonsmooth Payoff

Let a firm have two sales managers, each specializing in a different market for its product. Let it have two production facilities, one producing at low cost and another, more costly, to be used as a standby. This second facility can be visualized as a separate plant or as the use of the same plant at "overtime" periods, which involves higher wages. A conveniently simple case (J. Marschak 1959) is offered by a shipyard firm with two docks (a new one and an old, less efficient one) and two markets ("East" and "West"). Each sales manager is offered a price for a ship to be delivered in his market. The prices offered in each of the two markets are the two state variables. There are two decision variables, each of them taking one of two values: either accept or reject the order.

Of the nine information structures entered in Table 4.1, we shall confine ourselves to the following five:[2]

$\begin{bmatrix} 0 & 0 \\ 0 & 0 \end{bmatrix}$, to be called *routine*

$\begin{bmatrix} 1 & 1 \\ 1 & 1 \end{bmatrix}$, to be called *centralized complete information*

$\begin{bmatrix} 1 & 0 \\ 0 & 1 \end{bmatrix}$, to be called *decentralized information*

$\begin{bmatrix} 1 & 0 \\ 1 & 0 \end{bmatrix}$ and $\begin{bmatrix} 0 & 1 \\ 0 & 1 \end{bmatrix}$, to be called *centralized incomplete information*

We shall now study the profits (gross payoffs) associated with each information structure; assumptions about organizational cost will be introduced later. Let

$$k = \text{the cost of building a ship in the new dock}$$
$$k + d = \text{the cost of building a ship in the old dock}$$
$$k + x_E = \text{the price offered in the East}$$
$$k + x_W = \text{the price offered in the West}$$
$$a_i = \begin{matrix} 1 \\ 0 \end{matrix} \quad \begin{matrix} \text{if the order in the } i\text{th market is accepted} \\ \text{if the order in the } i\text{th market is not accepted} \end{matrix} \left\{ i = E, W \right\}$$

---

2. See Chapter 6 for further elaboration.

The pair $x = (x_E, x_W)$ is the pair of prices, measured from the minimum cost k. For a given $x = (x_E, x_W)$, the profit $u = \omega(x, a_E, a_W)$ is[3]

$$\omega(x, 1, 1) = (k + x_E) + (k + x_W) - k - (k + d) = x_E + x_W - d$$

$$\omega(x, 1, 0) = (k + x_E) - k = x_E$$

$$\omega(x, 0, 1) = (k + x_W) - k = x_W$$

$$\omega(x, 0, 0) = 0,$$

or in tabular form as in Table 4.2.

TABLE 4.2

a_W \\ a_E	1	0
1	$x_E + x_W - d$	x_W
0	x_E	0

ASSUMED DISTRIBUTION; NUMERICAL ASSUMPTIONS

We shall assume the simple 2×2 distribution of prices defined in (2.2) and (2.3) of Chapter 3. Moreover, we shall specify all the givens numerically and thus forego the task of studying various subcases; the numerical example will suffice to bring out the essentials of the problem. Assume that

$k = 20, d = 15$
$m = $ mean of $x_E = $ mean of $x_W = 10$,
$s_E = $ standard deviation of $x_E = 9$,
$s_W = $ standard deviation of $x_W = 1$,
$r = $ correlation coefficient $= .6$.

Then the prices take the values $p_E = k + m \pm s_E$ ($= 39$ or 21) and $p_W = k + m \pm s_W$ ($= 31$ or 29); and since $(1 + r)/4 = .4$, the assumed joint probabilities are as shown in Table 4.3.

TABLE 4.3

x_W \\ x_E	19	1
11	.4	.1
9	.1	.4

p_W \\ p_E	39	21
31	.4	.1
29	.1	.4

3. In a more general case, when more than one unit can be produced in each plant so that a_E and a_W are real numbers bounded by capacity c, $u = x_E a_E + x_W a_W - d \cdot \max(0, a_E + a_W - c)$. See McGuire 1961 and Chapter 5, Section 4 below.

For each of the four possible pairs x_E and x_W, the previous table (Table 4.2) of profits as a function of a_E and a_W becomes Table 4.4.

TABLE 4.4

x_E	x_W	Profits	Probabilities
19	11	$\dfrac{15 \mid 11}{19 \mid 0}$	.4
19	9	$\dfrac{13 \mid 9}{19 \mid 0}$	.1
1	11	$\dfrac{-3 \mid 11}{1 \mid 0}$	.1
1	9	$\dfrac{-5 \mid 9}{1 \mid 0}$	.4

ROUTINE CASE

Consider first the *routine* structure $\begin{bmatrix} 0 & 0 \\ 0 & 0 \end{bmatrix}$, that is let the same team

action be used regardless of prices. The expected profit U for each of the four possible team actions is as in Table 4.5.

TABLE 4.5

$a_E\ a_W$

0 0	$U =$		$= 0.0$
1 0	$U = (.5)(19) + (.5)(1)$		$= 10.0$
0 1	$U = (.5)(11) + (.5)(9)$		$= 10.0$
1 1	$U = (.4)(15) + (.1)(13) + (.1)(-3) + (.4)(-5) =$		5.0

Thus the best expected profit under routine structure is 10.0 units. It is achieved if only one of the two orders is accepted and the old dock is kept idle. Let us see how the (gross) expected payoff can be raised by using information. Take first the extreme case.

CENTRALIZED COMPLETE INFORMATION

Using the tabulation of profits in Table 4.4, the team chooses for each pair of prices the best pair of actions, that is, the one yielding maximum profit. Averaging these over the four price situations, we obtain the expected profit. In each row of Table 4.6 (i.e., for each price situation), the maximum profit is circled.

TABLE 4.6 CENTRALIZED COMPLETE INFORMATION

		Team Action (a_E, a_W)			Max Profit	Probability	Best Team Action
x_E	x_W	(0, 0)	(1, 0)	(0, 1)	(1, 1)			
19	11	0	⑲	11	15	19	.4	(1, 0)
19	9	0	⑲	9	13	19	.1	(1, 0)
1	11	0	1	⑪	−3	11	.1	(0, 1)
1	9	0	1	⑨	−5	9	.4	(0, 1)

Average max profit = 14.2.

Thus the best team decision rule is to accept one order only, either East or West, depending on whether x_E is high or low. The resulting maximum expected profit is 14.2. The *value* of centralized complete information, that is, its advantage over the routine case, is 14.2 − 10.0 = 4.2.

CENTRALIZED INCOMPLETE INFORMATION

We shall consider two such information structures: (1) both members know only x_E, and (2) both members know only x_W.

1. If both members know only x_E, the best team action rule follows from the result just obtained for the case of centralized complete information, since the added knowledge of x_W was shown to be without effect on the choice of the best team action. (This was, of course, due to the smallness of the variance of the western price.) Thus, with the numerical values of our example, centralized incomplete information such that x_E is the only observed variable is as profitable as centralized complete information. It has the same expected profit (= 14.2). Presumably it has lower cost.

2. If both members know only x_W, we must choose the pair of actions a_W and a_E that will achieve the maximum conditional expected profit (circled) in Table 4.7 given that x_W is high (= 11); and, similarly, given that it is low (= 9). The conditional probabilities $P(x_E|x_W)$ and the marginal probabilities $P(x_W)$ are, of course, derived from Table 4.3.

Here the best rule of action is: Accept the western order only if the western price is low; otherwise accept the eastern order. We chose our numerical data deliberately to produce this paradox. In the West, the high price is only two units above the low price; in the East, the assumed variance is much stronger. Since the means are the same, and the assumed correlation is positive and sufficiently strong, it pays, on the average, to accept orders from the East whenever the western price is high (and the estimated eastern price still higher) and to accept the western order whenever the western price is low (and the estimated eastern price still lower). The resulting expected profit is 12.2.

TABLE 4.7   CENTRALIZED INCOMPLETE INFORMATION
(about Western Price Only)

$$x_E = 19 \quad x_E = 1$$

$x_W = 11$ $P(x_W) = .5$		$P(x_E\|x_W) =$ .8	.2	
				Conditional
a_E	a_W	Profits		Expected Profits
0	0	0	0	0.0
1	0	19	1	(15.4)
0	1	11	11	11.0
1	1	15	−3	11.4

$x_W = 9$ $P(x_W) = .5$		$P(x_E\|x_W) =$ .2	.8	
				Conditional
a_E	a_W	Profits		Expected Profits
0	0	0	0	0.0
1	0	19	1	4.6
0	1	9	9	(9.0)
1	1	13	−5	−1.4

Maximum Expected Profit = (15.4)(.5) + (9.0)(.5) = 12.2.

DECENTRALIZED INFORMATION

In this case, the western (eastern) member knows only the western (eastern) price. We shall call it "his" price. Each member can apply one of four rules of action: (1) "always accept order" (*A*), (2) "accept order when my price is high" (*H*), (3) "accept order when my price is low" (*L*), and (4) "never accept order" (*N*). There are therefore $4 \times 4 = 16$ team action rules. The corresponding expected profits are computed and tabulated in Table 4.8 in the following manner: In each of the 16 cells corresponding to a team action rule, a corner is occupied by the profit obtained for each of the four possible pairs of prices, arranged as in the probability distribution table, Table 4.3. Most of the 16 team action rules are inadmissible, being dominated by one or more other action rules that promise a higher profit at some price pairs and a lower profit at no price pairs. For the remaining, admissible team action rules, the expected profit is shown in the center of the cell and is circled. The highest expected profit

($=12.5$) is circled twice. It is yielded by the action rule: "The western member accepts order only when he is offered a low price; the eastern member accepts order only when he is offered a high price." (See the remark above about the "paradox.") This, then, is the best team action rule under decentralized information.

TABLE 4.8   DECENTRALIZED INFORMATION
East accepts order

α_W \ α_E	always (A)	if eastern price high (H)	if eastern price low (L)	never (N)
always (A)	15 −3 13 −5	15 11 ⑫ 13 9	11 −3 9 −5	11 11 9 9
if western price high (H)	15 −3 19 1	15 11 ⑨ 19 0	11 −3 0 1	11 11 0 0
if western price low (L)	19 1 13 −5	19 0 ⦿12.5 13 9	0 1 9 −5	0 0 9 9
never (N)	19 1 ⑩ 19 1	19 0 19 0	0 1 0 1	0 0 0 0

In the following summary (Table 4.9), for illustrative purposes we shall make the same assumptions about organizational cost as in Section 7. It will be recalled that we use "profit" and "gross payoff" interchangeably.

TABLE 4.9   COMPARISON OF FIVE INFORMATION STRUCTURES

Information Structure	Gross Expected Payoff	Information Value	Organizational Cost	Net Expected Payoff
1. Routine	10.0	0	0	10.0
2. Decentralized	12.5	2.5	$2c$	$12.5 - 2c$
Centralized incomplete:				
3. x_W known to both	12.2	2.2	$c + c'$	$12.2 - (c + c')$
4. x_E known to both	14.2	4.2	$c + c'$	$14.2 - (c + c')$
5. Centralized complete	14.2	4.2	$2(c + c')$	$14.2 - 2(c + c')$

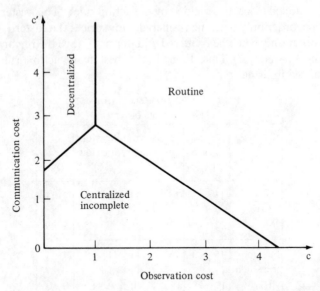

FIGURE 4.1. Optimal information structures for different cost combinations.

It so happens that, in our example, for any positive information cost, centralized incomplete information about x_E is better than the other type of centralized incomplete information and also better than centralized complete information. But to choose between the remaining three information structures, (1), (2), or (4), one would have to know more about the actual cost c of information and c' of communication. (See Table 4.10 and Figure 4.1.)

TABLE 4.10   OPTIMAL INFORMATION STRUCTURES

Routine	if $c \geqq \max(1.25, 4.2 - c')$
Decentralized	if $c \leqq \min(1.25, c' - 1.7)$
Centralized Incomplete	
(x_E known to both)	otherwise

9. PERSON-BY-PERSON SATISFACTORY TEAM DECISION RULES

We shall use Example 4A of the preceding section to illustrate a principle that can sometimes help to find the optimal decision rule for the team with a given information structure.

We see in Table 4.8, calculated for the case of decentralized information, that the optimal team decision rule ("East accepts at high price only, West accepts at low price only") has the following obvious property: This rule yields a higher, or at least not lower, profit than do other rules in the same *row* (i.e., all other team decision rules that prescribe that West should accept at low price only) and also yields a higher, or at least not lower, profit than other rules in the same *column* (i.e., all other team decision rules that make East accept at high price only). This is obvious, since the considered team decision rule is optimal in comparison with *all* other team rules whether or not in the same row or the same column. Such a rule is "person-by-person satisfactory": a team decision rule, $\alpha = (\alpha_W, \alpha_E)$ in our case, will be called *person-by-person* (p.b.p.) *satisfactory* if it cannot be improved by changing one of its components (i.e., α_W alone or α_E alone). As already remarked, an optimal team rule is always person-by-person satisfactory. But the converse is not true. For example, Table 4.8 contains the following rule: "East accepts always, West never." This rule is not optimal, since its payoff (10) is lower than the maximal one (12.5). But it is person-by-person satisfactory, since it dominates all the rules in the same column ("East accepts always") and the same row ("West never accepts"). For brevity, we shall sometimes write p.b.p. instead of person-by-person.

In order to find an optimal team decision rule, one need not compare all possible team decision rules, but only those that are p.b.p. satisfactory.

In Example 4B of the next section, p.b.p. satisfactoriness will not only be necessary, but will also be sufficient for optimality; a more general class of payoff functions for which this is the case will be defined in Chapter 5. Our present example, in which the p.b.p. satisfactoriness is not a sufficient condition for optimality, will merely help to elucidate the general method of searching for an optimum among the set of p.b.p.-satisfactory rules.

Let the pair $(\tilde{\alpha}_W, \tilde{\alpha}_E)$ denote a team decision rule that is p.b.p. satisfactory. Consider, for a while, $\tilde{\alpha}_W$ (a row of Table 4.8) as fixed. Then, to find $\tilde{\alpha}_E$ is to solve the one-person problem stated in Chapter 2, Section 5: one has to find, for each observation made (or, more generally, each message received) by the eastern member, that action a_E which maximizes the conditional expected profit, given that observation. In our case (that of decentralized information), the eastern member is informed only about x_E, and the western member is informed only about x_W. For each of the actions a_E (1 and 0), and each of the values of x_E (19 and 1), the conditional expected profit is

(9.1) $$\psi_E(x_E, a_E) = E\{\omega[x_E, x_W, a_E, \alpha_W(x_W)]|x_E\}.$$

This is to be maximized with respect to a_E, first when x_E is high, then when x_E is low. This yields the function $\tilde{\alpha}_E$, the best individual rule for the eastern member, when his partner's rule is tentatively fixed at $\tilde{\alpha}_W$. In this manner one obtains, for each assumed row $\tilde{\alpha}_W$, a tentative team decision rule $(\tilde{\alpha}_W, \tilde{\alpha}_E)$, a row-optimal rule. An analogous process yields, for each column, the column-optimal team rule. A rule that is both row-optimal and column-optimal is, by definition, person-by-person satisfactory.

Under other conditions, the procedure might be simpler. If the payoff function were concave and differentiable with respect to a_E and a_W, we should differentiate the corresponding expression $\psi_W(x_W, a_W)$ with respect to a_W, for each x_W; and similarly for a_E. We should then let the two partial derivatives vanish simultaneously, thus satisfying a necessary condition for the maximum. Such a procedure will be feasible in our next example, 4B. In our present example, with the payoff function nondifferentiable, other simplifying properties will be exploited: namely there are only two values for each action variable and for each information variable.

We shall use the payoff table (Table 4.2), remembering that $d = 15$.

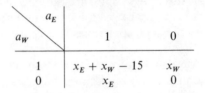

We note that, when $x_E = 19$, East is doing best by accepting the order, regardless of West's individual rule of decision: high eastern price exceeds the cost in either dock. Thus, always $\tilde{\alpha}_E(19) = 1$. On the other hand, when the eastern price is low, $x_E = 1$, we shall have to consider each of West's four possible rules, one by one, and look up our payoff table to find East's best rule:

1. If West never accepts ($a_W = 0$), then $\tilde{\alpha}_E(1) = 1$, since $x_E = 1 > 0$.
2. If West always accepts ($a_W = 1$), then $\tilde{\alpha}_E(1) = 0$, since $x_W - 14 < x_W$.
3. If West accepts at high price only, we compute the conditional expected profit for each a_E, using conditional probabilities .8 and .2 as weights, according to the assumed 2×2 probability distribution of Table 4.3, as shown in Table 4.11.
4. If West accepts at low price only, we make a similar computation, shown in Table 4.12.

We summarize East's best rules, obtained so far with West's rule fixed:
1. If West never accepts, East should always accept.
2. If West uses any other rule, East should accept at high price only.

TABLE 4.11

$x_E = 1$				$a_E = 1$	$a_E = 0$
x_W	$P(x_W\|x_E)$	a_W		Profits	
11	.2	1	$11 + 1 - 15 = -3$		11
9	.8	0	1		0
Conditional expected profits:			.2		(2.2)
		Best $\alpha_E(1) = 0$			

TABLE 4.12

$x_E = 1$				$a_E = 1$	$a_E = 0$
x_W	$P(x_W\|x_E)$	a_W		Profits:	
11	.2	0	1		0
9	.8	1	$9 + 1 - 15 = -5$		9
Conditional expected profits:			-3.8		(7.2)
		Best $\alpha_E(1) = 0$			

Thus only two rules for East have to be considered (i.e., only the first two columns of Table 4.8). We shall derive for West those rules that best combine with each of the two rules for East, and show that they correspond to the last two rows of Table 4.6.

If East always accepts, the payoff table (Table 4.2) shows, since $x_W < 15 = d$, that West should never accept: The cost in the old dock exceeds any price obtainable in the West. Thus the team decision rule *West never accepts, East always accepts* is person-by-person satisfactory.

TABLE 4.13

$x_W = 11$				$a_W = 1$	$a_W = 0$
x_E	$P(x_E\|x_W)$	a_E		Profits:	
19	.8	1	$11 + 19 - 15 = 15$		19
1	.2	0	11		0
Conditional expected profits:			14.2		(15.2)
		Best $\alpha_W(11) = 0$			

$x_W = 9$				$a_W = 1$	$a_W = 0$
x_E	$P(x_E\|x_W)$	a_E		Profits:	
19	.8	0	9		0
1	.2	1	$9 + 19 - 15 = 13$		19
Conditional expected profits:			(9.8)		3.8
		Best $\alpha_W(9) = 1$			

There remains the case in which East accepts at high price only. What should be West's rule? The profits at each of the possible prices in the West are entered in Table 4.13.

Thus when East's rule is "accept only at high price," then West's rule should be "accept only at low price." This is consistent with the result obtained when West's rule was the fixed one. We thus obtain the second p.b.p.-satisfactory rule for the team: *East accepts at high price, West at low price.*

We can now compare the expected payoffs yielded by each of these rules (none of the other 14 rules need be considered); they are 10.0 and 12.5, as seen on Table 4.8. Hence only the second p.b.p.-satisfactory team rule is optimal. We thus obtain the same result as in Section 8.

10. EXAMPLE 4B: TWO-PERSON TEAM WITH QUADRATIC PAYOFF

In Example 3E, a single person has to decide about two physically distinct action variables: he chooses simultaneously the quantities (a_1 and a_2) of the two inputs on the basis of some information about prices. We shall now replace a single decision-maker by a team of two, each to decide upon only one of the action variables, on the basis of his individual information. The environment is, as before, characterized by two state variables, the deviations (x_1 and x_2) of the two input prices from their respective means. The payoff function, after the appropriate choice of units and origins, discussed in Example 3E, retains its simple form

$$(10.1) \quad u = \omega(x_1, x_2, a_1, a_2) = - a_1{}^2 - a_2{}^2 + 2qa_1a_2 - a_1x_1 - a_2x_2,$$

but a_1, a_2 are now chosen by two different persons. The payoff (profit) to the team is quadratic; moreover, we assume $-1 < q < 1$ to make it strictly concave (see Chapter 3, Section 3). The payoff is nonadditive except when $q = 0$.

INFORMATION STRUCTURE

The ith member can decide about a_i on the basis of four different information structures [00], [10], [01], and [11]. Hence there are $4 \times 4 = 16$ information structures each represented by a matrix: the ith row of such a matrix (as in Table 4.1) represents the information available to the ith person. When the two rows are identical, the profits are the same as those obtained in the single-person example (3E). This is the "shared information" case, represented by each of the four matrices:

$$\begin{bmatrix} 00 \\ 00 \end{bmatrix}, \quad \begin{bmatrix} 10 \\ 10 \end{bmatrix}, \quad \begin{bmatrix} 01 \\ 01 \end{bmatrix}, \quad \begin{bmatrix} 11 \\ 11 \end{bmatrix}.$$

It is true that, even for these information structures, the computation of the net payoff will introduce new problems not present in the single-person case; for the cost of information in our new setup will be due not only to the expense of observation, but also to that of communication. For example, $\begin{bmatrix} 1 & 0 \\ 1 & 0 \end{bmatrix}$ may be implemented by letting both team members observe the same variable x_1; or if person 1 "specializes" in x_1, by letting him observe it and inform person 2.

PERSON-BY-PERSON-SATISFACTORY TEAM DECISION RULES

We have seen in Section 9 that every optimal team decision rule is also person-by-person satisfactory and that the converse is, in general, not true. However, it will be shown in Chapter 5 that, if the payoff function is differentiable and concave in the action variables, then every person-by-person-satisfactory team decision rule is also optimal. Now, our quadratic payoff function ω in (10.1) is indeed differentiable, and if $q^2 < 1$, ω is also concave (see Chapter 3, Section 3). Therefore, for each information structure a person-by-person-satisfactory rule will also be optimal.

To bring out the essential features of optimization in the case of a quadratic and concave two-person team, let us recall, as a matter of contrast, the reasoning applied (in Example 3E) to the case of a single person when the payoff function of his two action variables is quadratic and concave. We shall take up the various information structures one after another. When $\eta = [00]$ (routine information), the optimal decision rule was that constant pair $(\hat{a}_1, \hat{a}_2)$ which made both partial derivatives $\partial Eu/\partial a_i$ vanish. That is, we solved, for $\hat{a}_1$ and $\hat{a}_2$ simultaneously, the two equations

$$(10.2) \qquad \frac{\partial Eu}{\partial a_i}\bigg]_{a_i = \hat{a}_i} = 0 \qquad i = 1, 2.$$

In the case of complete information $\eta = [11]$, the optimal decision rule was a pair $(\hat{a}_1, \hat{a}_2)$, each $\hat{a}_i$ being a function of both external variables x_1 and x_2. Considering x_1 and x_2 as given, we obtain the best pair of action variables $\hat{a}_1 = \hat{a}_1(x_1, x_2), \hat{a}_2 = \hat{a}_2(x_1, x_2)$ by solving with respect to $\hat{a}_1, \hat{a}_2$ the two equations

$$(10.3) \qquad \frac{\partial u}{\partial a_i}\bigg]_{a_i = \hat{a}_i} = 0 \qquad i = 1, 2.$$

Finally, in the case of incomplete information the optimal decision rule was the pair of functions $(\hat{a}_1, \hat{a}_2)$ of a single variable. For example, when the incomplete information was [10], this variable was x_1, so that $\hat{a}_1 = \hat{a}_1(x_1), \hat{a}_2 = \hat{a}_2(x_1)$. One obtains these functions by considering x_1 as given, and solving for $\hat{a}_1$ and $\hat{a}_2$ the pair of equations,

(10.4) $$\frac{\partial E(u|x_1)}{\partial a_i}\Bigg]_{a_i = \hat{a}_i} = 0 \qquad i = 1, 2.$$

The maximands Eu, u, $E(u|x_1)$ that appear in each of the three equation systems, (10.2), (10.3), and (10.4), can all be regarded as special cases of the conditional expected payoff, given the information:

$$y = \eta(x) = \begin{cases} \text{constant} & \text{when } \eta = [00] \\ x_1, x_2 & \text{when } \eta = [11] \\ x_1 & \text{when } \eta = [10], \end{cases}$$

respectively. We can rewrite the conditional expected payoffs in the form

(10.5) $$\psi_1(a_1, y) = E\{\omega[x, a_1, \alpha_2(y)] | \eta(x) = y\}$$
$$\psi_2(a_2, y) = E\{\omega[x, \alpha_1(y), a_2] | \eta(x) = y\}.$$

The equations to be solved are

(10.6) $$\frac{\partial \psi_i(a_i, y)}{\partial a_i}\Bigg]_{a_i = \hat{a}_i} = 0 \qquad i = 1, 2.$$

Associating each value of y with the corresponding value of $\hat{a}_i$, we obtain the functions $\hat{a}_i$ ($i = 1, 2$).

As we proceed from a single-person to a two-person team, each action variable a_i (now associated with an individual person i) becomes dependent on information $y_i = \eta_i(x)$, which in general varies with i. Therefore the conditional expected payoffs (10.5) must be redefined:

(10.7) $$\psi_1(a_1, y_1) = E\{\omega[x, a_1, \alpha_2(y_2)] | \eta_1(x) = y_1\}$$
$$\psi_2(a_2, y_2) = E\{\omega[x, \alpha_1(y_1), a_2] | \eta_2(x) = y_2\}.$$

These have to be maximized person-by-person. The procedure can be most easily stated if we assume for a while that y_1 and y_2 can each take a finite number of values:

$$y_1 = y_{11}, y_{12}, \ldots, y_{1h}, \ldots, y_{1H},$$
$$y_2 = y_{21}, y_{22}, \ldots, y_{2k}, \ldots, y_{2K}.$$

The corresponding values of the two action variables, generated by some pair of functions (α_1, α_2) can be denoted thus:

$$a_1 = a_{11}, a_{12}, \ldots, a_{1h}, \ldots, a_{1H},$$

$$a_2 = a_{21}, a_{22}, \ldots, a_{2k}, \ldots, a_{2K},$$

where, for example, $a_{1h} = \alpha_1(y_{1h})$. (We shall not attempt, in this chapter, to extend the proof to y_1, y_2 continuous; but see Chapter 5.) The person-by-person-satisfactory[4] team decision rule $\hat{\alpha}_1, \hat{\alpha}_2$ can be expressed as the set of H numbers $\hat{a}_{1h}(h = 1, \ldots, H)$ and the set of K numbers $\hat{a}_{2k}(k = 1, \ldots, K)$, obtained by solving the $H + K$ equations with respect to these unknowns:

(10.8)

$$\left. \frac{\partial \psi_1(a_{1h}, y_{1h})}{\partial a_{1h}} \right]_{a_{1h} = \hat{a}_{1h}} = 0 \qquad h = 1, \ldots, H,$$

$$\left. \frac{\partial \psi_2(a_{2k}, y_{2k})}{\partial a_{2k}} \right]_{a_{2k} = \hat{a}_{2k}} = 0 \qquad k = 1, \ldots, K.$$

Associating $\hat{a}_{11}$ with $y_{11}, \ldots, \hat{a}_{1H}$ with y_{1H}, we obtain the function $\hat{\alpha}_1$; and associating $\hat{a}_{21}$ with $y_{21}, \ldots, \hat{a}_{2K}$ with y_{2K}, we obtain the function $\hat{\alpha}_2$.

We shall now apply these considerations explicitly to our quadratic case. The first of the two conditional expected payoffs in (10.7), with a_1 and y_1 fixed at some values a_{1h}, y_{1h}, is

(10.9) $\quad \psi_1(a_{1h}, y_{1h}) = -a_{1h}^2 - E\{\alpha_2^2(y_2)|y_{1h}\} + 2qa_{1h}E\{\alpha_2(y_2)|y_{1h}\}$

$$-a_{1h}E\{x_1|y_{1h}\} - E\{\alpha_2(y_2)x_2|y_{1h}\} \qquad h = 1, \ldots, H.$$

It is understood that "$|y_{1h}$" is written for brevity, instead of "$|\eta_1(x) = y_{1h}$." The K expressions for $\psi_2(y_{2k}, a_{2k})$, $k = 1, \ldots, K$ are analogous to (10.9). To find the team decision rule $(\hat{\alpha}_1, \hat{\alpha}_2)$ that maximizes, person-by-person, the conditional expected payoff for a given team information structure (η_1, η_2), we differentiate partially. The resulting $H + K$ equations can be written as follows:

(10.10)

$$-2\hat{a}_{1h} + 2qE\{\hat{a}_2(y_2)|y_{1h}\} = E\{x_1|y_{1h}\} \qquad h = 1, \ldots, H$$

$$2qE\{\hat{a}_1(y_1)|y_{2k}\} - 2\hat{a}_{2k} = E\{x_2|y_{2k}\} \qquad k = 1, \ldots, K.$$

Each of these two sets of equations can be rewritten in condensed form:

(10.11)

$$-2\hat{\alpha}_1(y_1) + 2qE\{\hat{\alpha}_2(y_2)|y_1\} = E\{x_1|y_1\}$$

$$2qE\{\hat{\alpha}_1(y_1)|y_2\} - 2\hat{\alpha}_2(y_2) = E\{x_2|y_2\}.$$

4. In general (e.g., Section 9), we denote the p.b.p.-satisfactory rule by $\tilde{\alpha}$, and the truly optimal rule by $\hat{\alpha}$. But when the payoff function is differentiable and concave, the two coincide.

For economic interpretation consider, for example, the first equation ($h = 1$) of the first line of (10.10). The expression on the right-hand side, $E\{x_1|y_{11}\}$, is the conditional expectation of the price of the first input, and that on the left-hand side is the conditional expectation of the marginal product of the first input given that the first member's information is y_{11}. Thus the classical rule of equating the marginal product of each input to its price is retained in a generalized form, while taking account of the possible incompleteness of the team member's information about the prices of inputs as well as about the other member's action.

ASSUMED PROBABILITY DISTRIBUTION

We have already assumed that the information variables y_1 and y_2 take only a finite number of values. We are considering only information structures in which a team member is informed about one or both or none of the observables. It is natural, therefore, to use in our example the "simple 2×2 distribution" of (x_1, x_2) described in (2.2) of Chapter 3. Thus $H = K = 2$.

THE CASE OF DECENTRALIZED INFORMATION

Let us begin with the case (see also Section 8 above)

$$\eta = \begin{bmatrix} 10 \\ 01 \end{bmatrix}.$$

In this case, for each $i(= 1, 2)$, $y_i = x_i(= s_i \text{ or } -s_i)$, so that

$$y_{11} = s_1, y_{12} = -s_1, y_{21} = s_2, y_{22} = -s_2,$$
$$a_{11} = \alpha_1(s_1), a_{12} = \alpha_1(-s_1), a_{21} = \alpha_2(s_2), a_{22} = \alpha_2(-s_2).$$

To use (10.10), note that

$$E(x_1|y_{11}) = E(x_1|x_1 = s_1) = s_1,$$
$$E(x_1|y_{12}) = E(x_1|x_1 = -s_1) = -s_1, \text{ etc.}$$

and, applying the results of Chapter 3, Section 2, we evaluate, for example,

$$E\{\alpha_2(y_2)|y_{11}\} = E\{\alpha_2(y_2)|x_1 = s_1\}$$
$$= \alpha_2(s_2) \Pr(x_2 = s_2|x_1 = s_1) + \alpha_2(-s_2) \Pr(x_2 = -s_2|x_1 = s_1)$$
$$= \frac{a_{21}(1 + r)}{2} + \frac{a_{22}(1 - r)}{2}.$$

Equations (10.10) become

(10.12) $-2\hat{a}_{11} + q(1 + r)\hat{a}_{21} + q(1 - r)\hat{a}_{22} = +s_1$

(10.12′) $-2\hat{a}_{12} + q(1 - r)\hat{a}_{21} + q(1 + r)\hat{a}_{22} = -s_1$

(10.13) $q(1 + r)\hat{a}_{11} + q(1 - r)\hat{a}_{12} - 2\hat{a}_{21} = +s_2$

(10.13′) $q(1 - r)\hat{a}_{11} + q(1 + r)\hat{a}_{12} - 2\hat{a}_{22} = -s_2.$

Adding the first two equations, and adding the last two equations, we obtain, respectively

$$\hat{a}_{11} + \hat{a}_{12} = q(\hat{a}_{21} + \hat{a}_{22})$$

$$q(\hat{a}_{11} + \hat{a}_{12}) = (\hat{a}_{21} + \hat{a}_{22}),$$

so that, since $q^2 \neq 1$, $\hat{a}_{11} = -\hat{a}_{12}$, $\hat{a}_{21} = -\hat{a}_{22}$ [that is, $\hat{a}_i(s_i) = -\hat{a}_i(-s_i)$: opposite information will call for opposite and equal action]. Substituting into (10.12), (10.13) and solving the resulting pair of equations, we obtain

$$\hat{a}_{11} = \frac{s_1 + qrs_2}{-2(1 - q^2r^2)} = s_1 \cdot \frac{1 + qrs_2/s_1}{-2(1 - q^2r^2)} = -\hat{a}_{12},$$

$$\hat{a}_{21} = \frac{s_2 + qrs_1}{-2(1 - q^2r^2)} = s_2 \cdot \frac{1 + qrs_1/s_2}{-2(1 - q^2r^2)} = -\hat{a}_{22}.$$

Thus (as in Example 3E) the decision functions are linear with no constant term,

(10.14) $\hat{\alpha}_i(y_i) = b_i y_i = b_i x_i \qquad i = 1, 2,$

where

(10.15) $$b_i = -\frac{1 + qrs_j/s_i}{2(1 - q^2r^2)} \qquad i \neq j.$$

For economic interpretation, consider first the symmetric case. Write $b_i = b_i^0$ when $s_1 = s_2$; then

(10.16) $$b_i^0 = \frac{-1}{2(1 - qr)} \qquad i = 1, 2.$$

Thus when both prices are equally uncertain, the optimal input of kind i changes in the direction opposite to the change in its price: for b_i^0 is negative, since $qr < 1$. Furthermore, b_i^0 increases (in absolute value) as qr increases, consistent with the following reasoning. Suppose the correlation r is close to $+1$. Then when the first member observes a low price of the first input, he is on the average justified in estimating the other price also to be low and in assuming therefore that his colleague has decided on a high input of the kind *he* controls; this in turn calls for a high input by the first member if q is large and positive (high complementarity) or for a low input if q is large in absolute value and negative (high interference).

By comparing the effects $(-b_i$ and $-b_i{}^0)$ of prices on corresponding inputs in the symmetric and the asymmetric cases, we may study the effect of the relative degree of uncertainty about the environmental variables, measured by $[1 - (s_j/s_i)]$:

$$b_i = b_i{}^0 + qr(1 - s_j/s_i)/2(1 - q^2r^2).$$

The first term on the right-hand side represents, as in (10.16), the effect of the price change regardless of relative uncertainties. The second term does depend on the relative uncertainties about x_i and x_j. If the uncertainty about x_i is greater than that about x_j $(s_i > s_j)$, then the smaller (s_j/s_i), the greater the second term is in absolute value; greater relative uncertainty about x_i leads to greater "caution" of the ith member.[5]

This correction for relative uncertainty may be strong enough to lead to a "paradox" analogous to the one shown in the shipyard example (Section 8 of this chapter). The coefficient b_1 (say) defined in (10.15) becomes positive if $qr < 0$ and $s_1/s_2 < |qr|$. That is, if the first team member controls the input with the less volatile price $(s_1 < s_2)$, he may do well to respond to a rise in this price by increasing the input, provided that the prices are strongly positively correlated and there is strong interference between inputs.

The reader may also find it instructive to compare (10.15) with (8.14) in Chapter 3, which gives the optimal decision rule for a single person who controls both inputs while knowing the price of only one of them.

All such economic interpretations of mathematical results may be compared with the results of the reader's "intuition." Even in the simple cases treated so far, some of the mathematical results seem to outrun those of an intuitive and discursive argument.

AN ALTERNATIVE APPROACH

The linearity of the optimal decision function suggests for the case considered an alternative use of the person-by-person maximization principle. This approach will not only simplify the computations for the case of the particular (and discrete) probability distribution we have used,

5. It will be recalled that the ratio s_1/s_2 does not depend on the choice of money unit but does depend on the chosen units of output and input quantities: they were chosen so as to reduce the quadratic profit function to the form (10.1).

but can also be extended to the important case of normal distribution of environmental variables. The approach consists in proving that linear decision functions satisfy the maximizing conditions (10.10) and in finding the coefficients of those functions.

Still considering the case of decentralized information, $y_i = x_i$, we put tentatively: $\alpha_i(y_i) = b_i x_i$. Then (10.11) becomes

$$-2b_1 x_1 + 2q \cdot E\{b_2 x_2 | x_1\} = x_1,$$

$$2q \cdot E\{b_1 x_1 | x_2\} - 2b_2 x_2 = x_2.$$

Inserting from the regression equation (2.4) of Chapter 3,

$$(10.17) \qquad\qquad E(x_i | x_j) = x_j \cdot r(s_i / s_j),$$

we obtain a pair of linear equations in the unknowns b_1, b_2:

$$-s_1 x_1 \cdot b_1 + q r s_2 x_1 \cdot b_2 = s_1 x_1 / 2,$$

$$q r s_1 x_2 \cdot b_1 - s_2 x_2 \cdot b_2 = s_2 x_2 / 2.$$

Since this is to hold for any values of x_1 or x_2, we can equate the co-efficients of x_1 (or x_2) on each side of each equation:

$$-s_1 \cdot b_1 + q r s_2 \cdot b_2 = s_1 / 2,$$

$$q r s_1 \cdot b_1 - s_2 \cdot b_2 = s_2 / 2.$$

The existence of a solution validates the tentative assumption that the person-to-person-satisfactory decision functions α_i are linear. In fact, the solution is (10.15), as is easily verified.

EXTENSION TO THE CASE OF A NORMAL DISTRIBUTION

The regression equation (10.17), which was derived for the case of a special discrete distribution, holds also for the normal distribution with zero means (Chapter 3, Section 2). Hence the result (10.15), obtained from the maximizing equations (10.11), holds also for the case of a normal distribution. For the general discrete case, these equations summarized the set of $H + K$ linear equations (10.10). When the states of the world x and the information signals y_i are normally distributed, the averages (expectations) are expressed by integrals. It follows from Theorem 5 of Chapter 5 that (10.11) remains in force in this case.

We are therefore permitted, continuing our study of the two-person quadratic team, to assume either the simple 2×2 distribution or the normal distribution with the same results. (A generalization of the normal distribution case to quadratic teams with more than two members will be pursued in Chapter 5.)

APPLICATION TO OTHER INFORMATION STRUCTURES

In the case of decentralized information, $\begin{bmatrix} 1 & 0 \\ 0 & 1 \end{bmatrix}$, we have exploited the linearity of the optimal decision function in the quadratic case with a normal distribution (or with the simple 2×2 distribution). We can apply the same method to any other of the 16 information structures, including those in which an information variable y_i is not a single number but a vector (an action is taken on the basis of knowledge of both x_1 and x_2). Consider, for example, the information structure $\begin{bmatrix} 1 & 1 \\ 0 & 1 \end{bmatrix}$: person 1 has complete information, person 2 has only partial information. Again, assume tentatively that

$$\hat{\alpha}_1(y_1) \equiv \hat{\alpha}_1(x_1, x_2) = b_{11}x_1 + b_{12}x_2$$

$$\hat{\alpha}_2(y_2) \equiv \hat{\alpha}_2(x_2) = b_2 x_2$$

and find the three coefficients b_{11}, b_{12}, b_2 (if they exist). Equations (10.11) become

$$-2(b_{11}x_1 + b_{12}x_2) + 2qE\{b_2 x_2 | x_1, x_2\} = E\{x_1 | x_1, x_2\},$$

$$2qE\{(b_{11}x_1 + b_{12}x_2)|x_2\} - 2b_2 x_2 = E\{x_2 | x_2\}.$$

Now $E\{x_2 | x_1, x_2\} = E\{x_2 | x_2\} = x_2; E\{x_1 | x_1, x_2\} = x_1$. Hence

$$-b_{11} \cdot x_1 - b_{12} \cdot x_2 + qb_2 \cdot x_2 = x_1/2$$

$$qb_{11}r(s_1/s_2) \cdot x_2 + qb_{12} \cdot x_2 - b_2 \cdot x_2 = x_2/2,$$

by (10.17). Equating the coefficients of x_1 and those of x_2 in each equation, we obtain

$$-b_{11} = 1/2, \ -b_{12} + qb_2 = 0 \qquad \text{from the first equation, and}$$

$$qr(s_1/s_2)b_{11} + qb_{12} - b_2 = 1/2 \qquad \text{from the second equation.}$$

This is solved by

$$b_{11} = -1/2; b_2 = -\frac{(1 + qrs_1/s_2)}{2(1 - q^2)};$$

$$b_{12} = -\frac{q(1 + qrs_1/s_2)}{2(1 - q^2)}.$$

Hence the person-by-person-satisfactory decision rule (which, in the

TABLE 4.14

Network	Information Structure	Best Decision Rules				Net Expected Payoff
		Member 1: Coefficient of		Member 2: Coefficient of		
		x_1	x_2	x_1	x_2	
1 □ □	$\begin{bmatrix}00\\00\end{bmatrix}$	0	0	0	0	0
2 × □	$\begin{bmatrix}10\\00\end{bmatrix}$	$-1/2$	0	0	0	$1/4 - c$
3 × → □	$\begin{bmatrix}10\\10\end{bmatrix}$	$-1/2 \cdot \dfrac{1+rq}{1-q^2}$	0	$-1/2 \cdot \dfrac{r+q}{1-q^2}$	0	$\dfrac{1+2rq+r^2}{4(1-q^2)} - c - c'$
4 ×	$\begin{bmatrix}10\\01\end{bmatrix}$	$-1/2 \cdot \dfrac{1}{1-rq}$	0	0	$-1/2 \cdot \dfrac{1}{1-rq}$	$\dfrac{1}{2(1-rq)} - 2c$
7 × → ×	$\begin{bmatrix}10\\11\end{bmatrix}$	$-1/2 \cdot \dfrac{1+rq}{1-q^2}$	0	$-1/2 \cdot \dfrac{q(1+qr)}{1-q^2}$	$-1/2$	$\dfrac{(1+rq)^2}{4(1-q^2)} + 1/4 - 2c - c'$
9 × ↔ ×	$\begin{bmatrix}11\\11\end{bmatrix}$	$-1/2 \cdot \dfrac{1}{1-q^2}$	$-1/2 \cdot \dfrac{q}{1-q^2}$	$-1/2 \cdot \dfrac{q}{1-q^2}$	$-1/2 \cdot \dfrac{1}{1-q^2}$	$\dfrac{1+rq}{2(1-q^2)} - 2 - 2c$

NOTE: These results are, of course, consistent with those of the next two chapters if the transformations (3.5) of Chapter 5 are carried out. In particular, replace q by $-q$; and, in the last column, because of the change in units for x_i, multiply the gross expected profit by 4.

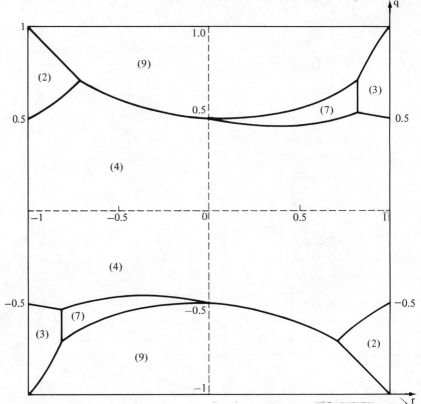

FIGURE 4.2 Regions of (r, q) plane in which each network is best. $c = c' = 1/12$.

quadratic concave case is also optimal) is

$$a_1 = -(1/2)x_1 - (1/2)\frac{q(1 + qrs_1/s_2)}{1 - q^2}x_2$$

(10.18)

$$a_2 = -(1/2)\cdot\frac{1 + qrs_1/s_2}{1 - q^2}\cdot x_2$$

It is interesting to compare this result with (8.7) of Chapter 3, where a single person determined both inputs, on the basis of the knowledge of both prices. In (10.18), the first input is *also* based on the knowledge of both prices, but the decision rule (of the first team member, the one who controls this input) is quite different from that in the single-person case. Note in particular the role of the regression coefficient rs_1/s_2. It is used, as it were, by the second member, who must estimate the price x_1 (unknown to him) on the basis of the known price x_2, for x_1 will influence his partner's decision and hence, by complementarity, the effect of his own decision. This estimate influences his own decision, and therefore in turn, his partner's decision. Only when there is no complementarity ($q = 0$) does the team decision rule coincide with that of the single person, namely, $a_i = -x_i/2$.

In summarizing the results in Table 4.14, we shall consider only the symmetrical case $s_1 = s_2 = 1$. We can therefore omit one-half of those cases of Table 4.1 that are obtainable by interchanging members 1 and 2. Moreover, as in Example 4A, we shall consider only teams with "co-specialization": member i is an "expert" about the variable x_i and observes it at cost c while the cost of his observing x_j is prohibitive. The cost of one-way communication is c'; the cost of two-way communication is $2c'$.

We shall stop here and shall leave the further analysis of the results to the reader. He will note especially how the optimality of a given network depends on the parameters q and r on the one hand, and on the observation and communication costs on the other. For example, fixing c and c' at some levels, he may study the regions of the (q, r) plane in which a given network would be optimal. Figure 4.2 gives an example of this.

11. Cases in which the Information Structure Concept Is Not Applicable

When discussing the single-person decision problem in Chapter 2, Section 12, we showed that it is not always possible to express the net expected payoff as the difference between gross expected payoff and the sum of expected information and decision costs,

$$(11.1) \qquad E\omega\{x, \alpha[\eta(x)]\} - E\tilde{\gamma}(x, \alpha, \eta).$$

Instead, for each value of x, a net payoff function, $\omega^*(x, \alpha, \eta)$, is defined and its expected value maximized.

In particular, this difficulty may arise even in a sequential decision problem for a "single person" if the person's action at one time affects his information at subsequent times. This is typical of problems of inventory control, investment, and sequential sampling in statistics.

In the multi-person case, the formulation (11.1) may be too restrictive for an additional reason, namely, one person's action may affect another's information. For example, a scout's action, taken on the basis of his own observations, may consist of a message to his chief; these messages form a part of the information on which the chief bases his subsequent actions.

Let η_1 and η_2 denote the information functions of the scout and his chief, respectively, and let α_1 and α_2 represent their decision functions. For each i, the set of decision functions α_i that are feasible is of course restricted by the choice of η_i. But, in addition, the set of information functions η_2 that are feasible may be restricted by the particular action $a_1 = \alpha_1[\eta_1(x)]$ taken by person 1 (the scout). In particular η_2 may simply be

$$\eta_2(x) = \alpha_1[\eta_1(x)].$$

In this case it would not be possible to formulate the team problem as one of choosing a best pair $(\hat{\alpha}_1, \hat{\alpha}_2)$ of decision functions for a given (fixed) pair (η_1, η_2) of information functions.

In the next three chapters, we analyze team decision problems in which assumption (11.1) is made explicitly or implicitly. The consideration of the more general case is deferred to Chapter 8, in which we use the concept of a "network."

CHAPTER 5

Best Decision Functions

1. INTRODUCTION

In this chapter, we consider problems of determining the best team decision function for a given information structure. The motivation for considering such problems has been given in Chapter 4; thus the concern in this chapter is primarily technical. The methods developed here will be used in Chapters 6 and 7 to analyze and evaluate specific classes of information structures.

The concept of a person-by-person-satisfactory team decision function was introduced in Chapter 4. In Section 2 of the present chapter, we show that if for every state of the world the payoff function is a concave, differentiable function of the team action variables, then every person-by-person satisfactory team decision function is optimal.

The person-by-person principle provides a way of characterizing optimal decision functions in a limited, but still fairly broad, class of cases. Further progress in characterizing optimal decision functions is possible if one considers even more limited classes of problems. These limitations can be on the payoff function, on the probability distribution, on the set of feasible decision functions, or on the information structure. In Sections 3 and 4, we consider two special classes of payoff functions, *quadratic* and *concave polyhedral*. In the first case, the person-by-person principle applies to give some fairly explicit characterizations of optimal decision functions. This will facilitate the study (in Chapters 6 and 7) of the organizational consequences of changes in the various parameters of the situation. In the second case (concave polyhedral), the person-by-person principle typically does not apply, but the techniques of linear programming provide a general method of solution; however, the effects of changes in the conditions are not as easily discerned. In addition to showing how, in the concave polyhedral case, the problem of finding an optimal team

155

decision function can be transformed into a linear programming problem, we apply the duality theory of linear programming to obtain Lagrangian multipliers that can be interpreted as "random prices." For the special case of a linear payoff function, the formulation in Section 4 provides one approach to "linear programming under uncertainty."

Since during the discussion of any particular problem the information structure will be fixed, we shall use the notation

$$\Omega(\alpha) = E\omega(x, \alpha[\eta(x)])$$

to denote the expected payoff for any particular decision function α. A decision function $\hat{\alpha}$ is optimal if it maximizes $\Omega(\alpha)$ in the set of decision functions available to the team.

2. PERSON-BY-PERSON SATISFACTORY DECISION FUNCTIONS

A team decision function is defined to be *person-by-person satisfactory* if it cannot be improved by changing any one component α_i alone. More formally, for any decision function $\tilde{\alpha}$, let

(2.1) $\Omega_i(\alpha_i, \tilde{\alpha}) = \Omega(\tilde{\alpha}_1, \ldots, \tilde{\alpha}_{i-1}, \alpha_i, \tilde{\alpha}_{i+1}, \ldots, \tilde{\alpha}_n);$

then $\tilde{\alpha}$ is person-by-person satisfactory (p.b.p.s.) if, for every i,

(2.2) $\Omega(\tilde{\alpha}) = \max_{\alpha_i} \Omega_i(\alpha_i, \tilde{\alpha})   i = 1, \ldots, n.$

An optimal decision function is *a fortiori* person-by-person satisfactory, but the converse is not, in general, true. This section describes a condition under which p.b.p. satisfactoriness guarantees optimality.

The concept of p.b.p. satisfactoriness is useful in much the same way that it is useful to be able to characterize (when possible) the maximum of a function of several variables as being attained at a point at which the several partial derivatives vanish, that is, at a point at which the function attains a maximum in each variable alone. In the case of the team problem, the "variables" in question are actually the several component decision functions.

The conditions (2.2) for p.b.p. satisfactoriness further suggest a process of *adjustment* whereby one might hope, starting from any team decision function, to approach an optimal decision function by changing the team decision function *one component at a time*. The convergence of such a person-by-person adjustment process to an optimal team decision function can be demonstrated under certain assumptions, but we shall not pursue this topic here.

MAXIMIZING CONDITIONAL EXPECTATIONS

In a one-person decision problem, the action prescribed by an optimal decision function is an action that maximizes the conditional expected payoff, given the observation (see Chapter 2, Section 5).

In the case of a p.b.p.s. decision function, each condition of (2.2) can be throught of as referring to a one-person problem, namely, the problem that person i faces when the decision functions of all persons j different from i are fixed at $\tilde{\alpha}_j$. For any action a_i of person i, and any value y_i of his information variable, the conditional expected payoff is

$$(2.3) \qquad \psi_i(a_i, y_i) \equiv E\{\omega[x, \tilde{\alpha}_1(y_1), \ldots, a_i, \ldots, \tilde{\alpha}_n(y_n)]|y_i\}.$$

Thus $\tilde{\alpha}$ is person-by-person satisfactory if and only if for every i and every y_i, $\tilde{\alpha}_i(y_i)$ maximizes $\psi_i(a_i, y_i)$. In particular, if a_i is a real variable, and ψ_i is differentiable in a_i, then the above maximum will occur at a value of a_i for which $\partial\psi_i/\partial a_i = 0$. This motivates the following definition: A team decision function α is *stationary* if, for every i and every y_i,

$$(2.4) \qquad \left.\frac{\partial\psi_i(a_i, y_i)}{\partial a_i}\right|_{a_i = \alpha_i(y_i)} = 0.$$

A CONDITION UNDER WHICH EVERY PERSON-BY-PERSON-SATISFACTORY DECISION FUNCTION IS OPTIMAL

THEOREM 1. *For each i let a_i be a real variable, and suppose that for every x, ω is a concave, differentiable function of $a = (a_1, \ldots, a_n)$; then any stationary team decision function is optimal.*[1]

Sketch of Proof. Let $\tilde{\alpha}$ be stationary, let ε be any other team decision function; define the function f by

$$f(t) = \Omega(\tilde{\alpha} + t\varepsilon),$$

where t is any real number. Because the function ω is concave and differentiable in a, the function f is concave and differentiable in t. Let $\omega_i(x, a)$ denote the partial derivative of ω with respect to a_i; then the derivative

---

1. The theorem remains valid if the team action variable, a, is constrained to lie in a convex set, and the stationary team decision function takes all its values in the interior of that set. An analogous theorem can also be proved for the case in which the action variables of the team members are vectors, and there are separate constraints on the actions of the individual members.

of f with respect to t is[2]

$$f'(t) = \frac{d}{dt} E\omega(x, \tilde{\alpha} + t\varepsilon)$$

$$= \sum_{i=1}^{n} E\omega_i(x, \tilde{\alpha} + t\varepsilon)\varepsilon_i.$$

(The change in the order of the operations of differentiation and expectation is valid here because the sets $X, Y_1, \ldots, Y_n$ are finite.) Hence

(2.5) $$f'(0) = \sum_{i=1}^{n} E\omega_i(x, \tilde{\alpha})\varepsilon_i.$$

For every i,

$$E\omega_i(x, \tilde{\alpha})\varepsilon_i = \sum_{y_i \in Y_i} E[\omega_i(x, \tilde{\alpha})\varepsilon_i | \eta_i(x) = y_i] \operatorname{Prob}[\eta_i(x) = y_i].$$

Since ε_i is a function of y_i, this last equals

(2.6) $$E\omega_i(x, \tilde{\alpha})\varepsilon_i = \sum_{y_i \in Y_i} \varepsilon_i(y_i) E[\omega_i(x, \tilde{\alpha}) | \eta_i(x) = y_i] \operatorname{Prob}[\eta_i(x) = y_i].$$

The stationarity condition (2.4) can be rewritten as follows by interchanging the operations of differentiation and expectation:

$$E[\omega_i(x, \tilde{\alpha}) | \eta_i(x) = y_i] = 0 \qquad \text{every } i \text{ and } y_i.$$

Substitution of this in (2.5) gives

$$f'(0) = 0.$$

Hence $f(t)$ has a maximum at $t = 0$; hence, for any decision function γ of the form $\gamma = \tilde{\alpha} + t\varepsilon$,

(2.7) $$\Omega(\gamma) = f(t) \leq f(0) = \Omega(\tilde{\alpha}).$$

Now any team decision function γ can be put in the form $\gamma = \tilde{\alpha} + t\varepsilon$ for some ε and t. Thus the argument leading to (2.7) shows that, for any team decision function γ,

$$\Omega(\gamma) \leq \Omega(\tilde{\alpha});$$

that is, $\tilde{\alpha}$ is optimal.

2. Recall that, for notational compactness, we write

$$E\omega(x, \alpha) \quad \text{for } E\omega(x, \alpha_1[\eta_1(x)], \ldots, \alpha_n[\eta_n(x)]),$$

and similarly for other expectations. Note also that the symbols $\mathscr{Y}$ and $\mathscr{Z}$ of Part One will be henceforth replaced by Y and Z.

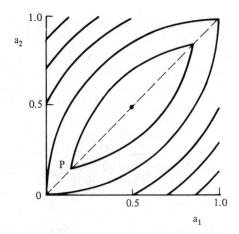

FIGURE 5.1. Person-by-person satisfactoriness is not sufficient for optimality.

A condition of differentiability seems to be essential to the above result,
as the following example suggests.

Consider a team of two members, whose payoff function is independent
of x, with contour lines as on Figure 5.1, say

$$(2.8) \qquad \omega(a_1, a_2) = \min\{-a_1{}^2 - (a_2 - 1)^2, -(a_1 - 1)^2 - a_2{}^2\}.$$

It is easily verified that any (a_1, a_2) for which $a_1 = a_2$ is person-by-person
satisfactory (e.g., the point P in Figure 5.1), whereas the maximum of ω
is attained only at $a_1 = a_2 = 1/2$. Note that in this example ω is actually
strictly concave.

For an extension of Theorem 1 to the case of an infinite X, see Radner
1962.

3. Teams with Quadratic Payoff Functions

In this section we shall explore the consequences of assuming that, for
every state of the world, the payoff is a quadratic function of the team
action variables. Particular attention will be given to the case in which
(1) the coefficients of the second degree terms do not depend upon the
state of the world, and (2) the relevant random variables are normally
distributed. In this case, the optimal decision variables will be shown to be
linear functions of the information variables, and an explicit algorithm
for their computation will be given.

A quadratic payoff function may be thought of as an approximation.
for each state of the world, to an arbitrary smooth payoff function in the

neighborhood of the best team action, say $\beta(x)$, corresponding to the state of the world x.

In a quadratic formulation, the variances and correlations of the information variables have an especially important role (whatever the probability distribution). In fact, the theory of the quadratic team has interesting connections with the statistical theory of regression (see Radner 1962).

Almost all of the essential features of the "quadratic team" are present in the two-person case. We shall therefore first present a fairly complete treatment of this case, which will be followed by a brief discussion of the quadratic team with any number of members.

THE TWO-PERSON CASE

Suppose that there are two real action variables, a_1 and a_2, and that the payoff function is given by

$$(3.1) \qquad \omega(x, a) = \lambda(x) + 2\mu_1(x)a_1 + 2\mu_2(x)a_2$$
$$- v_{11}(x)a_1{}^2 - 2v_{12}(x)a_1a_2 - v_{22}(x)a_2{}^2,$$

where λ, μ_1, and v_{ij} are all real-valued functions of the state of the world, x.

It is reasonable to confine our attention to situations in which there is a maximum payoff for every fixed x; for this reason, we shall make the assumption that $v_{11}(x)$, $v_{22}(x)$, and

$$\begin{vmatrix} v_{11}(x) & v_{12}(x) \\ v_{12}(x) & v_{22}(x) \end{vmatrix}$$

are positive for every x.

THEOREM 2. *The optimal decision functions* $\hat{\alpha}_1$ *and* $\hat{\alpha}_2$ *are determined by the following conditions: for every* y_1 *and* y_2,

$$(3.2) \qquad \begin{cases} \alpha_1(y_1)E(v_{11}|y_1) + E(\alpha_2 v_{12}|y_1) = E(\mu_1|y_1) \\ E(\alpha_1 v_{21}|y_2) + \alpha_2(y_2)E(v_{22}|y_2) = E(\mu_2|y_2). \end{cases}$$

Sketch of Proof.[3] The conditions of Theorem 1 (Section 2) are satisfied here, so that the person-by-person rule can be applied, in its special form of stationarity [condition (2.4)]. This last directly yields (3.2) above.

If, as we have been assuming, the state of nature, x, can take on only a finite number of values, then (3.2) represents a system of linear equations as follows.

3. For an extension to the case of an infinite set X, see Radner 1962.

Suppose that

1. The possible values of x are $x_1, \ldots, x_M$.
2. For $i = 1, 2$, the possible values of the information variable y_i are $y_{i1}, \ldots, y_{iM_i}$.
3. The conditional probability that $y_j = y_{jm}$ given that $y_i = y_{ih}$ is $p_{jm}{}^{ih}$.
4. The value $\alpha_i(y_{ih})$ is denoted by a_{ih}.

Then, according to (3.2), the values $a_{11}, \ldots, a_{1M_1}$ and $a_{21}, \ldots, a_{2M_2}$ are to be chosen to satisfy the following $(M_1 + M_2)$ linear equations:

$$a_{1h}E(v_{11}|y_{1h}) + \sum_{m=1}^{M_2} a_{2m}E(v_{12}|y_{1h}, y_{2m})p_{2m}{}^{1h} = E(\mu_1|y_{1h})$$

$$h = 1, \ldots, M_1$$

(3.3)

$$\sum_{h=1}^{M_1} a_{1h}E(v_{21}|y_{1h}, y_{2m})p_{1h}{}^{2m} + a_{2m}E(v_{22}|y_{2m}) = E(\mu_2|y_{2m})$$

$$m = 1, \ldots, M_2.$$

In Example 4B (Chapter 4, Section 10) the coefficients of the quadratic terms were constant, and the following interpretation was offered: a_1 and a_2 denote inputs in a production process, x_1 and x_2 denote the prices of the inputs, the production function is quadratic in the inputs, and by suitable choices of origins and units the payoff function can be put in the form [see (10.1) of Chapter 4]:

(3.4) $$\omega(x, a) = -x_1 a_1 - x_2 a_2 - a_1{}^2 + 2q a_1 a_2 - a_2{}^2.$$

Comparing this with the general formulation in (3.1), we see that

(3.5)
$$\begin{cases} \lambda(x) = 0, & \mu_1(x) = \dfrac{-x_1}{2}, & \mu_2(x) = \dfrac{-x_2}{2} \\ v_{11}(x) = v_{22}(x) = 1, & v_{12}(x) = -q. \end{cases}$$

Suppose, in this example, that each price x_i can have only one of M values $x_{ij}(j = 1, \ldots, M)$ and that the joint probabilities are

(3.6) $$\Pr(x_1 = x_{1j}, x_2 = x_{2k}) = \phi_{jk}.$$

Suppose further that the decision about each input is made only on the basis of knowledge about the corresponding price; that is, assume "decentralized information" as in Example 4B.

(3.7) $$\eta_i(x) = x_i.$$

Each decision function α_i will have the form

(3.8) $\alpha_i(x_{im}) = a_{im}$ $i = 1, 2;$

that is, a_{im} is the level of input i to be set by person i if he finds out that the price of his input is x_{im}. The numbers a_{im} are to be determined so as to maximize the expected payoff; their optimal values are, by (3.3), determined by the following system of $2M$ equations:

$$a_{1j} - q \sum_{m=1}^{M} a_{2m} \Pr(x_{2m}|x_{1j}) = -x_{1j}/2 \qquad j = 1, \ldots, M$$

(3.9)

$$-q \sum_{m=1}^{M} a_{1m} \Pr(x_{1m}|x_{2k}) + a_{2k} = -x_{2k}/2 \qquad k = 1, \ldots, M.$$

EXAMPLE 4B RECONSIDERED

In Example 4B, we specialized further at one point by assuming the simple 2×2 joint probability distribution [(2.2) of Chapter 3].

(3.10)

x_2 \ x_1	-1	$+1$
-1	$\dfrac{1+r}{4}$	$\dfrac{1-r}{4}$
$+1$	$\dfrac{1-r}{4}$	$\dfrac{1+r}{4}$

(Recall that, in this simple distribution, x_1 and x_2 have the same marginal distributions with the values $+1$ and -1 equally likely, and with means 0, variances 1, and correlation r.) The optimal decision functions, that is, the solutions of (3.9), were found to be

(3.11)
$$\begin{cases} a_{11} = a_{21} = \dfrac{1}{2(1-rq)} \\[3mm] a_{12} = a_{22} = \dfrac{-1}{2(1-rq)}. \end{cases}$$

It is interesting to compare these decision functions with those that would be optimal in the following two extreme situations:

1. *Complete information*—each person knows the value of both x_1 and x_2 before taking action, that is $\eta_i(x) = (x_1, x_2)$.

2. *No information*—each person takes action with only knowledge of the probability distribution of x_1 and x_2, that is, $\eta_i(x)$ constant.

These are, of course, the situations discussed in Examples 3E and 4B.

The results for the three information structures are summarized in Table 5.1, which shows for each person the action that is actually taken for each of the four possible states of the world, under each information structure.

TABLE 5.1. OPTIMAL DECISION FUNCTIONS FOR THREE
INFORMATION STRUCTURES

(x_1, x_2)	Complete Information $\eta_i(x) = (x_1, x_2)$		Decentralized Information $\eta_i(x) = x_i$		No Information η_i constant	
	a_1	a_2	a_1	a_2	a_1	a_2
$(-1,-1)$	$\dfrac{1}{2(1-q)}$	$\dfrac{1}{2(1-q)}$	$\dfrac{1}{2(1-rq)}$	$\dfrac{1}{2(1-rq)}$	0	0
$(-1,1)$	$\dfrac{1}{2(1+q)}$	$\dfrac{-1}{2(1+q)}$	$\dfrac{1}{2(1-rq)}$	$\dfrac{-1}{2(1-rq)}$	0	0
$(1,-1)$	$\dfrac{-1}{2(1+q)}$	$\dfrac{1}{2(1+q)}$	$\dfrac{-1}{2(1-rq)}$	$\dfrac{1}{2(1-rq)}$	0	0
$(1,1)$	$\dfrac{-1}{2(1-q)}$	$\dfrac{-1}{2(1-q)}$	$\dfrac{-1}{2(1-rq)}$	$\dfrac{-1}{2(1-rq)}$	0	0

THE TWO-PERSON CASE CONTINUED—NORMALITY
AND LINEAR DECISION FUNCTIONS

We shall now show that if
1. the coefficients of the quadratic terms in (3.1) are constant, independent of x, and
2. the coefficients of the linear terms, and the information variables, are normally distributed,
then the optimal decision functions are linear.

This result will be used later to analyze the influence of the variability and correlation of the information variables on the choice of optimal information structures.[4]

4. The assumption of normality violates the assumption of finite X that we have been making all along; see Radner 1962 for a rigorous proof.

According to assumption (1) above, the functions v_{ij} in (3.1) are constant. Let $v_{12} = -q$, and let the units of a_1 and a_2 be chosen so that $v_{11} = v_{22} = 1$. This gives us the form of the payoff function

$$(3.12) \quad \omega(x, a) = \lambda(x) + 2\mu_1(x)a_1 + 2\mu_2(x)a_2 - a_1^2 + 2qa_1a_2 - a_2^2.$$

The requirement that $\omega(x, a)$ have a maximum in a, for every x, is met by requiring that $q^2 < 1$. Indeed, by differentiating (3.12) with respect to a_1 and a_2, we get the conditions for a maximum as

$$(3.13) \quad \begin{aligned} a_1 - qa_2 &= \mu_1(x) \\ -qa_1 + a_2 &= \mu_2(x). \end{aligned}$$

The solution of this gives the best values of a_1 and a_2 for any given value of x as

$$(3.14) \quad \left\{ \begin{aligned} a_1 &= \frac{\mu_1(x) + q\mu_2(x)}{1 - q^2} \equiv \beta_1(x) \\ a_2 &= \frac{q\mu_1(x) + \mu_2(x)}{1 - q^2} \equiv \beta_2(x). \end{aligned} \right.$$

[Compare this with (8.7) of Chapter 3.][5]

Now suppose that η_1 and η_2 are the information functions for persons 1 and 2, respectively. It will simplify the exposition to assume that η_1 and η_2 are scalar-valued functions, but the extension to vector-valued functions (each person learning about several variables) is easy. Denote the random variable $\eta_i(x)$ by y_i, and let

$$(3.15) \quad \text{Correlation}(y_1, y_2) \equiv r.$$

There is no loss of generality in assuming that $Ey_i = 0$ and that $\text{Variance}(y_i) = 1$.

We now proceed to show that the optimal team decision functions are linear.

First, we shall write the person-by-person satisfactoriness condition for the present case [see (3.2)]:

$$(3.16) \quad \left\{ \begin{aligned} \alpha_1(y_1) - qE(\alpha_2|y_1) &= E(\mu_1|y_1) \\ -qE(\alpha_1|y_2) + \alpha_2(y_2) &= E(\mu_2|y_2). \end{aligned} \right.$$

We next show that changing μ_1 and μ_2 by adding constants results in a change of the optimal α_1 and α_2 by adding constants. Let m_1 and m_2

---

5. Henceforth, unless otherwise noted, the symbol β_i will be used to denote the optimal decision function for person i under *complete* information.

be any two numbers, and let c_1 and c_2 be the solutions of

(3.17)
$$\begin{cases} c_1 - qc_2 = m_1 \\ -qc_1 + c_2 = m_2. \end{cases}$$

It follows that, if α_1 and α_2 satisfy (3.16), then

(3.18)
$$\begin{cases} \alpha_1(y_1) + c_1 - qE(\alpha_2 + c_2|y_1) = E(\mu_1 + m_1|y_1), \\ -qE(\alpha_1 + c_1|y_2) + \alpha_2(y_2) + c_2 = E(\mu_2 + m_2|y_2). \end{cases}$$

In other words, when the constants m_1 and m_2 are added to μ_1 and μ_2, respectively, the constants c_1 and c_2 must be added to α_1 and α_2, respectively, to obtain new optimal decision functions.

Hence, there is no important loss of generality in assuming that $E\mu_1 = E\mu_2 = 0$, and this will now be done.

We next show that there exists a solution $(\hat{\alpha}_1, \hat{\alpha}_2)$ to (3.16) of the form

(3.19)
$$\begin{cases} \hat{\alpha}_1(y_1) = b_1 y_1 \\ \hat{\alpha}_2(y_2) = b_2 y_2. \end{cases}$$

In order to prove this, we substitute (3.19) into (3.16) and look for values of b_1 and b_2 that satisfy that condition;

(3.20)
$$\begin{cases} b_1 y_1 - qb_2 E(y_2|y_1) = E(\mu_1|y_1) \\ -qb_2 E(y_1|y_2) + b_2 = E(\mu_2|y_2). \end{cases}$$

Since the μ_i and the y_i are normally distributed with zero means, and the y_i have unit variances,

(3.21)
$$\begin{cases} E(\mu_i|y_i) = d_i y_i \\ E(y_i|y_j) = r y_j, \end{cases}$$

where

$$d_i = \text{Covariance}(\mu_i, y_i),$$
$$r = \text{Correlation}(y_1, y_2).$$

(See Mood and Graybill [1963], Chapter 9.)

The substitution of (3.21) in (3.20) gives

$$b_1 y_1 - qrb_2 y_1 = d_1 y_1$$
$$-qrb_1 y_2 + b_2 y_2 = d_2 y_2,$$

for all y_1 and y_2. Therefore

(3.22)
$$\begin{cases} b_1 - qrb_2 = d_1 \\ -qrb_1 + b_2 = d_2, \end{cases}$$

which has the solution

(3.23)
$$b_1 = \frac{d_1 + qrd_2}{1 - q^2r^2}$$
$$b_2 = \frac{d_2 + qrd_1}{1 - q^2r^2}.$$

If we drop the assumption that $E(\mu_i) = 0$, and now add the solution of (3.17), with $m_i = E(\mu_i)$,

(3.24)
$$\begin{cases} c_1 = \dfrac{E\mu_1 + qE\mu_2}{1 - q^2} \\ c_2 = \dfrac{E\mu_2 + qE\mu_1}{1 - q^2}, \end{cases}$$

we have, taking (3.23) and (3.24) together, the solution to our problem, as summarized in the following theorem.

THEOREM 3. *If the payoff function is given by (3.12) and if μ_1, μ_2, y_1, and y_2 are normally distributed with $Ey_i = 0$, $\mathrm{Var} y_i = 1$, $Ey_1y_2 = r$, and $\mathrm{Cov}(\mu_i, y_i) = d_i$, then the optimal decision functions $\hat{\alpha}_1$ and $\hat{\alpha}_2$ are linear,*

(3.25) $\hat{\alpha}_i(y_i) = c_i + b_i y_i,$

and the coefficients b_i and c_i are given by (3.23) and (3.24).

EXAMPLE

Consider Example 4B in its extension to the case of a normal distribution. Here x_1 and x_2 are the deviations of the input prices from their respective means, and a_1 and a_2 are the deviations of the levels of input from those values that would be best if the input prices had their mean values ($x_i = 0$). As before, denote the variance of x_i by $s_i{}^2$ and the correlation between x_1 and x_2 by r.

For the case of "decentralized information," we take

(3.26) $y_i = x_i/s_i,$

in order to standardize the information variables as in the statement of Theorem 3. Then $d_i = s_i/2$, and the application of Theorem 3 immediately gives

$$\hat{\alpha}_1(y_1) = -\left[\frac{1 + qrs_2/s_1}{2(1 - q^2r^2)}\right]x_1$$

(3.27)

$$\hat{\alpha}_2(y_2) = -\left[\frac{1 + qrs_1/s_2}{2(1 - q^2r^2)}\right]x_2.$$

The solution to the "full information" case is, of course, given by (3.14), which in the present example takes the form:

$$\hat{\alpha}_1(x_1, x_2) = -\frac{x_1 + qx_2}{2(1 - q^2)}$$

(3.28)

$$\hat{\alpha}_2(x_1, x_2) = -\frac{x_2 + qx_1}{2(1 - q^2)}.$$

It is left to the reader to verify that the solution to the "no information" case is given by $\hat{\alpha}_1 = \hat{\alpha}_2 = 0$. The reader should compare the results of this example with those of the previous example (Table 4.1).

THE GENERAL CASE

In this section, we shall generalize the results on the two-person case to the case of any (finite) number of team members. The reader who has difficulty with linear algebra may do well to skip this section and go on to the next, with the assurance that the two-person results are generalizable.

Suppose that there are n real action variables $a_1, \ldots, a_n$, and that the payoff function is

(3.29) $$\omega(x, a) = \lambda(x) + 2 \sum_{i=1}^{n} \mu_i(x)a_i - \sum_{i,j=1}^{n} v_{ij}(x)a_i a_j,$$

where the λ, μ_1, and v_{ij} are all real-valued functions of the state of the world x. As before, we confine our attention to situations in which there is a maximum payoff for every fixed x; for this reason, we make the assumption that the matrix $((v_{ij}[x]))$ is positive definite for every x.

THEOREM 4. *If the payoff function is given by* (3.29), *and if* $y_i = \eta_i(x)$ $(i = 1, \ldots, n)$ *are the information functions for the team, then the optimal decision functions* $\alpha_1, \ldots, \alpha_n$ *are determined (uniquely) by the following conditions:*

(3.30) $$\alpha_i(y_i)E(v_{ii}|y_i) + \sum_{j \neq i} E(\alpha_j v_{ij}|y_i) = E(\mu_i|y_i) \qquad i = 1, \ldots, n.$$

Proof. The theorem follows directly from the sufficiency of stationarity for optimality in this case [see (2.4) and Theorem 1, in Section 2].

If the set X of the states of nature is finite (as we have been assuming, strictly speaking), then (3.30) represents a system of linear equations whose unknowns are the values of the decision functions α_i for the various values of y_i. This has already been exemplified by (3.3) above. More generally, (3.30) represents a system of integral equations. That system may have no solution, but if it does, it will be unique. The mathematical questions associated with the case of an infinite set of states of nature are discussed in Radner 1962.

One specific case of an infinite X, namely, normal distributions, is noteworthy, however, for the linearity of the optimal decision functions.

THEOREM 5. *If*
1. *the functions v_{ij} in (3.29) are constants, $v_{ij}(x) = q_{ij}$;*
2. *the information functions η_i are vector-valued, with*

$$(3.31) \qquad \eta_i(x) = (y_{i1}, \ldots, y_{iM_i}) \equiv y_i;$$

3. *the functions μ_i and η_i are jointly normally distributed, with*

$$\dot{E} y_{ih} = 0$$

$$(3.32\text{a}) \qquad \text{Variance}(y_{ih}) = 1$$

$$\text{Correlation}(y_{ih}, y_{jk}) = r_{hk}{}^{ij}, \qquad r_{hk}{}^{ii} = 0 \qquad \textit{for } h \neq k$$

$$E\mu_i = m_i$$

$$(3.32\text{b}) \qquad \text{Covariance}(\mu_i, y_{ih}) = d_{ih};$$

then the optimal decision functions $\alpha_1, \ldots, \alpha_n$ are linear,

$$(3.33) \qquad \alpha_i(y_i) = \sum_{h=1}^{M_i} b_{ih} y_{ih} + c_i,$$

where the coefficients b_{ih} and c_i are determined by the systems of linear equations:

$$(3.34) \qquad \sum_{j=1}^{n} q_{ij} \sum_{k=1}^{Mj} r_{kh}{}^{ji} b_{jk} = d_{ih} \qquad i = 1, \ldots, n, h = 1, \ldots, M_i$$

$$(3.35) \qquad \sum_{j=1}^{n} q_{ij} c_j = m_i \qquad i = 1, \ldots, n.$$

Remark. There is no loss of generality in assuming (3.32a), since the given function η_i can always be transformed into a function that has these properties without essentially changing the information structure.

Sketch of Proof. The proof is based upon the person-by-person principle. (For a complete proof of the present theorem see Radner 1962.) We first consider the special case in which $E\mu_i = 0$. Just as in the corresponding theorem for the two-person case, we shall show that there are linear functions in the form of (3.33), with $c_i = 0$, that satisfy the condition of stationarity [(2.4) of Section 2]. We first note that

(3.36)
$$E(y_{jk}|y_i) = \sum_h r_{kh}{}^{ji} y_{ih}$$

$$E(\mu_i|y_i) = \sum_h d_{ih} y_{ih}.$$

Using (3.36), we find that the condition of stationarity applied to decision functions of the form (3.33) immediately gives

(3.37)
$$\sum_j q_{ij} \sum_k b_{jk} \sum_h r_{kh}{}^{ji} y_{ih} = \sum_h d_{ih} y_{ih},$$

for every $i = 1, \ldots, n$, and every value of y_{ih}, $h = 1, \ldots, M_i$. By equating the coefficients of y_{ih} on each side of (3.37), we get (3.34). It can be shown that, if the matrix $((q_{ij}))$ is positive definite, then so is the matrix of coefficients of the unknowns b_{ij} in (3.34) (see Radner 1962), and therefore (3.34) has a unique solution. A second application of the stationarity condition now shows that, if $E\mu_i = m_i$, then the c_i must be given by (3.35).

4. CONCAVE POLYHEDRAL PAYOFF FUNCTIONS: LINEAR PROGRAMMING UNDER UNCERTAINTY

A polyhedral function is a generalization to the case of several variables of a piecewise linear function of one variable. In this section, we shall show how the problem of finding a best team decision function for a given information structure can be transformed into a linear programming problem if the team payoff function is concave and polyhedral.

We shall begin with a discussion of a very simple example; this will be followed by a general treatment.

The introduction of the complications of uncertainty and team structure into a programming problem tends to result in a substantial increase in the size of the problem. On the other hand, joint constraints on the actions of team members with different information may result in very restrictive constraints on the decision functions available to the team, thus simplifying the problem. This section closes with a discussion of a class of cases in which such simplification is possible.

EXAMPLE 5A: A TEAM WITH A CONCAVE POLYHEDRAL
PAYOFF FUNCTION

Suppose that a firm has n salesmen, each of whom goes out at the beginning of the period to get orders. Assume that the ith salesman faces an unlimited demand at price $(1 + x_i)$; on the basis of knowledge of that price, but not of the prices faced by the other salesmen, he must decide on the quantity a_i that he will accept in orders. The orders of all the salesmen are filled centrally, and the unit cost depends upon the total quantity ordered. The unit cost is 1 if the total quantity ordered does not exceed a certain limit c; but, for the amount by which the total quantity ordered exceeds c the unit cost is $(1 + d)$, with $d > 0$. (Compare Example 4A in Chapter 4.)

Thus the action variable for the ith salesman is a nonnegative real number a_i; the state of nature is specified by the n-tuple $x = (x_1, \ldots, x_n)$; and the payoff function is

$$(4.1) \qquad \omega(x, a) = \begin{cases} \displaystyle\sum_{i=1}^{n} a_i x_i & \text{if } \displaystyle\sum_{i=1}^{n} a_i \le c \\[2ex] \displaystyle\sum_{i=1}^{n} a_i x_i - d\left(\sum_{i=1}^{n} a_i - c\right) & \text{if } \displaystyle\sum_{i=1}^{n} a_i \ge c \end{cases}$$

$$= \min\{\textstyle\sum a_i x_i, \sum a_i(x_i - d) + dc\}.$$

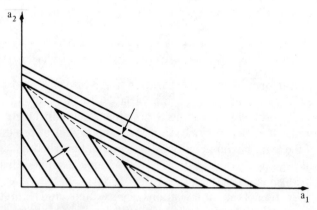

FIGURE 5.2. Contours of a concave polyhedral function.

Figure 5.2 shows contours of ω for fixed x and $n = 2$. The arrows indicate the directions in which the payoff is increasing. (We have assumed that $x_i < d$ for all states of the environment; otherwise there would be some states in which profit had no upper bound.)

The state of nature x will be supposed to be subject to the probability density function ϕ.

The information structure is

(4.2) $$\eta_i(x) = x_i.$$

The team decision problem can therefore be formulated as follows:

Problem 1. Choose nonnegative functions $\alpha_1, \ldots, \alpha_n$ to maximize

$$E\omega(x, \alpha[\eta(x)]) = \sum_x \omega(x, \alpha_1[x_1], \ldots, \alpha_n[x_n])\phi(x).$$

We shall now show that the optimal team decision functions can be found by solving the following associated linear programming problem. (Recall that x is assumed to be restricted to a finite set of possible values.)

Problem 2. Choose nonnegative functions $\alpha_1, \ldots, \alpha_n$ and a function ε of x, to maximize

$$E\varepsilon(x) \equiv \sum_x \varepsilon(x)\phi(x)$$

subject to the constraints

(4.3)
$$\varepsilon(x) \leq \sum_i \alpha_i(x_i)x_i \qquad \text{for all } x$$

$$\varepsilon(x) \leq \sum_i \alpha_i(x_i)(x_i - d) + dc \qquad \text{for all } x.$$

(Note that, because x is restricted to a finite set, the functions $\varepsilon, \alpha_1, \ldots, \alpha_n$ are each characterized by a finite sequence of numbers, so that Problem 2 is a finite-dimensional linear programming problem.)

For an optimal team decision function $\hat{\alpha}$, consider the function

(4.4) $$\hat{\varepsilon}(x) = \omega(x, \hat{\alpha}[\eta(x)]).$$

By (4.1), for every x, $\hat{\varepsilon}$ and $\hat{\alpha}$ satisfy (4.3). On the other hand, if α is any team decision function and ε is any function of x, with both satisfying (4.3), then

(4.5) $$\varepsilon(x) \leq \omega(x, \alpha[\eta(x)]) \qquad \text{for every } x,$$

and hence

(4.6) $$E\varepsilon(x) \leq E\omega(x, \alpha[\eta(x)] \leq E\omega(x, \hat{\alpha}[\eta(x)]) = E\hat{\varepsilon}(x).$$

In other words, of all functions ε for which there exists a team decision function α such that ε and α satisfy (4.3), the function $\hat{\varepsilon}$ has the largest expected value.

On the other hand, if any such function ε has an expected value as large as $E\hat{\varepsilon}$, then it follows from (4.5) and (4.4) that the corresponding team decision function α is as good as $\hat{\alpha}$.

Thus we have shown that α is a solution of Problem 1 if and only if (α, ε) is a solution of Problem 2.

In the example just presented there were no constraints on the action variables other than that of nonnegativity. Other linear constraints can easily be handled by the above method—by simply adding them to both maximization problems (1 and 2). This is so even if the constraints have random parameters. For example, if the maximum total quantity that the hypothetical firm just described can supply, *at any cost*, is c' (possibly a random variable), and if the firm insists on *making sure that all orders are filled*, then the constraint

(4.7) $\sum_i \alpha_i(x_i) \leqq c'$ for all x (and possibly all c')

is simply added to both Problems 1 and 2 above.

EXAMPLE 5B: A TEAM WITH A LINEAR PAYOFF FUNCTION

The simplest case of a polyhedral function is a linear function. In this case the original team decision problem is already in the linear programming form, and there is no need to go to the associated problem (Problem 2 above).

Consider Example 5A above, with the modification that supply is restricted absolutely to be no greater than c. Thus

(4.8) $\omega(x, a) = \sum a_i x_i,$

(4.9) $a_i \geqq 0, \quad \sum a_i \leqq c.$

Here the team decision problem is: Choose nonnegative functions $\alpha_1, \ldots,$ α_n to maximize

(4.10) $E\omega(x, \alpha[\eta(x)]) = \sum_x \sum_i \alpha_i(x_i) x_i \phi(x)$

subject to

(4.11) $\sum_i \alpha_i(x_i) \leqq c$ for every x.

Note that (4.10) and (4.11) are linear in the functions $\alpha_1, \ldots, \alpha_n$.

It may help the reader to see in more detail the special case in which $n = 2$ and in which x_1 and x_2 can each take on one of two values, x_{i1} and x_{i2}. Let the probability that $x_i = x_{im}$ be denoted by p_{im} and let $\alpha_i(x_{im})$ be denoted by $a_{im}(i, m = 1, 2)$; then this team decision problem is: Choose nonnegative numbers a_{im} $(i, m = 1, 2)$ to maximize

(4.12)
$$\sum_i \sum_m a_{im} x_{im} p_{im}$$

subject to the constraints

(4.13)
$$\begin{array}{llll}
a_{11} & + a_{21} & & \leqq c \\
a_{11} & & + a_{22} & \leqq c \\
& a_{12} + a_{21} & & \leqq c \\
& a_{12} & + a_{22} & \leqq c.
\end{array}$$

PERSON-BY-PERSON SATISFACTORY DECISION FUNCTIONS

A person-by-person satisfactory decision function is not, in general, optimal if the payoff function is polyhedral. However, the fact that person-by-person satisfactoriness is a necessary condition for optimality is often helpful.

In Example 5B, the person-by-person principle leads almost immediately to an explicit solution if one further assumption is made.

For any fixed i, the conditional expectation of $\omega(x, \alpha[\eta(x)])$ given x_i is [see (4.8)]:

(4.14)
$$\alpha_i(x_i)x_i + \sum_{j \neq i} E[\alpha_j(x_j)x_j | x_i].$$

Hence, for α to be person-by-person satisfactory $\alpha_i(x_i) = 0$ if $x_i < 0$; if $x_i > 0$, then $\alpha_i(x_i)$ must be equal to the largest value of a_i for which

(4.15)
$$a_i + \sum_{j \neq i} \alpha_j(x_j) \leqq c$$

for every x such that x_i has the given value. *If it is assumed that the range of every variable x_k is independent of* the values of the other variables, then in (4.15) all combinations of x_j's are possible, so that $\alpha_i(x_i)$ must equal some one number $\bar{a}_i$ for all $x_i > 0$. Hence, in order for α to be person-by-person satisfactory, it must be of the form

(4.16)
$$\alpha_i(x_i) = \begin{cases} 0 & \text{if } x_i < 0 \\ \bar{a}_i & \text{if } x_i > 0 \end{cases} \qquad i = 1, \dots, n,$$

where $\bar{a}_1, \dots, \bar{a}_n$ are nonnegative numbers, satisfying

(4.17)
$$\sum_i \bar{a}_i \leqq c.$$

For such a team decision function,

(4.18) $\Omega(\alpha) = \sum_i \bar{a}_i E(x_i | x_i > 0).$

Hence for the optimal team decision function α, $\bar{a}_i = c$ for some one i for which $E(x_i | x_i > 0)$ is a maximum, and $\bar{a}_j = 0$ for all $j \neq i$. In other words, in the optimal team decision function under the constraint that has been assumed, only one salesman ever accepts any orders (the others are "fired"); he accepts an order equal to the full capacity of the firm whenever the price exceeds the unit cost, and otherwise accepts no orders at all.

GENERAL FORMULATION

A function f of n real variables will be called *concave polyhedral* if there exist linear functions $f_1, \ldots, f_M$ such that

(4.19) $f = \min_{1 \leq m \leq M} f_m.$

An example is given by (4.1), in which ω, for every fixed x, is a concave polyhedral function of a with $M = 2$. A concave polyhedral function is a generalization to the case of several variables of a concave piecewise linear function of one variable.

Consider a team decision problem such that, for every state of nature, the payoff function is concave polyhedral in the action variables, that is, for every x,

(4.20) $\omega(x, a) = \min_{1 \leq m \leq M} \lambda_m(x, a),$

where $\lambda_1, \ldots, \lambda_M$ are, for every x, linear functions of a. Suppose further that the action variables are constrained by the conditions

(4.21) $a_i \geq 0 \qquad i = 1, \ldots, n$

(4.22) $\sum_{i=1}^{n} \delta_{ki}(x) a_i \leq \gamma_k(x) \qquad$ for every x, $k = 1, \ldots, K,$

where δ_{ki} and γ_k are given functions of the state of nature x.

Problem 1 (*Team Decision Problem*). Choose nonnegative functions $\alpha_1, \ldots, \alpha_n$ (where α_i is a function of y_i) to maximize

(4.23) $E \min_{1 \leq m \leq M} \lambda_m(x, \alpha[\eta(x)])$

subject to

(4.24) $\sum_{i=1}^{n} \delta_{ki}(x)\alpha_i[\eta_i(x)] \leq \gamma_k(x). \qquad$ for every x, $k = 1, \ldots, K.$

Associated with Problem 1, we consider another problem.

Problem 2 (Associated Linear Programming Problem). Choose functions $\varepsilon, \alpha_1, \ldots, \alpha_n$ (where ε is a function on X and α_i is a nonnegative function on Y_i, to maximize $E\varepsilon(x)$ subject to the constraints

$$(4.25) \qquad \varepsilon(x) \leq \lambda_m(x, \alpha[\eta(x)]) \qquad \text{for every } x, m = 1, \ldots, M,$$

$$(4.26) \qquad \sum_{i=1}^{n} \delta_{ki}(x)\alpha_i[\eta_i(x)] \leq \gamma_k(x) \qquad \text{for every } x, k = 1, \ldots, K.$$

THEOREM 6. *A team decision function α is optimal (i.e., is a solution of Problem 1) if and only if there is a function ε such that (α, ε) is a solution of Problem 2.*

The proof of Theorem 6 follows the line of reasoning of the example of Section 4.2 so closely that it will be omitted.

Note that, if the space X has N elements and if for each i the space Y_i has N_i elements, then the number of "unknowns" in Problem 2 equals $(N + \Sigma_i N_i)$, which is not greater than $N(n + 1)$. The number of individual constraints in (4.25) and (4.26) together is at the most $N(M + K)$.

In the special case in which $M = 1$ (i.e., in which the payoff function is linear in the action variables for every x), Problem 1 is already in the linear programming form, and there is no need to go to Problem 2.

THE CASE OF INFORMATION VARIABLES
WITH INDEPENDENT RANGES

If the ranges of variation of the different information variables are "independent," in a sense that will be made precise, and if the payoff function is linear in the action variables, then there will generally follow from this a reduction in the "size" of the resulting linear programming problem of finding an optimal team decision function.

If we assume that the set of states of the world is finite, the functions $\eta_1, \ldots, \eta_n$ are said to have *independent ranges* if every n-tuple of values $(y_1, \ldots, y_n)$ has positive probability. If $\eta_1, \ldots, \eta_n$ are the information functions, then this means that any one team member cannot rule out, on the basis of his own information, any combination of values of the information variables of other team members that was a priori possible.

Consider the team decision problem with a *linear* payoff function: maximize $(x)\alpha_i[\eta_i(x)] \leq \gamma_k(x)$

$$(4.27) \qquad E \sum_i v_i(x)\alpha_i(\eta_i[x])$$

subject to the constraint that, for every x, $\alpha(\eta[x]) = (\alpha_1[\eta_1(x)], \ldots,$

$\alpha_n[\eta_n(x)])$ lies in the (convex) set $\kappa(x)$ defined by the linear inequalities (4.24) and the condition that $\alpha_i \geqq 0$.

Suppose that the functions $\kappa, \eta_1, \ldots, \eta_n$ have independent ranges.[6] For any α, and for each i, let $[\underline{a}_i, \bar{a}_i]$ be the smallest closed interval such that

(4.28) $\mathrm{Prob}\{\underline{a}_i \leqq \alpha_i \leqq \bar{a}_i\} = 1,$

and let $I(\alpha)$ be the Cartesian product of the intervals $[\underline{a}_i, \bar{a}_i]$, $i = 1, \ldots, n$. (For $n = 2$, I is a rectangle; for $n = 3$, a rectangular parallelopiped, etc.)

It follows from the convexity of $\kappa(x)$ and the independence of the ranges of $\kappa, \eta_1, \ldots, \eta_n$, that the requirement that $\alpha(\eta[x])$ be in $\kappa(x)$ for every x is equivalent to the requirement that $I(\alpha)$ be contained in

(4.29) $$\bar{\kappa} = \bigcap_x \kappa(x).$$

[That is, $\bar{\kappa}$ is the largest set that is contained in all the sets $\kappa(x)$.]

Given any particular rectangle I in n-dimensional space we may ask what is the best α such that $I(\alpha) = I$? Applying the person-by-person satisfactoriness condition, one finds that α must satisfy:

(4.30) $$\alpha_i(y_i) = \begin{Bmatrix} \bar{a}_i \\ \underline{a}_i \end{Bmatrix} \text{ as } E(v_i|y_i) \begin{Bmatrix} > \\ < \end{Bmatrix} 0.$$

Hence the best expected payoff corresponding to the rectangle I is

(4.31) $$\Omega^*(I) \equiv \sum_i (\bar{a}_i \bar{d}_i + \underline{a}_i \underline{d}_i),$$

where

(4.32)
$$\bar{d}_i = E[v_i | E(v_i|y_i) > 0] \, \mathrm{Prob}\{E(v_i|y_i) > 0\}$$
$$\underline{d}_i = E[v_i | E(v_i|y_i) < 0] \, \mathrm{Prob}\{E(v_i|y_i) < 0\}.$$

Thus the original problem has been reduced to one of maximizing $\Omega^*(I)$, which is linear in the $\underline{a}_i$ and $\bar{a}_i$, subject to the condition that I be contained in $\bar{\kappa}$.

If in the original constraints (4.24) the functions δ_{ki} and γ_k are all non-negative, then the above problem is even more greatly simplified. In that case, it is easy to see that all the $\underline{a}_i$ must be zero (recall that all the $\underline{a}_i$ are nonnegative); furthermore, if the $\underline{a}_i$ are zero, then $I(\alpha)$ is in $\bar{\kappa}$ if and only if $(\bar{a}_1, \ldots, \bar{a}_n)$ is in $\bar{\kappa}$.

---

6. Note that κ is indeed a function, namely, a function from X to a set of convex subsets of n-dimensional Euclidean space.

Hence the problem reduces to one of choosing $\bar{a}_1, \ldots, \bar{a}_n$ so as to maximize

$$\sum \bar{d}_i \bar{a}_i$$

subject to the constraint that $(\bar{a}_1, \ldots, \bar{a}_n)$ be in $\bar{\kappa}$.

DUALITY AND SHADOW PRICES

Associated with a linear programming problem there is a saddle point problem involving the use of "Lagrangian multipliers"; furthermore, these multipliers can be interpreted as prices (see Arrow, Hurwicz, and Uzawa 1958, Chapter 1; Dantzig 1963, Chapter 6, Section 5, and Chapter 12; and Koopmans 1951, Chapter 3). We now show how the multipliers for the team problem with a concave polyhedral payoff function can be interpreted as random prices.

To apply the well-known saddle point theorem of linear programming, we first rewrite (4.25) and (4.26) of Problem 2 in a more standard form. Let each linear function $\lambda_m(x, a)$ in (4.20) be expressed as

$$(4.33) \qquad \lambda_m(x, a) = \sum_i \lambda_{mi}(x) a_i.$$

Also, let $\phi(x)$ denote the probability of the state x. Without loss of generality, we may assume that for all x,

$$(4.34a) \qquad \phi(x) > 0$$

$$(4.34b) \qquad \omega(x, \hat{\alpha}[\eta(x)]) > 0,$$

where $\hat{\alpha}$ denotes the optimal team decision function.[7]

With these conventions and notation, we can restate Problem 2 in the form: Choose nonnegative functions $\varepsilon, \alpha_1, \ldots, \alpha_n$ (where ε is a function on X and α is a function on Y_i) to maximize

$$(4.35) \qquad \sum_x \phi(x)\varepsilon(x)$$

subject to

$$(4.36a) \quad \varepsilon(x) - \sum_{i=1}^{n} \lambda_{mi}(x)\alpha_i[\eta_i(x)] \leqq 0 \qquad \text{all } x \in X, m = 1, \ldots, M,$$

$$(4.36b) \quad \sum_{i=1}^{n} \delta_{ki}(x)\alpha_i[\eta_i(x)] \leqq \gamma_k(x) \qquad \text{all } x \in X, k = 1, \ldots, K.$$

---

7. If $\phi(x) = 0$ for any state x, then that state can be eliminated from X; hence (4.34a). Inequality (4.34b) can be achieved by adding a suitably large constant to the payoff function.

Let the Lagrangian multipliers corresponding to the constraints (4.36a) be denoted[8] by $\xi_m(x)$, and those corresponding to (4.36b) by $\zeta_k(x)$. The *Lagrangian function*[9] is, from (4.35) and (4.36),

$$(4.37) \qquad L(\varepsilon, \alpha; \xi, \zeta) \equiv \sum_x \phi(x)\varepsilon(x) + \sum_x \sum_k \gamma_k(x)\zeta_k(x)$$

$$- \sum_x \sum_m \xi_m(x)\{\varepsilon(x) - \sum_i \lambda_{mi}(x)\alpha_i[\eta_i(x)]\}$$

$$- \sum_x \sum_k \zeta_k(x) \sum_i \delta_{ki}(x)\alpha_i[\eta_i(x)].$$

According to the saddle point theorem of linear programming, $(\hat{\varepsilon}, \hat{\alpha})$ is a solution of Problem 2 if and only if there exist nonnegative $\hat{\xi} = (\hat{\xi}_1, \ldots, \hat{\xi}_M)$ and $\hat{\zeta} = (\hat{\zeta}_1, \ldots, \hat{\zeta}_K)$ such that $(\hat{\varepsilon}, \hat{\alpha}; \hat{\xi}, \hat{\zeta})$ is a max-min saddle point of L, that is

$$(4.38) \qquad L(\varepsilon, \alpha; \hat{\xi}, \hat{\zeta}) \leq L(\hat{\varepsilon}, \hat{\alpha}; \hat{\xi}, \hat{\zeta}) \leq L(\hat{\varepsilon}, \hat{\alpha}, \xi, \zeta)$$

for all nonnegative $\varepsilon, \alpha, \xi, \zeta$ (where α is a team decision function based on the given information structure).

Notice that $L(\varepsilon, \alpha, \hat{\xi}, \hat{\zeta})$ is linear in ε and α and that $L(\hat{\varepsilon}, \hat{\alpha}; \xi, \zeta)$ is linear in ξ and ζ. The coefficients of $\varepsilon(x)$ and $\alpha_i(y_i)$ in $L(\varepsilon, \alpha; \hat{\xi}, \hat{\zeta})$ are, respectively,

$$(4.39\text{a}) \qquad \mu_0(x) \equiv \phi(x) - \sum_m \hat{\xi}_m(x),$$

$$(4.39\text{b}) \quad \mu_i(y_i) \equiv \sum_{x \in y_i} \left[\sum_m \hat{\xi}_m(x)\lambda_{mi}(x) - \sum_k \hat{\zeta}_k(x)\delta_{ki}(x) \right] \qquad i = 1, \ldots, n.$$

The coefficients of $\xi_m(x)$ and $\zeta_k(x)$ in $L(\hat{\varepsilon}, \hat{\alpha}; \xi, \zeta)$ are, respectively,

$$(4.40\text{a}) \qquad v_m(x) \equiv -\hat{\varepsilon}(x) + \sum_i \lambda_{mi}(x)\hat{\alpha}_i[\eta_i(x)],$$

$$(4.40\text{b}) \qquad \psi_k(x) \equiv \gamma_k(x) - \sum_i \delta_{ki}(x)\hat{\alpha}_i[\eta_i(x)],$$

Hence, since $(\hat{\varepsilon}, \hat{\alpha}; \hat{\xi}, \hat{\zeta})$ is a min-max saddle point of L, we have the duality conditions of linear programming:

$$(4.41\text{a}) \qquad \mu_0(x) \leq 0$$

$$(4.41\text{b}) \qquad \mu_0(x)\hat{\varepsilon}(x) = 0$$

$$(4.42\text{a}) \qquad \mu_i(y_i) \leq 0$$

$$(4.42\text{b}) \qquad \mu_i(y_i)\hat{\alpha}_i(y_i) = 0$$

---

8. This notation is for the purpose of this section only.
9. See Arrow, Hurwicz, and Uzawa 1958, pp. 4, 5.

(4.43a) $$v_m(x) \geqq 0$$

(4.43b) $$v_m(x)\hat{\xi}_m(x) = 0$$

(4.44a) $$\psi_k(x) \geqq 0$$

(4.44b) $$\psi_k(x)\hat{\zeta}_k(x) = 0.$$

In particular, (4.43a) is a repetition of the constraint (4.36a), and (4.43b) implies that the multiplier $\xi_m(x)$ is zero if the corresponding constraint in (4.36a) is not effective $[v_m(x) > 0]$, that is if for state x and for the optimal decision function, the payoff $\omega(x, \alpha[\eta(x)])$ is not on the "linear piece" $\lambda_m(x, a)$.

Similarly, (4.44a) is a repetition of the constraint (4.36b), and (4.44b) implies that the multiplier $\zeta_k(x)$ is zero if the corresponding constraint is not effective $[\psi_k(x) > 0]$.

To interpret the multipliers as random (state-dependent) prices, we make the scale transformation

(4.45)
$$\tilde{\xi}_m(x) = \frac{\xi_m(x)}{\phi(x)}$$

$$\tilde{\zeta}_k(x) = \frac{\zeta_k(x)}{\phi(x)}.$$

The coefficient $\mu_i(y_i)$ of $\alpha_i(y_i)$ in L can be rewritten

(4.46)
$$\mu_i(y_i) = \sum_{x \in y_i} \left[\sum_m \tilde{\xi}_m(x)\phi(x)\lambda_{mi}(x) - \sum_k \tilde{\zeta}_k(x)\phi(x)\delta_{ki}(x) \right]$$

$$= E\left[\sum_m \tilde{\xi}_m(x)\lambda_{mi}(x) - \sum_k \tilde{\zeta}_k(x)\delta_{ki}(x) \,\middle|\, \eta_i(x) = y_i \right] \text{Prob}\{\eta_i(x) = y_i\}.$$

The convention (4.34b) implies that $\hat{\varepsilon}(x) > 0$ for all x; hence the duality conditions (4.41) imply that $\mu_0(x) = 0$, that is

$$\sum_m \tilde{\xi}_m(x) = \phi(x) \qquad \text{all } x \in X$$

or

(4.47) $$\sum_m \tilde{\xi}_m(x) = 1 \qquad \text{all } x \in X.$$

Consider the typical situation in which for each x the payoff $\omega(x, \hat{\alpha}[\eta(x)])$ lies on exactly *one* "linear piece" $\lambda_m(x, a)$; in this case, for each x exactly one of the $\tilde{\xi}_m(x)$ will be unity, and all the others zero. Thus the $\tilde{\xi}_m(x)$

indicate on which linear piece the payoff lies, and

(4.48) $$\tilde{\lambda}_i(x) \equiv \sum_m \tilde{\xi}_m(x)\lambda_{mi}(x)$$

is the *marginal payoff* corresponding to the action variable a_i, in state x, using the optimal decision function.[10]

Using (4.48), we can rewrite the coefficient $\mu_i(y_i)$ [see (4.46)] as

(4.49) $\mu_i(y_i) = E\left[\tilde{\lambda}_i(x) - \sum_k \zeta_k(x)\delta_{ki}(x) \;\middle|\; \eta_i(x) = y_i\right]\text{Prob}\{\eta_i(x) = y_i\}.$

In the usual price interpretation of the Lagrangian multipliers $\zeta_k(x)$, we imagine that for each pair (k, x) there is a "resource," and that $\gamma_k(x)$ is the amount of the (k, x) resource available to the team. Further, we imagine that, if action i has the value a_i in state x, then a quantity $\delta_{ki}(x)a_i$ is used up. The constraint (4.36b) can then be interpreted as a condition that the total quantity used of the (k, x) resource cannot exceed the available supply $\gamma_k(x)$. If $\tilde{\lambda}_i(x)$ is interpreted as marginal "gross revenue," and $\zeta_k(x)$ as the "price" of resource (k, x), then the expression

$$\tilde{\lambda}_i(x) - \sum_k \zeta_k(x)\delta_{ki}(x)$$

can be interpreted as the "marginal profit" for the team member i, in state x, using the optimal decision function. Similarly, the expression

(4.50) $$E\left[\tilde{\lambda}_i(x) - \sum_k \zeta_k(x)\delta_{ki}(x) \;\middle|\; \eta_i(x) = y_i\right] \equiv \tilde{\mu}_i(y_i)$$

in (4.49) can be interpreted as the *conditional expected marginal profit for team member i given the information signal* y_i. From the duality conditions (4.42), we see that $\tilde{\mu}_i(y) \geq 0$ and that $\alpha_i(y_i) = 0$ if $\tilde{\mu}_i(y) < 0$.

Our duality or "profit" conditions are the probabilistic analogue of the set of rules Koopmans (1951, Chapter 3) gives for the maintenance of a best activity vector by a price mechanism under conditions of certainty, and are related to the welfare economics of competitive equilibrium under uncertainty (see Arrow 1953, Debreu 1959, Chapter 11, and Radner 1968).[11] It should be emphasized that it is the price *function* $\tilde{\zeta}_k$ that would be used by the ith member in calculating his conditional expected profit, and not just the value $\tilde{\zeta}_k(x)$ in any one state.

10. If $\omega(x, \hat{a}[\eta(x)])$ lies on more than one linear piece, then (4.48) is a weighted average of "slopes" $\lambda_{mi}(x)$, and thus can still be interpreted as a marginal payoff corresponding to a_i.

11. An extension of the duality theory to the case of an infinite set X of states has been given by Fisher (1962).

The duality conditions can be viewed as a refinement of the condition of person-by-person satisfactoriness, specially adapted to the concave polyhedral case. In this case, the condition of person-by-person satisfactoriness is necessary, but not sufficient, for optimality, whereas the duality conditions are both necessary and sufficient.

CHAPTER 6

The Evaluation of Information in Organizations

1.Introduction   2.Case of quadratic payoff function reviewed   3.Optimal decision functions and value of information in the quadratic case   4.Observation, communication, computation   5.Complete communication, complete information, routine   6.No communication; complete informational decentralization   7.Partitioned communication   8.Dissemination of independent information   9.Error in instruction   10.Complete communication of erroneous observations   11.Management by exception: Reporting exceptions   12.Management by exception: Emergency conference   13.Comparisons among the several information structures   14.Interaction, team size, returns to scale

1. INTRODUCTION

In this chapter we describe, evaluate, and compare certain elementary information structures in teams. Some of these information structures (for example, complete information, complete decentralization) are of interest because they are in a sense extreme; they are useful as bases of comparison with other information structures. The others represent simplified models that are suggested by common organizational devices. The reader will recognize the primitive character of these models.

The entire discussion in this chapter is restricted to the case in which the payoff to the team is a quadratic function of the action variables, for each possible state of the world, that is, for each specification of the values of the uncontrolled variables in the environment. The methods used here were developed in Chapter 5. Some discussion of the case of a team decision problem with a concave polyhedral payoff function was also presented in Chapter 5. However, in that case explicit formulas for the values of particular information structures appear to be very difficult to obtain, making it more difficult than in the quadratic case to derive conclusions about the relative values of the several information structures described below.

For the convenience of the reader, we recall in Sections 2 and 3 the formulation of the team decision problem with a quadratic payoff function (Chapter 4) and the characterization of optimal decision functions and of the value of information in the quadratic case. In Section 4, we describe the information structures that are studied in the following sections. The chapter closes with a comparison of the values of those information structures.

2. CASE OF QUADRATIC PAYOFF FUNCTION REVIEWED

As already mentioned, in the team decision problems to be considered in this chapter, the action variables will be taken to be real variables, and the payoff to the team to be a quadratic function of the action variables for every state of the world. Thus let the action variable of team member i be denoted by a_i (real), $i = 1, \ldots, n$; let the state of the environment be denoted by x, where x is an element of some set X; and let the payoff to the team be

$$(2.1) \qquad \omega(x, a) = \mu_0 + 2a'\mu(x) - a'Qa,$$

where a denotes the (column) vector with coordinates a_i for $i = 1, \ldots, n$, μ is a vector-valued function on X, and Q is a fixed positive definite $n \times n$ matrix. It will be shown that, without loss of generality one can take μ_0 equal to 0. A probability measure π on X expresses the uncertainty about which state of the world actually obtains.

The information upon which the several team members base their decisions is expressed as follows. For each $i = 1, \ldots, n$, let Y_i be some set; Y_i represents the set of alternative "signals" that can be received by person i. Also, for each i, let η_i be a function from X to Y_i, called the *information function* for person i. The n-tuple $\eta = (\eta_1, \ldots, \eta_n)$ will be called the *information structure* for the team. The function η_i determines the signals that person i receives under the alternative states of the world. Thus

$$(2.2) \qquad y_i = \eta_i(x).$$

Finally, the actions of the team members are to be determined according to *decision functions* α_i, where α_i is a real-valued function on Y_i, that is,

$$(2.3) \qquad a_i = \alpha_i(y_i).$$

The vector α of decision functions α_i will be called the *team decision function*. Given an information structure η, a best team decision function is one that maximizes the expected payoff,

$$(2.4) \qquad \Omega(\eta, \alpha) = E\omega(x, \alpha_1[\eta_1(x)], \ldots, \alpha_n[\eta_n(x)]).$$

Beyond the choice of the best decision functions for given information structures, it is of interest to compare alternative information structures in terms of the maximum expected payoff that can be derived from their use. We take as an origin for measurement the maximum expected payoff for the "null" information structure, which provides no information beyond the knowledge of π itself. Recall that, if utility is linear in outcome, then the *value* of an information structure η may be defined by (see Chapter 2, Section 11)

$$(2.5) \qquad V(\eta) = \max_{\alpha} \Omega(\eta, \alpha) - \max_{\alpha} E\omega(x, a).$$

In this chapter, a number of information structures suggested by various organizational devices will be analyzed from the point of view of determining their values and the corresponding optimal decision functions.

If X is not finite, then a more detailed specification of the problem is required. Let X be a measurable space (see, e.g., Halmos 1950, p. 73), with probability measure π; for each $i = 1, \ldots, n$, Y_i is a measurable space, η_i is a measurable function from X to Y_i; and α_i is a real-valued Borel measurable function on Y_i.

3. Optimal Decision Functions and Value of Information in the Quadratic Case

In this section, the main tools of analysis for the following sections are reviewed. Most of these results come from Chapter 5, Section 3.

The first tool characterizes the best team decision function for a given information structure in terms of the *stationarity* conditions, which in turn derive from the *person-by-person satisfactoriness* condition. The following theorem is a restatement of Theorem 4, Chapter 5, Section 3, for the case in which the coefficients of the quadratic terms are constants.

THEOREM 1. *For any information structure η, the unique almost every-where*[1] *best team decision function is the solution of*

$$(3.1) \qquad q_{ii}\alpha_i + \sum_{j \neq i} q_{ij}E(\alpha_j|\eta_i) = E(\mu_i|\eta_i) \qquad i = 1, \ldots, n.$$

(If X is infinite, we must add to the hypothesis the condition that $E\mu_i^2 < \infty$, $i = 1, \ldots, n$; see Radner 1962. Throughout this chapter, we make this assumption.)

As a corollary to Theorem 1, we have the following result on the value of an information structure.

COROLLARY 1. *If $\hat{\alpha}$ is an optimal team decision function with respect to an information structure η, then*

$$(3.2) \qquad V(\eta) = E\hat{\alpha}\mu - (E\hat{\alpha})'(E\mu).$$

---

1. The uniqueness of the best decision function is, of course, only almost everywhere (a.e.), i.e., two best decision functions will differ at most on a set of states of probability measure zero.

A second corollary concerns the expected value of an optimal decision function.

COROLLARY 2. *If $\hat{\alpha}$ is optimal for some η, then*

$$(3.3) \qquad\qquad E\hat{\alpha} = Q^{-1}E\mu.$$

(See the end of this section for proofs of the two corollaries.)

It follows from these last results that there is no essential loss of generality in assuming $E\mu = 0$, since adding or subtracting a constant vector to μ does not change the value of any given information structure. To see this, consider two team decision problems, one with μ and the other with $\bar{\mu}$, with

$$\bar{\mu}(x) = \mu(x) + c \qquad \text{for all } x,$$

where c is any given (constant) vector. (In particular, we could take $c = -E\mu$.) Let the corresponding optimal team decision functions be α and $\bar{\alpha}$, respectively. The optimality conditions for $\bar{\alpha}$ corresponding to (3.1) are

$$(3.1') \quad q_{ii}\bar{\alpha}_i + \sum_{j \neq i} q_{ij}E(\bar{\alpha}_j|\eta_i) = E(\bar{\mu}_i|\eta_i) = E(\mu_i|\eta_i) + c_i \qquad i = 1, \ldots, n.$$

Let $\bar{a}$ be a constant vector satisfying

$$\sum_j q_{ij}\bar{a}_j = c_i \qquad i = 1, \ldots, n,$$

that is,

$$\bar{a} = Q^{-1}c.$$

It follows immediately from (3.1) and (3.1') that

$$\bar{\alpha} = \alpha + \bar{a} = \alpha + Q^{-1}c,$$

and from (3.2) that $V(\eta)$ is the same for the two problems.

In what follows we shall adopt the convention that $E\mu = 0$. As consequences of this convention, we have

$$(3.4) \qquad\qquad V(\eta) = E\hat{\alpha}'\mu.$$

$$(3.5) \qquad\qquad E\hat{\alpha} = 0.$$

The second theorem deals with the important special case in which the information variables and the random coefficients μ_i are normally distributed (see Theorem 5, Chapter 5, Section 3).

THEOREM 2. *Suppose that* $\eta_1, \ldots, \eta_n$ *are vector-valued, and that* $\eta_1, \ldots, \eta_n$ *and* $\mu_1, \ldots, \mu_n$ *are jointly normally distributed; then for the optimal team decision function,* α_i *is a linear function of* y_i.

Proof of Corollaries 1 and 2 of Theorem 1. We first prove Corollary 2. By (6.8) of Chapter 2, on iterated expectations, if we take the expected value of (3.1) we get, for the optimal team decision function, $\hat{\alpha}$,

$$\sum_j q_{ij} E\hat{\alpha}_j = E\mu_i \qquad i = 1, \ldots, n,$$

which can be written in matrix form as

$$(3.6) \qquad\qquad\qquad QE\hat{\alpha} = E\mu.$$

Solving (3.6) for $E\hat{\alpha}$, we get (3.3).

To prove the first corollary, we first multiply (3.1) by $\hat{\alpha}_i$:

$$(3.7) \qquad q_{ii}\hat{\alpha}_i^2 + \sum_{j \neq i} q_{ij}\hat{\alpha}_i E(\hat{\alpha}_j|\eta_i) = \hat{\alpha}_i E(\mu_i|\eta_i).$$

Since $\hat{\alpha}_i$ is a function of η_i, (3.7) can be rewritten

$$(3.8) \qquad E\left(\sum_j q_{ij}\hat{\alpha}_i\hat{\alpha}_j|\eta_i\right) = E\left(\mu_i\hat{\alpha}_i|\eta_i\right) \qquad i = 1, \ldots, n.$$

Taking the expected value of (3.8) and summing on i, we obtain

$$E\sum_{ij} q_{ij}\hat{\alpha}_i\hat{\alpha}_j = E\sum_i \mu_i\hat{\alpha}_i,$$

or

$$(3.9) \qquad\qquad\qquad E\hat{\alpha}'Q\hat{\alpha} = E\mu'\hat{\alpha}.$$

From (2.1), the expected payoff for a team decision function α is

$$\Omega(\eta, \alpha) = 2E\mu'\alpha - E\alpha'Q\alpha - \mu_0.$$

Hence, by (3.9), the expected payoff for the optimal decision function, $\hat{\alpha}$, is

$$(3.10) \qquad\qquad\qquad \Omega(\eta, \hat{\alpha}) = E\mu'\hat{\alpha} - \mu_0.$$

In particular, if there is no information (η_i constant, $i = 1, \ldots, n$), and $\hat{a}$ is the corresponding best (constant) team action, then (3.10) implies

$$\max_a E\omega(x, a) - \mu_0 = E\mu'\hat{a} = \hat{a}'E\mu - \mu_0.$$

Note that, by Corollary 2,

$$E\hat{\alpha} = \hat{a} = Q^{-1}E\mu,$$

so that

$$(3.11) \qquad\qquad\qquad \hat{a}'E\mu = (E\hat{\alpha})'E\mu.$$

Hence the *value* of the information structure η is [see (2.5)]

$$V(\eta) = E\mu'\hat{\alpha} - (E\mu)'\hat{\alpha} = E\mu'\hat{a} - (E\mu)'(E\hat{a}).$$

Since μ_0 does not enter equations (3.1) to (3.5), we may take μ_0 equal to zero.

4. OBSERVATION, COMMUNICATION, COMPUTATION

The several information structures to be considered in the following sections can all be viewed as being generated by certain processes of observation, communication, and computation. Suppose that there are n persons, and that person i observes a random variable $\zeta_i(x)$ and takes action a_i. If there is no communication among the persons, then person i's information function is $\eta_i(x) = \zeta_i(x)$. On the other hand, if there is complete communication among persons, then $\eta_i(x) = \zeta(x) \equiv [\zeta_1(x), \ldots, \zeta_n(x)]$. Alternatively, the latter information structure could be generated by all persons communicating their observations to a central agency, which computes the best actions and communicates them to the corresponding persons. (In either case the team would be a *centralized* one in the sense of Chapter 4, Section 6.) Still different information structures are generated if errors are introduced into the communications to or from the central agency or between team members.

Rarely does one encounter in a real organization the extremes of no communication or complete communication just described. Rather, one finds that numerous devices are used to bring about a partial exchange of information. The usefulness of such devices is, of course, measured by the excess of the additional value (expected payoff) they contribute, over the costs of installing and operating them. Some simple devices of this kind will be examined in the following sections. For example, if each person i disseminates some contraction of his own observation, say $\tau_i[\zeta_i(x)]$, to all other persons in the team, then the resulting structure is

$$(4.1) \qquad\qquad \eta_i = (\zeta_i, \tau) \qquad i = 1, \ldots, n,$$

where $\tau = (\tau_1, \ldots, \tau_n)$. A different type of *partial decentralization* is achieved by partitioning the persons into groups, with complete communication within groups and no communication between groups.

A third type of partial decentralization is suggested by the phrase "management by exception." For example, suppose that the possible values of person i's observation are partitioned into two subsets, R_i and $\bar{R}_i$, labeled *exceptional* and *ordinary*, respectively. Suppose further that, whenever person i's observation is ordinary, he bases his action upon that observation alone, whereas whenever his observation is exceptional he reports it to a central agency, or manager, who then decides the values of all action variables corresponding to exceptional observations on the basis of all those exceptional observations. The information thus generated is, for each i,

$$(4.2) \qquad \eta_i(x) = \begin{cases} \zeta_i(x) & \text{if } \zeta_i(x) \in \bar{R}_i \\ \{\zeta_j(x)\}_{\zeta_j(x) \in R_j} & \text{if } \zeta_i(x) \in R_i, \end{cases}$$

and might be called *reports of exceptions*.

In certain of the information structures investigated in this chapter, it is assumed that the observation functions $\zeta_1, \ldots, \zeta_n$ are statistically independent. This does not mean that the information functions η_i for the several team members are statistically independent; on the contrary, such dependence is introduced when communication takes place. It would also be of interest, of course, to study the effect of dependence among the observations themselves. However, as the reader will soon see, the picture is complicated enough with independent observations, and it has seemed best at this time to leave the study of dependent observations for certain structures to a separate investigation.

A special case of interest is the one in which

$$(4.3) \qquad \zeta_i(x) = \mu_i(x),$$

where $\mu_i(x)$ is the coefficient of a_i in the quadratic payoff function (2.1). This will be called the case of *cospecialization of action and observation*, since in this case each person observes, in a sense, the first-order effect of his own action variable upon the team payoff.

In order to see more clearly the effects of interactions between action variables in the payoff function (as measured by the coefficients q_{ij} for $i \neq j$), it will from time to time be of interest to consider the special case in which

$$(4.4) \qquad q_{ij} = q_{ii}^{1/2} q_{jj}^{1/2} q \qquad i \neq j.$$

By suitable changes in units of the action variables, this can be transformed into the case

$$(4.5) \qquad q_{ij} = \begin{cases} 1 & i = j \\ q & i \neq j. \end{cases}$$

This will be called the case of *identical interaction*. It is noteworthy that, in order for the matrix $((q_{ij}))$ of (4.5) to be positive definite, it is necessary and sufficient that

$$(4.6) \qquad -\frac{1}{n-1} < q < 1,$$

which in this case is equivalent to [2]

$$(4.7) \qquad -1 < \frac{\partial^2 \omega}{2\partial a_i \partial a_j} < \frac{1}{n-1}.$$

We shall continue the study of processes of observation, communication and computation in Chapter 8. It will be shown there that the concept of *information structure* is not in fact adequate to characterize all such processes, and we shall be led to formulate the more general concept of *network*. (See also Chapter 4, Section 11.)

5. COMPLETE COMMUNICATION, COMPLETE INFORMATION, ROUTINE

Complete communication among the team members results in providing all team members with the same information on which to base their decisions. Should this resulting common information be sufficient to determine the best possible decision function (that is, the decision function that would be optimal if every member had full information about the state of the world), then the team will be said to have *complete information*. At the other extreme is the case in which the team members base their decisions upon the knowledge of the probability distribution of the states of the world only, which corresponds to *no* observation at all. This will be called the case of *routine*.

These three special cases are typically too extreme to be of practical interest in an organization of any complexity. Nevertheless, they are useful as base lines from which one can measure the effects of other information structures. Thus, in (2.5), the *value* of an information structure η has been defined as the maximum expected payoff using η, minus the maximum expected payoff using the routine information structure. From the other side, it is of interest to calculate the *loss* due to using η as compared with complete communication or complete information.

In the special case of cospecialization of action and observation (see Section 4), complete communication is equivalent to complete information, as will be shown below.

COMPLETE COMMUNICATION

Denoting the observation of person i by $\zeta_i(x)$, as in the previous section, the information structure called *complete communication* is defined by

$$(5.1) \qquad \eta_i(x) = \zeta(x),$$

2. One might say that the actions of the several team members are complementary or substitutes depending on whether q is negative or positive. In the figures of this chapter, only positive values of q are considered since, for large n, only small absolute values of q negative are admitted by constraint (4.6).

where

(5.2) $$\zeta(x) \equiv [\zeta_1(x), \ldots, \zeta_n(x)].$$

For the case of the quadratic payoff function (2.1), the best decision function is a linear transformation of the conditional expectation of μ given ζ. This is easily seen by applying Theorem 1, whose condition (3.1) reduces in this case to

(5.3) $$\sum_j q_{ij}\alpha_j = E(\mu_i|\zeta), \qquad i = 1, \ldots, n,$$

or more concisely,

(5.4) $$Q\alpha = E(\mu|\zeta).$$

The optimal team decision function under complete communication is therefore

(5.5) $$\hat{\alpha} = Q^{-1}E(\mu|\zeta).$$

COMPLETE INFORMATION

In the special case in which $\zeta(x) = x$, the team has *complete information,* that is,

(5.6) $$\eta_i(x) = x \qquad i = 1, \ldots, n.$$

For this case, (5.5.) implies that the best team decision function is

(5.7) $$\beta = Q^{-1}\mu.$$

Henceforth the symbol β will denote the best decision function under complete information as given by (5.7). Note that $\beta(x)$ depends upon x through μ only; hence complete knowledge of μ is sufficient to allow each team member to use β. From this it follows that, in the case of cospecialization of observation and information, complete communication is equivalent to complete information.

ROUTINE

Routine is defined by

(5.8) $\eta_i(x) = $ constant (independent of x) $i = 1, \ldots, n.$

Under routine, any team decision function is a constant vector, say a, and the best such constant vector is

(5.9) $$\hat{a} = Q^{-1}E(\mu),$$

as is easily seen by applying Theorem 1. Recall, however, the normalizing assumption $E(\mu) = 0$, which with (5.9) implies

(5.10) $$\hat{a} = 0.$$

It follows immediately from (5.10) that the maximum expected value under routine is zero. *Thus with the normalization $E(\mu) = 0$, the value of any information structure (2.3) and maximum expected payoff under that structure become identical.*

The value of complete information is easily inferred from (3.4) to be

(5.11) $$V_1 = E\mu'Q^{-1}\mu.$$

Also, from (3.4), the value of complete communication is

(5.12) $$V_\zeta = E[E(\mu|\zeta)'Q^{-1}E(\mu|\zeta)].$$

The loss due to using complete communication, relative to complete information, is obtained by subtracting (5.12) from (5.11), which yields

(5.13) $$L_\zeta = E\{[\mu - E(\mu|\zeta)]'Q^{-1}[\mu - E(\mu|\zeta)]\}.$$

THE CASE OF IDENTICAL INTERACTION

Consider now the special case of identical interaction, as in (4.5):

$$q_{ij} = \begin{cases} 1 & i = j \\ q & i \neq j. \end{cases}$$

Let $\bar{s}_n$ denote the average variance of $\mu_1, \ldots, \mu_n$, and $\bar{\bar{s}}_n$ denote the average covariance of different μ_i and μ_j, that is,

(5.14) $$\bar{s}_n \equiv \frac{1}{n}\sum_i s_{ii}, \qquad \bar{\bar{s}}_n \equiv \frac{1}{n(n-1)}\sum_{i \neq j} s_{ij}.$$

One can show (see below) that the value of complete information in this case is

(5.15) $$V_1 = \frac{n}{1-q}\left[(\bar{s}_n - \bar{\bar{s}}_n) - \frac{(q\bar{s}_n - \bar{\bar{s}}_n)}{(1 + [n-1]q)}\right].$$

It is interesting to note that, for large n, the second term in the square brackets in (5.15) is small relative to the first term, so that we have the approximation

$$V_1 \approx \frac{n(\bar{s}_n - \bar{\bar{s}}_n)}{1 - q}.$$

Hence if, for large n, both $\bar{s}_n$ and $\bar{\bar{s}}_n$ are approximately independent of n, say

$$\bar{s}_n \approx \bar{s}, \qquad \bar{\bar{s}}_n \approx \bar{\bar{s}},$$

then, in the special case considered, *returns to scale for complete information approach a constant as the size of the team gets large*, and during this approach returns to scale are increasing or decreasing according as $q\bar{s}$ is greater than or less than $\bar{\bar{s}}$.

These last remarks concerning returns to scale implicitly assume that the coefficient q remains constant as the team size, n, increases. Other hypotheses are, of course, interesting; this question is explored in Section 14. However, in Section 5 through 13, whenever the effect of increasing n is considered, it is assumed that q is held constant.

For the case in which the μ_i are uncorrelated, (5.15) reduces to

$$(5.16) \qquad V_1 = \frac{n\bar{s}_n[1 + (n - 2)q]}{[1 - q][1 + (n - 1)q]}$$

$$= \bar{s}_n f(n, q),$$

where

$$(5.17) \qquad f(n, q) \equiv \frac{n[1 + (n - 2)q]}{[1 - q][1 + (n - 1)q]}.$$

These last formulas will appear useful in later sections.

In the case of identical interaction, as in (4.5), one can verify directly that the inverse of Q, which will be denoted by $((q^{ij}))$, is given by

$$(5.18) \qquad q^{ij} = \begin{cases} \dfrac{1 + (n - 2)q}{D} & i = j \\[3mm] \dfrac{-q}{D} & i \neq j, \end{cases}$$

where

$$(5.19) \qquad D \equiv (1 - q)[1 + (n - 1)q].$$

From (5.11), (5.18), and (5.19) one can compute the value of complete information in this special case, obtaining

$$(5.20) \qquad V_1 = \frac{[1 + (n - 2)q]}{D} \sum_{i=1}^{n} s_{ii} - \frac{q}{D} \sum_{k \neq j} s_{ij},$$

where

$$(5.21) \qquad s_{ij} = E\mu_i\mu_j.$$

This can be rewritten in the form (5.15). If the limits

(5.22) $$\bar{s} \equiv \lim_{n \to \infty} \bar{s}_n \qquad \bar{\bar{s}} \equiv \lim_{n \to \infty} \bar{\bar{s}}_n,$$

exist, then

(5.23) $$\lim_{n \to \infty} \left(\frac{V_1}{n} \right) = \frac{\bar{s} - \bar{\bar{s}}}{1 - q}.$$

Furthermore, in the special case in which $\bar{s}_n$ and $\bar{\bar{s}}_n$ are *constant* (with respect to n), the approach to the limit in (5.23) is either monotonically increasing or monotonically decreasing according as $q\bar{s}$ is greater than or less than $\bar{\bar{s}}$.

6. NO COMMUNICATION; COMPLETE INFORMATIONAL DECENTRALIZATION

In the absence of communication, the information of team member i is

(6.1) $$\eta_i = \zeta_i,$$

where ζ_i is his own observation. Without further specification of the ζ_i, it does not appear that anything interesting beyond Theorem 1 can be said about the solution. Two specializations will be considered here: first, the case of statistically independent observations; and second, the case of cospecialization of observation and action.

In the case of independent observations, it will be shown that the value of the information structure is the sum of the values that the components η_i would have in "one-person" problems with payoff functions

(6.2) $$2\mu_i(x)a_i - q_{ii}a_i^2.$$

Specifically, we shall show that the value of such an information structure is

(6.3) $$V_2 = \sum_{i=1}^{n} \frac{1}{q_{ii}} E[E(\mu_i|\zeta_i)^2].$$

Consider now the effect of adding the assumption of cospecialization ($\zeta_i = \mu_i$). In this case (6.3) becomes

(6.4) $$V_2 = \sum_i \frac{s_{ii}}{q_{ii}},$$

where, as before, $s_{ii} = E\mu_i^2$. This will be called the case of *complete informational decentralization*, that is,

(6.5) $$\begin{cases} \eta_i = \zeta_i \text{ (no communication)} & i = 1, \ldots, n \\ \zeta_i = \mu_i \text{ (cospecialization)} & i = 1, \ldots, n \\ \mu_1, \ldots, \mu_n \text{ independent.} \end{cases}$$

The values of the coefficients q_{ii} are not, of course, invariant under a change of units in which the variables a_i are measured; by appropriate changes of units, together with corresponding changes of the coefficients μ_i and corresponding changes in their variances and covariances s_{ij}, one can achieve

$$(6.6) \qquad\qquad q_{ii} = 1 \qquad i = 1, \ldots, n,$$

and also

$$(6.7) \qquad\qquad V_2 = \sum_i s_{ii}.$$

Hence, for constant $\bar{s}_n$ (see Section 5), the value of the information structure (6.5) is simply proportional to n, that is, *complete informational decentralization exhibits constant returns to scale.*

Even without the assumption of independence of observations, further information about the solution in the case of cospecialization of action and observation can be obtained under the further assumption that $\mu_1, \ldots, \mu_n$ are normally distributed. As before, let $s_{ij} \equiv E\mu_i\mu_j$, let H be the matrix with elements $h_{ij} \equiv q_{ij}s_{ij}$, and let s be the vector with coordinates $s_{11}, \ldots, s_{nn}$. We shall show that the value of the information structure "no communication" is then

$$(6.8) \qquad\qquad V_2 = s'H^{-1}s.$$

In the special case of "identical interaction" and "identical correlation," (6.8) reduces to a simple and revealing formula. Assume that

$$(6.9) \qquad\qquad q_{ij} = \begin{cases} 1 & \text{if } i = j \\ q & \text{if } i \neq j; \end{cases}$$

$$(6.10) \qquad\qquad s_{ij} = \begin{cases} 1 & \text{if } i = j \\ r & \text{if } i \neq j; \end{cases}$$

where $-(1/n - 1) < q < 1$ and $-(1/n - 1) \leq r \leq 1$. Then the value as given by (6.8) reduces to

$$(6.11) \qquad\qquad V_2 = \frac{n}{1 + (n - 1)qr}.$$

If $qr \neq 0$, then V_2 approaches $(1/qr)$ as a limit as n gets large. On the other hand, if $qr = 0$, then $V_2 = n$. In other words, in this special case of "identical interaction" and "identical correlation" with cospecialization of action and observation, *the value of no communication approaches a (finite) limit as the number of variables n increases without limit, if neither the interaction nor the correlation is zero.*

To demonstrate (6.3), first note that, if $\eta_1, \ldots, \eta_n$ are statistically independent, then for any team decision function α,

(6.12) $$E(\alpha_j | \eta_i) = E\alpha_j \qquad i \neq j.$$

In other words, person i's information does not help him to predict person j's action. By (3.5), then, any *optimal* team decision function α satisfies

(6.13) $$E(\alpha_j | \eta_i) = 0 \qquad i \neq j.$$

Applying this to condition (3.1) of Theorem 1, we obtain

(6.14) $$q_{ii}\alpha_i = E(\mu_i | \eta_i) \qquad i = 1, \ldots, n,$$

(6.15) $$\alpha_i = \left(\frac{1}{q_{ii}}\right) E(\mu_i | \eta_i) \qquad i = 1, \ldots, n,$$

for the optimal team decision rule. Equation 6.3 now follows easily using (3.4) and, of course, (6.1).

We now consider the case of cospecialization, with the further assumption of normality of $\mu_1, \ldots, \mu_n$ but without the assumption of independence of observations. By Theorem 2, components of the optimal team decision rule are each linear, that is, for some constants $b_1, \ldots, b_n$,

(6.16) $$\alpha_i = b_i \mu_i \qquad i = 1, \ldots, n.$$

Hence, again using the normality,

(6.17) $$E(\alpha_j | \eta_i) = b_j \left(\frac{s_{ij}}{s_{ii}}\right) \mu_i.$$

Applying (6.16) and (6.17) to (3.1) of Theorem 1, we find that

(6.18) $$q_{ii}b_i\mu_i + \sum_{j \neq i} q_{ij}b_j \left(\frac{s_{ij}}{s_{ii}}\right) \mu_i = \mu_i \qquad i = 1, \ldots, n.$$

Since (6.18) must hold for (almost) all values of μ_i,

(6.19) $$q_{ii}b_i + \sum_{j \neq i} q_{ij}b_j \left(\frac{s_{ij}}{s_{ii}}\right) = 1 \qquad i = 1, \ldots, n,$$

which can be rewritten

(6.20) $$\sum_j q_{ij}s_{ij}b_j = s_{ii} \qquad i = 1, \ldots, n.$$

Let $H \equiv ((q_{ij}s_{ij}))$, $s \equiv$ the vector with coordinates $s_{11}, \ldots, s_{nn}$, and $b \equiv$ the vector with coordinates $b_1, \ldots, b_n$. Then the solution of (6.20) can be expressed as

(6.21) $$b = H^{-1}s.$$

Note that since $((q_{ij}))$ is positive definite and $((s_{ij}))$ is nonnegative semidefinite, H is positive definite. [H is the so-called Hadamard product of $((q_{ij}))$ and $((s_{ij}))$; see Halmos 1958, Section 85.]

To get the value of the information structure in this case, applying (3.4), we find that

$$V_2 = E \sum_i \alpha_i \mu_i$$

(6.22)
$$= E \sum b_i \mu_i{}^2$$

$$= b's.$$

By (6.21), this last gives a value of

(6.23) $$V_2 = s'H^{-1}s.$$

7. PARTITIONED COMMUNICATION

The results for no communication, with independent observations, extend easily to the case in which the team members are partitioned into a set of groups I_k such that complete communication takes place within each group but no communication takes place between groups. Thus let

(7.1) $$\zeta^k \equiv \{\zeta_i\}_{i \in I_k};$$

then the information structure under discussion is defined by

(7.2) $$\eta_i(x) = \zeta^k \qquad \text{if } i \in I_k.$$

The results of this section might be thought of as describing certain types of partial informational decentralization.

Denoting by α^k and μ^k the vectors consisting of those components of α and μ, respectively, corresponding to the kth group, and by Q_k the corresponding submatrix of Q, then by reasoning similar to that of Section 6 the reader can verify easily that the best team decision function is

(7.3) $$\alpha^k = Q_k{}^{-1}E(\mu^k|\zeta^k),$$

and that the value of this information structure is

(7.4) $$V_3 = \sum_k E[E(\mu^k|\zeta^k)'Q_k{}^{-1}E(\mu^k|\zeta^k)]$$

(with $\zeta_1, \ldots, \zeta_n$ assumed independent; actually, for this result, it is sufficient that the ζ^k be independent).

In the case of cospecialization of action and observation (4.3), the information structure (7.2) reduces to

(7.5) $$\eta_i = \mu^k \qquad \text{if } i \in I_k,$$

and yields a value, by (7.4), of

(7.6) $$V_3 = \sum_k \sum_{i \in I_k} q_k{}^{ii} s_{ii},$$

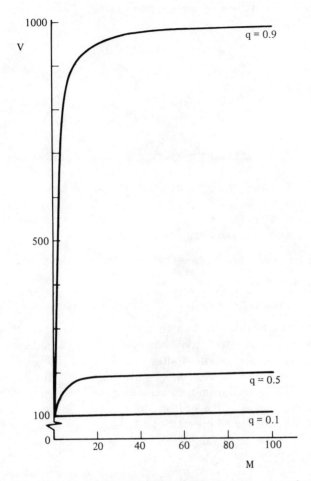

FIGURE 6.1. Value of information for groups of
equal size. $n = 100$.

where

(7.7) $$Q_k^{-1} \equiv ((q_k^{ij}))$$

(recall that $\mu_1, \ldots, \mu_n$ are uncorrelated).

In the special case of identical interaction (4.5), the value (7.6) reduces to

(7.8) $$V_3 = \sum_k \bar{s}_k f(M_k, q),$$

where M_k is the number of persons in group k,

$$(7.9) \qquad \bar{s}_k \equiv \frac{1}{M_k} \sum_{i \in I_k} s_{ii},$$

and $f(M_k, q)$ is given by (5.17) [apply (5.18)]. In particular, if all groups are of equal size M, then the value is

$$(7.10) \qquad V_3 = \bar{s}\left(\frac{n}{M}\right) f(M, q)$$

where $\bar{s} \equiv (1/n) \Sigma s_{ii}$ [compare with the value of complete information in (5.23)].

Figure 6.1 shows V_3 as a function of M, for $\bar{s} = 1$, $n = 100$, and three different values of q.

On the other hand, if a group (say the first) has M members, and each of the rest has only *one* member, then the value is

$$(7.11) \qquad V_3 = \bar{s}_1 f(M, q) + \sum_{i \notin I_1} s_{ii}.$$

8. Dissemination of Independent Information

As noted in the last section, partitioning of persons (or action variables) is one way of moving away from complete informational decentralization toward identical information. Another way is provided by the system that will be called here *dissemination of information*. Specifically, consider a situation in which each team member communicates some function of his observations, that is, some statistic, to a "central agency," which then compiles (but does not "process") all these reports and distributes this compilation to all the members.

We shall show that *the value of such an information structure can be expressed exactly as a sum of two parts, one part attributable to the disseminated information and one part attributable to the undisseminated information.*

To define the information structure precisely, for each i suppose the observation function ζ_i takes values in some set Z_i, and let τ_i be a function on Z_i. The variable $t_i = \tau_i(z_i)$ is to be interpreted as the ith member's report to the central agent. Let $\tau(x) = [\tau_1(x), \ldots, \tau_n(x)]$; then define the information structure by

$$(8.1) \qquad \eta_i(x) = [\zeta_i(x), \tau(x)] \qquad i = 1, \ldots, n.$$

The variable $t = (t_1, \ldots, t_n)$ is to be interpreted as the compilation sent out by the central agent to all the team members. We consider here only the case in which the observations ζ_i are statistically independent. We also omit the possibility that the central agent further reduces the compilation $\tau(x)$ to some summary statistic before sending it out to the team members. (The "central agent" here does not himself directly control any action variable.)

Define $\tilde{\mu}_i$ and $\bar{\mu}_i$ by

$$\begin{aligned}\tilde{\mu}_i(y_i) &= E(\mu_i|y_i)\\ \bar{\mu}_i(t) &= E(\mu_i|t).\end{aligned}$$

(8.2)

We shall show that the optimal decisions functions are

$$(8.3)\qquad \alpha_i(y_i) = E(\beta_i|t) + \frac{1}{q_{ii}}[\tilde{\mu}_i(y_i) - \bar{\mu}_i(t)],$$

where, as in Section 5, β is the best team decision function under complete information and is given by (5.7) as $\beta = Q^{-1}\mu$.

The corresponding expected payoff will be shown to be

$$(8.4)\qquad V_4 = E\bar{\mu}'Q^{-1}\bar{\mu} + \sum_i \frac{1}{q_{ii}}(E\tilde{\mu}_i{}^2 - E\bar{\mu}_i{}^2),$$

which can be shown to be equivalent to

$$(8.5)\qquad V_4 = E\bar{\mu}'Q^{-1}\bar{\mu} + \sum_i \frac{1}{q_{ii}}E[\mathrm{Var}(\tilde{\mu}_i|t)].$$

Note that the first term of (8.5) is the maximum expected payoff that could be obtained if all team members had only the information function τ; whereas the second term is a weighted sum of terms, each of which measures the degree to which that person can predict his μ_i better on the basis of y_i than on the basis of t alone.

Again, before demonstrating these facts, we shall consider a special case. Suppose (in addition to the assumptions already made) that the μ_i are independent, and that each μ_i is independent of $\{\zeta_j\}_{j\neq i}$. (This would be the case if, for example, each person's observation $\zeta_i(x)$ consisted of an estimate of $\mu_i(x)$, both μ_i and the error being independent of the μ_j and the errors of the other persons.) It is shown below that, in this case,

$$(8.6)\qquad \tilde{\mu}_i = E(\mu_i|\zeta_i),$$

and that the value of the information structure is

$$(8.7)\qquad V_4 = \sum_i q^{ii}E\bar{\mu}_i{}^2 + \sum_i \frac{1}{q_{ii}}(E\tilde{\mu}_i{}^2 - E\bar{\mu}_i{}^2),$$

where, as before, $((q^{ij})) = Q^{-1}$.

Again, as in (8.4), the first sum in (8.7) is the maximum expected payoff that could be obtained if all team members had *only* shared information τ; whereas the second term measures the additional value of each individual's knowing the part of his own observation that he did not share.

Another interpretation of (8.7) is suggested by rearranging the terms to give

$$(8.8) \qquad V_4 = \sum_i \frac{E\mu_i^2}{q_{ii}} + \sum_i \left(q^{ii} - \frac{1}{q_{ii}} \right) E\bar{\mu}_i^2.$$

The first sum in (8.8) is what the maximum expected payoff would be if the ith member knew only ζ_i (see Section 6 on no communication); the second sum is the additional value attributable to dissemination of $\tau_1, \ldots, \tau_n$.

Turn now to the derivation of the optimal team decision function and expected payoffs. We shall use the following lemma, the proof of which is given in Radner 1962.

LEMMA. *Let A, C, and G be independent random variables (not necessarily real); let B be a contraction of A,[3] and D a contraction of C; and let F be a real random variable defined by $F = f(A, D, G)$, where f is some given measurable function; then*

$$(8.9) \qquad E(F|B, C, G) = E(F|B, D, G).$$

In the present situation, the above lemma applies to give

$$(8.10) \qquad E(\alpha_j|y_i) = E(\alpha_j|\tau) \qquad \text{if } i \neq j.$$

This can be seen by taking (in the notation of the lemma)

$$(8.11) \qquad \begin{aligned} A &= \zeta_j \\ B &= \tau_j \\ C &= \zeta_i \\ D &= \tau_i \\ G &= \{\tau_k\}_{k \neq i, j} \\ f &= \alpha_j \end{aligned}$$

From (8.10) it follows that condition (3.1) of Theorem 1 reduces, in this case, to

$$(8.12) \qquad q_{ii}\alpha_i + \sum_{j \neq i} q_{ij}E(\alpha_j|\tau) = \tilde{\mu}_i \qquad i = 1, \ldots, n.$$

3. That is, the partition induced by A is as fine as that induced by B; see Chapter 2, Section 6.

Applying the lemma again to $\tilde{\mu}_i$, we find that the conditional expectation of (8.12) given τ is

(8.13)
$$\sum_j q_{ij} E(\alpha_j | \tau) = \bar{\mu}_i \qquad i = 1, \dots, n.$$

We subtract (8.13) from (8.12):

$$q_{ii}[\alpha_i - E(\alpha_i | \tau)] = \tilde{\mu}_i - \bar{\mu}_i$$

(8.14)
$$\alpha_i = E(\alpha_i | \tau) + \frac{1}{q_{ii}}(\tilde{\mu}_i - \bar{\mu}_i).$$

On the other hand, solving (8.13) for $E(\alpha | \tau)$, we obtain

(8.15)
$$E(\alpha | \tau) = Q^{-1} E(\mu | \tau) = E(\beta | \tau).$$

Substitution of this into (8.14) gives the *best team decision function*,

(8.16)
$$\hat{\alpha}_i(y_i) = E(\beta_i | t) + \frac{1}{q_{ii}}[\tilde{\mu}_i(y_i) - \mu_i(t)],$$

from which the values as given by (8.4) and (8.5) easily follow.

Equation 8.6 follows directly from the lemma, under the assumptions of the special case, by taking

(8.17)
$$A = (\mu_i, \zeta_i), B = \zeta_i, C = \{\tau_j\}_{j \neq i}, D \text{ constant}, f = \mu_i.$$

9. ERROR IN INSTRUCTION

Consider a team with complete communication to a central agent, in which the best team decision, $\beta_i(x)$, is computed by the central agent, and each team member is sent a message instructing him about the appropriate action $\beta_i(x)$. Suppose, however, that the actual message received by member i is not the correct value $\beta_i(x)$ but a value equal to the correct value plus some random error. To be precise, suppose that the information to member i is given by

(9.1)
$$y_i = \eta_i(x) = \beta_i(x) + \varepsilon_i(x),$$

where $\beta_i(x)$ is the best decision function for i under complete information (Section 5) and $\varepsilon_i(x)$ is an error term.

Each team member can, of course, simply follow the "instruction" y_i with the error, as he receives it. Indeed, this might at first appear to be the correct procedure if ε_i is independent of β_i, and has mean zero. However, we shall show that the team can do better if each team member is provided with a decision rule that adjusts the received instruction in a suitable way. It will be shown that the proper adjustment for any one person depends in general upon all the interactions q_{ij}, and that *even if only some of the team members' instructions are erroneous, all team members should typically make some adjustments.*

Throughout this section, we shall assume that

, 1. $\beta(x)$ and $\varepsilon(x)$ are normally distributed.
  2. β and ε are independent of each other.
  3. The components ε_i are (mutually) independent.

There is no loss of generality in further assuming that

4. $E\beta = E\varepsilon = 0$.

We first give the results for this information structure, including those for certain special cases, deferring the proofs to the end of the section.

First, denote the relevant variances and covariances by

$$(9.2) \qquad\qquad r_{ij} = E\beta_i\beta_j,$$

$$(9.3) \qquad\qquad t_i^2 = E\varepsilon_i^2.$$

Further, define the numbers f_{ij}, v_i, f^{ij}, and b_i by

$$(9.4) \qquad\qquad f_{ij} = \begin{cases} q_{ii}(r_{ii} + t_i^2) & \text{if } i = j \\ q_{ij}r_{ij} & \text{if } i \neq j. \end{cases}$$

$$(9.5) \qquad\qquad v_i = q_{ii}t_i^2,$$

$$(9.6) \qquad\qquad ((f^{ij})) = ((f_{ij}))^{-1},$$

$$(9.7) \qquad\qquad b_i = 1 - \sum_j f^{ij}v_j.$$

We shall show that the best team decision function is

$$(9.8) \qquad\qquad \alpha_i(y_i) = b_iy_i,$$

and that the resulting value of this information structure is

$$(9.9) \qquad\qquad V_5 = \sum_{ij} f_{ij}b_ib_j.$$

Thus each adjustment factor b_k depends upon all the parameters q_{ij}, r_{ij}, and t_i^2.

Note that, if all the error variances are very small, then the best decision b_iy_i is very close to y_i (set all $t_i^2 = 0$). On the other hand, if the error variances are very large, compared to the variances r_{ii} of the β_i, then b_i will be close to zero.

It is also interesting that even if, for some particular i, the error variance t_i^2 is zero, the adjustment factor b_i will in general be *different from* 1. In other words, error in the instructions to some team members should cause other team members to adjust their actions accordingly, *even if the latter are receiving error-free instructions.*

A SPECIAL CASE

Before demonstrating these results, consider the special case in which all interactions are identical, all correlations between different β_i and β_j are identical, and all error variances are identical, that is,

(9.10)
$$q_{ij} = \begin{cases} 1 & i = j \\ q & i \neq j \end{cases}$$

$$r_{ij} = \begin{cases} 1 & i = j \\ c & i \neq j \end{cases}$$

$$t_i^2 = t^2.$$

Having taken $r_{ii} = 1$, the parameter t is to be interpreted as the *ratio* of the error variance to the (common) variance of the β_i.

In this case, the adjustment factor b_i [see (9.7)] reduces to

(9.11)
$$b_i = 1 - \frac{t^2}{1 + t^2 + (n - 1)qc},$$

and the value of the information structure is

(9.12)
$$V_5 = \frac{n[1 + (n - 1)qc]^2}{1 + t^2 + (n - 1)qc}.$$

Thus the term

(9.13)
$$\frac{t^2 y_i}{1 + t^2 + (n - 1)qc},$$

is the "correction" subtracted by person i from the instruction y_i that he receives. Here it is quite easy to see that, if there are no errors ($t^2 = 0$), then the correction is zero; whereas as t^2 gets large, the correction tends to cancel out the information completely, that is, $t^2/[1 + t^2 + (n - 1)qc]$ tends to 1.

Similar remarks apply to the value V_5 [see (9.12)]. When $t^2 = 0$, one gets the value of complete information

(9.14)
$$N[1 + (n - 1)qc];$$

but when t^2 gets large, the value V_5 approaches zero.

Proof of results. By Theorem 2, the components of the optimal team decision function are linear, say,

(9.15) $$\alpha_i(y_i) = b_i y_i.$$

Hence condition (3.1) is

(9.16) $$q_{ii}b_i y_i + \sum_{j \neq i} q_{ij}b_j E(y_j | y_i) = E(\mu_i | y_i) \qquad i = 1, \ldots, n.$$

From assumptions 1, 2, and 3, it follows that

(9.17)
$$E(\eta_j | y_i) = \frac{r_{ij} y_i}{r_{ii} + t_i^2} \qquad i \neq j$$

$$E(\beta_j | y_i) = \frac{r_{ij} y_i}{r_{ii} + t_i^2} \qquad \text{all } i \text{ and } j.$$

The function β is related to μ by

(9.18) $$\mu_i(x) = \sum_j q_{ij}\beta_j(x),$$

since β is the optimal team decision function under complete information [condition (5.7)]. The substitution of (9.17) and (9.18) in the stationarity condition (9.16) gives

(9.19) $$q_{ii}b_i + \sum_{j \neq 1} q_{ij}b_j\left(\frac{r_{ij}}{r_{ii} + t_i^2}\right) = \sum_j q_{ij}\left(\frac{r_{ij}}{r_{ii} + t_i^2}\right),$$

which reduces to

(9.20) $$q_{ii}(r_{ii} + t_i^2)(b_i - 1) + \sum_{j \neq i} q_{ij}r_{ij}(b_j - 1) = -q_{ii}t_i^2.$$

The solution of this system for the values $(b_i - 1)$ gives (9.7), which completes the derivation of the best team decision function. The value (9.9) is obtained, with some straightforward algebra, by substituting the decision function of (9.7) and (9.8) in the payoff function and taking the expected value.

To derive the results for the special case (9.10), we use the fact that the inverse of an $n \times n$ matrix $((m_{ij}))$ of the form

(9.21) $$m_{ij} = \begin{cases} u & i = j \\ w & i \neq j, \end{cases}$$

is

(9.22) $$m^{ij} = \begin{cases} \dfrac{u + (n - 2)w}{D} & i = j \\ \dfrac{-w}{D} & i \neq j, \end{cases}$$

where

(9.23) $$D = (u - w)[u + (n - 1)w].$$

[Compare with (5.18) and (5.19).]

The matrix $((f_{ij}))$ of (9.4) is of this form (9.21), under the assumptions (9.10); hence the inverse is

(9.24)
$$f^{ij} = \begin{cases} \dfrac{1 + t^2 + (n - w)qc}{D} & i = j \\[2ex] \dfrac{-qc}{D} & i \neq j, \end{cases}$$

$$D = (1 + t^2 - qc)[1 + t^2 + (n - 1)qc].$$

Simple algebra now yields (9.11) and (9.12) from the general expressions (9.7) and (9.9).

10. Complete Communication of Erroneous Observations

In the preceding section, we considered the effects of errors in instructions from a central decision agency to the individual team members. In this section, we shall consider the effects of errors in the *information provided by the team members to such a central agency.*

For this information structure, we consider only the case of cospecialization of action and observation ($\zeta_i = \mu_i$). Suppose that each team member sends a message consisting of the value $\mu_i(x)$ plus an error $\varepsilon_i(x)$ to a central agency. On the basis of the messages received from all n team members, the central agency then computes the best decision for each team member and communicates this to him (error-free). Note that in this case all n decisions are based upon the *same* information. To be precise, the information structure to be discussed is

(10.1) $\eta_i(x) = [\mu_1(x) + \varepsilon_1(x), \ldots, \mu_n(x) + \varepsilon_n(x)]$ for all i.

Note that this information structure is formally equivalent to that of complete communication of *observations* $\mu_i + \varepsilon_i$; in particular, the results for this structure follow directly from those of Section 5, which are repeated here for convenience. The best team decision function is

(10.2) $\alpha(y) = Q^{-1}E(\mu|y),$

with a corresponding value

(10.3) $V_6 = E\{E(\mu|y)'Q^{-1}E(\mu|y)\} = \sum_{ij} q^{ij} \, \text{Cov}[E(\mu_i|y), E(\mu_j|y)],$

where $((q^{ij}))$ is the inverse of the matrix $((q_{ij}))$.

Various special cases are of interest. If the μ_i and ε_i are all statistically independent, then

(10.4) $$E(\mu_i|y) = E(\mu_i|\mu_i + \varepsilon_i).$$

If, further, the μ_i and ε_i are normally distributed (with means that can be taken to be zero), then,

(10.5) $$E(\mu_i|\mu_i + \varepsilon_i) = \frac{s_{ii}}{s_{ii} + t_i^2}(\mu_i + \varepsilon_i),$$

where $s_{ii} = E(\mu_i^2)$ and $t_i^2 = E(\varepsilon_i^2)$. In this case, the best team decision function and corresponding value are, respectively,

(10.6) $$\alpha_i = \sum_j q^{ij}\left(\frac{s_{jj}}{s_{jj} + t_j^2}\right)(\mu_j + \varepsilon_j),$$

(10.7) $$V_6 = \sum_i q^{ii}\left[\frac{s_{ii}}{1 + (t_i^2/s_{ii})}\right].$$

If one further specializes by assuming that

$$E\mu_i^2 = s^2$$

$$E\varepsilon_i^2 = t^2$$

(10.8)

$$q_{ij} = \begin{cases} 1 & i = j \\ q & i \neq j, \end{cases}$$

the value becomes

(10.9) $$V_6 = \frac{ns^2[1 + (n-2)q]}{(1 + t^2/s^2)(1 - q)[1 + (n-1)q]}.$$

The reader can verify that, for $t^2 = 0$ (no error), V_6 equals the value of complete information, whereas as (t^2/s^2) gets large, V_6 approaches zero as a limit.

The results (10.2) and (10.3) follow directly from (5.6) and (5.12). The special case (10.9) is similar to that discussed in the previous section.

11. MANAGEMENT BY EXCEPTION: REPORTING EXCEPTIONS

The term *management by exception* covers a number of organizational devices whereby the decision about a given action variable is normally made on the basis of relatively few information variables, but may be made on the basis of more information if the original information variables take on *exceptional* values. In this and the next section, we analyze two such management by exception devices. The first might be called *reporting exceptions*, or more accurately, if somewhat colloquially, "passing the buck." The second device, discussed in the next section, can be described as *emergency conference*. The comparison of the various information structures considered in this chapter, which is made in Section 13, tends to confirm the widely held belief that management by exception can provide a relatively efficient way of utilizing information.

We shall analyze these particular management-by-exception information structures in the context of cospecialization of action and observation ($\zeta_i = \mu_i$). Before giving a precise definition of reports of exceptions, the following description may be helpful. Suppose that, for each team member i, the range of possible values of $\mu_i(x)$ is divided into two parts, "ordinary" values and "exceptional" values. Let R_i denote the set of exceptional values. If, in a particular instance, member i observes $\mu_i(x)$ to be *not* exceptional, that is, not in R_i, then he chooses a value of his action variable a_i on the basis of $\mu_i(x)$ only, according to some decision function. On the other hand, if he observes $\mu_i(x)$ to be exceptional, that is, in R_i, then he reports that value to a central agency. The central agency then makes the decision about the values of the decision variables of all team members i who have reported exceptional observations, on the basis of all those exceptional observations.

More precisely, the information structure to be analyzed in this section is defined as follows. For each i, let R_i be a given subset of the real line [the exceptional values of $\mu_i(x)$]; and for each state of nature, let $J(x)$ be the set of all j such that $\mu_j(x) \in R_j$. Then the information structure η is defined by

$$(11.1) \qquad \eta_i(x) = \begin{cases} \mu_i(x) & \text{if } \mu_i(x) \notin R_i \\ \{\mu_j(x)\}_{j \in J(x)} & \text{if } \mu_i(x) \in R_i. \end{cases}$$

Note that (11.1) defines a class of information structures, a particular structure being determined by a particular choice of the exception sets $R_1, \ldots, R_n$.

Such an information structure can, of course, be described in a somewhat more general context than the one used here. The basic idea is that the variables directly observed by member i have exceptional and ordinary values: if they are ordinary, he makes the decisions about his action variables just on the basis of that information; if they are exceptional, the decisions are made by an agent on the basis of all the exceptional information (and possibly other information as well).

In what follows, it is assumed that the variables $\mu_i(x)$ are statistically independent, with means zero and variances s_i^2. It is also assumed that each $\mu_i(x)$ has a distribution that is symmetrical about its mean, zero. Likewise, we only consider exceptional sets R_i that are symmetrical around zero; that is, if m is in R_i, then so is $-m$.

It will be seen that, in this case, the following parameters are of central importance in evaluating the information structure corresponding to a particular choice of $R_1, \ldots, R_n$:

(11.2)
$$p_i \equiv \text{Prob}[\mu_i(x) \in R_i]$$
$$s_{Ri}^2 \equiv \text{Var}[\mu_i(x)|\mu_i(x) \in R_i].$$

Thus p_i is the frequency with which the variable $\mu_i(x)$ turns out to be exceptional; and s_{Ri}^2 is the conditional variance of $\mu_i(x)$, given that it is exceptional. The larger p_i, the more frequently the action variable a_i is determined by the central agent, and the larger will be the (gross) expected payoff. Of course, the greater the frequency of exceptions, the more costly one can expect such an information structure to be.

It will also appear that, other things being equal, the larger the conditional variances s_{Ri}^2, the larger the gross expected payoff. This is plausible, in view of the quadratic payoff function. The precise result is this: Given the probabilities $p_1, \ldots, p_n$, the optimal choice of R_i is that which maximizes s_{Ri}^2, and this is achieved by taking R_i to be the complement of an interval symmetric around zero. Note that, in this case, the values in R_i are indeed "exceptional," in the usual sense of being farther from the average than the "ordinary" values.

Before deriving the formulas for the best decision rules and the value of this type of information structure, we present the results of some numerical computations. For the purposes of these computations, it is assumed that

(11.3)
$$q_{ij} = \begin{cases} 1 & i = j \\ q & i \neq j, \end{cases}$$

(11.4) $\mu_i(x)$ is normally distributed, with mean 0
                     and variance 1, for each i.

(This is the special case of identical interaction that has been discussed in several previous sections.)

Taking all the exception sets R_i to be identical, and choosing them in the best way (subject to the constraint of symmetry), we calculate the values of the information structures for various values of the parameters: q, degree of interaction; n, number of action variables; p, probability of a value of $\mu_i(x)$ being exceptional. The parameters q and n are to be thought of as "technological," whereas p is a parameter of the information structure, to be chosen by the organizer.

It should be noted that the parameters s_{Ri}^2 [see (11.2)] are all equal, because the sets R_i are identical; furthermore, their common value is determined by p, once the distribution of $\mu_i(x)$ is given, and the best choice of R_i is made. It might also be noted that the effect of assuming the variances of the $\mu_i(x)$ to be, say, s^2 instead of 1, would be to multiply all the computed values by s^2.

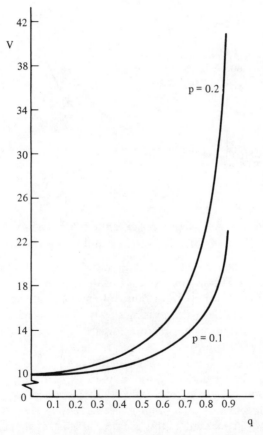

FIGURE 6.2. Reports of exceptions: V as a function
of q for $n = 10$ and $p = 0.1, 0.2$.

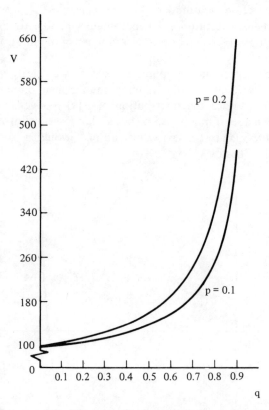

FIGURE 6.3. Reports of exceptions: V as a function
of q for $n = 100$ and $p = 0.1, 0.2$.

First, we consider the effect of changing the interaction parameter, q.
Figures 6.2 and 6.3 show the value, V, of the information structure, as a
function of q, for different pairs of values of p and n. As the figures illustrate,
the value is greater, the larger q, rising slowly when q is near zero and then
more rapidly as q approaches 1. Note, too, that the increment in value due
to going from $p = .1$ to $p = .2$ is larger, the larger q.

Figure 6.4 shows the effect of changing p, the relative frequency of
exceptions, for fixed values of q and n. As one would expect, the value V
increases with p; however, each successive increment of p produces a
smaller increment of value, so that p has *decreasing marginal value*. This
latter effect is quite marked, in this example at least, so that a frequency of
exceptions of $1/3$ has achieved almost 80 percent of the possible increase
in value.

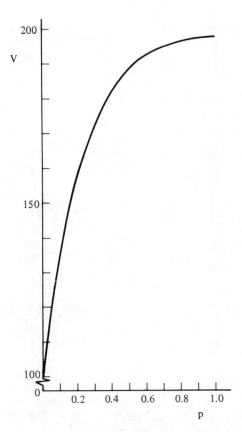

FIGURE 6.4. Reports of exceptions: V as a function
of p for $n = 100$ and $q = 0.5$.

Turning to Figure 6.5, which shows the effect of changing n, one sees
that as n increases, with p and q fixed, *the value V increases more than
proportionately*. This is illustrated in the figure by plotting (V/n) as a function of n (the lower curve). Recall that, under these particular assumptions,
the value of *complete* information also increases more than proportionately
with n [see (5.16) and (5.17)]; this is shown by the upper curve in Figure 6.5.
As inspection of the two curves shows, (V/n) approaches a constant much
more rapidly for complete information than for reports of exceptions.

As n increases, the expected number of exceptions, np, increases proportionately. If the costs of dealing with these exceptions were proportional
to the average number of exceptions, then we would have here an example

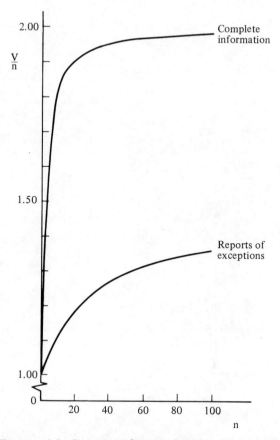

FIGURE 6.5. Reports of exceptions and complete
information: V/n as a function of
n for $q = 0.5$ and $p = 0.1$.

of increasing returns to scale in the size of the organization arising from
the use of this type of information structure.

Finally, Figure 6.6 shows the effect of increasing n while simultaneously
decreasing p, so that the expected number of exceptions, np, remains
constant. These curves show that, although in this case total value increases with n, it does so less than proportionately to n. As n increases
without limit, the ratio V/n decreases to the limiting value 1, which is the
value of V/n for complete decentralization in this case.

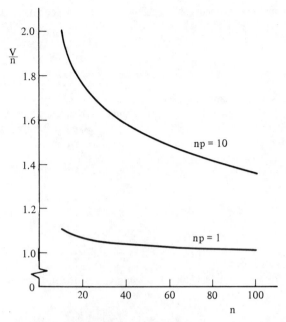

FIGURE 6.6. Reports of exceptions: V/n as a function of n for $q = 0.5$ and $np = 1, 10$.

DERIVATION OF BEST DECISION FUNCTIONS

Assume that

1. The distribution of each μ_i is symmetric around its mean, which can be taken to be zero.
2. Each exception set R_i is symmetric around zero.
3. $\mu_i, \ldots, \mu_n$ are statistically independent.

Recall that $J(x)$ denotes, for each x, the set of indices of those variables $\mu_j(x)$ that have exceptional values, that is,

$$(11.5) \qquad\qquad J(x) \equiv \{j | \mu_j(x) \in R_j\}.$$

Denote by $\mu^J(x)$ the vector of those coordinates of μ for which j is in $J(x)$; and denote by $Q_{J(x)}$ the matrix of those elements q_{ij} of Q for which i and j are in $J(x)$. In this notation, the information structure to be analyzed can be described by

$$(11.6) \qquad\qquad \eta_i(x) = \begin{cases} \mu_i(x) & \text{if } i \notin J(x) \\ \mu^J(x) & \text{if } i \in J(x). \end{cases}$$

Consider now the particular team decision function $\hat{\alpha}$ defined by

(11.7)
$$\hat{\alpha}_i(y_i) = \begin{cases} \dfrac{\mu_i(x)}{q_{ii}} & \text{if } i \notin J(x) \\[2mm] [Q_{J(x)}^{-1}\mu^J(x)]_i & \text{if } i \in J(x). \end{cases}$$

In other words, the decision function $\hat{\alpha}$ just defined directs team member i: (1) to take that action that would be appropriate under "complete decentralization," if he observes an *un*exceptional value of μ_i; and (2) to take that action that would be appropriate under "partitions with independent information," with i in the group $J(x)$ if he observes an exceptional value of μ_i.

We shall now show that $\hat{\alpha}$ satisfies (3.1) and is therefore optimal.

First note that

(11.8)
$$E(\alpha_j|\eta_i) = \begin{cases} 0 & \text{if } i \notin J(x) \\ 0 & \text{if } i \in J(x), \, j \notin J(x) \\ [Q_J^{-1}\mu^J]_j & \text{if } i \in J(x), \, j \in J(x). \end{cases}$$

This follows from the independence and symmetry of the μ_i distribution and the symmetry of the sets R_i. Therefore, if $i \notin J(x)$

(11.9)
$$\sum_j q_{ij}E[\hat{\alpha}_j|\eta_i] = q_{ii}\left(\frac{\mu_i}{q_{ii}}\right) = \mu_i;$$

and if $i \in J(x)$,

(11.10)
$$\sum_j q_{ij}E[\hat{\alpha}_j|\eta_i] = \sum_{j \in J} q_{ij}[Q_J^{-1}\mu^J]_j = \mu_i.$$

Then (11.9) and (11.10) together verify that $\hat{\alpha}$ satisfies (3.1) and is therefore optimal.

COMPUTATION OF THE VALUE OF THE INFORMATION STRUCTURE

According to (3.4), the expected payoff yielded by the best team decision function $\hat{\alpha}$ is

(11.11)
$$V_7 = E \sum_j \mu_j \hat{\alpha}_j.$$

We shall now show that V_7 is given by (11.23) below. Given any particular set K,

(11.12)
$$E\{V|J(x) = K\} = E\left[\sum_{j \in K} \mu_j \alpha_j \Big| J(x) = K \right]$$

$$= E\{(\mu^K)'Q_K^{-1}\mu^K | \mu_j(x) \in R_j \text{ for } j \in K\}$$

$$+ \sum_{i \notin K} \frac{1}{q_{ii}} E\{\mu_i^2 | \mu_i(x) \in \bar{R}_i\}.$$

Define

(11.13)
$$s_{0i}^2 \equiv E\{\mu_i^2 | \mu_i(x) \notin R_i\}$$
$$s_{Ri}^2 \equiv E\{\mu_i^2 | \mu_i(x) \in R_i\}$$

(11.14) $q_K^{ii} \equiv$ ith diagonal element of Q_K^{-1}.

Then (recalling that the μ_j are independent), we find that

(11.15) $E\{(\mu^K)'Q_K^{-1}\mu^K | \mu_j \in R_j \text{ for } j \in K\} = \sum_{j \in K} q_K^{jj} s_{Rj}^2,$

and (11.12) can be rewritten,

(11.16) $E\{V | J(x) = K\} = \sum_{j \in K} q_K^{jj} s_{Rj}^2 + \sum_{j \notin K} \left(\frac{1}{q_{jj}} \right) s_{0j}^2.$

We denote by p_j the probability that $\mu_j(x)$ is exceptional, that is,

(11.17) $p_j \equiv \text{Prob}\{\mu_j(x) \in R_j\}.$

Then the probability, for a given set K, that $J(x) = K$ is

(11.18) $P(K) = \prod_{j \in K} p_j \prod_{j \notin K} (1 - p_j),$

and taking the expected value of (11.16), we obtain

(11.19) $V_7 = \sum_{\text{all } K} P(K) \left[\sum_{j \in K} q_K^{jj} s_{Rj}^2 + \sum_{j \notin K} \left(\frac{1}{q_{jj}} \right) s_{0j}^2 \right].$

This last can be put into a more useful form if we interchange the order of summation over the sets K and the index j of the team members, thus,

(11.20)
$$V_7 = \sum_{j=1}^{n} \left[\sum_{K \ni j} P(K) q_K^{jj} s_{Rj}^2 + \sum_{K \not\ni j} P(K) \frac{1}{q_{jj}} s_{0j}^2 \right]$$
$$= \sum_{j=1}^{n} \left[s_{Rj}^2 \sum_{K \ni j} P(K) q_K^{jj} + \left(\frac{1}{q_{jj}} \right) s_{0j}^2 \sum_{K \not\ni j} P(K) \right].$$

First we note that

(11.21) $\sum_{K \not\ni j} P(K) = (1 - p_j).$

Second, we can write

(11.22) $\sum_{K \ni j} P(K) q_K^{jj} = E[q_{J(x)}^{jj}],$

where by convention we take $q_K^{jj} = 0$ if $j \notin K$. The substitution of these last two equations in (11.20) gives

(11.23) $V_7 = \sum_{j=1}^{n} \left[s_{Rj}^2 E(q_{J(x)}^{jj}) + s_{0j}^2 (1 - p_j) \left(\frac{1}{q_{jj}} \right) \right].$

This is the formula we shall use in the further analysis of the value of this information structure.

We can now show that, given p_j, the best set R_j is the complement of an interval (symmetric around zero, by assumption). First, by the symmetry assumptions, the variance of μ_j is related to the conditional variances s_{Rj}^2 and s_{Oj}^2 by

(11.24) $$s_j^2 = p_j s_{Rj}^2 + (1 - p_j) s_{Oj}^2.$$

Therefore, choosing the sets R_j to maximize V_7 for given probabilities p_j is equivalent to choosing the conditional variances s_{Rj}^2 and s_{Oj}^2 to maximize V_7, subject to (11.24) and $s_{Rj}^2, s_{Oj}^2 \geq 0$. This can be done by making s_{Rj}^2 as large as possible if

(11.25) $$E\{q_{J(x)}^{jj}|J(x) \ni j\} \geq \frac{1}{q_{jj}}.$$

Now note that, since the matrix Q is positive definite (and hence so is every Q_J),

(11.26) $$q_J^{jj} q_{jj} \geq 1 \qquad \text{all } j \in J,$$

with strict inequality unless $J = \{j\}$ or $q_{jk} = 0$ for all $k \neq j$. Condition (11.25) is therefore always satisfied.

Consider now a special case. Suppose that all the variances s_i^2, s_{Ri}^2, and s_{Oi}^2 are the same and equal to s^2, s_R^2, and s_O^2, respectively, and suppose that all the sets R_i are identical with $p_i = p$. Let $M(x)$ denote the number of elements in $J(x)$; then $M(x)$ has the binomial distribution $B(p, n)$. Define $f^*(M)$ and $g(M)$ by

(11.27)
$$f^*(M) \equiv E\left\{ \sum_{j \in J(x)} q_{J(x)}^{jj} \middle| M(x) = M \right\}$$

$$g(M) \equiv E\left\{ \sum_{j \notin J(x)} \left(\frac{1}{q_{jj}} \right) \middle| M(x) = M \right\}.$$

Now (11.23) for V_7 reduces to

(11.28) $$V_7 = s^2 \left[\frac{s_R^2}{s^2} E f^*(M[x]) + \left(\frac{s_O^2}{s^2} \right) E g(M[x]) \right].$$

In particular, in the case of *identical interaction*

(11.29) $$q_{ij} = \begin{cases} 1 & \text{if } i = j \\ q & \text{if } i \neq j, \end{cases}$$

it follows from (5.14) and (5.2) that

(11.30)
$$f^*(M) = \frac{M[1 + (M - 2)q]}{(1 - q)[1 + (M - 1)q]} \equiv f(M, q),$$

$$g(M) = n - M,$$

so that V_7 is given by

(11.31) $$V_7 = ns^2 \left[\left(\frac{s_R^2}{s^2} \right) \frac{Ef[M(x), q]}{n} + (1 - p) \left(\frac{s_0^2}{s^2} \right) \right].$$

This is the formula used in the computation of the numerical results described earlier in this section with $s^2 = 1$ and the μ_i normally distributed. There seems to be no convenient closed expression for $Ef[M(x), q]$.

Under the assumption of normality, with $s^2 = 1$, we find the following relationship between p, s_R^2, and the interval $[-r, r]$ that defines the complement of R:

(11.32) $$p = 2 \int_r^\infty \varphi(t)\, dt,$$

(11.33) $$s_R^2 = \frac{2r\varphi(r)}{p} + 1,$$

where $\varphi(t) = 1/\sqrt{2\pi} \exp\{-t^2/2\}$. Formula (11.33) is derived easily, using integration by parts. From (11.24), of course, we have

(11.34) $$ps_R^2 + (1 - p)s_0^2 = 1.$$

VALUE OF INFORMATION FOR LARGE n

In the special case covered by (11.31), $(1/n)f(M, q)$ can be written

(11.35) $$\frac{f(M, q)}{n} = \frac{(M/n)\{(1/n) + [(M - 2)/n]q\}}{(1 - q)\{(1/n) + [(M - 1)/n]q\}}.$$

Hence, by the law of large numbers,

(11.36) $$\lim_{n \to \infty} \frac{Ef[M(x), q]}{n} = \frac{p}{1 - q}.$$

Together with (11.31), this last implies

(11.37) $$\lim_{n \to \infty} \frac{V_7}{n} = s^2 \left[\frac{p}{1 - q} \left(\frac{s_R^2}{s^2} \right) + (1 - p) \left(\frac{s_0^2}{s^2} \right) \right].$$

12. MANAGEMENT BY EXCEPTION: EMERGENCY CONFERENCE

In the last section, it was assumed that the decisions about only those variables corresponding to "exceptional" information were taken jointly, whereas the decisions about the other variables were taken independently. Another management-by-exception type of information structure, which might be labeled *emergency conference*, stipulates that, whenever any information variable takes on an exceptional value, *all* decisions are taken jointly. More precisely, we shall analyze the following information structure:

$$(12.1) \qquad \eta_i(x) = \begin{cases} \mu_i(x) & \text{if for } every\ j,\ \mu_j(x) \notin R_j \\ \mu(x) & \text{if for } some\ j,\ \mu_j(x) \in R_j, \end{cases}$$

where $R_i, \ldots, R_n$ are given subsets of the real line.

Let $\tilde{R}$ be the set of states of nature x for which at least one of the values $\mu_j(x)$ is exceptional, that is,

$$(12.2) \qquad \tilde{R} \equiv \{x | \text{for some } j,\ \mu_j(x) \in R_j\}.$$

It is clear that, when the state of nature x is in $\tilde{R}$, then the team is in a situation of complete information, whereas when x is *not* in $\tilde{R}$, then the team is in a situation of complete decentralization facing a conditional distribution μ given that x is not in R. If $\mu_1, \ldots, \mu_n$ are independent, as we shall assume in this section, then they will also be conditionally independent given that $x \notin \tilde{R}$.

As before, it turns out that the important parameters of the exception sets R_i are

$$(12.3) \qquad p_i = \text{Prob}\{\mu_i(x) \in R_i\},$$

$$(12.4) \qquad s_i^2 = \text{Var}(\mu_i),$$

$$(12.5) \qquad s_{Oi} = \text{Var}[\mu_i | \mu_i(x) \notin R_i].$$

Indeed, we shall show that (assuming, as we can without loss of generality, that $E\mu = 0$) the value of the information structure (12.1) is

$$(12.6) \qquad V_8 = \sum_i q^{ii} s_i^2 - \sum_i \left[q^{ii} - \frac{1}{q_{ii}} \right] s_{Oi}^2 \, \text{Prob}\{x \notin \tilde{R}\},$$

where $((q^{ij})) = Q^{-1}$, and

$$(12.7) \qquad \text{Prob}\{x \notin \tilde{R}\} = \prod_i (1 - p_i).$$

It will also be shown that, given $p_i, \ldots, p_n$, the best choices of the sets R_i are the complements of intervals.

In particular, if

$$(12.8) \qquad \begin{cases} p_i = p, \\ s_i^2 = s, \qquad s_{Oi}^2 = s_O^2 \\ q_{ij} = \begin{cases} 1 & i = j \\ q & i \neq j, \end{cases} \end{cases}$$

then (12.6) reduces to

(12.9) $V_8 = s^2 f(n, q) - s_0^2 (1 - p)^n \{ f(n, q) - n \},$

where $f(n, q)$ is given by (5.17).

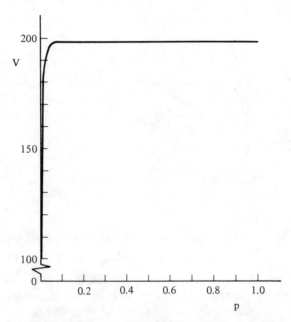

FIGURE 6.7. Emergency conference: V as a function of p for $q = 0.5$ and $n = 100$.

Figure 6.7 shows the value of emergency conference as a function of p, for $q = .5$ and $n = 100$, as given by (12.9). Note that the value rises extremely rapidly for small values of p, so that by the time p has reached .05, the increase in value over $p = 0$ is 97 percent of the total possible increase ($p = 1$). This is to be expected when n is fairly large, since it takes only one exception to convene the entire conference and bring about a state of complete information. The probability that one or more exceptions will occur is $1 - (1 - p)^n$.

Figure 6.8 shows V/n as a function of n (with n varying from 1 to 100), for $q = .5$, and $p = .01$ and .1. As n increases, for fixed (positive) p, the probability of a conference, that is, of at least one exception's occurring, converges rapidly to 1. With $p = .1$, by the time n has reached 40 one is practically in a situation of complete information.

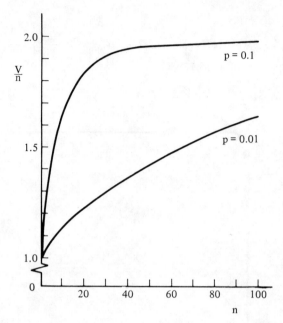

FIGURE 6.8. Emergency conference: V/n as a function of n for $q = 0.5$ and $p = 0.01, 0.1$.

The last remarks suggest looking at how V/n behaves as a function of n, when the probability of a conference is kept constant. Figures 6.9 and 6.10 show two such curves (for $q = .5$), the first with $1 - (1 - p)^n$ held constant at .99 and the second with $1 - (1 - p)^n$ held constant at .90. These figures reveal that, for any given value of the probability of a conference, there is a value of n that maximizes V/n. In other words, with the probability of a conference fixed, there are *decreasing returns to scale* after some point. This is in contrast with the corresponding case for reporting exceptions, as exemplified in Figure 6.5. Note that the decreasing returns to scale in the present case occur even though the average *size* of the conference $n[1 - (1 - p)^n]$ is increasing. If the average size of the conference were to be held constant, the tendency toward decreasing returns to scale would be more marked. This last situation is the one that is comparable to Figure 6.6.

BEST TEAM DECISION FUNCTIONS

Consider now the information structure of (12.1) with arbitrary sets $R_1, \ldots, R_n$, and assume that

(12.10) $\mu_i, \ldots, \mu_n$ independent,

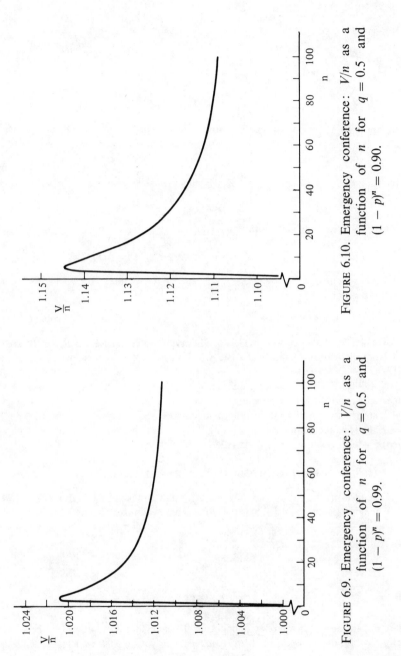

FIGURE 6.9. Emergency conference: V/n as a function of n for $q = 0.5$ and $(1 - p)^n = 0.99$.

FIGURE 6.10. Emergency conference: V/n as a function of n for $q = 0.5$ and $(1 - p)^n = 0.90$.

(12.11) $E(\mu_i) = 0, \text{Var}(\mu_i) = s_i{}^2.$

Define m^0 and a^0 by

(12.12) $m_i{}^0 = E\{\mu_i | \mu_i(x) \notin R_i\}.$

(12.13) $a^0 = Q^{-1}m^0.$

By applying Theorem 1, it can be shown that the best team decision function $\hat{a}$ is given by

(12.14) $\hat{a}_i(y_i) = \begin{cases} a_i{}^0 + \dfrac{\mu_i(x) - m_i{}^0}{q_{ii}} & \text{if } x \notin \tilde{R} \\[2ex] [Q^{-1}\mu(x)]_i & \text{if } x \in \tilde{R}. \end{cases}$

The proof is routine, and is omitted.

VALUE OF THE INFORMATION STRUCTURE

Again we consider the two cases $x \notin \tilde{R}$ and $x \in \tilde{R}$ separately, by writing the value of information as

(12.15) $V_8 = E[\omega(x, \alpha[y])] = E\{\omega | x \notin \tilde{R}\} \text{Prob}(x \notin \tilde{R}) + E\{\omega | x \in \tilde{R}\} \text{Prob}(x \in \tilde{R}).$

Because $\hat{a}$ satisfies condition (3.1) of Theorem 1 in each case ($x \notin \tilde{R}$, $x \in \tilde{R}$) separately, one can apply (3.4) to each case. After some calculation, this application yields (12.6).

Note that, since Q is positive definite, $q^{ii} \geq 1/q_{ii}$, so that the term in brackets on the right-hand side of (12.6) is nonnegative. The quantity $q^{ii}s_i{}^2$ is the value of *complete* information under the current assumptions.

In the special case described by (12.8), it follows easily from (5.4) that the value V_8 reduces to the expression given in (12.9).

BEST CHOICE OF THE EXCEPTION SETS

Given the probability of a conference, we find that the choice of the sets $R_i, \ldots, R_n$ that maximizes the value (12.6) is the choice that minimizes

(12.16) $\sum_i \left(q^{ii} - \dfrac{1}{q_{ii}} \right) s_{i0}{}^2$

subject to

(12.17) $\prod_i (1 - p_i) = \text{Prob}\{x \in \tilde{R}\}$

(the p_i and the $s_{0i}{}^2$ being related, of course. In particular, if we are given the values of $p_i, \ldots, p_n$, *the expression* (12.16) *is minimized by taking each set* R_i *to be the complement of some interval, symmetric around zero* (*the mean of* μ_i). This characteristic is therefore true of the best choice given only the value of $\text{Prob}\{x \notin \tilde{R}\}$.

In the case of symmetric sets R_i, one has $a^0 = m^0 = 0$, so that the best team decision function is given by

$$(12.18) \qquad \alpha_i(y_i) = \begin{cases} \dfrac{\mu_i(x)}{q_{ii}} & \text{if } x \notin \tilde{R} \\[2mm] [Q^{-1}\mu(x)]_i & \text{if } x \in \tilde{R}. \end{cases}$$

13. Comparisons Among the Several Information Structures

In this section, we shall present comparisons among the several information structures that have been considered in the previous sections. These comparisons will be made for the special case of cospecialization of action and observation, with identical interactions, and independent observations with identical variances.

The first set of comparisons is among the following four information structures: (1) partition into equal groups, (2) partition into groups with only one group having more than one member, (3) emergency conference, and (4) reports of exceptions. As will be seen, these four structures are comparable in the sense that structures (3) and (4) can be viewed as resulting from variable partitioning into groups, the particular partition used depending upon the information signals that are actually received by the team members. It will be seen that, if one compares structures of the above four types with the same average group size, then the above list is in the order of increasing value.

This result can be explained heuristically as follows. Under the assumptions described above, the "technology" of the team exhibits increasing returns to scale; that is, under complete information, value per person, V/n, increases as n increases (see Section 5). With independent observations, partition of the team is equivalent to substituting for the original team a collection of smaller teams, with the same total number of members. Because of the increasing returns to scale, if the number of groups is given, the best allocation of the members to the groups is achieved by assigning as many members as possible to one group, leaving the rest of the groups with one member each. This accounts for the greater value of (2) as against (1) in the above comparison.

The superiority of (3) and (4) over (1) and (2) is plausible, when one sees that structures (3) and (4) have something of the character of a two-stage sequential analysis. Additional information is brought to bear on decisions only under circumstances in which additional information is more than ordinarily helpful. In this respect, "reports of exceptions" is more selective than "emergency conference," since it brings the additional information to bear upon only those action variables that are associated with the unusual observations, rather than upon all the action variables. Indeed, it will be shown that for large values of n, "emergency conference" is approximately no better than fixed groups with only one group having more than one member.

The second comparison is between error in instruction (Section 9) and complete communication of erroneous observation (Section 10). It will be seen that, if one compares structures of the two types that have the same ratio of variance of error to variance of message, then error in observation is preferable to error in instruction. This is related to the fact that, under complete information with nonzero interaction, the optimal decision rules for the several members are correlated (Section 5). In the case of error in observation, the complete, error-free communication makes possible any desired degree of correlation between the decisions of different team members; whereas the error in instruction introduces a lack of correlation between the information on which different decisions must be based.

GENERAL REMARKS ON COMPARISONS OF INFORMATION STRUCTURES

Before going into the detailed comparisons of this section, some general remarks may be helpful. Ideally, one would want to compare information structures on the basis of net value of information, namely gross value of information minus the cost of both the information and the associated best decision function. Therefore, any comparison between the gross values of two information structures is meaningful only in the context of some assumption about the relative costs of the two structures. Although no explicit discussion of costs is presented here, certain assumptions are implicit in the comparisons made below. Thus, in the comparisons among information structures based upon fixed or variable partitions into groups, the implicit assumption is that costs depend upon the average group size. On the other hand, the comparison between error in instruction and error in observation is meaningful if the costs depend upon the ratio of the variance of the error to the variance of the message.

FIXED AND VARIABLE PARTITIONS

Consider now the case of cospecialization of action and observation, (4.3), together with the special assumptions of identical interactions, (4.4) and (4.5), and independent, normally distributed observations μ_i with identical variances. There is no further loss of generality in assuming that the μ_i all have means zero and variances one.

The two fixed-partition information structures to be considered are (1) partitions into equal groups, and (2) partitions such that at the most one group has more than one member. Under the above assumptions, the values for these two types of structure are given, respectively, by

(13.1) $$V_3 = \left(\frac{n}{M}\right) f(M, q),$$

(13.2) $$V'_3 = f(M, q) + (n - M),$$

[see (7.10) and (7.11)]; where in the first case M denotes the number of persons in each group, and in the second case M denotes the number of persons in the one group that can possibly have more than one member; and where the function $f(u, v)$, as in (5.17), is defined by

(13.3) $$f(u, v) = \frac{u[1 + (u - 2)v]}{[1 - v][1 + (u - 1)v]}.$$

The two variable-partition information structures to be considered are *emergency conference* (Section 12) and *reports of exceptions* (Section 11), with values given, respectively, by

(13.4) $$V_8 = f(n, q) - s_0^2(1 - p)^n[f(n, q) - n],$$

(13.5) $$V_7 = s_R^2 E f(M, q) + n(1 - p)s_0^2,$$

[see (12.9) and (11.31)]; where p is the probability that a value of an observation $\mu_i(x)$ is exceptional, s_0^2 is the conditional variance of μ_i given that it is not exceptional, s_R^2 is the conditional variance μ_i given that it is exceptional, and in (13.5) M has the binomial distribution $B(p, n)$. Recall that, as in (11.34),

(13.6) $$p s_R^2 + (1 - p)s_0^2 = 1,$$

and that s_R^2 and s_0^2 are determined by p [see (11.32) and (11.33)].

To compare the values of the above four types of information structure, we shall compare structures that, roughly speaking, have the same average group size. It will be more convenient, however, to consider explicitly, for any fixed n, the average number of groups associated with the information structure. Thus, for the case of partitions into equal groups of size M, the number of groups is

(13.7) $$G = \frac{n}{M},$$

whereas for the case of one large group, of size M, the number of groups is

(13.8) $G = n - M + 1$.

For the two variable-partition cases, the number of groups is a random variable. For emergency conference, the expected number of groups is

(13.9) $EG = n(1 - p)^n + 1 - (1 - p)^n$;

for reports of exceptions, the expected number of groups is

(13.10) $EG = n(1 - p) + p$.

Figure 6.11 shows value V as a function of G (or EG) for the above four types of information structure with $n = 100$ and $q = .5$. In the fixed partition cases, G is varied by varying M; in the variable partition cases EG is varied by varying p. As the figure shows, "reports of exceptions" gives the highest value (for G different from 1 or n); "emergency conference" gives a barely higher value than fixed groups with one of size M; and these two in turn give a higher value than fixed equal groups.

The relations among the above four types of information structure emerge quite clearly and simply for large values of n. Suppose that, as n increases without limit, the (average) number of groups increases proportionately, so that $G = \gamma n$ (or $EG = \gamma n$). It is easily verified, using (13.1) to (13.10), that the limits, as n increases without limit, of value per person, V/n, for the four types of information structure are

(13.11) $\lim \dfrac{V_3}{n} = \dfrac{1 - \gamma q}{1 - q} - \dfrac{\gamma(1 - \gamma)q}{\gamma + (1 - \gamma)q}$,

(13.12) $\lim \dfrac{V_3'}{n} = \lim \dfrac{V_8}{n} = \dfrac{1 - \gamma q}{1 - q}$,

(13.13) $\lim \dfrac{V_7}{n} = \dfrac{1 - \gamma q}{1 - q} + \dfrac{\gamma(1 - s_o^2)q}{1 - q}$.

In (13.13), the limit value s_o^2 corresponds to $p = 1 - \gamma$. It is clear that the above three limiting values are in order of increasing magnitude, except when $q = 0$, $\gamma = 0$, or $\gamma = 1$, in which case all three limiting values are equal.

COMMUNICATION ERRORS

Consider now the two information structures, *error in instruction* (Section 9) and *error in observation* (Section 10). The discussion will proceed under the same special assumptions of (1) cospecialization, (2)

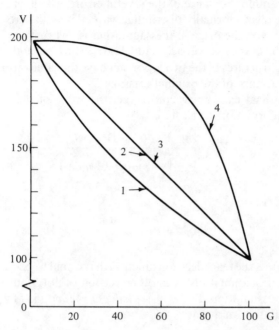

FIGURE 6.11. Comparisons among fixed and vari-
able partitions: V as a function of
fixed or average number of groups,
G.
Curve 1: Fixed groups, equal size.
Curve 2: Fixed groups, one of size M.
Curve 3: Emergency conference.
Curve 4: Reports of exceptions.

identical interactions, and (3) independent and normally distributed
observations μ_i with identical variances. However, in this case the variance
of μ_i will be denoted by s^2.

The two information structures of Sections 9 and 10 are comparable
in that they are both concerned with complete communication in which
errors are introduced. In the one case, however, the errors are introduced
at the points at which the processed observations, that is, the instructions,
are being communicated from the central agent to the team members;
whereas, in the second case, the errors are introduced before the processing
of information, that is, in the communication of observations to the
central agent. For the purpose of the comparison to be made here, let t^2

denote the common variance of the several errors, which will be assumed to be independent, normally distributed variables, with zero means, and uncorrelated with the original messages (that is, instructions or observations) to which they have been added. It seems natural to compare information structures of the two types that have the same ratio of variance of error to variance of the original message.

For the special case being considered, the value of the "error in instruction" information structure is

$$(13.14) \qquad V_5 = \frac{nw[1 + (n - 1)q(c/w)]^2}{1 + \left(\dfrac{t^2}{w}\right) + (n - 1)q(c/w)},$$

where

$$(13.15) \qquad E\beta_i\beta_j = \begin{cases} w & \text{if } i = j \\ c & \text{if } i \neq j, \end{cases}$$

and $\beta = Q^{-1}\mu$ is the team decision function that would be best for complete information. Equation 13.14 is another version of (9.12) but without the normalizing assumption that $w = 1$. Using (5.14) and (5.15) we can, after some computation, arrive at

$$(13.16) \qquad \frac{c}{w} = -\left(\frac{(n - 2)q^2 + 2q}{(n - 1)q^2 + [1 + (n - 2)q]^2}\right),$$

$$(13.17) \qquad w = s^2\left(\frac{(n - 1)q^2 + [1 + (n - 2)q]^2}{[1 - q]^2[1 + (n - 1)q]^2}\right).$$

From (13.14) to (13.17), it follows that

$$(13.18) \qquad \lim_{n \to \infty} \left(\frac{V_5}{n}\right) = \frac{s^2}{1 + r - q},$$

where

$$(13.19) \qquad r = \frac{t^2}{w}.$$

Note that r is the ratio of the variance of the error to the variance of signal to which the error is added.

The value of the "error in observation" information structure is, from (10.9),

$$(13.20) \qquad V_6 = \frac{ns^2[1 + (n - 2)q]}{[1 + (t^2/s^2)][1 - q][1 + (n - 1)q]},$$

$$(13.21) \qquad \lim_{n \to \infty} \left(\frac{V_6}{n} \right) = \frac{s^2}{(1 + r')(1 - q)},$$

where

$$(13.22) \qquad r' = \frac{t^2}{s^2}.$$

By comparing (13.18) and (13.21) we see that, if $r = r'$, then

$$(13.23) \qquad \lim_{n \to \infty} \left(\frac{V_5}{n} \right) \leq \lim_{n \to \infty} \left(\frac{V_6}{n} \right),$$

with strict inequality if r and q are strictly positive.

14. Interaction, Team Size, Returns to Scale

At various points in this chapter, we have considered how the value of a particular information structure varies as the number of team members increases. In particular, we have studied this question in the special case of *identical interaction*, which by appropriate choice of units can be expressed as

$$(14.1) \qquad q_{ij} = \begin{cases} 1 & i = j \\ q & i \neq j \end{cases}$$

[see (4.4) and (4.5)]. We assumed that as n, the number of team members, increased, the interaction coefficient, q, remained constant.

We shall argue below, by means of an example, that this last assumption (q constant as n increases) is plausible in some situations, but there may be others in which it is not. For example, there are probably many situations in which the average interaction decreases as the team size increases. A particular hypothesis of this type has been proposed by Selten,[4] namely, that the total interaction remains constant, which in this case translates into

$$(14.2) \qquad n(n - 1)q = k,$$

for some constant k independent of n. We shall call this the *constant total interaction* hypothesis, in contrast to the *constant individual interaction* hypothesis of constant q, and we shall see that the two hypotheses may have different implications for the way in which the value of a particular information structure varies with team size.

---

4. Private communication.

First we recall that, in order for the matrix (14.1) to be positive definite, it is necessary and sufficient that

(14.3) $$-\frac{1}{n-1} < q < 1.$$

Hence the constant individual interaction hypothesis can hold for all n only if q is nonnegative, that is, only if the *interaction coefficient*, $\partial^2 \omega / \partial a_i \partial a_j$ is zero or negative. If the constant total interaction hypothesis is to hold for all $n(\geq 2)$, then (14.3) implies that $|k| < 2$.

Consider now the case in which $\mu_1, \ldots, \mu_n$ are uncorrelated, which came up quite often in the previous sections, and let us first contrast how the value of complete information varies with team size under the two hypotheses. From (5.16), the value is

(14.4) $$V_1 = \bar{s}_n f(n, q)$$

where

$$f(n, q) \equiv \frac{n[1 + (n - 2)q]}{[1 - q][1 + (n - 1)q]}$$

and

$$\bar{s}_n = \frac{1}{n} \sum_{i=1}^{n} \text{Var}(\mu_i).$$

We shall suppose that, as n increases, the average variance, $\bar{s}_n$, approaches a limit, say $\bar{s}$. Under the constant *individual* interaction hypothesis, we saw that

$$\lim_{n \to \infty} \frac{V_1}{n} = \frac{\bar{s}}{1 - q},$$

with V_1/n increasing if $\bar{s}_n$ is constant and $q > 0$. We described this by saying that, in this case, returns to scale for complete information approach a constant as the size of the team gets large, and during this approach the returns to scale are *increasing* (although more and more slowly).

On the other hand, under the hypothesis of constant *total* interaction, we have, from (14.2) and (14.4),

$$\lim_{n \to \infty} \frac{V_1}{n} = \bar{s},$$

and it is straightforward to verify that V_1/n is decreasing as n increases. Thus, in the limit, returns to scale are also constant (although the limiting constant of proportionality is different) but returns to scale are *decreasing* during the approach to the limit.

Adopting the hypothesis of constant total interaction does not qualitatively change the conclusions of Sections 6 to 12 but it does alter the asymptotic comparisons of information structures made in Section 13. Indeed, under this hypothesis, the four "partition" information structures have the same asymptotic value, and the two "error" structures have the same asymptotic value. This is plausible if one notes that the coefficient

$$q = \frac{k}{n(n-1)}$$

is going to zero like $1/n^2$ as n increases, so that, for large n, the effect of interaction is essentially wiped out. (The specific calculations are left to the reader.)

We close this section with an example of a team decision problem in which the hypothesis of constant individual interaction is satisfied. This example is a modification of the sales force example of Chapter 5, Section 4 (Example 5A). Let the team consist of n salesmen, and let the demand function facing salesman i be

$$p_i = \gamma_i - ba_i,$$

where p_i is the price at which he can sell the quantity a_i. Suppose that the cost function for the team is

$$c_1\left(\sum_i a_i\right) + c_2\left(\sum_i a_i\right)^2.$$

Therefore, if salesman i sells the quantity $a_i, (i = 1, \ldots, n)$, then the net profit to the team will be

$$\sum_i (\gamma_i - c_1)a_i - \sum_i (b + c_2)a_i^2 - \sum_{\substack{i,j \\ i \neq j}} c_2 a_i a_j.$$

If $\gamma_1, \ldots, \gamma_n$ are random variables, and b, c_1, and c_2 are constants, then we have a special case of the quadratic payoff function (2.1), with

$$\mu_i \equiv \gamma_i - c_1$$

$$q_{ii} = b + c_2$$

$$q_{ij} = c_2 \qquad i \neq j.$$

If we assume that adding new salesmen (e.g., by adding new sales territories) does not alter b, c_1, or c_2, then we have a case of constant (identical) individual interaction.

CHAPTER 7

The Team in a Dynamic Environment

1.Introduction   2.The single-person problem with a quadratic payoff function
3.Single person, autoregressive environment, delayed information   4.Proper team,
autoregressive environment, delayed information   5.Periodic recovery of delayed
complete information   6.Substitution of timeliness for completeness

1. INTRODUCTION

TREATMENT OF TIME IN A TEAM DECISION PROBLEM

Thus far, our treatment of the team decision problem has been static,
not in the sense that consideration of time has been excluded by our formulation of the decision problem, but rather in the sense that the special
features of a decision problem associated with time have not been explicitly examined.

From a certain point of view, the introduction of time into a decision
problem requires no change in the formulation of Chapter 4. Decisions
about actions taken at different times are typically based on different
information. To express this, we may simply consider actions taken at
different times as corresponding to different team members. Thus, if
$a_i(t)$ denotes the action of person i at time $t(t = 1, \ldots, T)$, and if $x(t)$
denotes the state of the world at time t, then the team action variable for
the complete problem (with nT persons) is

(1.1) $$a = [a_1(1), \ldots, a_n(1), a_1(2), \ldots, a_n(T)],$$

and the state of the world for the complete problem is

(1.2) $$x = [x(1), \ldots, x(T)].$$

In particular, a "single-person sequential (dynamic) decision problem"
looked at in this way can be interpreted as a team decision problem. The
reason for singling out the time index for special treatment is that there is
usually associated with the time element some special feature of the structure of information, of the statistical properties of the state of the world,
or of the payoff function.

In what follows, we shall maintain explicit reference to time by retaining the notation in which $a_i(t)$ denotes the action of a person i at time t, and $y_i(t) = \eta_i(x, t)$ denotes the information on the basis of which action $a_i(t)$ is taken, according to a decision function $\alpha_i(\cdot, t)$, that is,

$$a_i(t) = \alpha_i[\eta_i(x, t), t].$$

(For brevity, we shall occasionally suppress the argument x and speak of the function $\eta_i(t)$.) Implicit in the everyday concept of time is the constraint that the information $y_i(t)$ can depend at most on the history of the world up through time t, that is, $[x(1), \ldots, x(t)]$.

Perhaps the most common feature of the structure of information in time is generated by the presence of *memory*. A sequence $\{\eta(\cdot, t)\}$ of (one-period) information structures will be said to have *memory* if, for each t, $\eta(\cdot, t + 1)$ *is as fine as* $\eta(\cdot, t)$. (See Chapter 2, Section 6.) However, memory is in general costly, and is therefore not a universal feature of dynamic decision problems. Indeed, the question of how much memory to provide for in any given situation (e.g., when to throw away files) is a special case of the general problem of choice of an information structure.

A typical feature of the statistical properties of the sequence of states $\{x(t)\}$ is the tendency of the statistical dependence between states at different times to become weaker, in some sense or other, as the difference in time increases. A consequence of this is that information about the distant past is less valuable than information about the recent past.[1]

An interesting class of stochastic processes $x(t)$ is the class of *Markov processes*, in which the conditional distribution of the *future*, $x(t + 1)$, $x(t + 2)$, and so forth, given the *present* and *past*, $x(t)$, $x(t - 1)$, and so forth, is a function of the present, $x(t)$, only. It should be pointed out, however, that if $z(t) = \zeta[x(t)]$ is a sequence of values of some function ζ on successive states $x(t)$, then even if $\{x(t)\}$ is a Markov process, the sequence $\{z(t)\}$ need not be a Markov process (and will typically not be). Hence, if each $z(t)$ is an observation on the corresponding state $x(t)$, then the fact that $\{x(t)\}$ is a Markov process does not imply that it is of no value to include past observations $z(s)$, $s < t$, in addition to the current observation $z(t)$, in the information upon which the decision $a(t)$ is to be made.

Turning to the influence of time in the payoff function, we note that the interaction between action variables at different times tends to be weaker the greater the difference in time. If this is the case, there will be less need for coordination of actions that are distant in time than of actions that are

---

1. This tendency toward weaker dependence need not be monotonic; if $x(t)$ is real-valued and one measures dependence by the correlation function $R(s, t)$, then for fixed t, $R(t, t + d)$ will typically approach 0 as d increases, but not necessarily monotonically.

close in time. In particular, if the payoff function is additive in time (i.e., if there is no interaction between actions at different times), the sequential decision problem can be dealt with as a succession of one-period problems, provided that there are no constraints linking actions at different times.

PAYOFF FUNCTIONS ADDITIVE IN TIME

For most of this chapter, we limit ourselves to the case in which there is no interaction between actions taken at different times. Our main interest in this case is to study *the team in a changing environment*. In other words, we wish to study a succession of team decision problems of the type discussed in Chapters 5 and 6, with the environment, and information about the environment, changing through time. In particular, we wish to study the effects of delays in the receipt and use of information, and the possibilities of substituting incomplete but slightly delayed information for more complete but more delayed information.

Consider a payoff function, with dated action vectors as in (1.1) but with no interaction through time,[2] that is,

$$(1.3) \qquad\qquad \omega(x, a) = \sum_{t=1}^{T} \omega_t[x, a(t)].$$

As above, let $\alpha(\,\cdot\,, t)$ denote the n-tuple $[\alpha_1(\,\cdot\,, t), \ldots, \alpha_n(\,\cdot\,, t)]$ of decision functions corresponding to time t; this may be called the *team decision function for time t*. Similarly, there is an information structure $\eta(\,\cdot\,, t) = [\eta_1(\,\cdot\,, t), \ldots, \eta_n(\,\cdot\,, t)]$ for the team at time t. If the payoff function is additive, as in (1.3), then it follows immediately that the best sequence of team decision functions, $\{\alpha(\,\cdot\,, t)\}$, is such that, for each t, $\hat{\alpha}(\,\cdot\,, t)$ is best for the "one-period" decision problem with payoff function ω_t and information structure $\eta(\,\cdot\,, t)$. This additive decomposition also applies to comparisons of the values of alternative information structures.

DELAY

Suppose that, at time t, the available information about the state of the world is some function of the states of the world up to and including the time $(t - \tau)$. We shall then say that the information has delay τ. The delay τ is a variable that depends (possibly) upon the team member, the time t, and the states of the world up to and including time t. In this and following sections, we shall elaborate on the concept of delay and on the circumstances under which it arises; we shall investigate the losses due to certain patterns of delay, under alternative simple assumptions about

2. See Koopmans 1960 for a discussion of preferences that can be represented in this form.

the stochastic process generating the state of the world; and we shall explore some problems of achieving the optimal balance between delay and incompleteness of information.

Formally, let $x(t)$ denote the state of the world at time t, and let $\bar{x}(t)$ denote the complete history of the states of the world up to and including time t. We shall say that an information structure exhibits *simple delay* if, for each i,

(1.4) $$\eta_i(x, t) = \tilde{\eta}_i[\bar{x}(t - \tau)],$$

where $\tilde{\eta}_i$ is a fixed function, for each i.

At first glance, (1.4) may appear to place little, if any, restriction on the information structure, but the fact that the function $\tilde{\eta}_i$ does not have time directly as an argument is indeed a restriction. For example, if the state of the world is described by two coordinates, and if information at time t always consists of the value of the first coordinate at time $(t - 1)$, then we have a case of simple delay. However, if we modify the information structure of the example by letting the information at every tenth period (say) consist of the values of *both* coordinates in the previous period, then we no longer satisfy condition (1.4). We shall primarily be concerned with examples of simple delay, with one important exception (Sections 5 and 6).

If we consider the case of simple delay, the amount of delay, τ, can in principle depend upon i, t, and $\bar{x}(t)$. If it is a periodic function of t, it is natural to describe it as *periodic delay*.

Delays are typically caused by the time necessary to perform the various aspects of information processing: observation, communication, and computation. Delays can also be caused indirectly whenever a team limits the frequency with which the actions are changed (because changing actions may in itself be costly). While the action is being held constant, the world is changing, so that there is effectively a delay between observation and action.

Delays can usually be reduced at the expense of increased costs. (As is usual with regard to costs, we have little empirical information on which to base reasonable theories.) On the other hand, delays can also often be reduced by contenting oneself with less complete information.

For example, information may consist of a sample of observations. By spending more time, a larger sample can be obtained. However, suppose that, until the sampling has stopped, a decision based only upon *a priori* information must be in effect. The improvement in the final decision because of increasing the sample size must be balanced against the loss that results from keeping the *a priori* decision (decision based on *a priori* information only) in force for a longer period.[3]

As a second example, communication and computation delay can be reduced by partitioning the team into groups (with little or no communication between groups), but with a resulting loss due to less complete information (see Section 6 of this chapter).

Computational delay can be reduced by not carrying certain computations to completion, at the expense of providing less accurate solutions to computational problems (see T. Marschak 1959 and 1968).

Delays may cause losses because, until the delayed action is taken, some other action (*a priori* action, or "inaction") is in force, as in the first example given above. Such losses will be experienced even if the payoff-relevant aspect of the environment is not changing during the interval of delay.

Delays may also cause losses because, during the interval of the delay, the payoff-relevant aspect of the environment is changing, and by the time the action is taken it is no longer appropriate. Since our main interest in this chapter is to study the team in a changing environment, we shall concentrate on this second type of loss.

The comparison of information structures developed in Chapter 2, Section 8, and in particular the concept of garbling, throws some light on the economic effect of message delays. Consider a single-person decision problem in time with the payoff function additive in time. Let Z_t be a payoff-adequate partition of the set X of states of nature for the payoff function ω_t. The event z_t in Z_t will, of course, depend at most on $\bar{x}_t$, the history of the world up to time t.

Suppose the decision-maker's information at time t consists in being informed of which event z_θ occurred at time $\theta(\theta \leq t)$, that is,

$$(1.5) \qquad\qquad \eta(x, t) = z_\theta.$$

Consider two alternative values of θ, say θ' and θ'', with $\theta' > \theta''$, and let

$$Y' = Z_{\theta'}, \; Y'' = Z_{\theta''}.$$

Y' is the partition of X corresponding to the information structure (1.5) for $\theta = \theta'$, and similarly for Y''.

We note in passing that, if $\theta' = t$, then Y' is complete information about the payoff relevant description of nature for the decision at time t; hence Y' is trivially at least as valuable as Y''. Are there more general conditions

---

3. By citing this example, we of course do not intend to imply that there are not also situations in which one can modify the decision as each observation in the sample is obtained. See Chapter 2, Sections 9 and 10; and Sections 3 and 4 of the present chapter.

for which the same conclusion is valid? We shall show that, *if the sequence* $\{z_t\}$ *is a Markov process, then* Y' *is at least as valuable as* Y''.

If the event sequence $\{z_t\}$ is a Markov process, then for any (finite or infinite) sequence of dates $t_1 > t_2 > t_3 \ldots$,

(1.6) $$\text{Prob}(z_{t_1}|z_{t_2}, z_{t_3}, \ldots) = \text{Prob}(z_{t_1}|z_{t_2}).$$

It follows from this Markov property that, for any z_t in Z_t, y' in Y', and y'' in Y'',

(1.7) $$\text{Prob}(z_t|y', y'') = \text{Prob}(z_t|y').$$

By (8.8) and (8.4) of Chapter 2, Section 8, this is equivalent to the *garbling* condition:

(1.8) $$\text{Prob}(y''|z_t, y') = \text{Prob}(y''|y')$$

Hence, by the corollary to the theorem of Chapter 2, Section 8, Y' is at least as valuable as Y''.

We might call Y' (and Y'') *delayed complete* information, since Y' gives complete information about the payoff-adequate description of X for the decision at some time $\theta \leq t$. We have just shown that, if $\{z_t\}$ is a Markov process, then increasing the delay of complete information decreases, or at least cannot increase, its value. This conclusion will in general no longer be valid if the information is not complete. For example, Y'', although more delayed than Y', might be sufficiently finer than Y' to make up for the greater delay. Nor will the conclusion be valid in general if $\{z_t\}$ is not a Markov process; for example, the statistical dependence between z_θ and z_t might be a periodic function of θ, for fixed t.

CHAPTER SUMMARY

The chapter consists of two parts: the first part is concerned with a single person in a dynamic environment (Sections 2 and 3), and the second part with a "proper team" in a dynamic environment. By a proper team, we mean one in which different actions at the same time are not all based on the same information.

The analysis in the whole chapter is restricted to the case of a quadratic payoff function; for the proper team we also assume that the payoff function is additive in time.

In Section 2, we derive the optimal decision rule for the single-person problem and apply it to prove the Simon-Theil theorem on certainty equivalents. This theorem states that the solution of a single-person, dynamic decision problem, with a quadratic payoff function, can be obtained by solving instead a sequence of decision problems, one for each time t, in which at each time t the random coefficients in the quadratic payoff function are replaced by the conditional expectation of those coefficients given the information at time t. This theorem is valid under the condition that the information structure has memory, in the sense defined above. The Simon–Theil theorem does not appear to be generalizable to the case of a proper team, even with a quadratic payoff function, nor to the case of a single person with a nonquadratic payoff function.

From Section 3 onward, we consider the case in which the random coefficients in the quadratic payoff function form a first-order linear autoregressive process in time. For the single person the results are well known from the theory of prediction and extrapolation. Two special cases call for special attention: the case in which the autoregressive process is stable, and the case of *Brownian motion*, in which the coefficients are formed by the successive addition of independent increments.

The contrast between the stable case and the nonstable case of Brownian motion is especially significant in the problems with incomplete information, and in particular for the proper team problem. In the case of stability, the coefficients tend to stay near a mean value, and the expected loss per unit time due to the incompleteness of the information approaches an upper bound as t increases. In the Brownian motion case, however, the expected loss per unit time depends upon the time. In the particular case in which the coefficients are normally distributed and the information functions are linear (we call this the *special* Brownian motion case), the expected loss per unit time because of the incompleteness of the information increases linearly as a function of time. In such a situation, it periodically becomes worthwhile to obtain complete information about the coefficients, possibly with some delay, whatever the cost of doing so (Section 5).

In Sections 3 and 4, we give special attention to the effect of delay on the value of information, and we exhibit a decomposition of the loss at any given time because of the use of delayed incomplete information into the loss due to the delay and the loss due to the incompleteness of the information.

Finally, we explore the situation in which the team's information can be made more complete only by increasing the delay with which the team members receive it, and we derive conditions for an optimal balance between timeliness and completeness of information. We apply these conditions to the problem of partitioning the team into equal groups (Chapter 6, Section 7), under the assumption that the larger the group size, the longer the delay in achieving complete exchange of information within the group. We find that, in the above case of stable coefficients, the optimal group size is independent of the size of the team; whereas, in the special Brownian motion case, the optimal group size increases with the size of the team but not at the same rate.

2. THE SINGLE-PERSON PROBLEM WITH A QUADRATIC PAYOFF FUNCTION

Consider a "single person" who must make decisions sequentially with respect to a (finite) sequence of action vectors $a(1), \ldots, a(T)$, the payoff function being

$$(2.1) \qquad \omega(x, a) = 2 \sum_{t=1}^{T} \mu(x, t)'a(t) - \sum_{s,t=1}^{T} a(s)'Q(s, t)a(t),$$

where for each x, s, and t, $\mu(x, t)$ is a vector and $Q(s, t)$ is a matrix. We assume that the square matrix made up of the blocks $Q(s, t)$ is positive definite. Suppose further that, at time t, the person's action $a(t)$ is to be based on the information $y(t) = \eta(x, t)$ according to some decision function $\alpha(\cdot, t)$, that is,

$$(2.2) \qquad a(t) = \alpha(y[t], t) = \alpha(\eta[x, t], t).$$

For a fixed information structure $\eta = [\eta(\cdot, 1), \ldots, \eta(\cdot, T)]$ the person is to choose the best sequence $\alpha(\cdot, 1), \ldots, \alpha(\cdot, T)$ of decision functions, that is, the decision functions that maximize the expected payoff.

As we noted in Section 1, this decision problem can from a formal point of view be regarded as a "team decision problem," with the person's decisions at different dates t corresponding to different members of the team.

It follows immediately, from Theorem 4 of Chapter 5, that the optimal decision functions $\tilde{\alpha}(\cdot, t)$ are determined (uniquely) by the following conditions:

$$(2.3) \sum_{t=1}^{T} Q(s, t)E[\alpha(\cdot, t)|\eta(\cdot, s)] = E[\mu(\cdot, s)|\eta(\cdot, s)] \qquad s = 1, \ldots, T.$$

This is the form taken by the "person-by-person satisfactoriness" condition in this case.

In the formulation of Chapter 5, each member of the team has a single numerical action variable. In the present case there is a vector-valued action variable, $a(t)$, for each member (i.e., each time). But the result of Chapter 5, Theorem 4, can easily be generalized to the case of vector-valued action variables by grouping together into a single vector all of the numerical action variables based on the same information.

MEMORY AND CERTAINTY-EQUIVALENTS IN THE
QUADRATIC CASE (THE SIMON–THEIL THEOREM)

Suppose that the decision-maker's information structure η has *memory* in the sense defined in Section 1; that is, if $s \leq t$, then $\eta(\,\cdot\,, t)$ is at least as fine as $\eta(\,\cdot\,, s)$. We shall show that there is a second decision problem associated with the original one such that:

(2.4a) The payoff function is the same, except that in (2.1) each function $\mu(\,\cdot\,, t)$ is replaced by some function $\tilde{\mu}(\,\cdot\,, t)$ of the *initial information variable*, $y(1) = \eta(x, 1)$;

(2.4b) The optimal decision function at time 1, say $\alpha(\,\cdot\,, 1)$, for the new problem is the same as that for the original problem.

The function $\tilde{\mu}(\,\cdot\,, t)$ that replaces $\mu(\,\cdot\,, t)$ is accordance with (2.4a) is called the "certainty-equivalent" of $\mu(\,\cdot\,, t)$. *We shall show that the certainty-equivalent of $\mu(\,\cdot\,, t)$ can be taken to be* $E[\mu(\,\cdot\,, t)|y(1)]$. This property of the quadratic payoff function was originally stated by Simon (1956) and Theil (1957).

It should be emphasized that the optimal decision functions, $\tilde{\alpha}(\,\cdot\,, t)$, for $t = 2, \ldots, T$, will typically not be the same as the optimal decision functions for $t = 2, \ldots, T$ in the original problem [say $\hat{\alpha}(\,\cdot\,, t)$]. The former are sometimes called the *planned decisions*. These plans must typically be revised when new information becomes available, as follows.

At time $t = 1$, the decision-maker knows $y(1) = \eta(x, 1)$; he therefore knows $\tilde{\mu}[y(1), 1], \ldots, \tilde{\mu}[y(1), T]$ and can solve the second problem to obtain the decisions $\tilde{\alpha}(t) \equiv \tilde{\alpha}[y(1), t], t = 1, \ldots, T$ (hence the term *certainty-equivalent*, since at time 1 he knows (is certain of) all the parameters of the second problem). Since (as we shall show), $\tilde{\alpha}(\,\cdot\,, 1) = \hat{\alpha}(\,\cdot\,, 1)$, the best decision at time 1 is $\tilde{\alpha}(1)$.

Fixing $a(1) = \tilde{\alpha}(1)$ in the payoff function (2.1) determines a new quadratic function in the action variables $a(2), \ldots, a(T)$. A *new* certainty-equivalent problem can then be formulated at *time* 2, leading to the determination of the best action at time 2, and so forth.

Finally, one can show that the planned decisions at time 1 are the mathematical expectations of the optimal decisions given the information at time 1, that is,

(2.5) $\tilde{\alpha}[y(1), t] = E\{\hat{\alpha}[y(t), t]|y(1)\}$ $t = 2, \ldots, T.$

The importance of the certainty-equivalence theorem is that it enables the decision-maker to substitute for the problem of determining T decision *functions*, $\hat{\alpha}(\,\cdot\,, 1), \ldots, \hat{\alpha}(\,\cdot\,, T)$, the problem of determining T

decisions, $a(1), \ldots, a(T)$. Thus it is not necessary to determine the best decision at a time t for any value of the information signal $y(t)$ except the one actually observed. On the other hand, to obtain the best decision at time 1 requires solving a problem with T variables $(\tilde{a}(1), \ldots, \tilde{a}(T))$; to obtain the best decision at time 2 requires solving a problem with $(T - 1)$ variables, and so forth.

For example, if the decision-maker observes at each time t a variable that can take on one of K values, and he remembers all past observations, then his information signal, $y(t)$, at time t can in principle take on one of K^t different values. Suppose that his action variable at each time t is one-dimensional; then his decision function $\alpha(\,\cdot\,, t)$ at time t can effectively be represented by a vector with K^t coordinates, and his sequence $[\alpha(\,\cdot\,, 1), \ldots, \alpha(\,\cdot\,, T)]$ of decision functions by a vector of

$$(2.6) \qquad \sum_{t=1}^{T} K^t = \frac{K(K^{T-1} - 1)}{K - 1}$$

coordinates. On the other hand, there are T variables $\tilde{a}(1), \ldots, \tilde{a}(T)$ in the certainty-equivalent problem at time 1, $(T - 1)$ variables in the certainty-equivalent problem at time 2, and so forth; all in all there are

$$(2.7) \qquad \sum_{t=1}^{T} (T - t + 1) = \frac{T(T + 1)}{2}$$

variables in all the certainty-equivalent problems taken together. Note that, asymptotically, (2.6) increases like K^{T-1}, whereas (2.7) only increases like T^2.

Unfortunately, it does not appear that the certainty-equivalence theorem generalizes in any convenient way to the case of a proper team, nor to nonquadratic payoff functions.

To prove the certainty-equivalence theorem, take the conditional expectation of condition (2.3), which determines the optimal decision functions, given $\eta(\,\cdot\,, 1)$. This gives

$$\sum_t Q(s, t) E\{E[\hat{a}(\,\cdot\,, t)|\eta(\,\cdot\,, s)]|\eta(\,\cdot\,, 1)\} = E\{E[\mu(\,\cdot\,, s)|\eta(\,\cdot\,, x)]|\eta(\,\cdot\,, 1)\} \qquad s = 1, \ldots, T.$$

(2.8)

Since $\eta(\,\cdot\,, s)$ is as fine as $\eta(\,\cdot\,, 1)$, for each s, it follows from the theorem on iterated expectations that, for any function f on X,

$$E\{E[f|\eta(\,\cdot\,, s)]|\eta(\,\cdot\,, 1)\} = E[f|\eta(\,\cdot\,, 1)].$$

In particular,

$$E\{E[\hat{a}(\,\cdot\,, t)|\eta(\,\cdot\,, s)]|\eta(\,\cdot\,, 1)\} = E[\hat{a}(\,\cdot\,, t)|\eta(\,\cdot\,, 1)],$$

$$E\{E[\mu(\,\cdot\,, s)|\eta(\,\cdot\,, s)]|\eta(\,\cdot\,, 1)\} = E[\mu(\,\cdot\,, s)|\eta(\,\cdot\,, 1)].$$

Substituting these into (2.8), we obtain

(2.9) $\sum_t Q(s, t)E[\hat{\alpha}(\cdot, t)|\eta(\cdot, 1)] = E[\mu(\cdot, s)|\eta(\cdot, 1)]$ $s = 1, \ldots, T.$

Define

(2.10)
$$\tilde{\alpha}(\cdot, t) \equiv E[\hat{\alpha}(\cdot, t)|\eta(\cdot, 1)]$$
$$\tilde{\mu}(\cdot, t) \equiv E[\mu(\cdot, t)|\eta(\cdot, 1)];$$

then (2.9) becomes

(2.11) $\sum_t Q(s, t)\tilde{\alpha}(\cdot, t) = \tilde{\mu}(\cdot, s)$ $s = 1, \ldots, T.$

But this is the condition that determines the optimal decision functions in a problem with payoff function

$$\tilde{\omega}(x, a) = 2 \sum_t \tilde{\mu}(x, t)'a(t) - \sum_{s,t} a(s)'Q(s, t)a(t),$$

and in which all decisions are based on complete information about $\tilde{\mu}(\cdot, 1), \ldots,$ $\tilde{\mu}(\cdot, T)$; see Chapter 6, Section 5. Note, however, that from (2.10)

$$\tilde{\alpha}(\cdot, 1) = E[\hat{\alpha}(\cdot, 1)|\eta(\cdot, 1) = \hat{\alpha}(\cdot, 1),$$

so that $\tilde{\alpha}(\cdot, 1)$ is the optimal decision function *at time* 1 for the original problem.

Note that, in the proof, we only used the fact that $\eta(\cdot, t)$ is as fine as $\eta(\cdot, 1)$ for all t. However, to continue the process at time 2, we would need that $\eta(\cdot, t)$ is as fine as $\eta(\cdot, 2)$ for all $t \geq 2$, and so forth.

3. Single Person, Autoregressive Environment, Delayed Information

INTRODUCTION

Although our primary interest is in the team, it may be helpful to continue our review of single-person problems. We shall study some results on the effects of delayed information in a succession of single-person decision problems. These results are well known from the theory of prediction and extrapolation. We shall take up in turn the following cases:

1. Delayed complete information, with a one-dimensional action variable.
2. Delayed incomplete information, with a multidimensional action variable.

In both cases, we shall assume that the quadratic payoff function is additive in time, as in (1.3), and indeed with the matrix $Q(t, t)$ of interaction coefficients constant in time. The coefficients $\mu(x, t)$, on the other hand, will be assumed to form a linear first-order autoregressive process (this concept will be explained below). In particular, we shall consider two special cases: (1) the case in which the process is stable; (2) the case of Brownian motion, in which the $\mu(x, t)$ are formed by the successive addition of independent increments.

As we shall see, the distinction between the stable case and that of Brownian motion is especially significant in the problems with incomplete information. In the case of stability, the coefficients $\mu(x, t)$ tend to stay near a "normal," or mean, value, and the conditional variance of $\mu(x, t)$, given the initial value $\mu(x, 0)$, approaches an upper bound as t increases. Therefore the expected loss per unit time due to the incompleteness of the information also approaches an upper bound as t increases.

In the Brownian motion case, on the other hand, the variance of $\mu(x, t)$ increases linearly in t, and therefore the expected loss per unit time due to the incompleteness of the information also increases linearly in t. A consequence of this is that it periodically becomes worthwhile to obtain complete information about $\mu(x, t)$, possibly with some delay. This aspect of the problem is further explored in Section 5.

ONE-DIMENSIONAL ACTION VARIABLE

Consider now a single-person decision problem, with a one-dimensional action variable $a(t)$ in each period $t = 0, 1, \ldots, T$, and with a quadratic payoff function that is additive in time [see 1.3)] such that

$$(3.1) \qquad \omega_t[x, a(t)] = 2\mu(x, t)a(t) - q[a(t)]^2 \qquad q > 0.$$

We shall assume that the coefficients $\mu(x, t)$, which we shall abbreviate as $\mu(t)$, form a first-order linear autoregressive process, that is to say,

$$(3.2) \qquad \mu(t) = w\mu(t - 1) + \varepsilon(t),$$

where w is a constant (the autoregression coefficient), where the $\varepsilon(t)$ are independent and identically distributed, and $\varepsilon(t)$ is independent of $\mu(t - 1), \mu(t - 2), \ldots$, and so forth. Let the variance of $\varepsilon(t)$ be denoted by v. There is no essential loss of generality in assuming that the $\mu(t)$ and $\varepsilon(t)$ have zero means. Thus

$$(3.3) \qquad E\mu(t) = E\varepsilon(t) = 0 \qquad \mathrm{Var}\ \varepsilon(t) = v.$$

For this process, the state of the environment, x, could be taken to be the infinite sequence, $[\mu(0), \varepsilon(1), \varepsilon(2), \ldots]$.

PROPERTIES OF THE FIRST-ORDER LINEAR
AUTOREGRESSIVE PROCESS

We first give a short summary of the properties of the $\mu(t)$ process. We shall typically think of time as starting at $t = 0$; the solution of (3.2) for $\mu(t)$ in terms of $\mu(0)$ and $\varepsilon(1), \ldots, \varepsilon(t)$ is

$$\mu(1) = w\mu(0) + \varepsilon(1),$$

$$\mu(2) = w^2\mu(0) + \varepsilon(2) + w\varepsilon(1), \text{ etc.}$$

(3.4)

$$\mu(t) = w^t\mu(0) + \sum_{m=0}^{t-1} w^m\varepsilon(t - m).$$

From (3.3) and (3.4) one easily obtains the variances

(3.5) $$\operatorname{Var} \mu(t) = w^{2t} \operatorname{Var} \mu(0) + \sigma_t^2,$$

where

(3.6) $$\sigma_k^2 \equiv v \sum_{m=0}^{k-1} w^{2m}.$$

More generally, $\mu(t)$ is related to $\mu(s)$ by

(3.7) $$\mu(t) = w^{t-s}\mu(s) + \sum_{m=0}^{t-s-1} w^m\varepsilon(t - m) \qquad s \leqq t.$$

One can easily show from (3.7) that the conditional mean and variance of $\mu(t)$ given $\mu(s)$ are

$$E[\mu(t)|\mu(s)] = w^{t-s}\mu(s),$$

(3.8)

$$\operatorname{Var}[\mu(t)|\mu(s)] = \sigma_{t-s}^2.$$

One can classify the members of this family of processes according to the value of the autoregression coefficient w.

If $w = 0$, then the successive $\mu(t)$ are *independent and identically distributed*.

More generally, if $|w| < 1$, then as t gets large the *distribution* of $\mu(t)$ approaches that of the random variable

(3.9) $$\sum_{m=0}^{\infty} w^m\bar{\varepsilon}(m),$$

where the $\bar{\varepsilon}(m)$ are independent and identically distributed with the same distribution as the $\varepsilon(t)$; the limiting variance of $\mu(t)$ is, from (3.5),

$$(3.10) \qquad\qquad \bar{v} \equiv \frac{v}{1 - w^2}.$$

Thus, in this case, the process tends toward a statistical equilibrium or "steady state." We shall call this the *stable case*. In particular, if $\mu(0)$ already has the same distribution as (3.9), then the process is *stationary*, and all of the $\mu(t)$ are identically distributed, with variance $\bar{v}$, as in (3.10).

If $w = 1$, then $\mu(t)$ equals $\mu(0)$ plus a sum of independent and identically distributed random variables. In particular, if $\mu(0) \equiv 0$, then we shall call this the case of *Brownian motion*:

$$(3.11) \qquad\qquad \mu(t) = \sum_{m=1}^{t} \varepsilon(m).$$

The variance of $\mu(t)$ increases linearly with t, thus:

$$(3.12) \qquad\qquad \text{Var } \mu(t) = tv.$$

If $w = -1$, the process is similar to Brownian motion but with an oscillation. If $|w| > 1$, then the process is *explosive* in the sense that the variance increases geometrically with time. In what follows, we shall restrict our attention to the cases $|w| < 1$ and $w = 1$.

A stochastic process $\{x(t)\}$ is said to be *stationary* if the joint distribution of any finite number of the variables is invariant under a translation of the time index t, that is, for any $t_1, \ldots, t_n$ and any t, the joint distribution of $x(t_1 + t), \ldots, x(t_n + t)$ is the same as the joint distribution of $x(t_1), \ldots, x(t_n)$. If we extend the sequence of independent and identically distributed random variables $\varepsilon(t)$ backward indefinitely, and rewrite (3.4) with an arbitrary starting time t_0, we get, from (3.7),

$$\mu(t) = w^{t-t_0}\mu(t_0) + \sum_{m=0}^{t-t_0-1} w^m \varepsilon(t - m) \qquad t_0 \leq t.$$

If $|w| < 1$, then as t_0 tends toward $-\infty$ with t fixed, $\mu(t)$ converges to

$$\bar{\mu}(t) = \sum_{m=0}^{\infty} w^m \varepsilon(t - m)$$

almost surely (use Theorem D, Section 46, of Halmos 1950), and it can be verified that the process $\{\bar{\mu}(t)\}$ is stationary. Note that every $\bar{\mu}(t)$ has the same distribution as does the random variable (3.9). If $\mu(0)$ already has this same distribution, then it is clear that the $\{\mu(t)\}$ process will be stationary.

We have called the case in which $|w| < 1$, *stable*, since the corresponding non-stochastic difference equation is stable in this case (see Robinson 1959, p. 106);

however, there appears to be no standard terminology for this case. In the auto-regressive process that we are considering, stability is a necessary, but not sufficient, condition for the process to be stationary.

The term *Brownian motion* is usually applied to the continuous time process in which successive increments are independent and normally distributed. Here, on the other hand, time is discrete and we do not assume normality.

VALUE AND LOSS WITH DELAYED INFORMATION

Suppose that the action at time t is chosen on the basis of information about the μ-process that is delayed d periods; to be precise,

$$(3.13) \qquad \eta(x, t) = \mu(t - d) \qquad d \geq 0.$$

It is an easy consequence of the principle of maximizing conditional expectation in the quadratic case [see Chapter 2, Section 5, or (5.5) of Chapter 6] that the best decision function for period t is proportional to the conditional expectation of $\mu(t)$ given $\mu(t - d)$, namely,

$$(3.14) \qquad \alpha[\mu(t - d), t] = \left(\frac{1}{q}\right) w^d \mu(t - d).$$

[Recall that the payoff function is given by (3.1).] The expected payoff in period t, using the best decision function, is [see (5.11) of Chapter 6]

$$(3.15) \qquad (1/q) w^{2d} \, \mathrm{Var}[\mu(t - d)].$$

Since the maximum expected payoff with no information at all is zero, (3.15) also gives the *value* of the delayed information,

$$(3.16) \qquad V_t(d) = (1/q) w^{2d} \, \mathrm{Var}[\mu(t - d)].$$

The expected payoff in this expression is shown as depending on the delay d of the information. In particular, for zero delay, the value is

$$(3.17) \qquad V_t(0) = (1/q) \, \mathrm{Var}[\mu(t)].$$

This is the maximum possible value, that is, the value of complete information (see Chapter 6, Section 5).

Expression (3.16) for the value of delayed information can be rewritten

$$(3.18) \qquad V_t(d) = w^{2d} V_{t-d}(0),$$

or alternatively,

$$\frac{V_t(d)}{V_t(0)} = w^{2d} \frac{\mathrm{Var}[\mu(t - d)]}{\mathrm{Var}[\mu(t)]}.$$

The expected *loss* due to delay is easily calculated to be [subtracting $V_t(d)$ from $V_t(0)$]:

$$(3.20) \qquad\qquad L_t(d) = \frac{\sigma_d{}^2}{q}$$

[use (3.16), (3.17), (3.5), and (3.6)]. *Notice that the loss at date t because of using delayed information depends on the delay but not on t.*

TABLE 7.1   VALUE AND LOSS FOR DELAYED INFORMATION, AS A FUNCTION OF THE DELAY (d) AND THE TIME (t): ONE-DIMENSIONAL CASE

Type of $\mu(t)$ process	Value $V_t(d)$	Loss $L_t(d)$	Limit of loss as $d \to \infty$
Independent	$\dfrac{v}{q}$ if $d = 0$ 0 if $d \geq 1$	0 if $d = 0$ $\dfrac{v}{q}$ if $d \geq 1$	$\dfrac{v}{q}$
Stable case	$\dfrac{1}{q}[w^{2t}\, \mathrm{Var}\, \mu(0) + w^{2d}\sigma^2_{t-d}]$	$\dfrac{v(1 - w^{2d})}{q(1 - w^2)}$	$\dfrac{v}{q(1 - w^2)}$
Brownian motion	$\dfrac{(t - d)v}{q}$	$\dfrac{dv}{q}$	∞

Table 7.1 gives the value and loss as a function of delay for the three cases of independence, stability, and Brownian motion. In the case of independence, any positive delay is as bad as no information at all. In the stable case (which of course includes independence as a special case), the loss increases toward a limit, $v/q(1 - w^2)$, as the delay, d, increases. In Brownian motion, on the other hand, the loss is proportional to the delay. As we shall show, this important distinction between the stable and the Brownian motion cases carries over to the proper team.

MULTIDIMENSIONAL ACTION VARIABLE AND μ-PROCESS; DELAYED INCOMPLETE INFORMATION

If the problem just considered is generalized to the extent that the action variable is a real vector, the results are somewhat more complicated but qualitatively similar. In particular, the stable case still has the feature that the loss due to delay remains bounded as the delay increases without limit, while in the Brownian motion case the loss depends on the delay.

If the μ-process is also vector-valued, as in the quadratic payoff function (2.1), then one is naturally led to consider the situation in which decisions are based upon information that is not only *delayed* but *incomplete*, in the sense that, even if it were undelayed, the information in question would still be incomplete. We retain for the time being, however, the assumption that all decisions in any given time period are based upon the same information. We shall calculate the best decision functions and the expected payoff, and identify the separate losses due to delay and incompleteness of the information.

Suppose that the one-period payoff function is

$$(3.21) \qquad \omega_t[x, a(t)] = 2\mu(t)'a(t) - a(t)'Qa(t),$$

where $a(t)$ is the n-dimensional action variable, $\mu(t)$ is a random vector, and Q is a fixed positive definite matrix. The coefficient vector $\mu(t)$ is assumed to be determined by a linear first-order autoregressive process,

$$(3.22) \qquad \mu(t) = w\mu(t-1) + \varepsilon(t),$$

where w is a scalar constant,[4] the vectors $\varepsilon(t)$ are independent and identically distributed, and $\varepsilon(t)$ is independent of $\mu(t-1), \mu(t-2), \ldots$, and so forth. There is no essential loss of generality in further assuming that the $\mu(t)$ and $\varepsilon(t)$ have zero means. The matrix of variances and covariances of the coordinates of $\varepsilon(t)$ will be denoted by v. Thus

$$(3.23) \qquad E\mu(t) = E\varepsilon(t) = 0 \qquad \mathrm{Var}\ \varepsilon(t) = v.$$

Under these assumptions, (3.4) to (3.8) also describe the properties of the vector-valued, μ-process, and the classification of cases (independent, stable, Brownian motion, etc.) applies as well. The symbol $\mathrm{Var}\ \mu(t)$ must be interpreted as the matrix of variances and covariances of the vector $\mu(t)$.

Let the information structure at time t be

$$(3.24) \qquad \eta(x, t) = \tilde{\eta}[\mu(t-d)],$$

where $\tilde{\eta}$ is a fixed function and d is the delay. We may interpret

$$(3.25) \qquad z(s) \equiv \tilde{\eta}[\mu(s)]$$

as an observation, possibly incomplete, of the μ-process at time s. This

4. The more general case in which w is a matrix will be treated in the fine print at the end of this section. However, the case in which w is a scalar already exhibits the influences of delay and incompleteness of information that we want to illustrate, but with a minimum of complication.

observation is available to the decision-maker, however, only with a delay d (see Section 1), so that the action at time t is based on the information

(3.26) $y(t) \equiv z(t - d)$.

It is important to distinguish at this point between information about $\mu(t - d)$ and information about the *entire path* of the μ-process up to and including the time $(t - d)$. We shall be analyzing the former situation; the latter situation involves finer information structure and hence larger value. It might be thought that, since $\mu(t)$ is a Markov process, information about $\mu(s)$ along the entire path leading up to the period $(t - d)$ is no more helpful than information about $\mu(t - d)$ alone. But even if $\mu(t)$ is a Markov process, the process $z(t)$ may not be, as was mentioned in Section 1. Thus knowledge of the path $z(s)$, $s \leq t - d$, leading up to time $(t - d)$ will in general lead to a higher expected payoff than knowledge of $z(t - d)$ alone.

One might say that we are going to deal with an information structure that exhibits both delay and lack of memory. In certain special cases, however, the observation process $z(t)$ *will* have the Markov property, in which case lack of memory will not result in any loss.

Let $\tilde{\mu}(s)$ denote the regression of $\mu(s)$ on $z(s)$, that is,

(3.27) $\tilde{\mu}(s) = E[\mu(s)|z(s)]$.

We shall show that the best decision function at time t based on the observation $z(t - d)$ is

(3.28) $\alpha[y(t), t] = w^d Q^{-1} \tilde{\mu}(t - d)$

and that the value of this information structure is

(3.29) $V_t(d) = w^{2d} \operatorname{trace}\{Q^{-1} \operatorname{Var} \tilde{\mu}(t - d)\}$.

We shall also show that the loss $L_t(d)$ due to the delay and incompleteness of the information can be expressed as

(3.30) $L_t(d) = [\text{loss due to using } complete \text{ information with}$

delay d at time $t]$

$+ w^{2d} \cdot [\text{loss due to using } undelayed\ incomplete$

information at time $(t - d)]$.

Let $\delta(s)$ denote the "residual" in the regression of $\mu(s)$ on $z(s)$, that is

(3.31) $\delta(s) \equiv \mu(s) - \tilde{\mu}(s)$.

It is well known from regression theory that

(3.32) $\text{Var } \mu(s) = \text{Var } \tilde{\mu}(s) + \text{Var } \delta(s).$

[The terms $\text{Var } \tilde{\mu}(s)$ and $\text{Var } \delta(s)$ are sometimes called the *explained* and *unexplained* variances, respectively.] We shall show below that the exact expression for the loss $L_t(d)$ corresponding to (3.30) is

(3.33) $L_t(d) = \left(\sum_{m=0}^{d-1} w^{2m} \right) \text{trace } Q^{-1}v + w^{2d} \text{trace } Q^{-1} \text{Var } \delta(t-d).$

Table 7.2 gives the value and loss for the special cases of a *stationary* μ-process ($|w| < 1$) and *Brownian motion* ($w = 1$). We see again that, as the delay gets large, the loss approaches an upper bound in the stationary case; whereas it is unbounded in the Brownian motion case.

We see also that the loss is again independent of t in the stationary case, whereas in the Brownian motion case *the loss depends on t if the observation $z(t)$ is not complete* (i.e., if the variance of the residual $\delta(t)$ is not zero). In the Brownian motion case, the loss $L_t(d)$ depends on t through $\text{Var } \delta(t-d)$. There does not appear to be any simple general statement about how $\text{Var } \delta(t-d)$ depends on t for arbitrary $\tilde{\eta}$ and distribution of $\varepsilon(t)$. However, an interesting special case is the one in which $\tilde{\eta}$ is linear and the $\varepsilon(t)$ are normally distributed. In this case it can be shown (see below) that, for fixed d, $\text{Var } \delta(t-d)$ *increases linearly as a function of t*, and therefore so does $L_t(d)$. Indeed it can be shown that in this special case

(3.34) $L_t(d) = d \text{ trace } Q^{-1}v + (t-d) \text{ trace } Q^{-1} \text{Var } \delta(1).$

This case in which the $\varepsilon(t)$ are normally distributed and $\tilde{\eta}$ is linear will be called here the *special Brownian motion case*.

We now derive the best decision functions and the formulas for value and loss in the case of delayed incomplete information. We do this for the general first-order autoregressive process

(3.35) $\mu(t) = W\mu(t-1) + \varepsilon(t),$

where all the assumptions of (3.22) and (3.23) are made, with the exception that W is assumed to be a nonsingular matrix [rather than just a scalar as in (3.22)].

The relevant properties of the process (3.35) are similar to (3.4) to (3.8); however, with the interpretation of the variance as a matrix and a more general definition of $\sigma_t{}^2$. Thus

(3.36) $\mu(t) = W^{t-s}\mu(s) + \sum_{m=0}^{t-s-1} W^m \varepsilon(t-m),$

(3.37) $\text{Var } \mu(t) = W^t \text{Var}[\mu(0)](W')^t + S_t,$

TABLE 7.2 VALUE AND LOSS FOR DELAYED INCOMPLETE INFORMATION AS A FUNCTION OF THE DELAY (d) AND THE TIME (t): MULTI-DIMENSIONAL CASE

Type of μ-process	Value $V_t(d)$	Loss $L_t(d)$
General	$w^{2d} \text{trace}\{Q^{-1} \text{Var } \tilde{\mu}(t-d)\}$ or $V_t(d) = w^{2d}V_t(0)$	$\left(\dfrac{1-w^{2d}}{1-w^2}\right) \text{trace } Q^{-1}v + w^{2d} \text{trace}\{Q^{-1} \text{Var } \delta(t-d)\}$
Stationary case	$w^{2d} \text{trace}\{Q^{-1} \text{Var } \tilde{\mu}\}$ or $V_t(d) = V(d) = w^{2d}V(0)$	$\left(\dfrac{1-w^{2d}}{1-w^2}\right) \text{trace } Q^{-1}v + w^{2d} \text{trace}\{Q^{-1} \text{Var } \delta\}$
Brownian motion	$\text{trace}\{Q^{-1} \text{Var } \tilde{\mu}(t-d)\}$	$d \text{ trace } Q^{-1}v + \text{trace}\{Q^{-1} \text{Var } \delta(t-d)\}$
Brownian motion with linear $\bar{\eta}$ and Gaussian $\varepsilon(t)$	$(t-d) \text{trace}\{Q^{-1} \text{Var } \tilde{\mu}(1)\}$ or $V_t(d) = (t-d)V_1(0)$	$d \text{ trace } Q^{-1}v + (t-d) \text{trace } [Q^{-1} \text{Var } \delta(1)]$

(3.38)
$$S_k \equiv \sum_{m=0}^{k-1} W^m v(W')^m,$$

(3.39a)
$$E[\mu(t)|\mu(s)] = W^{t-s}\mu(s) \qquad s \leq t,$$

(3.39b)
$$\mathrm{Var}[\mu(t)|\mu(s)] = S_{t-s} \qquad s \leq t.$$

To obtain the best decision functions, we apply (5.5) of Chapter 6:

$$\hat{\alpha}[z(t-d), t] = Q^{-1}E[\mu(t)|z(t-d)].$$

Since $\mu(t-d)$ is at least as fine as $z(t-d)$, it follows from (6.8) of Chapter 2 that

(3.40)
$$\begin{aligned} E[\mu(t)|z(t-d)] &= E\{E[\mu(t)|\mu(t-d)]|z(t-d)\} \\ &= E[W^d\mu(t-d)|z(t-d)] \\ &= W^d E[\mu(t-d)|z(t-d)]. \end{aligned}$$

Define

(3.41)
$$\tilde{\mu}(s) = E[\mu(s)|z(s)];$$

then we have shown that the best decision function is

(3.42)
$$\hat{\alpha}[z(t-d), t] = Q^{-1}W^d\tilde{\mu}(t-d).$$

By (5.11) of Chapter 6, the corresponding expected payoff is

(3.43)
$$V_t(d) = \mathrm{trace}\{Q^{-1}W^d[\mathrm{Var}\ \tilde{\mu}(t-d)]W')^d\}.$$

This is also the *value* of the information structure. The maximum possible value, for zero delay $(d = 0)$ and $z(t) \equiv \mu(t)$, is

(3.44)
$$V_t^* \equiv \mathrm{trace}\{Q^{-1}\ \mathrm{Var}\ \mu(t)\}.$$

Subtracting (3.43) from (3.44), we obtain the *loss* due to the delay and incompleteness of the information at date t:

(3.45) $$L_t(d) = \mathrm{trace}\ Q^{-1}\ \mathrm{Var}\ \mu(t) - \mathrm{trace}\ Q^{-1}W^d\ \mathrm{Var}\ \tilde{\mu}(t-d)(W')^d.$$

If $z(t-d) = \mu(t-d)$, that is, if the observation is *complete*, then the loss is, from (3.45):

(3.46)
$$L_t^*(d) \equiv \mathrm{trace}\ Q^{-1}[\mathrm{Var}\ \mu(t) - W^d\ \mathrm{Var}\ \mu(t-d)(W')^d].$$

Using (3.37) and (3.38), we can reduce this to

(3.47)
$$\begin{aligned} L_t^*(d) &= \mathrm{trace}\ Q^{-1}(S_t - S_{t-d}) \\ &= \mathrm{trace}\ Q^{-1} \sum_{m-t-d}^{t-1} W^m v(W')^m. \end{aligned}$$

On the other hand, if the observation is incomplete but the information is *undelayed*, then the loss is

$$(3.48) \qquad L_t(0) = \text{trace } Q^{-1}[\text{Var } \mu(t) - \text{Var } \tilde{\mu}(t)].$$

We shall show that the general expression for the loss, $L_t(d)$, can be represented as a sum of two parts: a first part equal to the loss due to delayed complete information, and a second part similar to the loss due to undelayed incomplete information. [In the special case in which W is scalar, this second part is exactly equal to w^{2d} times the loss due to incompleteness, as in (3.33).] To see this, let $\delta(s) = \mu(s) - \tilde{\mu}(s)$ as in (3.31). Then (3.45) can be rewritten

$$(3.49) \qquad L_t(d) = [V_t^* - V_t^*(d)] + [V_t^*(d) - V_t(d)],$$

where

$$(3.50) \qquad V_t^*(d) = \text{trace } Q^{-1}W^d \text{ Var } \mu(t - d)(W')^d$$

is the value of delayed complete observation. The first term in brackets in (3.49) is therefore just equal to (3.46).

The second term in brackets in (3.49) equals, by (3.43), (3.50), and (3.32),

$$(3.51) \qquad \text{trace } Q^{-1}[W^d \text{ Var } \mu(t - d)(W')^d - W^d \text{ Var } \tilde{\mu}(t - d)(W')^d]$$

$$= \text{trace } Q^{-1}W^d \text{ Var } \delta(t - d)(W')^d.$$

This last is to be compared with (3.48), which by (3.32) can be rewritten

$$(3.52) \qquad \text{trace } Q^{-1} \text{ Var } \delta(t).$$

In particular, if $W = wI$, where w is a scalar and I is the identity matrix, then (3.51) reduces to

$$(3.53) \qquad w^{2d} \text{ trace } Q^{-1} \text{ Var } \delta(t - d),$$

which is equal to $w^{2d}L_{t-d}(0)$. Indeed, setting $W = wI$, we obtain all the results of the main part of the text in this section.

4. PROPER TEAM, AUTOREGRESSIVE ENVIRONMENT, DELAYED INFORMATION

INTRODUCTION

In this section, we extend our analysis of the previous section to deal with delayed information in a proper team, that is to say, delayed information such that different decisions made at the same time are based upon different information. Precisely, we shall analyze information structures of the type,

$$(4.1) \qquad \eta_i(x, t) = \tilde{\eta}_i[\mu(t - d)] \equiv z_i(t - d) \qquad i = 1, \ldots, n.$$

As we shall show, under the assumptions that we have been making about the μ-process, the best decision functions for delayed team information are proportional to the best decision functions for undelayed team information, the constant of proportionality depending on the delay. Also, as in the case of a single person, the loss due to delayed incomplete information can be decomposed into a loss due to the delay and a loss due to the team structure (incompleteness) of the information.

In particular, in the special Brownian motion case the loss due to the team structure of the information increases linearly with time. This leads us to consider in Section 5 the periodic recovery of delayed complete observation.

BEST DECISION FUNCTIONS, VALUE, AND LOSS

Let $\hat{a}_j(t)$ denote the best team decision functions at date t for the information structure (4.1), and let $\tilde{a}_j(t)$ denote the best team decision functions at date t for the special case in which the delay is zero ($d = 0$). We shall show that

(4.2) $$\hat{a}_j(t) = w^d \tilde{a}_j(t - d) \qquad j = 1, \ldots, n.$$

Also let $V_t(d)$ be the value of the information structure (4.1); we shall show that

(4.3) $$V_t(d) = w^{2d} V_{t-d}(0).$$

Let $\hat{V}_t(d)$ denote the value of the information structure in which each team member at time t receives a complete description of $\mu(t - d)$, that is, $z_i(t) = \mu(t - d)$ for each i (delayed complete observation). In particular, $\hat{V}_t(0)$ is the value of complete information for the team at time t. The loss at time t due to using the team information structure (4.1), compared with using complete information, is

(4.4) $$L_t(d) = \hat{V}_t(0) - V_t(d).$$

We shall now decompose this loss into the loss due to delay and the loss due to the team structure of the information. Applying (4.3) to the case in which $z_i(t) = \mu(t - d)$, we get

(4.5) $$\hat{V}_t(d) = w^{2d} \hat{V}_{t-d}(0),$$

and the corresponding loss is

(4.6) $$\hat{L}_t(d) = \hat{V}_t(0) - \hat{V}_t(d) = \hat{V}_t(0) - w^{2d} \hat{V}_{t-d}(0).$$

We can now write the loss $L_t(d)$ as

$$L_t(d) = \hat{V}_t(0) - \hat{V}_t(d)$$
$$= [\hat{V}_t(0) - \hat{V}_t(d)] + [\hat{V}_t(d) - V_t(d)]$$
$$= \hat{L}_t(d) + [w^{2d}\hat{V}_{t-d}(0) - w^{2d}V_{t-d}(0)]$$

(4.7) $$L_t(d) = \hat{L}_t(d) + w^{2d}L_{t-d}(0).$$

Note that $L_{t-d}(0)$ is the loss due to using the *undelayed* team information structure $\eta_i(t - d) = \tilde{\eta}_i(t - d)$ as compared with complete information.

To characterize the best decision functions, we apply the person-by-person satisfactoriness condition in the form that it takes for the quadratic case in Chapter 5, Theorem 4. This gives us the equations

(4.8) $$\sum_j q_{ij}E\{\hat{\alpha}_j[z_j(t - d), t]|z_i(t - d)\} = E\{\mu_i(t)|z_i(t - d)\} \qquad i = 1, \ldots, n.$$

From (3.40) of the last section,

(4.9) $$E[\mu_i(t)|z_i(t - d)] = w^d \tilde{\mu}_i(t - d),$$

where

(4.10) $$\tilde{\mu}_i(t) \equiv E[\mu_i(t)|z_i(t)].$$

Hence (4.8) can be rewritten

(4.11) $$\sum_j q_{ij}E\left\{\left(\frac{1}{w^d}\right)\hat{\alpha}_j[z_j(t - d), t]|z_i(t - d)]\right\} = \tilde{\mu}_i(t - d) \qquad i = 1, \ldots, n.$$

Setting $d = 0$ in (4.11), we obtain the equations that determine the decision functions $\tilde{\alpha}_j(t)$:

(4.12) $$\sum_j q_{ij}E\{\hat{\alpha}_j[z_j(t), t]|z_i(t)\} = \tilde{\mu}_i(t) \qquad i = 1, \ldots, n.$$

Hence the equations that determine the $\tilde{\alpha}_j(t - d)$ are

(4.13) $$\sum_j q_{ij}E\{\tilde{\alpha}_j[z_j(t - d), t - d]|z_i(t - d)\} = \tilde{\mu}_i(t - d) \qquad i = 1, \ldots, n.$$

A comparison of (4.11) and (4.13) shows that

(4.14) $$\tilde{\alpha}_j[z_j(t - d), t - d] = \left(\frac{1}{w^{2d}}\right)\hat{\alpha}_j[z_j(t - d), t] \qquad j = 1, \ldots, n,$$

since the solution of the system is unique (see Theorem 4, Chapter 5), thus proving (4.2)

From (3.4) of Chapter 6, we have

(4.15) $$V_t(d) = E\sum_i \hat{\alpha}_i(t)\mu_i(t).$$

By (4.2),

(4.16) $$E\hat{\alpha}_i(t)\mu_i(t) = w^d E\tilde{\alpha}_i(t - d)\mu_i(t).$$

Since $\tilde{\alpha}_i(t - d)$ is a function of $z_i(t - d)$, and $\mu_i(t - d)$ is as fine as $z_i(t - d)$, it follows that $\tilde{\alpha}_i(t - d)$ is constant for any given value of $\mu_i(t - d)$, so that

(4.17) $$E[\tilde{\alpha}_i(t - d)\mu_i(t)|\mu_i(t - d)] = \tilde{\alpha}_i(t - d)E[\mu_i(t - d)]$$
$$= \tilde{\alpha}_i(t - d)w^d\mu_i(t - d)$$

[use (3.8)]. Taking the expected value of both sides of (4.17) and applying the theorem on iterated expectations [(6.7) of Chapter 2], we get

(4.18) $$E\tilde{\alpha}_i(t - d)\mu_i(t) = w^d E\tilde{\alpha}_i(t - d)\mu_i(t - d).$$

Hence, combining (4.15), (4.16), and (4.18),

(4.19) $$V_t(d) = w^{2d} E \sum_i \tilde{\alpha}_i(t - d)\mu_i(t - d).$$

In particular, for $d = 0$,

(4.20) $$V_t(0) = E \sum_i \tilde{\alpha}_i(t)\mu_i(t).$$

Now (4.3) follows immediately from (4.19) and (4.20).

THE STATIONARY CASE

In the stationary case, the value of the team information structure is constant in time, and depends only on the delay and the structure of the information function $\tilde{\eta}$. Thus (4.3) becomes

(4.21) $$V(d) = w^{2d}V(0).$$

The value is the product of two terms: one depending on the delay alone (w^{2d}) and one on the information function $\tilde{\eta}$ alone $[V(0)]$.
Correspondingly, the loss can be written

(4.22) $$L(d) = \hat{V}(0) - V(d)$$
$$= (1 - w^{2d})\hat{V}(0) + w^{2d}[\hat{V}(0) - V(0)]$$
$$= (1 - w^{2d})\hat{V}(0) + w^{2d}L(0).$$

The loss (per unit time) is a weighted average of the value of complete undelayed information $[\hat{V}(0)]$ and the loss that would be caused by having the undelayed team information function $\tilde{\eta}$. The greater the delay, the greater the weight attached to the first term.

THE BROWNIAN MOTION CASE

Again the results are similar to those for the single person. The loss depends on t if the team information function $\tilde{\eta}$ is not complete. If the "shocks" $\varepsilon(t)$ are normally distributed and the information functions $\tilde{\eta}_i$ are linear (the special Brownian motion case) then again the value and loss are linear in t and d,

(4.23) $$V_t(d) = (t - d)V_1(0),$$

(4.24) $$L_t(d) = \hat{V}_t(0) - V_t(d)$$

$$= t\hat{V}_1(0) - (t - d)V_1(0).$$

This last one can be written in two ways. One way is

$$L_t(d) = d\hat{V}_1(0) + (t - d)[\hat{V}_1(0) - V_1(0)]$$

(4.25) $$= d\hat{V}_1(0) + (t - d)L_1(0).$$

Here $\hat{V}_1(0)$ is the value of complete information at time 1, and $L_1(0)$ is the loss at time 1 due to having undelayed team information $\tilde{\eta}$ rather than (undelayed) complete information.

Alternatively,

(4.26) $$L_t(d) = dV_1(0) + t[\hat{V}_1(0) - V_1(0)]$$

$$= dV_1(0) + tL_1(0).$$

Here $V_1(0)$ is the value at time 1 of the undelayed team information $\tilde{\eta}$.

5. PERIODIC RECOVERY OF DELAYED COMPLETE INFORMATION

The analysis in the last two sections of a team in an autoregressive environment brought out a contrast between two special cases: the stable case and the Brownian motion case. In the stable case, the value of a given information structure per unit time as a function of time, t, approaches a finite limit as t increases, and so does the loss (as compared with having complete information). The limiting value and loss are, of course, those of the corresponding stationary case.

On the other hand, in the special Brownian motion case, both the value per unit time of a given information structure (as compared with no information) and the loss per unit time (as compared with complete information) increase linearly with time. Recall (4.23) and (4.26),

(5.1) $$V_t(d) = (t - d)V_1(0).$$

(5.2) $$L_t(d) = dV_1(0) + tL_1(0).$$

However, the loss due to having delayed complete information[5] as compared with undelayed complete information depends only on the delay, not on the time:

(5.3) $\hat{L}_t(d(= d\hat{V}_1(0)$

[since applying (5.2), $\hat{L}_1(0) = 0$].

Hence, in the special Brownian motion case, *whatever be the cost of complete information, even delayed complete information, there is some time t such that it is worth having.* This remarkable feature of the special Brownian motion case derives essentially from the assumption of a quadratic payoff function, together with the fact that the variance of the special Brownian motion process increases linearly with time. Recall that, in the case of a quadratic payoff function, the expected loss due to incomplete information is a linear function of the variances and covariances of the *errors* in the actions of the team members (Chapter 6, Section 5). In the special Brownian motion case, the variances and covariances of these errors increase linearly in time for a given (linear) structure of information.

We suspect that this feature of the special Brownian motion case to which we have called attention is also characteristic of a much broader class of cases in which the payoff function is unbounded and the environment is nonstationary and, in some sense, also unbounded.

Suppose now (in the special Brownian case) that each team member receives complete information on $\mu(t_0)$. This has the effect of using t_0 as a new origin for the measurement of time and $\mu(t_0)$ as a new origin for the measurement of the μ-process. This is suggested by (3.6) and (3.8), with $w = 1$, since

$$E[\mu(t) - \mu(t_0)|\mu(t_0)] = 0 \qquad t \geq t_0$$
(5.4)
$$\text{Var}[\mu(t) - \mu(t_0)|\mu(t_0)] = (t - t_0)v \qquad t \geq t_0.$$

Indeed, it is easy to go farther and show that the conditional joint distribution of

(5.5) $\mu(t_0 + 1) - \mu(t_0), \mu(t_0 + 2) - \mu(t_0), \ldots$

given any sequence of observations on the μ-process up to and including time t_0, say $\mu(t_N), \mu(t_{N-1}), \ldots, \mu(t_1), \mu(t_0)$, with $t_N < t_{N-1} < \ldots < t_1 < t_0$,

5. According to the terminology of Chapter 6, delayed information cannot, strictly speaking, be *complete*. We shall, however, use the term *delayed complete information* to denote the case in which action at time t is based on knowledge, by all team members, of $\mu(t - d)$.

is the same as the joint conditional distribution of the variables (5.3) given $\mu(t_0)$ alone, and that this conditional joint distribution is the same as the joint distribution of $\mu(1), \mu(2), \ldots$ given $\mu(0) = 0$.

It follows from this that, if the team has complete information about $\mu(t_0)$, and at time $t > t_0 + d$ each team member i learns $\tilde{\eta}_i(x, t - d)$, then the loss as compared with having complete undelayed information at time t will be the same as the loss that would be incurred at time $(t - t_0)$ due to having the information $\tilde{\eta}(x, t - t_0 - d)$, as compared with having complete undelayed information at time $(t - t_0)$.

More precisely, consider the information structure

(5.6) $\qquad \eta_i(x, t) = [\mu(t_0), \tilde{\eta}_i(x, t - d)] \qquad t_0 < t - d, i = 1, \ldots, n.$

It follows from the above remarks that the loss at time t is equal to

(5.7) $\qquad\qquad L_{t - t_0}(d) = dV_1(0) + (t - t_0)L_1(0),$

where $L_t(d)$ and $V_1(0)$ are defined for the information structure (4.1).

Suppose that, at time t, the team had the opportunity to obtain complete information about $\mu(t_0)$, where $t_0 < t$. By how much would this additional information reduce the team's loss at time t? Subtracting (5.7) from (5.2), we find this reduction to be equal to $t_0L_1(0)$. (Recall that $L_1(0)$ is the loss that would be incurred at time 1 due to having undelayed information $\tilde{\eta}$ rather than complete information.) *Hence if complete information, even if delayed, can be made available to all team members at some given cost, it will eventually be worthwhile to do so, no matter what the given cost is.*

This suggests that we examine the effects of a policy in which the team *periodically* recovers complete, though possibly delayed, information. We consider a policy according to which the team receives information with structure $\tilde{\eta}$ every period, but with a delay of d_2 time units, and receives *complete* information every b periods, with delay d_1. To be precise, define

(5.8) $\qquad G(t) = \begin{cases} 0 & 0 \leq t < b + d_1 \\ kb & kb + d_1 \leq t < (k + 1)b + d_1, k \geq 1 \ (k \text{ integral}). \end{cases}$

Suppose that the information structure η is defined by

(5.9) $\qquad \eta_i(x, t) = (\mu[G(t)], \tilde{\eta}_i[\mu(t - d_2)]) \qquad i = 1, \ldots, n,$

where $\tilde{\eta}_1, \ldots, \tilde{\eta}_n$ are fixed information functions. We assume that $d_2 \leq d_1$.

For any *cycle* $kb + d_1 \leq t < (k + 1)b + d_1$ (and $k \geq 1$), the loss at time t is, from (5.7),

(5.10) $\qquad\qquad L_t = d_2V_1(0) + (t - kb - d_1)L_1(0).$

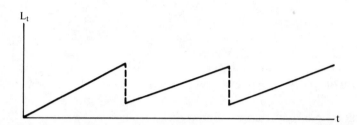

FIGURE 7.1. Periodic recovery of delayed complete information. Loss as a function of time.

This loss as a function of time fluctuates between fixed limits, as is shown in Figure 7.1.

From (5.10), *the average loss per unit time in any cycle* ($k \geq 1$) *is*

$$(5.11) \qquad \bar{L}(d_1, d_2) = d_2 V_1(0) + \left(\frac{b-1}{2} + d_1 \right) L_1(0).$$

If the team must pay a fixed cost c every time it obtains new complete information, we may ask, "What is the optimal cycle length b?" The net loss per unit of time over a cycle (after adding the cost of the delayed complete information) is

$$(5.12) \qquad\qquad\qquad \bar{L}(d_1, d_2) + \frac{c}{b}.$$

It is straightforward to determine from (5.11) and (5.12) that the optimal value of b is

$$(5.13) \qquad \hat{b} = \left[\frac{2c}{L_1(0)} \right]^{1/2} \qquad \frac{1}{\hat{b}} = \left[\frac{L_1(0)}{2c} \right]^{1/2}.$$

Thus the optimal *frequency* of recovery of delayed complete information is proportional to the square root of the difference in value between complete and incomplete information, and inversely proportional to the square root of the cost.

6. Substitution of Timeliness for Completeness

We now explore the situation in which the information structure $\tilde{\eta}$ can be improved only at the expense of increasing the delay with which the team receives the information $\tilde{\eta}$. We consider a family of information functions $\tilde{\eta}_g$, indexed by some parameter g, with the convention that the larger the value of g the better is $\tilde{\eta}_g$, that is, the larger the expected payoff when $\tilde{\eta}_g$ is used without delay. On the other hand, we suppose that the delay with which $\tilde{\eta}_g$ is available to the team also depends on g, for example, $d = D(g)$, in such a way that $D(g)$ is an increasing function of g.

In such a situation, there will typically be a point beyond which it does not pay to improve the information function $\tilde{\eta}_g$ (increase g) because the gain so obtained is more than offset by the loss due to increased delay.

The optimal balance between timeliness and completeness will depend on the particular family of information functions $\tilde{\eta}_g$, and on the delay function $D(g)$, as well as on the other characteristics of the team. We can at most illustrate the problem, and we have chosen for the illustration the family of information functions generated by partitioning the team members into groups of equal size, with complete communication within groups and no communication between groups. (We have already studied this simple type of information structure in Chapter 6, Section 7.) For this family of information structures, we can take the parameter g to be the group size in the partition.

Again we contrast the special case of stationary and Brownian motion environments. In addition to deriving a few more general results, we show that, in the stationary case, the optimal group size is independent of the size of the team, whatever be the delay function D. On the other hand, in the special Brownian motion case, the optimal group size does depend upon the size of the team; the form of this dependence is determined by the delay function D. For example, if the elasticity of delay with respect to group size is constant, say h, then as the number, n, of team members increases, the ratio of the optimal group size to the size of the team is asymptotically

$$\left[\frac{1}{nh}\right]^{1/(h+1)}$$

Here the optimal group size increases without limit as the team size increases, but at a slower rate, so that the ratio of optimal group size to team size approaches zero.

THE STATIONARY CASE

Consider a family of information functions $\tilde{\eta}_g$, indexed by a parameter g. Assume that g varies from 0 to $\bar{g} > 0$, and make the convention that $g = 0$ corresponds to no information, and that $g = \bar{g}$ corresponds to complete information. We make the further convention that the larger g, the better is $\tilde{\eta}_g$, when used without delay. Thus, using the notation of Section 4, we assume that

(6.1) $$V(0) = \beta(g)\hat{V}(0),$$

where $\hat{V}(0)$ is the value per unit time of undelayed complete information, $V(0)$ is the value of the information $\tilde{\eta}_g$ without delay, and β is a function of g such that

(6.2) $\qquad \beta(0) = 0, \qquad \beta(\bar{g}) = 1, \qquad \beta$ is monotone increasing.

On the other hand, we suppose that, to get a better information function $\tilde{\eta}_g$ one must accept a longer delay, that is,

(6.3) $$d = D(g),$$

where

(6.4) $\qquad D(0) = 0, \qquad D(\bar{g}) \equiv \bar{d}, \qquad D$ is monotone increasing.

In addition to deriving conditions for an optimal value of g, we shall show below that

1. It always pays to have some information (and some delay); that is, the optimal value of g is positive (provided $w > 0$); and

2. If D is convex and β is concave, then the optimal value of g is less than or equal to $\bar{g}$, according as the autoregression coefficient w is less than or greater than some critical value (in absolute value). In other words, if w is sufficiently small in absolute value, then the optimal balance between timeliness and completeness of information is such that information is less than complete and delay is less than the maximum. On the other hand, if w is sufficiently large in absolute value, then it is best to have complete information (with, by necessity, the maximum delay, $\bar{d}$).

It will be shown below that, if the optimal value of g is strictly less than $\bar{g}$, then it is the solution of

(6.5) $$\frac{\beta'(g)}{\beta(g)} = \log\left(\frac{1}{w^2}\right)D'(g).$$

Consider the family of information structures generated by *equal partitions* of the team members (Chapter 6, Section 7). In the special case of identical interaction ($q_{ii} = 1$, $q_{ij} = q$ for $i \neq j$) and uncorrelated $\mu_i(t)$ with equal variances, (5.23) and (7.10) of Chapter 6 give

(6.6) $$\beta(g) = \frac{1 + (g - 2)q}{1 + (g - 1)q} \cdot \frac{1 + (n - 1)q}{1 + (n - 2)q} \qquad g \geq 1,$$

where g is the number of persons in each set of the partition. A routine calculation yields[6]

$$(6.7) \qquad \beta'(g) = \frac{q^2}{[1 + (g - 1)q]^2}\left(\frac{1 + (n - 1)q}{1 + (n - 2)q}\right),$$

so that β is concave.

It seems reasonable to assume that $D(g)$ is increasing and convex. In order for each member i of a given group to learn the numerical value of μ_j for each j in his group, some process of observation and communication is required, which might be expected to take more time the larger the group. Furthermore, $D(g)$ is the delay from the observation $\mu(t - d)$ to the time t at which the *actions* based on the information about $\mu(t - d)$ are actually taken. Thus this delay also includes the time to compute the action, and this time, too, would be expected to be longer the larger the group.

From (6.6) and (6.7), we get

$$(6.8) \qquad \frac{\beta'(g)}{\beta(g)} = \frac{q^2}{[1 + (g - 1)q][1 + (g - 2)q]}.$$

Notice that, in this example, $\beta'(g)/\beta(g)$ is independent of the number, n, of team members. Hence, applying condition (4.35), *the optimal group size g is independent of the number of team members.*

From (4.3) and (6.1). and recalling that in the stationary case the value $V_t(d)$ is independent of t, it follows that the value of the information $\tilde{n}_g$, with delay $d = D(g)$, is

$$(6.9) \qquad f(g) \equiv w^{2d(g)}\beta(g)\hat{V}(0).$$

We note that, if $w > 0$, then $f(0) = 0$ and $f(g) > 0$ for $g > 0$; hence conclusion (1) above that it always pays to have some information (with the corresponding delay) if $w > 0$.

The derivative of f with respect to g is

$$(6.10) \qquad f'(g) = \left[\beta'(g) - \beta(g)D'(g)\log\frac{1}{w^2}\right]\hat{V}(0)w^{2D(g)}.$$

If β is strictly concave and D is strictly convex, then β' is decreasing and D' is increasing. Also, β is increasing, so that the term in the brackets on the right-hand side of (6.10), namely,

$$(6.11) \qquad \beta'(g) - \beta(g)D'(g)\log\frac{1}{w^2},$$

6. We ignore the fact that, strictly speaking, g must be an integer here.

is decreasing. Since

$$\hat{V}(0)w^{2D(g)} > 0$$

(we assume $w > 0$), it follows that the equation $f'(g) = 0$ has at the most one solution on the interval $(0, \bar{g}]$, and that any such solution is also determined by setting (6.11) equal to zero. We already know that $f'(0) > 0$ for $w > 0$. Inspection of (6.11) shows that, for w sufficiently small, $f'(g) = 0$ has a solution on $(0, \bar{g}]$, that this solution is an increasing function of w, that for some critical value of w less than one the solution reaches $\bar{g}$, and finally that for values of w greater than this critical value $f'(g)$ is positive on $(0, \bar{g}]$. Hence the optimal g is positive, it increases with w up to $\bar{g}$; it reaches $\bar{g}$ for some value of w less than one; and for larger w is equals $\bar{g}$. We have thus proved conclusion (2). Setting (6.11) equal to zero yields (6.5).

THE SPECIAL BROWNIAN MOTION CASE WITH PERIODIC RECOVERY OF COMPLETE INFORMATION

Let us pursue the problem of optimum balance between timeliness and completeness, for the special Brownian motion case, with periodic recovery of complete information (as in Section 5). Consider again a family of information structures η_g and a delay function $D(g)$, with all the properties assumed above, and suppose that, for the information structure $\tilde{\eta}_g$, the value of this information, undelayed, at time 1 is

$$(6.12) \qquad\qquad V_1(0) = \beta(g)\hat{V}_1(0),$$

where $\hat{V}_1(0)$ is the value of undelayed complete information at time 1, and β has the same properties (6.2) as before.

Recall that the average loss per unit time in any cycle is [see 5.9)]:

$$(6.13) \qquad \bar{L}(d_1, d_2) = d_2 V_1(0) + \left(\frac{b-1}{2} + d_1\right)L_1(0),$$

where b is the length of time between receipt of complete information, d_1 is the delay of the complete information when it is received, and d_2 is the delay of the information $\tilde{\eta}_g$ (which is received every period).

Since d_2 is the delay associated with the information $\tilde{\eta}_g$, we assume

$$(6.14) \qquad\qquad d_2 = D(g),$$

where D has the same properties (6.4) as before. The average loss per unit time over a cycle can therefore be expressed as

$$(6.15) \qquad L[d_1, D(g)] = \left[\frac{b-1}{2} + d_1\right][1 - \beta(g)] + D(g)\beta(g).$$

It is again easy to show that the optimal value of g is *positive*. The optimal value of g may be the maximum, but if it is less than the maximum, then it is the solution of

(6.16)
$$\frac{D'(g)}{D(g)} = \frac{\beta'(g)}{\beta(g)}\left[\frac{d_1 + (b - 1)/2}{D(g)} - 1\right],$$

provided D is convex and β is concave.

As an example, consider again the problem of optimal group size for equal partitions. The function β is the same, and therefore so is $\beta'(g)/\beta(g)$, which is independent of the team size, n. However, a difference arises in that the delay d_1 (needed to produce complete information) enters (6.16), and presumably d_1 would depend upon the size of the team. Indeed, $d_1 = D(n)$. How the optimal group size $\hat{g}$ varies with the team size n depends upon the form of the function D.

For example, suppose delay is proportional to group size, that is,

(6.17)
$$D(g) = cg.$$

Then, as we shall show, as the size of the team increases, the optimal group size increases, too, but only as fast as the square root of the team size. More generally, if the elasticity of delay with respect to group size is constant, say equal to $h \geq 1$, that is,

(6.18)
$$D(g) = cg^h \qquad h \geq 1,$$

then, as we shall show,

(6.19)
$$\frac{\hat{g}}{n} \sim \left[\frac{1}{nh}\right]^{1/(h+1)}.$$

so that optimal group size increases with the size of the team, but not as fast.

We may write the condition (6.16) for an interior solution $\hat{g}$ as follows, using the form (6.8) that β'/β takes for partitions and the form (6.18) for the delay function, recalling that the delay of complete information depends on the team size, that is, $d_1 = D(n)$:

$$\frac{h}{g} = \frac{q^2}{[1 + (g - 1)q][1 + (g - 2)q]}\left[\frac{cn^h + (b - 1)/2}{cg^h} - 1\right],$$

or

(6.20)
$$h = \frac{g^2 q^2}{[1 + (g - 1)q][1 + (g - 2)q]}\left[\frac{n^h + (b - 1)/2}{g^{h+1}} - \frac{1}{g}\right].$$

We can rewrite (6.20) as

$$(6.21) \qquad chg^{h-1} = \frac{q^2}{[1 + (g - 1)q][1 + (g - 2)q]}\left[cn^h + \frac{b - 1}{2} - cg^h\right].$$

If for an unbounded sequence $n_1, n_2, \ldots$, the corresponding sequence of $\hat{g}$'s were bounded, then for that sequence the left-hand side of (6.21) would be bounded but the right-hand side would be unbounded, a contradiction. Hence g must increase without bound as n does. From this and (6.20), it easily follows that

$$(6.22) \qquad\qquad\qquad \lim_{n \to \infty} \frac{n^h}{\hat{g}^{h+1}} = h$$

or

$$(6.23) \qquad\qquad\qquad \frac{\hat{g}}{n} \sim \left[\frac{1}{nh}\right]^{1/(h+1)}.$$

Hence, although $\hat{g}$ grows without bound as n increases, the "relative group size" $\hat{g}/n$ approaches zero. Notice that the asymptotic behavior of $\hat{g}$ is independent of q and c.

For example,

$$(6.24) \qquad \begin{cases} \text{if } h = 2 \quad \hat{g} \sim \left(\dfrac{1}{2}\right)^{1/3} n^{2/3}, \quad \dfrac{\hat{g}}{n} \sim \left(\dfrac{1}{2n}\right)^{1/3}; \\[2em] \text{if } h = 3 \quad \hat{g} \sim \left(\dfrac{1}{3}\right)^{1/4} n^{3/4}, \quad \dfrac{\hat{g}}{n} \sim \left(\dfrac{1}{3n}\right)^{1/4}. \end{cases}$$

CHAPTER 8

The Team Problem as a Problem of Optimal Networks

1. INTRODUCTION

In the foregoing chapters we have confined our discussion of a team's behavior to those aspects that can be described by the information function and the decision function. These two together determine the team action in response to any given state of nature. This relation between state of nature and action can be described by a single function, the *response function* ρ, defined by

$$(1.1) \qquad\qquad \rho(x) = \alpha[\eta(x)].$$

The response function ρ is the composition of the information function η and the decision function α. Inversely, (1.1) displays a decomposition of ρ into η and α.

This decomposition of the response function into information and decision functions has been useful in exploring certain aspects of the problem of organization. The concepts of information and decision functions seemed particularly suitable for the study of the gross expected utility. As will be recalled, we have found it convenient, though sometimes artificial, to regard the net value of a response function as a difference between the *gross* expected utility derived from that function and the cost of the organization used to realize, or implement, the function.

On the other hand, when we turn to the discussion of the means by which a particular response function is to be realized, and the associated costs, then the decomposition into information and decision functions may not be so helpful. (See also Chapter 4, Section 11.) Rather, it seems more helpful to think of the realization of any response functions as being brought about by combining the observation of events outside the organization with communication and computation within the organization.

The word *computation* is used here in the sense of a *function* or *transformation*; thus a man who responds to a complex stimulus with a simple response is in effect performing a computation, although he is not conscious of any explicit arithmetical or logical operations. Computation typically enters into the determination of an information variable as well as of a decision variable. For example, if the information consists of the arithmetic mean of several observations, then the computation of averaging must be performed to determine the message.

Communication may be involved when information variables are transmitted. Communication is also involved when actions are computed at one point in the organization but implemented at another.

In the next two chapters, we propose to give some attention to the question of organization costs, and for this purpose we find it useful to describe a team in terms of what we shall call a *network*. Although a precise definition of a network (in our sense) follows soon, it may be good to give here a rough description of what we have in mind. By an *element* of a network we shall mean something that transforms incoming messages into outgoing messages in a well-defined, though possibly stochastic, way. Messages coming in from nature are to be interpreted as observations, whereas messages going out to nature are what we have up to now called actions. Communication involves messages from one element to another. Computation may be performed in the transformation of incoming into outgoing messages. Errors of observation, communication, and computation are reflected in the stochastic nature of the elements. The network itself consists of elements connected to nature and to each other in a logically consistent way so as to result in a response function.

We have just described an *abstract network*, which is to be distinguished from the *implemented network*, consisting of the *instruments*, or physical objects (men, machines, etc.), that perform the functions indicated by the abstract network. There need be no one-to-one correspondence between the elements of the abstract network and the instruments of the implemented network. A single man may perform several functions of observation, computation, and communication, and be represented by several elements in the abstract network. Further, it will be seen below that, in a dynamic problem, it is natural to represent a single instrument in several time periods by several elements, just as in Chapter 7 a single individual in several time periods was represented by several team members. On the other hand, a whole department or office made up of many men and machines might for some purposes be represented by a single element of the abstract network used to describe the organization.

Thus a network realizes a response function, which in turn results in a certain gross expected utility. From the latter must be subtracted the cost of the network, the difference being the net expected utility. At this level, then, the problem of the organizer is to choose a network with maximum net expected utility.

In the above formulation, we do not yet take account of the costs that the organizer himself incurs in his effort to solve the problem of organization, nor do we discuss the means by which the organizer may organize the work of organizing the team; these problems are deferred to Chapter 9. It is generally recognized that a substantial part of the effort of some members of an organization is typically devoted to the job of organizing, so that in a sense the problem posed in this chapter is still too special. In another sense, however, the problem is too general. That is, it is too general for us to be able to say a great deal systematically about it.

In Section 2, we give a precise definition of our concept of a network, and in Section 3 we illustrate this concept with some simple examples. In Section 4, we give conditions under which the additional processing of messages at a point in a network cannot increase the gross payoff, and pooling of information cannot decrease it.

2. NETWORKS

NETWORK ELEMENTS

In the introductory section of this chapter we outlined the idea that a response function of a team is generated by a network, the elements of which transform incoming messages into outgoing messages. These messages are from or to nature, or from or to other elements. We wish now to make this idea more precise, and we first take up the concept of a network element.

The class of real-world objects that we wish to formalize in the abstract concept of a network element is a broad one. The reader may keep in mind the following representative examples:

Person
Computing machine
Department (of an organization)
Communications relay station
Thermostat.

In any particular context, the elements will be the building blocks from which the various alternative networks being considered are to be built, and the appropriate interpretation of the concept of element will depend upon the details in which the alternative networks differ.

In particular, in problems in which time plays a role, it will usually be useful to treat the same "person" or "machine" at two different times as two different elements. This important point is of course related to the treatment of time in Chapter 7, and will be discussed more fully below.

To every network element corresponds both an input variable and an output variable. The input variable is thought of as having two components, the first being a message from nature, and the second a (combined) message from other elements. The element determines the output message as a function of the two components of the input message.

The formalism just introduced would at first appear to be capable of describing only deterministic elements, i.e., elements in which there is a deterministic relation between inputs and outputs. Two ways of representing stochastic relations suggest themselves.

First, the stochastic character of the output variable may be traced back to the stochastic character of nature if the concept of nature is given a sufficiently broad interpretation. In particular, the message from nature may be described as having two stochastic components, say z' and e, where z' represents the message from the outside world and e represents the stochastic nature of the element. The variable e is sometimes called *noise* (in the channel) by communication engineers, while z' would correspond to *source*. The distinction between z' and e is that z' enters the payoff function (is relevant to the decision problem), whereas e does not. Thus a payoff adequate partition of the set of states of nature would reflect the variable z' but possibly not e.

Formally, then, an element can be described in terms of a functional relationship

$$(2.1) \qquad\qquad b = \beta(z', e, \tilde{b}),$$

where b denotes the output message, and $\tilde{b}$ denotes the combined input message from the other elements.[1] Further, if x denotes the complete description of nature, then we may denote the determination of z' and e by

$$(2.2) \qquad\qquad z' = \zeta'(x) \qquad e = \varepsilon(x).$$

This last takes note of the fact that typically an element is exposed to only some aspect of nature. We shall say that e represents *noise* if the conditional distribution of e given z' and $\tilde{b}$ is independent of z'.

For example, an element that simply transmits a numerical observation z', with an additive error e, would be represented by the transformation

$$(2.3) \qquad\qquad b = z' + e.$$

---

1. Note that the symbol β here has a completely different meaning than that used in Chapters 5 to 7.

Another way of describing the stochastic nature of an element is provided by the joint probability distribution of the combined message $\tilde{b}$ from the other elements, the message z' from the outside world, and the output message b.

It should be borne in mind, however, that the noise variables of different elements may be statistically dependent, so that the several joint distributions of $\tilde{b}$, z', and b may not suffice to describe the stochastic nature of the several elements of the network taken together. For example, the noise variables in a number of elements of a radio communication network may be correlated because of widespread electrical storms. One can, of course, describe such statistical dependence by the single joint distribution of all of the inputs and outputs of all of the elements in the network.[2]

NETWORKS

Having described what we mean by a network element, we are now in a position to define our concept of a network. Roughly speaking, a network is a collection of elements, together with a specification of the connections among them and between them and nature. This specification must be such as to generate a well-defined response function, that is, such that each state of the world results in a (unique) team action.

We suppose then that there are m elements; for each element i one has

(2.4)

$$Z_i = \text{the set of possible alternative messages } z_i$$
$$\text{from the outside world, and}$$

$$E_i = \text{the set of possible alternative values of}$$
$$\text{the noise variable } e_i.$$

The connections among the elements are to be described as follows. For each i and j, let B_{ij} denote the set of possible alternative messages that can be sent directly from element i to element j. Typically, some of the sets B_{ij} will be empty.

The possible messages *from* nature to an element i have already been described in the sets Z_i and E_i. The messages *to* nature from the network are what we have up to now called the team action variable denoted by an n-tuple, $a = (a_1, \ldots, a_n)$, of component action variables. We shall

---

2. A mathematically equivalent approach is suggested by D. Blackwell's (1953) concept of *stochastic transformation* and is used in Marschak 1971. Each element of the network is associated with a conditional probability distribution of its outputs, given its inputs. The joint distribution of all the inputs and outputs of all the elements of the network is then determined, given the distribution of the messages from nature.

think of the n action variables a_j as being assigned to the several elements, so that some, but not necessarily all, of the elements will have one or more action variables assigned to them. In our interpretation of these abstract concepts, there would typically be many elements without action variables in any but the simplest of organizations.

We denote by B_{i0} the set of possible alternative messages from element i to nature; that is, the set B_{i0} will either be empty or it will be the Cartesian product of some sets A_j, where for each $j = 1, \ldots, n$, A_j is the set of alternative values that can be taken on by the action variable a_j. For the sake of symmetry, we may denote by B_{0i} the set of possible alternative messages from nature to element i, that is, the Cartesian product of Z_i and E_i.

In terms of the notation already used to describe a single element, the set B_i of possible alternative output messages of element i is given by

$$(2.5) \qquad\qquad B_i = \prod_{j=0}^{m} B_{ij}.$$

On the other hand, the set $\tilde{B}_i$ of combined messages from other elements[3] is given by

$$(2.6) \qquad\qquad \tilde{B}_i = \prod_{k=0}^{m} B_{ki}.$$

Finally, for each element i, there is a function $\beta_i = (\beta_{i0}, \ldots, \beta_{im})$ that transforms input messages into output messages. We shall call β_i the *task function* of element i. For the sake of symmetry, we may denote the pair of functions (ζ_i, ε_i), corresponding to (2.2), by β_{0i}.

The whole system $\{B_{ij}, \beta_{ij}\}$, $(i, j = 0, \ldots, m)$ is to determine a response function according to the equations

$$(2.7) \qquad \begin{aligned} b_{ij} &= \beta_{ij}(b_{0i}, \ldots, b_{mi}) \qquad i = 1, \ldots, m; \; j = 0, \ldots, m \\ b_{0j} &= \beta_{0j}(x) \qquad j = 1, \ldots, m. \end{aligned}$$

In order to insure that the system of equations (2.7) does indeed determine a well-defined response function, we make the important assumption of *recursiveness*: There exists a numbering $i = 1, \ldots, m$ of the elements of the network such that, for every $i = 0, \ldots, m$,

$$(2.8) \qquad \begin{aligned} &\text{(a) if } 1 \leq j \leq i, \text{ then } B_{ij} \text{ is empty};\\ &\text{(b) } B_{00} \text{ is empty.} \end{aligned}$$

---

3. Formally, B_i and $\tilde{B}_i$ as defined in (2.5) include messages from an element to itself, but this is ruled out by (2.8a) below, which requires B_{ii} to be empty.

Condition (2.8a) says that, if the sets B_{ij}, $i, j = 1, \ldots, m$, are arranged in a square array with B_{ij} in the ith row and jth column, then all the sets that are on or below the diagonal are empty.

Two features of the formulation just proposed call for comments and clarification. First, note that (after suitable renumbering of the elements) the output of element i can depend at most on the state of nature, including noise, and on the outputs of elements with indices less than i. This recursive property of the network helps insure its consistency and is in accord with our intuitive notion of cause and effect.[4] In particular, if the same instrument (person or machine) operating at two distinct points of time is included in the system, then that instrument would be represented by two distinct elements with no messages going backwards in time.

Second, one may ask why any distinction at all is being made between the output messages b_i of the elements of the network and the action variables a_j. Are not the outputs b_i also actions? The distinction we have in mind is related to the distinction that is sometimes made between final and intermediate goods. Some of the activities in an organization enter directly as arguments of the payoff function, whereas others are intermediate in a chain or activities that finally result in actions that enter directly as arguments of the payoff function. We may call these two types of action variables *final* and *intermediate*, respectively. For example, in an insurance company the calculation of premiums is an intermediate activity, whereas the collection of premiums is a final activity. The classification of a particular activity in a particular organization as final or intermediate is, to some extent, a matter of convention and a question of research strategy for the person studying the organization. The relevance of the distinction for the present discussion is that, in this chapter, we shall assume that the space of final actions is given and consider the problem of choosing the best network, which includes the problem of choosing the best set of intermediate action variables.

Two devices are useful in visualizing the connections among the elements, and between the elements and the environment. The first is diagrammatic, as in Figures 8.1a, 8.1b. The elements $i = 1, \ldots, m$, are represented by points. A single arrow from a point i to a point j indicates that i sends messages directly to j; in other words, that B_{ij} is not empty. A double arrow into i indicates that i does receive messages from nature; a double arrow out of i indicates that i controls a final action

---

4. Thus we agree with the point of view that any cause and effect system that is described in sufficient detail will have this recursive feature (see Strotz and Wold 1960 and the references indicated there). Nevertheless, nonrecursive formulations have played an important role in the description of systems, parts of which are in some kind of equilibrium.

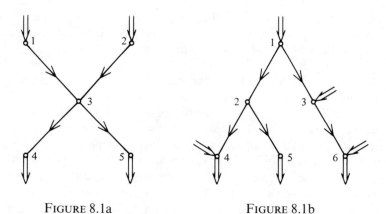

FIGURE 8.1a   FIGURE 8.1b

variable. A consequence of the recursiveness assumption is that there are no loops of single arrows.

A second device, which has already been mentioned, is to arrange the sets B_{ij} in a square array, with the set B_{ij} placed in row i and column j. If the set B_{ij} is empty, then we place the symbol ϕ in the corresponding position. Thus the array corresponding to Figure 8.1a is shown in Table 8.1.

TABLE 8.1

	0	1	2	3	4	5
0	ϕ	B_{01}	B_{02}	ϕ	ϕ	ϕ
1	ϕ	ϕ	ϕ	B_{13}	ϕ	ϕ
2	ϕ	ϕ	ϕ	B_{23}	ϕ	ϕ
3	ϕ	ϕ	ϕ	ϕ	B_{34}	B_{35}
4	B_{40}	ϕ	ϕ	ϕ	ϕ	ϕ
5	B_{50}	ϕ	ϕ	ϕ	ϕ	ϕ

Figure 8.2a shows a network representing a single individual who makes observations and decisions at three successive dates. The arrows from "1" to "2" and from "2" to "3" indicate memory. Figure 8.2b shows a network representing two individuals at four successive dates. The first person is represented by elements 1, 3, and 5; the second person by elements 2, 4, and 6. At the first and third dates, the first person makes

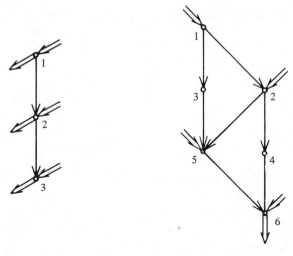

FIGURE 8.2a   FIGURE 8.2b

an observation, communicates to the second person, and stores something in his memory. At the second and fourth dates, person 2 operates similarly; in addition, he takes a final action at date four.

It is useful to distinguish certain classes of network optimization problems. *First,* suppose that:

1. The message sets B_{ij} are given for $i, j = 0, \ldots, m$.
2. The task functions β_{ij} are given for $i = 0, \ldots, m$, and $j = 1, \ldots, m$.
3. For each $i = 1, \ldots, m$, there is given a *set*, say $\mathscr{B}_{i0}$, of feasible task functions β_{i0}.

In this case, the functions determining the messages from nature to the network elements, and among the network elements, are given, but there remains a choice of the functions that determine the final actions (messages to nature). It is easy to see that for such a class of networks, say $\mathscr{N}$, *there is for each element a uniquely determined information structure,* in the sense that for each $i = 1, \ldots, m$ there is a function η_i such that

(2.9) $\tilde{b}_i = \eta_i(x).$

(Recall that $\tilde{b}_i$ is the combined incoming message to i from nature and all other elements.) For any given element i, the function η_i is the same for all networks in the class $\mathscr{N}$. We say, in this case, that *the class $\mathscr{N}$ of networks determines the (unique) information structure* $\eta = (\eta_1, \ldots, \eta_m)$. The problem of choosing a best network from the class $\mathscr{N}$ is equivalent to choosing a best team decision function $\alpha = (\alpha_1, \ldots, \alpha_m)$ for the given information structure $\eta = (\eta_1, \ldots, \eta_m)$, subject to the constraints

(2.10) α_i in $\mathcal{B}_{i0}$ $i = 1, \ldots, m$.

(In particular, $\mathcal{B}_{i0}$ may be the set of all functions from $\tilde{B}_i$ to B_{i0}.) This is the type of problem discussed in Chapters 4 to 6.

Second, suppose that the class $\mathcal{N}$ of networks is the union of a number of classes $\mathcal{N}_\eta$, each of which determines a unique information structure η. The choice of a best network is equivalent to the choice of a best information structure, together with the corresponding best team decision function.

Third, and more generally, suppose that:

1. The message sets B_{ij} are given for $i, j = 0, \ldots, m$.
2. For each $i = 0, \ldots, m$, there is a set of feasible task functions β_i from $\tilde{B}_i$ to B_i. (In particular, this includes the possibility of choice of the functions that determine the messages from nature—observation, noise.)

This third case includes the first two. But it also covers cases in which, roughly speaking, it is not possible to vary the decision function of an element (β_{i0}) without simultaneously varying some other element's information structure. For example, a given team member may be constrained to report his (final) action to another team member; thus i's choice of task function may be subject to the constraint

$$\beta_{ij}(\tilde{b}_i) = \beta_{i0}(\tilde{b}_i),$$

for some particular $j \neq 0$. (Examples C to E in Section 3 below come under this third case.)

Finally, and most generally, not even the message sets B_{ij} need be given, and there may be constraints that relate the feasible message sets to the feasible task functions. For example, just the final action variables may be given (the sets B_{i0}), together with a set of *instruments* with certain cost and capability characteristics; the job of organizing would consist in constructing a best network with the available instruments, taking as given the gross payoff function $\omega(x, a)$, and possibly the network costs. We shall discuss some aspects of this general network optimization problem in Chapter 9.

3. SOME NETWORKS FOR A TEAM WITH TWO FINAL ACTION VARIABLES

In this section, we analyze some simple examples of the problem of choosing a best network. The purpose of these primitive examples is to illustrate and clarify the formal relationships that have been described in general terms in the preceding sections. In each example, a class of networks is specified, and the network with the highest expected gross payoff is determined. Implicit in such a procedure is the assumption that all of the networks in any one class have the same cost.

All of the examples, with one exception, deal with the following case. There are two final action variables, denoted by a_1 and a_2, respectively, such that each variable can take on only the values -1 or $+1$. The payoff function is assumed to be:

$$(3.1) \qquad \omega(x, a) = \mu_1(x)a_1 + \mu_2(x)a_2 - qa_1a_2 \qquad q \geq 0,$$

where μ_1 and μ_2 are random variables, as is indicated by showing them dependent upon x, the state of nature.[5] Finally, to keep complications to a minimum, we assume that μ_1 and μ_2 are statistically independent, each having a continuous distribution that is symmetric around zero.

While considering these examples, it is useful to have in mind the maximum expected payoff that can be achieved with the action variables fixed, that is, with the *routine* information structure (see Chapter 6, Section 5). Such an information structure might be thought of as being generated by the degenerate network pictured in Figure 8.3.

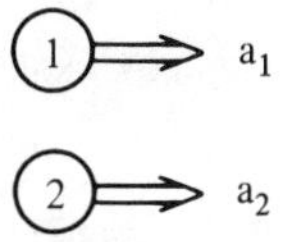

FIGURE 8.3. Routine.

It is easily seen that there are two optimal pairs of actions (a_1, a_2) in this case: $(1, -1)$ and $(-1, 1)$, each giving the expected payoff q. This follows from taking the expected value of the payoff function (3.1) with fixed a_1 and a_2:

$$E\omega(x, a) = a_1 E\mu_1 + a_2 E\mu_2 - qa_1a_2$$

$$= -qa_1a_2.$$

(Recall that each μ_i is assumed to have a distribution that is symmetric around 0, and hence $E\mu_i = 0$.) The network that produces the routine information structure is presumably the cheapest among all of those that are considered in this section.

5. The reader can easily verify that, if the payoff function is quadratic as in Chapter 5, (3.1), with the coefficients v_{ij} constant but with a_i restricted to the values ± 1, the payoff function can be written in the form just given, plus a constant term. See also Table 4.2 of the "shipyard" example of Chapter 4, where however a_i is equal to 1 or 0, not 1 or -1.

EXAMPLE 8A. TWO ELEMENTS IN PARALLEL

Consider the class of networks with two elements, say 1 and 2, such that element i has the variable μ_i as input, and the variable a_i as output. We may say that element i observes μ_i and takes the final action a_i. This is a simple-enough organization; it corresponds moreover to the information structure labeled "complete informational decentralization" in Chapter 6, Section 6. Any one of the networks in this class may be represented by the diagram of Figure 8.4.

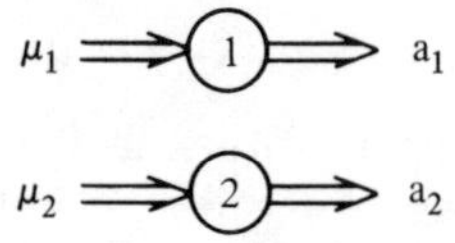

$$\mu_1 \Rightarrow \boxed{1} \Rightarrow a_1$$

$$\mu_2 \Rightarrow \boxed{2} \Rightarrow a_2$$

FIGURE 8.4 Two elements in parallel.

In terms of the notation introduced in Section 2,

B_{01}, B_{02} are each the set of real numbers,

(3.2) B_{10}, B_{20} each consist of the set $\{-1, +1\}$,

B_{12} and B_{21} are empty.

Corresponding to this class of networks is the class of response functions [see (1.1)]:

(3.3) $$\rho(x) = [\alpha_1(\mu_1), \alpha_2(\mu_2)],$$

where α_1 can be any function of μ_i that takes only the values ± 1. This corresponds exactly to the information structure

(3.4) $$\eta_i = \mu_i \qquad i = 1, 2.$$

Of course, one cannot in general characterize a class of networks by a single information structure.

Choosing the best network from the given class is in this case equivalent to choosing the best functions α_1 and α_2. We shall show that, for sufficiently small q, the best choice is[6]

(3.5) $$\alpha_i(\mu_i) = \begin{cases} -1 \\ \qquad \text{according as } \mu_i \begin{cases} < \\ = \\ > \end{cases} 0, \\ +1 \end{cases}$$

---

6. In the case of the intermediate equality, $\mu_i = 0$, in (3.5), it does not matter whether $\alpha_i(\mu_i) = +1$ or -1. In any case, this occurs with probability 0.

and that the corresponding (maximum) expected gross payoff is

(3.6) $$\Omega = E|\mu_1| + E|\mu_2|.$$

For example, if μ_i is normally distributed with mean 0 and variance s_i^2, then $E|\mu_i| = s_i\sqrt{2/\pi}$. If μ_i is rectangularly distributed on the interval $[-R_i, R_i]$, then $E|\mu_i| = R_i/2$.

On the other hand, for values of q that are large compared to the dispersions of μ_1 and μ_2, the solution is given approximately by

(3.5a) $$\alpha_1(\mu_1) = 1, \ \alpha_2(\mu_2) = -1 \ [\text{or} \ \alpha_2(\mu_2) = -\alpha_1(\mu_1) = 1],$$

(3.6a) $$\Omega = q;$$

in other words, the solution is approximately the same as that of the best routine network.

It is intuitively clear that two opposing factors are at work in determining the solution. The terms $\mu_i(x)a_i$ in the payoff function (3.1) make it desirable for a_i to have the same sign as μ_i. On the other hand, the interaction term $(-qa_1a_2)$ makes it desirable for a_1 and a_2 to have opposite signs. But inasmuch as μ_1 and μ_2 are uncorrelated (and with distributions symmetric around zero), these two requirements are incompatible, so that one or the other will dominate according to the magnitude of q relative to the dispersions of μ_1 and μ_2.

It will be seen that, whatever the magnitude of q, the optimal functions α_1 and α_2 have the following property: There are constants c_1 and c_2 such that

(3.7) $$\alpha_i(\mu_i) = \begin{cases} -1 \\ +1 \end{cases} \ \text{according as} \ \mu_i \begin{Bmatrix} < \\ > \end{Bmatrix} c_i \qquad i = 1, 2.$$

Proof of Results. To prove (3.7), we use the person-by-person satisfactoriness condition (Chapter 5, Section 2). Given α_2, the function α_1 must be chosen so that for each value of μ_1, the corresponding value of a_1 maximizes the conditional expected payoff

(3.8) $$\mu_1 a_1 + E[\mu_2\alpha_2(\mu_2)|\mu_1] - qa_1E[\alpha_2(\mu_2)|\mu_1]$$
$$= a_1(\mu_1 - qE[\alpha_2|\mu_1]) + E[\mu_2\alpha_2|\mu_1].$$

Hence

(3.9) $$\alpha_1(\mu_1) = \begin{cases} -1 \\ +1 \end{cases} \ \text{according as} \ (\mu_1 - qE[\alpha_2|\mu_1]) \begin{Bmatrix} < \\ > \end{Bmatrix} 0.$$

Recall that μ_1 and μ_2 are independent; therefore

$$E[\alpha_2|\mu_1] = E(\alpha_2),$$

and (3.9) can be rewritten in the form of (3.7), where $c_1 = qE(\alpha_2)$. By symmetry, we have the analogous result for α_2 with $c_2 = qE(\alpha_1)$.

It remains to determine the best values of the numbers c_1 and c_2. At this point (3.9) and a corresponding equation for $\alpha_2(\mu_2)$ may be substituted in the payoff function (3.1) to choose the values of c_1 and c_2 that maximize the expected payoff, or we may pursue the implications of person-by-person satisfactoriness. Thus, from (3.9) and the corresponding equation for $\alpha_2(\mu_2)$, we have

(3.10) $E\alpha_i = 1 - 2F_i(c_i)$

where F_i is the cumulative distribution function of μ_i. Hence,

$$c_1 = q[1 - 2F_2(c_2)]$$
(3.11)
$$c_2 = q[1 - 2F_1(c_1)].$$

Since μ_1 and μ_2 have distributions that are symmetric around zero, a solution of (3.11) is

(3.12) $c_1 = c_2 = 0.$

It can be shown that, if q is sufficiently small, then (3.12) is the only solution of (3.11), in which case (3.5) and (3.6) follow immediately. On the other hand, if q is outside the ranges of μ_1 and μ_2, then a solution of (3.11) is

(3.13) $c_1 = -c_2 = q,$

and another is

(3.14) $c_2 = -c_1 = q,$

and both of these are optimal. That is to say, in this case, the optimal procedure is for a_1 and a_2 to be fixed in advance, independently of the observed values of μ_1 and μ_2 and with opposite signs (recall $q \geq 0$). If q is very large, but not outside the ranges of μ_1 and μ_2 (e.g., if μ_1 and μ_2 have infinite ranges), then (3.13) and (3.14) will be approximate solutions.

In general, there may be many solutions to (3.11). By examining the second-order conditions for a maximum, one can show that a sufficient condition for $c_1 = c_2 = 0$ to be a local optimum is that

(3.15)
$$f_1(0) > 0, \quad f_2(0) > 0$$

$$q^2 < \frac{1}{4f_1(0)f_2(0)},$$

where f_i is the probability density function of μ_i.

EXAMPLE 8B. TWO ELEMENTS IN SERIES

Consider the class of networks with two elements, say 1 and 2, such that element 1 has the pair $\mu = (\mu_1, \mu_2)$ as input, element 2 has the pair $a = (a_1, a_2)$ of final action variables as output, and a *message*, $\gamma(\mu) \equiv [\gamma_1(\mu), \gamma_2(\mu)]$, is the output of 1 and the input of 2, with the constraint that $a_i = \gamma_i(\mu)$. This corresponds to the information structure labeled *complete information* in Chapter 6, Section 5, and could be represented by the diagram of Figure 8.5.

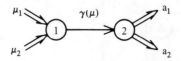

FIGURE 8.5. Two elements in series.

In terms of the notation introduced in Section 2,

$$(3.16) \quad \begin{cases} B_{01} \text{ is the space of pairs of real numbers,} \\ B_{12} = \{(1, 1), (-1, 1), (1, -1), (-1, -1)\}, \\ B_{20} = B_{12}, \\ B_{10} \text{ and } B_{02} \text{ are empty.} \end{cases}$$

Corresponding to this class of networks is the class of response functions,

$$(3.17) \qquad \rho(x) = [\gamma_1(\mu), \gamma_2(\mu)],$$

where γ_i can be any function of μ that takes on the values ± 1.

One might interpret this class of networks by saying that 1 observes μ_1 and μ_2, computes the actions a_1 and a_2, and then sends a corresponding "command" to 2, who simply follows orders.

Inspection of the payoff function (3.1) shows that the optimal pair (γ_1, γ_2) is given by

$$(3.18) \quad \gamma(\mu) = \begin{cases} (1, 1) \\ (-1, 1) \\ (1, -1) \\ (-1, -1) \end{cases} \text{according as} \begin{cases} \mu_1 + \mu_2 - q \\ -\mu_1 + \mu_2 + q \\ \mu_1 - \mu_2 + q \\ -\mu_1 - \mu_2 - q \end{cases} \text{is the largest.}$$

Condition (3.18) determines four regions in the (μ_1, μ_2) plane, which are shown in Figure 8.6, numbered 1 to 4 in the same order as in (3.18) (the boundaries are heavy solid lines).

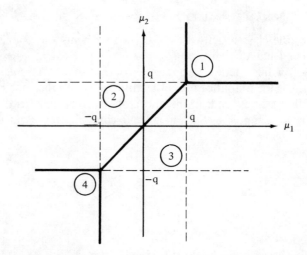

FIGURE 8.6. Optimal actions for regions of (μ_1, μ_2) plane.

A straightforward calculation leads to the following rather messy formula for the maximum expected (gross) payoff:

$$\Omega = 2 \int_q^\infty \mu_1 \, dF_1(\mu_1) + 2 \int_{\mu_2 = -q}^q \int_{\mu_1 = \mu_2}^q \mu_1 \, dF_1(\mu_1) \, dF_2(\mu_2)$$

$$(3.19) \qquad + 2 \int_q^\infty \mu_2 \, dF_2(\mu_2) + 2 \int_{\mu_1 = -q}^q \int_{\mu_2 = \mu_1}^q \mu_2 \, dF_2(\mu_2) \, dF_1(\mu_1)$$

$$- q[4F_1(-q)F_2(-q) - 1].$$

For example, if μ_i is rectangularly distributed on $[-R_i, R_i]$, with $q \leq R_i$ $(i = 1, 2)$, then (3.19) reduces to

$$(3.20) \qquad \Omega = \left(\frac{R_1 + R_2}{2}\right) + \frac{q^2}{2}\left(\frac{1}{R_1} + \frac{1}{R_2}\right) - \frac{q^3}{3}\left(\frac{1}{R_1 R_2}\right).$$

On the other hand, if $R_1 = R_2 = R$, and $q \geq R$, then the maximum expected payoff is

$$(3.21) \qquad \Omega = \frac{2R}{3} + q.$$

Figure 8.7 shows a graph of Ω as a function of q for the case $R_1 = R_2 = R$. The slope of the curve is 0 at $q = 0$, and 1 for $q \geq R$.

Since the maximum expected payoff under the routine information structure is q, the *value* of complete information in this case $(R_1 = R_2 = R)$

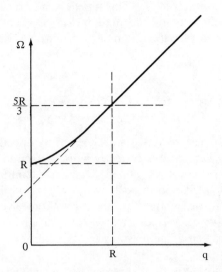

FIGURE 8.7. Maximum expected payoff.

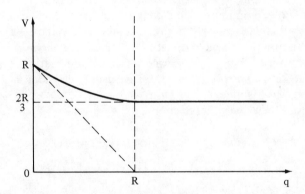

FIGURE 8.8. Value of information.

is obtained by subtracting q from (3.20) or (3.21), as the case may be, giving

$$(3.22) \qquad V = \begin{cases} R\left[1 - \left(\dfrac{q}{R}\right) + \left(\dfrac{q}{R}\right)^2 - \dfrac{1}{3}\left(\dfrac{q}{R}\right)^3\right] & \text{if } q \leqq R \\[3ex] \dfrac{2R}{3} & \text{if } q \geqq R. \end{cases}$$

Figure 8.8 shows a graph of V as this function of q. It is interesting that, in this example, the value of information *decreases* as the magnitude of the interaction term *increases* [compare this with (5.23) of Chapter 6, Section 5].

EXAMPLE 8C. TWO ELEMENTS IN SERIES,
WITH NOISY COMMUNICATION

Consider now a class of networks generated by introducing noise into the message from 1 to 2 in the series network of Example 8B. With such noise, the class of networks will no longer generate complete information; in fact *this class will not correspond to any single information structure.* As in Example 8B, we assume that the message received is accepted as determining the values of the final action variables without further adjustment. In this sense, the message can be interpreted as a "complete command."

More precisely, suppose that there are three elements, that element 1 receives (μ_1, μ_2) as input and sends $[\gamma_1(\mu), \gamma_2(\mu)]$ as output, where γ_1 and γ_2 are functions to be determined. The message $[\gamma_1(\mu), \gamma_2(\mu)]$ goes through a noisy communication channel, element 2, whose output is $[\varepsilon\gamma_1(\mu), \varepsilon\gamma_2(\mu)]$, where ε is a random variable with values ± 1. This last output is an input (message received) for element 3, which takes the final actions determined by $a_i = \varepsilon\gamma_i(\mu)$. An error in communication corresponds to $\varepsilon = -1$. Let $p = \text{Prob}(\varepsilon = -1)$; we need only consider $0 \leq p \leq 1/2$. We assume that ε is independent of μ_1 and μ_2.

In terms of the notation of Section 2,

(3.23)

B_{01} is the space of pairs of real numbers,

$B_{12} = \{(1, 1), (-1, 1), (1, -1), (-1, -1)\}$,

$B_{02} = \{1, -1\}$,

$B_{23} = B_{12}$,

$B_{30} = B_{12}$,

all other B_{ij} are empty.

The networks in this class may be represented by the diagram of Figure 8.9.

The corresponding response function is

(3.24) $$\rho(x) = [\varepsilon\gamma_1(x), \varepsilon\gamma_2(x)].$$

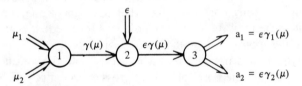

FIGURE 8.9. Series with noisy communication.

We shall show that the optimal functions γ_1 and γ_2 are determined by condition (3.18) with q replaced by

$$(3.25) \qquad c = \frac{q}{1 - 2p}.$$

Thus Figure 8.6 shows the regions in the (μ_1, μ_2) plane corresponding to the four alternative messages sent by 1 if one replaces q in that figure by c.

Similarly, let C be the expression obtained by replacing q by c in (3.19); then, as will be shown, the maximum expected payoff for this class of networks is

$$(3.26) \qquad \Omega = (1 - 2p)C.$$

For example, if μ_i is rectangularly distributed on $[-R_i, R_i]$, and $c \leq R_i$ $(i = 1, 2)$, then

$$\Omega = \left(\frac{R_1 + R_2}{2}\right)(1 - 2p) + \left(\frac{1}{R_1} + \frac{1}{R_2}\right)\frac{q^2}{2(1 - 2p)} - \left(\frac{1}{3R_1 R_2}\right)\frac{q^3}{(1 - 2p)^2}.$$

(3.27)

In particular, if $R_1 = R_2 = R$, and $c \leq R$, then

$$(3.28) \qquad \Omega = R(1 - 2p) + \frac{q^2}{R(1 - 2p)} - \frac{q^3}{3R^2(1 - 2p)^2}.$$

On the other hand, if $R_1 = R_2 = R$, and $c \geq R$, then

$$(3.29) \qquad \Omega = \left(\frac{2R}{3}\right)(1 - 2p) + q.$$

The graph of Ω as a function of q, as given by (3.28) and (3.29), is obtained from Figure 8.7 by replacing R with $R(1 - 2p)$. Similarly, $(\Omega - q)$ decreases from $R(1 - 2p)$, when $q = 0$, to $(2/3)R(1 - 2p)$, when $q \geq R(1 - 2p)$.

As one would suspect, the maximum expected payoff, Ω, decreases as p, the probability of error in communication, increases. Nevertheless, because we have assumed that the errors in the two coordinates of the message are perfectly correlated (i.e., that the sign of one coordinate is reversed if and only if the sign of the other is reversed), *it is still possible to control the interaction term*, $-qa_1a_2$, *without error*. Thus one can always fall back on a network that is no worse than the routine information structure from the point of view of gross expected payoff.

In the next subsection, by way of contrast, we study a class of networks in which the errors in the two coordinates are independent, and in this case one can no longer guarantee a network with expected payoff at least as large as q.

PROOF OF RESULTS

To prove the results described above, substitute $a_i = \varepsilon\gamma_i(\mu)$ into the payoff function (3.1), and take the expected value:

$$(3.30) \qquad E\omega = E[\varepsilon\gamma_i(\mu)\mu_1 + \varepsilon\gamma_2(\mu)\mu_2 - q\varepsilon^2\gamma_1(\mu)\gamma_2(\mu)].$$

Since ε is independent of μ, and $\varepsilon^2 = 1$, one can rewrite the above as (suppressing the argument μ of the functions γ_i)

$$
\begin{aligned}
(3.31) \qquad E\omega &= E[(E\varepsilon)\gamma_1\mu_1 + (E\varepsilon)\gamma_2\mu_2 - q\gamma_1\gamma_2] \\
&= E[(1 - 2p)\gamma_1\mu_1 + (1 - 2p)\gamma_2\mu_2 - q\gamma_1\gamma_2] \\
&= (1 - 2p)E[\gamma_1\mu_1 + \gamma_2\mu_2 - c\gamma_1\gamma_2],
\end{aligned}
$$

where $c \equiv q/(1 - 2p)$. Comparison of (3.31) with the expected payoff for the networks of Example 8B yields (3.26) and the corresponding optimal functions γ_1 and γ_2.

EXAMPLE 8D. SERIES-PARALLEL

Suppose that, in the networks discussed in the last subsection, each final action variable is assigned to a separate element instead of to the

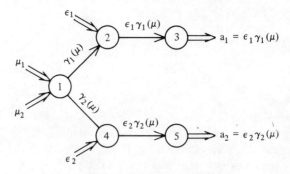

FIGURE 8.10. Series-parallel.

same element, with a separate communication channel to each from element 1 and with noise variables in each that are independent. The results in this case are similar to those of the last subsection, except that here it is possible to get a maximum expected payoff that is smaller than that for routine.

The networks to be studied are diagrammed in Figure 8.10.

Element 1 receives (μ_1, μ_2) as input, sends $\gamma_1(\mu)$ to element 2, and sends $\gamma_2(\mu)$ to element 4. Element 2, which is a communication channel from 1 to 3, also receives as input the noise variable $\varepsilon_1 (= \pm 1)$; its output to 3 is $\varepsilon_1 \gamma_1(\mu)$. Element 3 takes the final action $a_1 = \varepsilon_1 \gamma_1(\mu)$. A similar chain runs from 1 to 5 through 4, resulting in the final action $a_2 = \varepsilon_2 \gamma_2(\mu)$. We assume that $\varepsilon_1, \varepsilon_2, \mu_1, \mu_2$ are statistically independent and that

$$\text{Prob}(\varepsilon_i = -1) = p \qquad i = 1, 2;$$

that is the probability of error is the same for both channels.

The interpretation of two separate channels, and separate elements for the two final action variables, is not essential here. One might imagine a single channel as in Example 8B but with independent errors in the two coordinates. (More generally, one could study a single or double channel with an arbitrary joint distribution of $\mu_1, \mu_2, \varepsilon_1$, and ε_2.)

The response function generated by this class of networks is

$$(3.32) \qquad \rho(x) = [\varepsilon_1 \gamma_1(\mu), \varepsilon_2 \gamma_2(\mu)].$$

Using the method of Example 8C, the reader can easily verify that the solution in the present case is obtained from that of Example 8C by using the value $q(1 - 2p)$ for the constant c [instead of the value $q/(1 - 2p)$].

In particular, for the case of a rectangular distribution with $R_1 = R_2 = R$, we have for the maximum expected payoff,

$$(3.33) \qquad \Omega = \begin{cases} R(1 - 2p) + \dfrac{(1 - 2p)^3 q^2}{R} - \dfrac{(1 - 2p)^4 q^3}{3R^2} & \text{if } q(1 - 2p) \leq R; \\[4mm] \dfrac{2R(1 - 2p)}{3} + (1 - 2p)^2 q & \text{if } q(1 - 2p) \geq R. \end{cases}$$

Again, Ω is an increasing function of q and a decreasing function of p. However, in this case Ω falls to *zero* as p approaches $1/2$, so that for sufficiently small p the maximum expected payoff is less than for the routine information structure (unless $q = 0$).

This last result should be compared with that of Chapter 6, Section 9, concerning the information structure labeled *error in instruction*. In that example, a central agent computed what would be the best values of the action variables under complete information, but these values were transmitted through noisy channels to agents who "adjusted" the received instructions before taking the final actions. By contrast, in the present example, the elements assigned the task of taking the final actions are not allowed to make any adjustments ("theirs not to reason why; theirs but to do or die"). Rather, it is the central agent (element 1) that adjusts his messages to take account of the distortion that will take place in the channels.

All of which suggests the study of a modification of the present class of networks to allow the elements 3 and 5 to take final actions that are not equal to the messages received, in other words, that would allow them to perform computation. Such modification, on the other hand, would presumably increase the network costs. We do not, however, follow through this exercise here.

EXAMPLE 8E. SERIES: PARTIAL COMMAND

In the networks of Example 8C, all the work of observation and computation was performed by element 1, whereas element 3 simply translated his orders into final actions (element 2 was the communication channel). In this example, we study the effects of having element 1 *delegate* some of the work of observation and communication to element 3. If this has the effect of distributing more evenly the work of observation and communication, it also has the effect that the decision about a_1 is based on less information. On the other hand, no noise will now intervene between the observation μ_2 and the action a_2.

More precisely, we study the class of networks diagrammed in Figure 8.11.

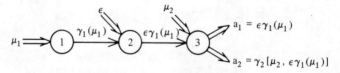

FIGURE 8.11. Partial command.

We shall also compare this class with the class obtained by interchanging the variables μ_1 and μ_2, and the variables a_1 and a_2.

The response function is

(3.34) $$\rho(x) = [\varepsilon\gamma_1(\mu_1), \gamma_2(\mu_2, \varepsilon\gamma_1[\mu_1])];$$

where $\varepsilon = \pm 1$, and is statistically independent of μ_1 and μ_2. The response function (3.34) may be rewritten:

(3.35)
$$a_1 = \varepsilon \gamma_1(\mu_1)$$
$$a_2 = \gamma_2(\mu_2, a_1).$$

The problem is to choose the best functions γ_1 and γ_2.

The interpretation is that element 1 observes μ_1 and sends an order, $\gamma_1(\mu_1)$, to element 3 through a noisy channel 2, fixing the nominal value of a_1. Element 3 receives the order as $\varepsilon \gamma_1(\mu_1)$ and uses this as the actual value of a_1; in addition, element 3 observes μ_2, and on the basis of the values of a_1 and μ_2, determines the value of a_2.

This interpretation of the message from elements 1 to 3 as an "order" is certainly not the only possible one. Figure 8.11 may simply represent the sequential nature of two decisions. The question of what makes a message an order or command is one that we defer to a later point.

We shall show that, for this class of networks, the best choice of γ_1 and γ_2 is

(3.36)
$$\gamma_1(\mu_1) = \begin{cases} -1 \\ +1 \end{cases} \qquad \text{according as } \mu_1 \begin{cases} < \\ > \end{cases} 0$$

$$\gamma_2(\mu_2, a_1) = \begin{cases} -1 \\ +1 \end{cases} \qquad \text{according as } \mu_2 \begin{cases} < \\ > \end{cases} a_1 q.$$

The maximum expected payoff is

(3.37)
$$\Omega_1 = (1 - 2p)E|\mu_1| + E|\mu_2 - q|,$$

where, as before, $p = \text{Prob}(\varepsilon = -1) = \text{Prob(error in communication)}$. The expected payoff Ω_1 is clearly decreasing as p increases from 0 to $1/2$; it is increasing as a function of q, since

(3.38)
$$\frac{\partial \Omega_1}{\partial q} = \frac{\partial E|\mu_2 - q|}{\partial q} = 2F_2(q) - 1 \geqq 0.$$

On the other hand, $(\Omega_1 - q)$ is decreasing as a function of q, since

(3.39)
$$\frac{\partial}{\partial q}(\Omega_1 - q) = 2[F_2(q) - 1] \leqq 0.$$

Nevertheless, it can be shown that

(3.40)
$$\Omega_1 \geqq q,$$

even if $p = 1/2$ (with strict inequality if q is not outside the range of μ_2).

This last point is plausible, since element 3 can control the sign of $a_1 a_2$, and therefore the sign of the interaction term.

It is of interest to compare this class of networks with that defined by interchanging μ_1 and μ_2, and a_1 and a_2, in Figure 8.11. Putting it more concretely, suppose that person A can cheaply observe μ_1 and person B can cheaply observe μ_2, but they are alike in other respects. Which one should be the "boss" in a network of the type under discussion?

It will be shown that, roughly speaking, in the case of noisy communication $(p > 0)$, the person who observes the variable with the *larger* dispersion should be the boss (i.e., should take the position of element 1), *provided that the dispersions of both variables are not too large.* On the other hand, if one or both variables have sufficiently large dispersions, then the person observing the variable with the *smaller* dispersion should be the boss. The larger the probability of error, the smaller the critical value of the dispersion that separates the two cases.

In the case of noiseless communication $(p = 0)$, the person observing the variable with the larger dispersion should be the boss, regardless of the sizes of the dispersions.

To put it another way, if there is not too much garbling in the transmission of commands, the man with the knowledge of the variable about which there is the most uncertainty should be the boss; but too much garbling of commands not only destroys that man's effectiveness in the "boss" position, but makes the greater uncertainty about his variable more dangerous.

Let Ω_2 denote the maximum expected payoff for the second class of networks (in which μ_2 is observed by element 1, etc.). By symmetry,

$$(3.41) \qquad \Omega_2 = (1 - 2p)E|\mu_2| + E|\mu_1 - q|.$$

Hence

$$(3.42) \qquad \Omega_1 - \Omega_2 = (E|\mu_2 - q| - (1 - 2p)E|\mu_2|)$$
$$- (E|\mu_1 - q| - (1 - 2p)E|\mu_1|)$$
$$= C_2 - C_1,$$

where

$$(3.43) \qquad C_i = E|\mu_i - q| - (1 - 2p)E|\mu_i|.$$

More definite results can be obtained by making special assumptions about the distributions of μ_1 and μ_2, as follows.

CASE OF RECTANGULAR DISTRIBUTION

Suppose that μ_i is rectangularly distributed on $[-R_i, R_i]$. Then, as will be shown,

$$(3.44) \qquad C_i = \begin{cases} \left| \left(q - \dfrac{R_i}{2} \right) \right| + pR_i & \text{if } R_i \leq q \\[2ex] \dfrac{q^2}{2R_i} + pR_i & \text{if } R_i \geq q. \end{cases}$$

The quantity C_i is first decreasing with R_i, and then increasing, reaching a maximum when $R_i = q/\sqrt{2p} \equiv R_0$. Hence

$$(3.45) \qquad \begin{aligned} &\text{(i) if } R_1, R_2 \leq R_0, \text{ then } \Omega_1 > \Omega_2 \text{ is equivalent} \\ &\quad\;\, \text{to } R_1 > R_2; \text{ whereas} \\[1ex] &\text{(ii) if } R_1, R_2 \geq R_0, \text{ then } \Omega_1 > \Omega_2 \text{ is equivalent} \\ &\quad\;\;\, \text{to } R_1 < R_2. \end{aligned}$$

CASE OF NORMAL DISTRIBUTION

Suppose that μ_i is normally distributed with mean zero and variance s_i^2. Then

$$(3.46) \qquad C_i = q \left[\Phi\!\left(\frac{q}{s_i} \right) - \frac{1}{2} \right] + s_i \varphi\!\left(\frac{q}{s_i} \right) - (1 - 2p)s_i\varphi(0),$$

where φ is the standard normal density and Φ is the standard normal cumulative distribution function. As s_1 increases, $(\Omega_1 - \Omega_2)$ first increases and then decreases, reaching a maximum in s_1 when

$$s_1^{\,2} = \frac{q^2}{- \log(1 - 2p)} \equiv s_0^{\,2}.$$

Furthermore,

$$(3.47) \qquad \begin{aligned} &\text{(i) if } s_1, s_2 \leq s_0, \text{ then } \Omega_1 > \Omega_2 \text{ is equivalent} \\ &\quad\;\, \text{to } s_1 > s_2; \text{ whereas} \\[1ex] &\text{(ii) if } s_1, s_2 \geq s_0, \text{ then } \Omega_1 > \Omega_2 \text{ is equivalent} \\ &\quad\;\;\, \text{to } s_1 < s_2. \end{aligned}$$

Thus the results for the normal case parallel those for the rectangular case, with s_i playing the role of R_i.

DISTRIBUTION OF μ_1 AND μ_2 DIFFERING BY A
SCALE PARAMETER

Both the normal and rectangular examples above are cases in which the distributions of μ_1 and μ_2 differ by a scale parameter. Let v be a random variable with a probability density function f that is symmetric around zero, and with variance 1. For $i = 1, 2$, suppose that μ_1 has the same distribution as $s_i v$, where s_i is some positive number; that is to say, the probability density of μ_i is

$$(3.48) \qquad\qquad f_i(\mu_i) = \left(\frac{1}{s_i}\right) f\left(\frac{\mu_i}{s_i}\right).$$

The variable μ_i will of course have mean zero and variance s_i^2.

We shall show that, if $p > 0$, then there is a critical number s_0, depending on p, such that

$$(3.49)$$

        (i) if $s_1, s_2 \leq s_0$, then $\Omega_1 > \Omega_2$ if and only if
        $s_1 > s_2$; whereas

        (ii) if $s_1, s_2 \geq s_0$, then $\Omega_1 > \Omega_2$ if and only if
        $s_1 < s_2$.

Furthermore, if s_2 is fixed at any value, then $\Omega_1 < \Omega_2$ for sufficiently large s_1.

On the other hand, if $p = 0$, then for all s_1 and s_2, $\Omega_1 > \Omega_2$ if and only if $s_1 > s_2$.

PROOF OF RESULTS

Substituting the second half of the response function (3.35) into the payoff function (3.1) and taking the expected value, we find that

$$(3.50) \qquad E\omega = E[\mu_1 a_1 + \mu_2 \gamma_2(\mu_2, a_1) - q a_1 \gamma_2(\mu_2, a_1)],$$

where it is understood that $a_1 = \varepsilon \gamma_1(\mu_1)$. Hence, given the function γ_1, it follows that the function γ_2 must be chosen so that $\gamma_2(\mu_2, a_1)$ maximizes the conditional expectation

$$E[\mu_1 a_1 + \mu_2 \gamma_2(\mu_2, a_1) - q a_1 \gamma_2(\mu_2, a_1)|\mu_2, a_1]$$

$$= a_1 E[\mu_1|\mu_2, a_1] + \gamma_2(\mu_2, a_1)(\mu_2 - q a_1).$$

Hence

$$(3.51) \qquad \gamma_2(\mu_2, a_1) = \begin{cases} -1 \\ +1 \end{cases} \text{ according as } \mu_2 - q a_1 \begin{Bmatrix} < \\ > \end{Bmatrix} 0.$$

Using this γ_2, and the given γ_1, one obtains the expected payoff

(3.52)
$$E\omega = E[a_1\mu_1 + |\mu_2 - qa_1|]$$
$$= E[\varepsilon\gamma_1(\mu_1)\mu_1 + |\mu_2 - q\varepsilon\gamma_1(\mu_1)|]$$
$$= E\{\mu_1\gamma_1(\mu_1)E(\varepsilon) + E_{\varepsilon,\mu_2}[|\mu_2 - q\varepsilon\gamma_1(\mu_1)|]\},$$

where E_{ε,μ_2} denotes expectation with respect to ε and μ_2 (recall that ε, μ_1, and μ_2 are independent). Hence $\gamma_1(\mu_1)$ equals (-1) or $(+1)$, according as

(3.53)
$$-\mu_1 E(\varepsilon) + E|\mu_2 + q\varepsilon| \begin{Bmatrix} > \\ < \end{Bmatrix} \mu_1 E(\varepsilon) + E|\mu_2 - q\varepsilon|,$$

or according as

(3.54)
$$\mu_1 \begin{Bmatrix} < \\ > \end{Bmatrix} \left[\frac{1}{2E(\varepsilon)} \right][E|\mu_2 + q\varepsilon| - E|\mu_2 - q\varepsilon|]$$

$$= \left[\frac{1}{2(1 - 2p)} \right][p(E|\mu_2 - q| - E|\mu_2 + q|)$$

$$+ (1 - p)(E|\mu_2 + q| - E|\mu_2 - q|)]$$

$$= \frac{1}{2}[E|\mu_2 + q| - E|\mu_2 - q|]$$

$$= 0.$$

(Recall that the distribution of μ_i is symmetric around 0.) Thus (3.36) has been verified.

From (3.52) we have

(3.55)
$$\Omega_1 = \max E\omega$$

$$= (E|\mu_1|)(E\varepsilon) + \frac{1}{2}E|\mu_2 - q\varepsilon| + \frac{1}{2}E|\mu_2 + q\varepsilon|$$

$$= (1 - 2p)E|\mu_1| + \frac{1}{2}p(E|\mu_2 - q| + E|\mu_2 + q|)$$

$$+ \frac{1}{2}(1 - p)(E|\mu_2 + q| + E|\mu_2 - q|).$$

But $E|\mu_2 + q| = E|\mu_2 - q|$, so that

(3.56)
$$\Omega_1 = (1 - 2p)E|\mu_1| + E|\mu_2 - q|,$$

which proves (3.37).

Note that, for any random variable v with density function f that is symmetric around 0,

(3.57)
$$E|v - q| = 2q \int_0^q f(t)\, dt + 2 \int_q^\infty tf(t)\, dt,$$

as can easily be verified. Hence $E|v - q| \geq q$, and

(3.58)
$$\frac{\partial}{\partial q} E|v - q| = 2 \int_0^q f(t)\, dt = 2F(q) - 1,$$

where F is the cumulative distribution function of v. This proves (3.38) to (3.40).

To prove the results on the comparison of Ω_1 and Ω_2, we discuss first the case of distributions differing by a scale parameter. If a random variable τ has the distribution of sv, where $s > 0$ [i.e., if the density function of τ is $(1/s)f(t/s)$], then analogous to (3.57) we have

(3.59)
$$E|\tau - q| = 2q \int_0^{q/s} f(t)\, dt + 2s \int_{q/s}^\infty tf(t)\, dt.$$

From this we easily calculate

(3.60)
$$\frac{\partial}{\partial s} E|\tau - q| = 2 \int_{q/s}^\infty tf(t)\, dt,$$

which is nonnegative, and nonincreasing as a function of s. In particular, setting $q = 0$,

(3.61)
$$E|\tau| = 2s \int_0^\infty tf(t)\, dt = sE|v|,$$

(3.62)
$$\frac{\partial}{\partial s} E|\tau| = 2 \int_0^\infty tf(t)\, dt = E|v|.$$

Define $C(s)$ by

(3.63)
$$C(s) = E|\tau - q| - (1 - 2p)E|\tau|;$$

then from (3.42) and (3.43),

(3.64)
$$\Omega_1 - \Omega_2 = C(s_2) - C(s_1).$$

From (3.59) to (3.62), we have

(3.65)
$$\frac{d}{ds} C(s) = 2\left[2p \int_0^\infty tf(t)\, dt - \int_0^{q/s} tf(t)\, dt \right],$$

so that $C(s)$ is a convex function of s that decreases for $s \leq s_0$, say, and increases for $s \geq s_0$. The remaining results now follow easily, including those for the rectangular and normal cases.

EXAMPLE 8F. SERIES: SEQUENTIAL ACTION

In the class of networks examined in Example 8E, the message from element 1 to 3 (through channel 2) had a dual function. First, it determined the value of the final action variable a_1; and second, it provided information about a part of nature, variable μ_1. The message from element 1 to 3 was interpreted as a "command."

We can imagine a closely related situation in which two decisions are to be taken in sequence, with the person making the first decision informing the other person which decision he has made, as in Figure 8.12.

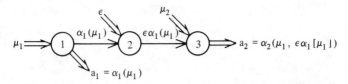

FIGURE 8.12. Sequential action, message about action taken.

Or, as an alternative, the message could be about the value of μ_1 observed, rather than about the decision made. This would be more informative but it could also be expected to be more expensive, since the action a_1 is only a zero–one variable, whereas the variable μ_1 can take on a continuum of possible values. The greater expense could be both in the transmission of the message, and in the subsequent computation by element 3. One would also expect the noise to take a different form, for example, additive. The resulting class of networks is diagrammed in Figure 8.13.

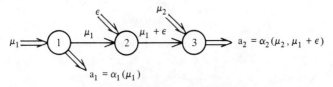

FIGURE 8.13. Sequential action, message about observation.

We shall analyze such a class of networks, but for mathematical convenience we take a problem that differs slightly from the one we have been considering in the examples of this section. Suppose that a_1 and a_2 are real-valued and that the payoff function is quadratic, as follows:

$$(3.66) \qquad \omega(x, a_1, a_2) = 2\mu_1 a_1 + 2\mu_2 a_2 - q_{11}a_1{}^2 - q_{22}a_2{}^2 - 2q_{12}a_1 a_2,$$

where $q_{ii} > 0$, $q_{11}q_{12} - q_{12}^2 > 0$. Suppose further that μ_1, μ_2, and the noise variable ε are independent and normally distributed with means zero and variances s_1^2, s_2^2, and t^2, respectively. The response function implied by Figure 8.13 is

(3.67)
$$a_1 = \alpha_1(\mu_1)$$
$$a_2 = \alpha_2(\mu_2, \mu_1 + \varepsilon),$$

where the decision functions α_1 and α_2 are to be determined.

The class of networks thus defined corresponds to a single information structure:

(3.68)
$$\eta_1 = \mu_1$$
$$\eta_2 = (\mu_2, \mu_1 + \varepsilon).$$

Applying Theorem 5 of Chapter 5, one easily finds that the best decision functions α_1 and α_2 are the linear functions

(3.69)
$$\alpha_1(\mu_1) = \left(\frac{q_{22}}{q_{11}q_{22} - k_1 q_{12}^2}\right)(\mu_1 + \varepsilon)$$

$$\alpha_2(\mu_2, \mu_1 + \varepsilon) = \left(\frac{1}{q_{22}}\right)\mu_2 - \left(\frac{k_1 q_{12}}{q_{11}q_{22} - k_1 q_{12}^2}\right)(\mu_1 + \varepsilon)$$

where

(3.70)
$$k_1 \equiv \frac{s_1^2}{s_1^2 + t^2}.$$

The corresponding maximum expected payoff is

(3.71)
$$V_1 = \frac{q_{22}s_1^2}{q_{11}q_{22} - k_1 q_{12}^2} + \frac{s_2^2}{q_{22}}.$$

Note that $k_1 = 1$ when there is no noise in the channel (element 2), and that k_1 tends towards 0 as the noise gets more important relative to the message, that is, as $t^2 \to \infty$ with s_1^2 fixed. The quantity

$$\frac{k_1}{1 - k_1} = \frac{s_1^2}{t_1^2}$$

is the *signal-to-noise ratio*. The parameter k_1 may be interpreted as the reliability of the channel.

We may again pose the question, "Given that one wants to use a network of the 'sequential' type being discussed, which decision should come first in the sequence?" To answer this, interchange the variables a_1 and a_2

and the variables μ_1 and μ_2 in the problem just discussed; this gives an expected payoff

$$(3.72) \qquad V_2 = \frac{q_{11}s_2{}^2}{q_{11}q_{22} - k_2 q_{12}{}^2} + \frac{s_1{}^2}{q_{11}},$$

where

$$(3.73) \qquad k_2 = \frac{s_2{}^2}{s_2{}^2 + t^2}.$$

To compare the two different cases requires some assumption about the variances of the noise variables in the two cases. One plausible assumption is that $k_1 = k_2 = k$, that is, that the signal-to-noise ratio is the same in each case. With this we find that

$$(3.74) \qquad V_1 - V_2 = \left(\frac{s_1{}^2}{q_{11}} - \frac{s_2{}^2}{q_{22}}\right)\left[\frac{k(q_{12}{}^2/q_{11}q_{22})}{1 - k(q_{12}{}^2/q_{11}q_{22})}\right].$$

Here the decision about a_1 or about a_2 should come first, according as $(s_1{}^2/q_{11})$ or $(s_2{}^2/q_{22})$ is the larger. This ordering is independent of the magnitude of the communication reliability parameter k, except for the limiting case $k = 0$, in which the ordering does not matter.

One can interpret the significance of the quantity $(s_i{}^2/q_{ii})$ as follows. The larger $s_i{}^2$ is, the greater the uncertainty about the variable μ_i, and therefore the more valuable it is for the team that i communicate that value to the other person. On the other hand, the larger q_{ii} is, the more sensitive is the payoff to departures of a_i from its best value (under complete information) and, therefore, the more valuable it is that a_i be determined on the basis of information about both μ_1 and μ_2, rather than on the basis of μ_i alone.

The quantity $(q_{12}{}^2/q_{11}q_{22})$ is a measure of the interaction between the two action variables in the payoff function (a measure that is invariant under changes of scale in the units used to measure the action variables). Equation 3.74 shows that the importance of choosing the best sequence of decisions increases with the interaction.

4. PROCESSING AND POOLING OF INFORMATION

In a network with given task functions, consider a *dyadic segment*, (i, k), in which the set B_i of outputs of the element i is identical with the set $\tilde{B}_k$ of inputs of the element k (see Figure 8.14).

The examples given in this and earlier chapters illustrate two important propositions, which in this section will be presented explicitly and proved:

under certain conditions, (A) information-processing never *increases* the gross expected payoff; (B) information-pooling never *decreases* the gross expected payoff.

FIGURE 8.14. Dyadic segment (i, k).

(A) GROSS PAYOFF LOSS THROUGH INFORMATION PROCESSING

Leaving the rest of the network unchanged, we change the segment thus: introduce a new element j between i and k as in Figure 8.15. Thus a message b_{ij} received by j from i is *processed* into a (generally different) message b_{jk}, from j to k, on which k will base his decision. For example,

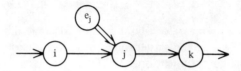

FIGURE 8.15. Introduction of noisy processing element j between elements i and k.

b_{ij} may be a report about the observations made by i, and b_{jk} may be a command given by j to k. Note that (as in Figure 8.9 with $i = 1, j = 2$, and $k = 3$) the message b_{jk} may be affected by noise, "garbled" in a sense defined in Chapter 2, Section 7. We shall show that the introduction of a processing element j will decrease, or at least never increase, the gross expected payoff, regardless of the payoff function and of the probabilities of the states of the world.

(B) GROSS PAYOFF GAIN THROUGH INFORMATION POOLING

Change the dyadic segment as follows: while preserving the input set B_i, introduce another element j and let the input of k consist of messages from both i and j (see Figure 8.16).

Thus message b_{ik} is *pooled* with message b_{jk}, to provide a basis for k's decisions. Again, each message may include previously introduced noise but the pooled message is not to include any further noise. We shall show that the pooling of messages will increase, or at least never

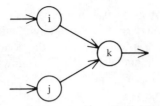

FIGURE 8.16. Pooling messages from i and j to k.

decrease, the gross expected payoff for any payoff function and any probability distribution of the states of the world.

However, if the pooled message is itself subject to further noise, then the pooling of the messages may well decrease the payoff.

PROCESSING

First consider the case in which the entire network consists at most of the elements $i, j,$ and k of Figure 8.15. The decision (action) of k will therefore be a *final* one (see Section 2), that is, it will impinge directly on nature. This decision will be based on the message received by k. On the other hand, the message received by i will be an observation, that is, it will come from nature, say $b_{0i} = \beta_{0i}(x)$.

In the case of no processing (Figure 8.14), the message sent by i and received by k is, say,

$$b_{ik} = \beta_{ik}(b_{0i})$$
$$= \beta_{ik}[\beta_{0i}(x)]$$
$$\equiv \eta(x).$$

The function η, then, describes how k's incoming messages depend indirectly on the state of nature, x.

In the case of processing (Figure 8.15), the message received by j is

$$b_{ij} = \eta(x),$$

whereas the message received by k from j is

$$b_{jk} = \beta_{jk}(b_{ij}, e_j)$$
$$\equiv \eta'(x).$$

The function β_{jk} describes how the message b_{ij} is processed, with the possible introduction of noise, before being sent to k. The function η' describes how, in the case of processing, k's incoming messages depend indirectly on the state of nature.

By our definition of noise (see above, Section 2), the noise variable $e_j \equiv \varepsilon_j(x)$ has the property that, if Z is a payoff-adequate partition of the set X of states of nature into sets z, then the conditional distribution of e_j given b_{ij} and z is independent of z. It follows that the conditional distribution of the pair (b_{ij}, e_j), and hence of $\beta_{jk}(b_{ij}, e_j)$, is independent of z. Hence the message $b_{jk} = \beta_{jk}(b_{ij}, e_j)$ is a *garbling* of the message b_{ij}, according to the definition in Chapter 2, Section 8; that is, the information structure η' is a garbling of the information structure η, relative to Z. [Recall that Y' is a garbling of Y if, for every y in Y, y' in Y, and z in Z, the conditional probability of y' given $z \cap y$ is independent of z.]

It follows from the corollary to the theorem of Chapter 2, Section 8, that η is at least as valuable an information structure as η'. We have thus shown that the introduction of processing cannot increase the expected payoff.

To extend the proposition to an entire network, we cannot apply the "garbling corollary" directly, but we can use a similar argument. Let k be a given element in the network, let $\tilde{B}_k$ be its set of alternative combined input messages from other elements and from nature, let C_k be its set of alternative combined output messages to other elements, and let A_k be its set of alternative primary actions (messages to nature).

Any task function for k can be described by a pair (γ_k, α_k) where

$$
\begin{aligned}
c_k &= \gamma_k(\tilde{b}_k) \qquad c_k \text{ in } C_k \\
a_k &= \alpha_k(\tilde{b}_k) \qquad a_k \text{ in } A_k.
\end{aligned}
$$
(4.1)

Suppose that the set of feasible functions γ_k is the set of all functions from $\tilde{B}_k$ to C_k, and that the set of feasible functions α_k is the set of all functions from $\tilde{B}_k$ to A_k, *whatever be the task functions of the rest of the elements in the network.*

Let K denote the set of all elements in the network other than k, and let a_K be the combined final action variable of the elements in K. For a given specification of the task functions of all elements except k, and of the functions that determine the messages coming into the network from nature, there exist functions η_k, η_K, and α_K, and a set Y_K, such that *for any choice of the function* γ_k,

$$
a_K = \alpha_K[\gamma_k(\tilde{b}_k), y_K]
$$
(4.2)

where

$$
\begin{aligned}
y_K &= \eta_K(x) \qquad y_K \text{ in } Y_K \\
\tilde{b}_k &= \eta_k(x) \qquad \tilde{b}_k \text{ in } \tilde{B}_k.
\end{aligned}
$$
(4.3)

As usual, we may associate with $\tilde{B}_k$ and η_k a partition, say Y_k, of X, and *indeed we shall identify $\tilde{B}_k$ with Y_k*. Similarly, we shall represent Y_K as a partition of X.

The effect of introducing into the network an element that processes the information coming into k is to replace the partition Y_k by a partition Y_k'. In keeping with the concept of noise suggested in Section 2, we shall assume that, if Z is a payoff-adequate partition of X, then for every y_k in Y_k, y_k' in Y_k', y_K in Y_K, and z in Z,

(4.4) $$P(y_k'|y_k, y_K, z) = P(y_k'|y_k).$$

Let (γ_k', α_k') be the task function for element k *with the processed information*, that is with the partition Y_k'; let the task functions of the other elements, and hence α_K and Y_K, be fixed. The expected payoff $\Omega(Y_k')$ is equal to

(4.5) $$\sum_{\substack{z \in Z \\ y_k' \in Y_k' \\ y_K \in Y_K}} P(z \cap y_k' \cap y_K)\omega[z, \alpha_k'(y_k'), \alpha_K(\gamma_k'[y_k'], y_K)] \equiv \Omega'.$$

From the properties of conditional probability, it follows that

$$P(z \cap y_k' \cap y_K) = \sum_{y_k} P(y_k)P(z \cap y_k' \cap y_K|y_k) = \sum_{y_k} P(y_k)P(y_k'|z \cap y_K \cap y_k)$$
$$\times P(z \cap y_K|y_k).$$

Using the hypothesis (4.4),

(4.6) $$P(z \cap y_k' \cap y_K) = \sum_{y_k} P(y_k)P(y_k'|y_k)P(z \cap y_K|y_k).$$

Applying (4.6) to the expression (4.5), we obtain

(4.7)
$$\Omega' = \sum_{y_k} P(y_k) \sum_{y_k'} P(y_k'|y_k) \sum_{z,y_K} P(z \cap y_K|y_k)\omega[z, \alpha_k'(y_k'), \alpha_K(\gamma_k'[y_k'], y_K)]$$
$$\leq \sum_{y_k} P(y_k) \max_{a,c} \sum_{z,y_K} P(z \cap y_K|y_k)\omega[z, a, \alpha_K(c, y_K)],$$

(remembering that $\sum_{y_k'} P(y_k'|y_k) = 1$). For each y_k in Y_k, let $\alpha_k(y_k)$ and $\gamma_k(y_k)$ be values of a and c, respectively, that maximize

$$\sum_{z,y_K} P(z \cap y_K|y_k)\omega[z, a, \alpha_K(c, y_K)];$$

then (4.7) can be rewritten as

$$\Omega' \leqq \Omega \equiv \sum_{y_k} P(y_k) \sum_{z,y_K} P(z \cap y_K|y_k)\omega[z, \alpha_k(y_k), \alpha_K(\gamma_k[y_k], y_K)]$$
$$= \sum_{y_k,z,y_K} P(z \cap y_k \cap y_K)\omega[z, \alpha_k(y_k), \alpha_K(\gamma_k[y_k], y_K)],$$

which is the expected payoff that results when element k uses the *unprocessed information*, Y_k, and the task functions α_k and γ_k. Hence the network can always do no worse using the unprocessed information than the processed information.

POOLING

The proposition that, under our assumptions, the pooling of messages cannot decrease the gross payoff follows directly from the fact that the pooled information is at least as fine as the unpooled information. In the unpooled case, the incoming message is b_{ik}, whereas in the pooled case the incoming message is (b_{ik}, b_{jk}). Any (task) function of b_{ik} can be reproduced by a (task) function of (b_{ik}, b_{jk}) that is, independent of b_{jk}, thus:

$$\beta'_k(b_{ik}, b_{jk}) \equiv \beta_k(b_{ik}).$$

Hence, if (1) the task function of element k can be varied independently of the task functions of the other elements, and (2) the set of task functions available (feasible) for element k is the set of all functions from $\tilde{B}_k$ to B_k, then the set of response functions that can be generated by the network with the pooled information includes all the response functions that can be generated by the network with the unpooled information. (This is essentially the same argument that was used in Chapter 2, Section 8, on comparison of information structures.)

CONSTRAINTS ON TASK FUNCTIONS

In proving that processing cannot increase the gross payoff—and that pooling cannot decrease it—we made two assumptions:

1. The task function of the element in question can be varied independently of the task functions in the rest of the network (including the functions that determine the inputs from nature).
2. The set of task functions feasible for the element in question is the set of all functions from its set of inputs to its set of outputs.

If these assumptions are satisfied for every element in the network, then one is in case 3 of the discussion at the end of Section 2, with the particular assumption (2) above *guaranteeing a sufficiently rich set of feasible task functions* at each element.

On the other hand, if the set of feasible task functions for the element in question, say k, is constrained in some manner so that (2) is not satisfied, then the processing of messages coming into k may *increase* the gross payoff, or pooling may *decrease* it.

To illustrate with an extreme case, suppose that k is the only element in the network, that its input message is a pair of nonnegative numbers, say $x = (x_1, x_2)$, that its output is a final action, say a, and that for any pair (x_1, x_2) the optimal action is $a = (x_1 + x_2)/2$, as would be the case, for example, if the payoff function were

$$\omega(x, a) = -\left(a - \frac{x_1 + x_2}{2}\right)^2.$$

Suppose, however, that the element k is extremely limited in its information processing capability, and can in fact perform only *one* operation, namely, select the maximum of two numbers. With such a constraint, it is obvious that there is some processing of the input (x_1, x_2) that would increase the gross payoff, for example, introduce an element j between nature and k with the task function

$$\beta_{jk}(x_1, x_2) = \left(\frac{x_1 + x_2}{2}, 0\right).$$

Whether the introduction of such a new element j would increase the *net* payoff or not would depend, of course, on its cost.

Similar considerations apply to the pooling of information. Indeed, it is only if one can ignore the costs of, or constraints on, task functions that one can guarantee that more information is better than (or at least no worse than) less information. We return to a more extended consideration of this point in the next chapter.

CHAPTER 9

Task Allocation, Organizing, and Leading

1. Constraints

Not all networks are feasible. A network may be not feasible because the *outputs b_{ij} of its elements* (each element being associated with some time period) cannot be produced during the stated period of time by any man or machine within the reach of the organizer of the team. Even supposing for a moment that financial resources are unlimited, one must recognize that there are limitations imposed by the laws of physics and of human physiology. In fact, one has to face the even narrower limitations due to cultural conditions. The technology and training prevailing in a given society seldom take advantage of all the possibilities offered by nature, including the nature of man.

The feasibility restrictions imposed upon the choice of networks are analogous to restrictions on methods of material production and transportation. For example, a system of assembly lines constituting a plant has the same formal structure as an organizational network, except that, in the case of an assembly line, the output of each element is not a signal but the result of some physical transformation or translocation. Each position (a worker, a tool) on the assembly line would be represented by a sequence of elements, one element for each time period of stated length. The output of each element is thus limited by the feasible maximum speed of some physical or physiological processes.

The case of team networks is similar. Not more than a certain number of symbols can be transmitted per unit of time, without error, or with errors of a specified kind and probability, by a given communication channel, human or inanimate. Not more than a certain number of computations of a given kind can be performed per unit of time by a given man or machine within a specified limit of errors, and the number of variables on which observations of a given degree of accuracy can be performed simultaneously is also limited.

The limitations of available men and machines explain why it pays to process information. This was shown in Chapter 8, Section 4. It may not be feasible to assign to the same man or machine the task of reading original reports (that are relatively fine or relatively errorless), and also the task of computing optimal decisions on the basis of such reports; thus it may be necessary to insert intermediaries and, hence, coarsen or garble the reports. Similarly, the constraints on available resources may also make it impossible to take full advantage of information pooling. A man (or machine) able to absorb messages from two sources and to make optimal decisions on the basis of this information may not exist for the type of messages and actions considered.

The loss in *gross* payoff due to delay of information or to garbling (see Chapters 7 and 8) can be a reason against processing information. The time needed to transmit messages from an element i to an element k directly is presumably shorter than the combined time needed for the transmission from i to an element j, the processing (computation) by j, and the retransmission from j to k (compare Figures 8.14 and 8.15). The insertion of j would thus diminish (or at least not increase) the gross expected payoff, both because the information will be *garbled* (or, as a special case, *coarsened*), and because it will be *delayed*. But again, such delays may be necessary because of the limited capacities of the instruments (men and machines) available for implementing the network.

Except in Chapter 6, we have treated the size of a team (the number of persons constituting it) as fixed. In our present, more general, context, such a restriction appears unnecessary. Neither the number of people, nor the number of machines, nor the number of elements (men or machines with a time subscript) need be restricted in advance; although, in particular cases, these numbers may be bounded for some reason: for example, the size of a small farm team may be limited by the size of the farmer's family. In general, those numbers are to be determined along with other properties of an optimal network, as expressed by the matrices $[B_{ij}]$, $[\beta_{ij}]$. These properties will include the description of the nature of each element: for example, whether it should be associated with a man of some particular kind, or a machine of some particular kind. Hence, if by the "size" of a team at a given time we mean the number of people assigned at that time to the tasks of observing, communicating, or computing on behalf of the team, then the team's size, too, is reflected in the relevant parts of the two matrices and will be determined as a result of maximizing the net expected payoff.

2. Costs

It was stated in Chapter 2, Section 12 that it is, in general, not possible to represent gross payoff as a sum of cost and net payoff, both measured in utility units. To be sure, this decomposition and the resulting simplification of analysis is possible in the important case in which (1) the results of the team's activities as well as the costs of installing and operating the network are money amounts, and (2) the expected value of the difference is maximized (which is to say that utility is identified with money).

If neither of the two assumptions is fulfilled, the optimal network is defined as one that maximizes, over the set of feasible networks, the expectation of the payoff; the latter being a function not only of the events and the final team action (which is yielded by the network), but also directly a function of the network itself.

An intermediate case is one in which it is possible to represent the results of team actions and the network costs as separate money amounts, but in which money is *not* identical with utility. In this case the maximand is not the expectation of the difference between the two amounts, but rather the expectation of some (nonlinear) function of this difference. In what follows, we shall make this intermediate assumption, as it will permit us to fix the ideas using ordinary principles of accounting. (A similar assumption about the results of actions and the costs of information structures was discussed in Chapter 2, Section 12, where it permitted us to define in a simple way the concept of *value of information.*)

For any given network, there are costs of providing and operating its elements. More precisely, we have in mind the costs of *intermediate* activities only (observation, communication, computation). We have called them the *organizational costs.* They are associated with men and machines producing intra-team signals. On the other hand, the costs associated with the *final* activities of the team—those impinging upon nature—have been already taken into account in computing the gross payoff. Thus the wages and capital charges associated with material production and transportation, and with communications sent to the world outside the team, are not included in organizational costs. This separation permits us to concentrate on the specific problems of organization as such, though there are helpful formal analogies between the economics of intra-team signals and the usual economics of material production.

It is useful to distinguish between fixed and variable costs. The variable costs of a network depend on the kind and frequency of observations, communications, and computations that actually take place. Thus, in our notation, variable costs depend on the actual signals b_{ij} transmitted from one element to another. These signals depend, of course, on the signal-transformation functions β_{ij} defined in Chapter 8, but they also depend on the state of the environment, the argument of the functions β_{0j}. Consequently the variable costs are random. For example, in the case of *management by exception* (Chapter 6, Sections 11 and 12), charges for those observations, communications, and computations that are to be made in emergency situations will arise if and only if certain events occur, defined beforehand as *emergency*. Variable network costs are exemplified by the wages of personnel hired for short periods or entitled to overtime bonuses, and by those costs of using rented equipment (such as telephones or computers) that are charged over and above a constant ("flat") rental.

Fixed costs, on the other hand, depend on the functions $\beta_{ij}(1, j = 0, \ldots)$ and hence on the sets B_{ij} of possible signals, not on the actual signals b_{ij}. Fixed costs are therefore nonrandom, being independent of the events. They are exemplified by salaries on long term contracts, by a part of income of a manager-owner, by capital charges on purchased equipment, and by long term rentals.

Because of its variable components, the total cost of providing and operating a network is, in general, a random variable. The function K that associates each network N with some amount $K(N)$ of expected cost may be called the *organizational cost function*. To discuss its properties, we may ask what changes can result from varying the task function of the ith element, that is, the set of functions $\beta_i = (\beta_{i0}, \beta_{i1}, \ldots)$ that characterizes its task (of observation, communication, computation). Such changes may, of course, imply changes in the domain or range of the task function, that is, in the sets $\tilde{B}_i$ or B_i of the potential messages received or sent by the element i.

A network element is associated with some man or machine (an *instrument*) and a given time period. Given the instrument, one task (β_i', say) will require more time than another (β_i, say) in order to be accomplished without errors. Possibly β_i' will require infinite time, which is another way of saying the instrument is altogether unable to accomplish this task without error. More generally, given the instrument, one task will require more time than another (possibly infinite time) to be achieved with errors of various kinds, occurring with probabilities not exceeding some fixed preassigned ("tolerance") limits. We shall then say that the former task is *more difficult* than the latter, given the man or machine considered, and given the tolerance limits. Substituting a more difficult task for a less difficult one will then (by definition) require more hours of a given man or machine, or delay some final action, or result in larger probabilities of more harmful errors. To some extent, these effects can be substituted for each other. Thus the harm due to errors can be diminished if the instrument is worked for a longer time, but this will increase the delay; or additions may be made to personnel and machinery, thus avoiding delays. In either case, additional rentals or wages are added to the cost. Instead, one may introduce a new instrument, which is more effective in the following sense: it will perform the same task with the same errors in shorter time, or with smaller errors in the same time. Men and machines that are more effective may be in relatively short supply, or can be produced only by a relatively costly effort of training a man or building a machine. In this case, under conditions of a market economy (perfect or imperfect), those men and the lenders or sellers of those machines will ask and receive higher salaries or rentals or prices. The economics of the market in services of, and facilities for, computation, observation, and communication is not fundamentally different from the economics of any other market of human services, and of purchased or rented equipment.

This applies also to the case in which the change in the task can be accomplished by substituting for the previously employed man or machine one of equal cost but different specialization. This is a concept that was touched upon in Chapter 4 in terms of information structures, and that we shall take up again presently, in terms of (implemented) networks.

3. SPECIALIZATION

In Chapter 4, Section 6, we have related specialization to the costliness of having very fine information handled by a single person. In Example 4B given later, it was preferable that the personnel manager should not be informed of details pertaining to finance (say).

Using the concept of *implemented networks* introduced in Chapter 8, we can now treat specialization in a more general way. The net payoff to the team depends on how certain kinds of activities are allocated among the various instruments. It will be recalled that these activities consist of receiving messages (from other instruments or, in the case of observations, from nature), of processing them into other messages (by computing), and of communicating these messages (to other instruments or, in the case of final actions, to nature).

For example, we may identify the two action-producing elements on each of the network diagrams of Chapter 8, Section 3, with two instruments: the personnel manager (and his staff) and the finance manager (and his staff). It would be somewhat artificial to insist that a_1 and a_2 be real-valued: for example, a_1 = the wage rate offered to the workers; a_2 = the interest rate offered to the lenders. We can, more broadly, consider the

set of all team actions as the Cartesian product of two sets, whose elements
are actions pertinent to personnel and to finance, respectively. Clearly,
there are many ways of factoring the set of team actions. For example,
instead of contrasting "personnel" and "finance" we might install one
manager for each of two geographic regions; or one manager for the cold,
the other (the vacation substitute) for the warm season; or one manager
to handle all affairs with outsiders whose name initials run from *A* through
L, and the other to handle all others. The reader will easily recall cases in
which each of such allocations of activities is indeed applied and is
presumably close enough to optimal. In any given case, some of those
allocations are so manifestly bad as to be not worth considering. (See
Section 6, on the cost of organizing.) For others, it pays to compare the
net expected payoffs they would yield. Sometimes this can be done by
comparing separately the gross payoffs (as was done in the examples of
Chapter 8) and the cost of each network. In any case, the results of comparison will reflect the gross payoff function, the probabilities of states of
Nature and thus, given the network, the joint probabilities of events and
messages (and thus of errors). But, in addition, the differences among the
net expected payoffs of alternative implemented networks will also depend
on the nature and cost of available instruments.

An instrument that is well adapted to messages of a certain class may
be altogether unable to handle messages of a different class, or it may
handle them with more harmful delays and errors. A man not proficient
in a foreign language or in some branch of chemical engineering is an
example.

In general, the cost of a machine that can handle several classes of
operations (whether information-processing or not) contrasts with that of
several machines, each equally effective in a different specialty, as follows:
The "all-purpose" machine will have to possess some additional device
to select each special operation as the need arises. But the cost of the
selection device may be offset by savings on some parts that are common
to all classes of operations. Also, a specialized machine will stand idle
more frequently than an all-purpose one.

In the case of information-processing machines, a class of operations
will usually be associated with messages having in common some property
that will call for a processing "routine" characteristic of its task function.
In a strongly specialized instrument, a unique routine is built in once and
for all; there is no need to specify the particular class of messages, since
no other messages will occur. In a more flexible instrument, several
routines can be applied, each activated by a different symbol. Repetitive
properties of messages can be exploited by economizing on symbols per

unit of time, since the repeated part is reduced to a single symbol. But the symbol representing each routine has to be stored in the instrument's memory, thus requiring additional capacity, and hence presumably increasing the cost. Does this apply to humans? Psychologists tell us of our tendency to group objects into patterns (Gestalts); these are classes of objects connected by some simple relation (of which similarity and contiguity are important cases). Patterns help one to memorize and to solve problems. A specialist responds quickly whenever he can identify a certain pattern. This can be exploited by letting each man deal only with messages that belong together in some easily recognizable manner.

We are so used to people's specialization that we hardly notice its economic consequences. We are seldom aware how inconvenient it would be if people would have their tasks assigned and reassigned at random, rather than in accordance with some principle of classification. Problems of optimal assignment become visible when two or more principles appear, at first sight, to be almost equally economical. Whether aid to foreign agriculture should be the job of the Secretary of State (together with all other foreign affairs) or of the Secretary of Agriculture (with all other agricultural matters) cannot be deduced from the dictionary definitions of the words "foreign" and "agricultural" alone. To answer such questions one has to compare the organizational cost of each kind of assignment, usually simultaneously with the comparison of gross payoffs, since these may also be affected by the choice.

Moreover, as in the case of inanimate data-processing instruments, a man who has several specialties, that is, can apply several "routines" (called "patterns" in this context), may or may not command a higher fixed cost (his salary) than the several narrower specialists that he might replace. Competent, versatile men are not in large supply, and may not be easy to train or even discover. Given the available resources, a certain compromise—the least costly specification of classes of messages—will be optimal.

It will be recalled that, for formal convenience, we defined network elements in such a way that a given person, or a given piece of equipment, may be represented by two or more elements, one element for each time period of stated length. Thus, when a person "memorizes," we represent this by a message sent from one element to another, both being associated with the same physical person. But, instead of memorizing, the person may transmit the message to another person, or a file or a machine, freeing his memory capacity to store other information. Clearly, both methods are encountered, and presumably each has its advantages. Adding a physically distinct link adds to the fixed costs and increases delays and the chance of errors. But overloaded memory also leads to errors and slows down operations.

So far we have discussed cost economies that may result from choosing the set $\tilde{B}_i$ (or the set B_i) of messages received (or sent) by the element as some "specialty," that is, as a set of messages related to each other by some common property or simple relation. Economies also arise if there is some simple relation between the elements of B_i and those of $\tilde{B}_i$. It so happens that the man who issues commands to the Pacific Fleet can be more easily informed about the situation in the Pacific than in the Atlantic.

In earlier chapters, $\tilde{B}_i$ was in effect replaced by the set of observations of nature made by member i, and B_i was replaced by the set A_i of (final) actions of that member. The above example of the Fleet commander was particularly suitable to that simple case, named there *cospecialization of action and observation*; see in particular Chapter 4, Section 7. Cost advantages of cospecialization influence the organizational cost function. Interesting cases arise when networks without cospecialization happen to be prohibitively costly; their cost is so large that, regardless of the payoff function, they can never be optimal. When used in conjunction with a particular payoff function, namely, a quadratic one, the cospecialization of action and observation admitted of a further interpretation: each member of the team is informed of the first-order effect of his action (as in (4.3) of Chapter 6.)

In the more general case, this latter implication need not apply. Nor need we limit the sets of messages received and sent by the ith element to those now denoted by B_{0i} (observations) and B_{i0} (final actions). For we can look, more generally, to important cases in which a given set of messages sent is most conveniently (i.e., most cheaply) combined with a certain set of messages received.

4. Subordination, Coordination, Delegation

Pure networks such as those presented in Chapter 8 are *implemented* if their elements, or groups of elements, are associated with *instruments*: men, machines, or collections of men and/or machines. One can interpret some properties of implemented networks in terms of the more conventional language applied to human organizations. To be sure, having dealt with teams only, we shall not be able to accommodate those aspects that arise out of conflicts of interest among members. On the other hand, it is obvious that a very great variety of pure and implemented team networks can be constructed. The resulting logical possibilities may prove much richer than those aspects that the conventional language tries to capture.

Any attempt to exactly match conventional terms with the logically possible relations would be artificial, if not impossible. Nor would this be very useful.

The "serial" and the "parallel" aspects of the pure networks illustrated in Chapter 8 might seem to match, respectively, the aspects of "subordination" and "coordination." We have, in fact, used the term *commands* in Examples 8B and 8C, when a simple arrangement in series was discussed. The element associated with a *commander* computes the action (assumed two-dimensional for the sake of later discussion). Whether or not it is economical to associate the next element in the series, the one performing the action, with a separate instrument called *subordinate* will clearly depend on the nature and cost of available instruments, as we have just explained in the preceding section on specialization.

It is easy to replace the (final) action (a_1, a_2), as in Examples 8B and 8C, by messages that the subordinate sends to elements further along the line, and similarly to replace the observation (μ_1, μ_2) of nature, by messages received from other elements of the network. That is, we can make full use of our general *task* concept and regard a scheme such as Figure 8.5 as a subnetwork. It will be understood that the optimal solution (for the function γ, in this case) would have to be obtained, ideally, for all subnetworks simultaneously; although, in practice, successive iterations part-by-part may be dictated by computational economy (see below, Section 7). Again, the cost and availability of instruments will determine how best to implement the subnetwork.

Note, however, that a serial arrangement may involve the transmission, not of a command but of something usually called *report*: the first element in the series (or subseries) may transform his information by merely condensing, translating, or manipulating it in some manner other than transforming it into a task for another element to perform. Again, the available instruments may or may not be such as to make the specialization of a *reporter* economically advantageous.

In Example 8E, the serial arrangement was enriched, in that command was replaced by *partial command* or *delegation*. This may be implemented in a network in which only some aspects of the subordinate's action are prescribed by the commander; he decides himself on other aspects in the light of all his information—which includes the command as well as the messages that he, but possibly not the commander, has received. The Chief of Staff may determine a general direction of troop movements, but the detail of individual routes is left for others to be determined subsequently. The delegation case (and its variants in Example 8F) is indeed more realistic than that of complete command. The lowliest subordinate, even one's horse or a simple automaton, is left a margin of decision to exploit information that is more easily available to the subordinate than to the boss, and to relieve the latter's tasks from trivia. Again, such a division of tasks is advantageous only given the nature and cost of available instruments.

The arrangement of network elements in parallel may be called for by advantages of specialization and simultaneous, rather than sequential, performance of certain tasks. This arrangement may, in turn, call for *coordination*. Thus in Example 8D, the action variables (or, more generally, tasks) are allocated to two different elements, numbered 3 and 5; we may associate them with two different instruments. The gross expected payoff is improved, compared with the case of *no coordinator* (Example 8A). This improvement may or may not be large enough to make coordination worthwhile.

Note, however, that, instead of having a coordinator, one might introduce partial exchange of communications between the two action-performing instruments suggested by those examples: for example, communication only from time to time (standing conference), as the need arises (*ad hoc* conferences), or only about some aspects of nature or of performed action. Some of these arrangements were treated in Chapter 6.

Thus, we see again that the variety of logical possibilities, and their actually observed counterparts, is richer than that covered by a few conventional terms such as "subordination," "authority," "responsibility," and "coordination."

5. Organizing as a Decision Problem

In preceding chapters, an *organizer* was faced with the problem of finding a network that would yield the highest net expected payoff—net, that is, of the costs of observation, communication, and computation incurred in the various parts (elements) of the network. No cost was charged to the activities of the organizer himself. He was a benevolent outsider. Alternatively, we can say that his activities were assumed to be, in effect, effortless, his problem-solving powers unlimited. In the present chapter, we shall try to dispose of this fictitious figure, the godlike organizer. More precisely, we shall retain the idea that the problem of optimal network is to be solved by someone, a person or a group of persons. But none of these will be assumed to have unlimited ability to solve problems as complex as that of determining a network, optimal relative to the goals usually associated with human organizations.

We retain our normative rather than descriptive approach, as stated in Chapter 1. In subsequent chapters we studied, in particular, the decision functions that maximize the gross expected payoff, given the information structure. We were thus able to compare the values of various information structures. In doing so, we neglected the costs of the network, apart from a few illustrative remarks on costs, made occasionally to keep the reader's perspective straight. Only in Sections 1 to 4 of the present chapter have we introduced the network costs in a more systematic fashion, to extend our normative study to the maximization of the net expected payoff of an implemented network. At that point, we took into account the limitations of its instruments (human beings, machines) in performing their activities, and hence the costs of such activities, in a going network set up by an all-wise organizer. We did not take into account the limitations of the organizer himself. In the present and subsequent sections, we do just this.

The organizer's problem clearly belongs to a special class: it is the problem of how best to solve a given problem. It also belongs to the class of big, or complex, problems. These two properties of the task of organizing can be discussed separately. Being a big problem, it may call for "delegation" and other devices discussed for big tasks in general. Being a problem of how to solve a problem, the organizing task faces us with a peculiar difficulty, which we shall discuss in the next section, and which we shall label "uncertainty about the outcome and cost of logical operations." In Sections 7 to 11, we shall take up the devices designed to meet the complexity of the organizing task. Section 12 and 13 relate this task to the concept of *leadership*.

6. UNCERTAINTY ABOUT THE OUTCOME AND COST OF LOGICAL OPERATIONS

This difficulty is encountered even in single-person problems. A person is given a task that he may perform more or less well, depending on the effort spent. More precisely, he has to choose an action that will maximize the expected utility of the outcome, account being taken of the cost of effort. For contrast's sake, suppose first the task is a physical one, and a simple one at that: chopping wood or carrying water. The conceptual scheme of Chapters 1 and 2 applies. A consistent person assigns a (net) utility to each combination of effort and outcome, and assigns a subjective probability to each of the possible effort-outcome pairs associated with a given method of accomplishing the task. He chooses the method with the highest (net) expected utility. In the special case in which net utility can be represented as the difference between the utility of outcome (payoff) and disutility of effort, or cost (Chapter 2, Section 12), the consistent person weighs the expected (gross) utility of outcome against the expected disutility of effort. Here, as usual, subjective probabilities will reflect the person's past experience, combined with any beliefs he had before acquiring experience (Chapter 1, Sections 9 to 10; Chapter 2, Sections 9 to 11).

But suppose the task is to compute the square root $\sqrt{x}$ of a positive number x. At how many digits shall the person stop if he wants to avoid the penalty of large errors and large exertions, measured according to his scale of utilities? In a case like this, it would first seem doubtful whether subjective probabilities could be applied.

The rules of logic and mathematics together with the postulates of consistent behavior imply that a consistent person acts as if he assigned probabilities to states of nature. This implies assigning probabilities to the outcomes of each action. But the same rules of logic and mathematics imply that, if the action is a logico-mathematical operation, the outcome is unique. A consistent man is a perfect logician and mathematician! His subjective probabilities are: 1, for the true outcome of a logico-mathematical operation; 0, for all its other outcomes. Thus he knows the error incurred by stopping the computation of $\sqrt{x}$ after a given number of digits, even before he starts computations. Or, pushing this thought further: a consistent man knows at once all the answers to logico-mathematical problems. The problem of how best to solve a problem does not arise.

It would seem, then, that the balancing of expected disutility of effort against expected utility of outcome, before deciding upon an action, does not apply when the task is logico-mathematical. If the decision-maker is not consistent, he has no utilities and subjective probabilities, and hence no expected utilities, to begin with. If he is consistent, his subjective probabilities of outcomes of logico-mathematical operations are 1 or 0.

And yet it is true that mathematicians do adorn their writing with phrases like "this conjecture is more probable than that one." They seem to imply willingness to take a bet, as if mathematical truth were a random event. (See one of our examples in Chapter 1, Section 10.) Is there a contradiction?

The question is of importance to us. The organizing problem as we have formulated it is indeed, at least in part, of a logical or mathematical nature. The organizer is to find whether it is worth his effort to make a more or less exhausting and exact computation of the net payoffs of various networks, on the basis of more complete or less complete information. The usual answer is that he "uses judgment," and this would be easy to interpret in terms of subjective probabilities, except for the difficulty that bars subjective probabilities from being applied to logico-mathematical problems.

Let us return to our simple example,[1] of the person trying to approximate $\sqrt{x}$. Let $0 < x < 1$, and denote by a (action) the number of digits to the right of the decimal point of the computed number. Let $f(x, a)$ be the computed number. Then the absolute value of the error is

$$|\sqrt{x} - f(x, a)| \equiv g(x, a),$$

say. For simplicity, assume the disutility of error to be equal to its size, and let the disutility of the effort (or time spent) in computing a digits be $\kappa(a)$, an increasing function of a. Then the payoff (in utils) is the following function of nature (represented by the number x) and action (represented by the positive integer a):

$$\omega(x, a) = -g(x, a) - \kappa(a).$$

We might make the problem more complicated by assuming x uncertain and having its subjective probability distribution; we would have to find an optimal decision rule $\hat{a}(x)$ instead of an optimal constant integer $\hat{a}$, say. The rule $\hat{a}$ would minimize the expected disutility of any future computation of square roots. Our difficulty is present, however, even when x is known. We cannot find an optimal value $\hat{a}$ of a in advance of computing $f(x, a)$ for various values of a.

For a given value of a, consider the particular function g defined above as being drawn at random from the set of all functions sharing those properties of g known to the problem-solver (for example, he knows that g is nonnegative and continuous in x). We can represent the error as $g(x, a, \theta)$, where θ is a random index characterizing a particular element of that set of functions. In other words, we redefine *nature* by adding θ to the list of random variables outside of the decision-maker's control. A state of nature is now defined, not as x, but as the pair (x, θ). In our particular case, it is usual (perhaps most sparing of further effort) to assume that $g(x, a, \theta)$, for x and a given, is uniformly distributed over the interval $[0, 10^{-a}]$. Then the conditional expected utility is

$$E[\omega(x, a, \theta)|(x, a)] = -(1/2) \cdot 10^{-a} - \kappa(a);$$

from this, the optimal value of a is computable. *We have, in effect, ignored some information about the function $f(x, a)$.* That information was accessible to us (for any a, however large) only at a cost, $\kappa(a)$. Instead, we used information about the (subjective) distribution of states of nature, nature being redefined to include the random parameter θ of the function g. By neglecting information (about the function f), the decision-maker about to

1. We are indebted to L. J. Savage for discussions of this subject.

perform a logical operation puts himself in the position of someone acting in the physical, uncertain world.

In a more general case, the cost function κ is not known; instead, a subjective probability distribution over a set of such functions is used.

To the extent that the organizer's problem is a logico-mathematical one, his "judgment" in cutting the organizing problem to a size that is feasible and not too expensive is, we believe, similar to that of a person's deciding to limit his computations to a certain number of digits. Like such a computer, the organizer is well advised to neglect his knowledge of some of the characteristics of his problem and to treat them instead as if they presented just another aspect (another dimension, or random variable) of the uncertain physical world. This aspect is described by subjective probabilities of payoffs and costs, which reflect his past experience, if any, in dealing with somewhat similar problems.

It should be emphasized that the approach just outlined is like a "rule of thumb," and is not guaranteed to be free from logical difficulties and inconsistencies. (Many of the remarks in this chapter are offered in the same spirit.) We are not aware of any systematic development of a theory of rational behavior under uncertainty about the outcome of logical operations, comparable to the theory of utility and subjective probability presented in Chapter 1.

7. Postponing Problem-Solving

Having extended the concept of *nature* (*world, environment*) in a manner that permits one to treat uncertainty about the outcome of logical operations on a par with uncertainty about physical nature, we can discuss the common device of postponing the solution of the problem we called "organizing," or, for that matter, of any "problem of how to solve a problem." The man trying to compute $\sqrt{x}$ approximately may find it preferable not to determine the number of digits (his action, a) in advance. Instead, he may decide that he will add more and more digits until he is satisfied that any further increase in the degree of approximation will not pay the additional effort. That is, he decides in advance on a strategy to be followed: on a succession of operations (each depending on previous outcomes) and a rule when to stop the operations. This "stopping rule" problem[2] is analogous to the decisions in the "dynamic case," treated in some detail in Chapter 7, where nature was not yet defined in the broader sense we have now introduced. It may pay to postpone action until more information is collected on some aspects of the environment, provided

---

2. See R. Radner 1964 for a discussion of stopping rule problems.

that the advantage of added information is not offset by the disadvantage due to the variability of other aspects of the environment. The latter may make the delayed action less than optimal (obsolete), although it would have been optimal if taken earlier. These considerations can be extended to the case in which some of the aspects of the environment are the uncertain outcomes of logical operations.

In particular, our organizer's action is to propose a network. He is uncertain about the costs of working out any such proposal. His judgment about the probabilities of those costs may recommend to him a strategy: start with some initial proposal, improve it step by step, each step depending on the results of the previous one, until further improvement of the network (the increment of its net value, not counting the cost of organizing) is not worth the additional effort.

8. "Earn While You Learn"

It may pay for the team to accept and put into effect the interim results of the organizer's activities, and to change the network later, following his later results. This is not possible with recommendations involving commitments of long duration, such as plant construction or long term contracts. But in many cases, you can indeed "earn while you learn."

Consider, for example, a complicated inventory problem, with many stages of production or transportation, many warehouses, and a great variety of storable items. There is uncertainty about the actual usage for any item at any time (*nature* in the original physical sense of Chapter 1). But there is also uncertainty about how long it will take, and what qualified personnel will be needed, to work out a tolerably good, or a very good, or an almost perfect, inventory policy. An inventory policy is a response rule in the sense of Chapter 8 and will need a network to be implemented. The subjective probabilities, to the organizer, may be such that, on the average, it is best to start by putting into effect a merely tolerable policy, the one worked out most quickly, yet giving some chances of profit. As time goes on, not only will the sample of usages increase in size, improving the estimate of their probability distribution, but also the logical problem dealing with the mathematical structure of the optimal policy will be closer to its solution. For both reasons, the policy will be revised and thus improved. But in the meantime some profits, though not maximal profits, will be collected. (Similar considerations will also apply, for example, to a portfolio policy, with investments earning while the response function is being improved.)

The network elements themselves—for example, the various jobs needed to implement a certain policy for a multibranch inventory—may have to be created, redefined, abolished, within the limits imposed by fixed plant, equipment, and long term contracts, in the process of a gradual solution of the organizing problem. A solution that would be perfect if the organizing effort were costless need not be approached, but a solution taking account of the organizing effort may be closely approached while the team's activities are going on.

This may have been the actual pattern of development of many efficient organizations. They have changed in time not only because they respond to a changing physical environment, but also because they had proceeded with operations while their organizing problem was being solved step by step, and an interim solution put into effect at each step. For in many cases, not to do anything is not the best choice. While the organizer postpones the complete solution of his problem (and may possibly never get to it), he may recommend to the team to go ahead and act on the basis of his incomplete solution, pending its improvement.

9. Reorganizing

Typically, the organizer does not "start from scratch." Rather, his problem is one of modifying some existing network, or the existing plan of a network, possibly a tradition. For, on the average, it may be costly (require too much effort of this particular organizer) to look for a network that is not, in some sense, proximate to a known one. The network values achieved are, in this sense, local rather than global maxima. An organizer who can, with moderate effort, consider the whole set of networks that are available and achieve a breakthrough, away from tradition and toward a more nearly global maximum, is a rare occurrence; hence, in a market economy, he is costly. (This is perhaps the essence of the current economic theory of entrepreneurial profit.)

10. Delegation of Organizing Activities

Earlier in this chapter, we discussed the costs associated with intermediate actions: observations, computations, and communications. The same results can be applied to the activity we consider now: that of organizing. We shall presently see that, in fact, many of the intermediate activities, especially those we described as computation, but some observations and communications as well, do characterize the organizing effort.

The costs of organizing may be such as to make it economical to split the organizing task among several people. The situation is not different, in principle, from that which calls for splitting any large task, whether manual or mental, among people; this was discussed in Sections 3 and 4.

The persons among whom the task of organizing is split constitute a team, for their activities are directed toward the same goal. This goal is to choose from the set of available networks one that will maximize the net expected payoff of the team that is being organized, taking into account the cost of organizing. We may, but need not, think of the organizing team as physically distinct from the team that is being organized. For expository purposes, we have, so far, represented them as distinct. Such a separation is, in fact, almost realized when a firm is being set up or reorganized following recommendations of a team of management consultants, or in the case of a Constituent Assembly, or when the statutes of some future government agency are being set up on paper. More usual is the case in which the network is being determined by the efforts of some of the same people who will participate in its current operations, once a network is constructed or modified. As stated in Sections 7 and 8, such a network may be a provisional one, the complete solution of the organizing problem having been postponed. Some organizing work is going on within the team while current operations have already started, using a temporary network that is being constantly changed. Thus some team members constantly contribute to improving the solution of the network problem.

This applies to many, perhaps the majority, of team members. Simple application of a prescribed rule, a task function, by each member is probably an exception rather than a rule, at least in our own culture (as distinct from the more traditional ones). Some activities of a bank teller, a ticket vendor, the worker on the assembly line, may be of such a nature. In the earlier parts of the book, for purposes of simpler exposition, we regarded such cases as typical. We now have to introduce the fact—which, very likely, is justified economically—that the task functions, rather than being prescribed by some outside organizer, are often determined by team members themselves, especially by those more remote from the level of final actions. Thus individual team members contribute to the solution of the network problem for the team. How these contributions are fitted together to yield the solution of the total problem, is an important question. Some of the discussion, in the present and the preceding chapters, of the case of a going network will apply, *mutatis mutandis*, to the case in which the network itself is being set up or revised.

The postponement of organizing, as described in Section 7 of this chapter, can be formally regarded as a case of delegation if we consider the same person at successive points of time as a sequence of several members of the organizing team, connected by one-way communication lines, directed from the present to the future (see Chapter 7). We have seen that postponement may make the organizing problem easier to solve, by reducing uncertainty about the outcome of logical operations. We can now add another reason for postponement: if the capacity of a person (or team) to solve a problem in one week is limited, or such quick achievement is only possible at a higher rate of effort, or at the price of larger errors, it may pay to extend the process of solution, by the same person (or team) over several weeks, by delegating it to his future self.

11. RESOLVING INCONSISTENCIES

On the face of it, actions of any two members of a team can be mutually inconsistent. Yet, strictly speaking, only organizing activities can be inconsistent; and we may be able to point to some modes of resolving such inconsistencies.

Two of a firm's truck drivers ($i = 1, 2$) come to its warehouse from two different departments of the firm, each driver being instructed to haul away a certain amount, a_i, of the same commodity. Suppose that

$$a_1 + a_2 > x,$$

where x is the stock available in the warehouse. The above inequality is inconsistent with the physical limitation

$$0 \leq a_1 + a_2 \leq x.$$

The apparent contradiction is resolved by distinguishing, as we do, between messages and final actions. Denote by b_i the amount that the driver i is *told* (by his department head) to haul away, as distinct from a_i, the amount he *does* haul away. Our situation is properly described, without any contradictions, thus:

$$0 \leq a_1 + a_2 \leq x < b_1 + b_2,$$

which implies, of course, that $a_i < b_i$ for at least one i. The decision rule for truck driver i will *not* be: $a_i = b_i$. (In fact, such a rule might prove physically nonfeasible even in the case of a single driver, when it should be: $a_i = \min(b_i, x)$, to provide for the case that the order exceeds the available stock.) In our case of two drivers, the rule may be

$$a_i = \min[b_i, xb_i/(b_1 + b_2)];$$

so that the stock, if it falls short of the sum of two orders, is allocated in proportion to each order. Such a decision rule implies, of course, that the information sent to i is *not*: $y_i = b_i$ but is, for example,

$$y_i = \begin{cases} (b_i) & \text{if } b_1 + b_2 \leq x \\ (b_1, b_2) & \text{otherwise.} \end{cases}$$

The same information structure can be combined with different decision rules, for example "first come first served"; or "driver 1 always has priority."

But note that, to realize the information structure just described, it may be convenient to insert a special third element into the network. For example, a warehouse clerk may receive messages b_1, b_2 from two departments and transform them into messages y_1, y_2 (as defined above) to the two drivers. The rule that "nobody should obey two leaders" (the "hierarchical" principle) may have, among its various meanings, this somewhat trivial one: inconsistencies between messages received by two elements of a network can be avoided if a third element has the task of resolving such inconsistencies, using some fixed rule.

A further device is a *court of appeal*. A certain network element is designated to be the receiver of messages about any inconsistency of messages. In response to this information, he produces a decision, a *ruling* that, unlike the standing rules stated above, varies from case to case. It resolves the inconsistency by determining what action (which may itself consist in sending a message) should be taken by the original receiver of the inconsistent messages.

With the help of standing rules and of rulings, every team member can find how to respond to any information, whether it does or does not contain inconsistent messages. If it does, its receiver will apply a standing rule of resolving such inconsistencies, or he will ask the court of appeal for a ruling. His decision (task) function must include the possibility of making such an appeal.

Since physical laws cannot be violated, some such devices as standing rules, rulings, hierarchy, even if not foreseen on paper, must in fact be used in any team. It is the job of the organizer—whether a single person or an organizing team—to make them as efficient as possible (e.g., by avoiding unnecessary costs or delays). The organizing team can also try to apply the same devices in the accomplishment of its own task. Thus the hierarchical principle, standing rules, and a court of appeal may be essential to any team in its capacity of the team organizing itself. Note, in particular, that the device of postponing the problem solution can be regarded as constituting a court of appeal in the shape of some organizing team member in some future period.

12. Leadership in Teams

It is convenient for our purposes and, we believe, agrees with ordinary language, to think of a leader as one who sets the *goal* and induces others to move toward it by following a *way* determined by the leader. In the special case of teams as distinct from general organizations, the goal is common to both leader and followers. It is the highest possible expected utility, computed on the basis of utilities (tastes) and personal probabilities (beliefs) common to the leader and all other members of the team. If tastes and beliefs were not the same for all, the leader would have to look for (optimal) *incentives*. These are conditions—promises of rewards and threats of punishment—with the following property: if each member tries to maximize *his* expected utility subject to those conditions, then the expected utility as viewed by the leader reaches as high a level as can be achieved, given the tastes and beliefs of the membership. The question of incentives did not arise in this book because we limited our purpose to the study of teams. A unique *goal* was assumed as given. But the question of *ways*, to be determined by the leader, remains. Every implemented network, that is, every possible allocation of tasks among men and machines, is one possible way to achieve the goal. Optimal task allocation has been, in fact, the subject matter of the present Part Two of the book. It has given rise to a rich variety of nontrivial problems, even though all the complications that might be due to conflicting goals were avoided. We feel that the proposed methods of stating and solving task allocation problems in the simple case of teams will retain their usefulness, or at least provide insight, in the more general case. In our Epilogue, we shall try to define optimal allocation of tasks as a subject matter of general organization theory, with the optimality (or goal) concept appropriately revised.

If the leader's function in a team is to determine the allocation of tasks, he is identical with the organizer, and all the preceding sections of this chapter apply. In particular, the activity of organizing must be regarded, in general, as a continuing one. To be sure, the device of routine may be worth applying to some aspects (coordinates) of the members' action variables: it may be convenient to determine their values (e.g., the office hours) once and for all. But, taken in its full meaning, as the complete predetermination of the members' actions, routine is of course a trivial case: a limiting case that we have set up mainly for its propaedeutic value. The routine solution, taken literally, almost never pays off, and is therefore seldom used. In large and complex organizations, the same tends to hold (as already emphasized in this chapter) for the somewhat more general case in which the actions are permitted to vary in response to varying information, but the decision rules (or, more generally, the task functions) are predetermined in advance.

Moreover, its very complexity, compared with the capacities of available men, calls for splitting up and delegating leadership activities. And, as is true of specialization in general (Section 3 of this chapter), specialization of one or several persons on leadership tasks only, may or may not increase the team's net expected payoff. It may or may not be desirable that the same person or persons fulfill the organizing tasks as well as other tasks of observation, computation, and communication. This will depend on the nature and costs of available men and machines.

In a different terminology, one might define leadership in teams, not by the content of its tasks—viz., the organizing task—but by the formal position in the network. But, a given position in a network (e.g., within some arrangement "in series" or "in parallel") may not preclude the task in question from being rather trivial, compared with the dignity and difficulty associated, in most minds, with leadership. We agree with people who have given serious thought to the matter[3] and who feel more comfortable with a language in which leadership tasks are in some sense *creative*. Such is the task of organizing, involving as it does the process of solving complex problems. This task remains difficult and creative when, in extending leadership from teams to general organizations, the problem of determining ways is extended to that of inducing goals.

3. We refer to our discussions with Leo Hurwicz and Herbert A. Simon, in particular.

PART THREE
EPILOGUE: OPTIMALITY AND
VIABILITY IN A GENERAL MODEL
OF ORGANIZATION

CHAPTER 10

Epilogue: Optimality and Viability in a General Model of Organization

1. INTRODUCTION

Let us now take a last look at the several-person decision problem, going beyond the special assumptions that characterize the team. As compared with the single-person decision problem, the general several-person problem has a number of new elements:

1. Individual members of the organization may differ with respect to possibilities of action, with respect to their information, and with respect to their preferences. Within the expected utility framework, we may distinguish, with regard to preferences, differences in beliefs about events from differences in preferences among (sure) consequences.
2. The multi-person character introduces the possibility of uncertainty about other members' actions as well as about the state of nature.
3. Differences among individuals with respect to preferences lead to a new problem of definition of optimality, both for the organization as a whole and for members of the organization.

In this chapter, we sketch a formal model for the several-person decision problem and discuss alternative concepts of optimality. It will be seen that there is no generally accepted criterion of optimality, and likewise no generally accepted way to characterize mutual uncertainty about individual behavior. These two points are clearly related. The concept of optimality will be replaced by a concept of *viability*, but it appears that, in order to make such a concept quite precise in any given several-person decision problem, it is necessary to have information about the particular possibilities of communication among the decision-makers during the process of organizing and about their anticipations regarding each other's behavior.

2. FORMAL STRUCTURE OF THE SEVERAL-PERSON DECISION PROBLEM

The description of the several-person decision problem that we give here is based upon, and is an extension of, the network model of the team given in Chapter 8. Let

> X be the set of alternative *states* of the environment,
> R be the set of alternative *outcomes* to the organization, and
> A be the set of alternative *acts* available to the organization; every act **a** is a function from X to R.

Acts are generated by *strategies*. Let β_i be a strategy of individual i ($i = 1, \ldots, n$), and let $\beta = (\beta_1, \ldots, \beta_n)$ be a joint strategy for the organization. In a way to be described below, every joint strategy determines an act for the organization; that is, if $\mathscr{B}$ is the set of available joint organization strategies, then there is a function, say $\mathbf{F}$, from $\mathscr{B}$ onto A.

Every member i is assumed to have a preference ordering, say $\precsim_i$ on the set A of available organization acts. It should be emphasized that the outcomes refer to the organization as a whole, so that an individual might be interested only in some aspect of a given outcome (e.g., his own consumption, as a component of an n-tuple of consumptions).

The generation of acts by strategies is assumed to take place by means of a system of observation, communication, computation and decision. Imagine that there is a sequence of elementary dates $t = 1, \ldots, T$ at which these activities take place, and let

> B_{ijt} = the set of alternative messages from i to j at date t,
> B_{0jt} = the set of alternative observations of the environment by j at date t (messages from the environment to j);
> B_{i0t} = the set of alternative decisions by i at date t (messages from t to the environment);
> β_{jt} = a function from

$$\underset{i=0}{\overset{n}{\times}} B_{i,j,t-1} \qquad \text{to} \qquad \underset{k=0}{\overset{n}{\times}} B_{jkt},$$

> $\beta_j = (\beta_{j1}, \ldots, \beta_{jT})$, a *strategy* for j.

A message sent at date t is to be thought of as being received at date $(t + 1)$. Messages that take more than one elementary time unit from sending to receipt may be thought of as passing through a sequence of "dummy" organization members (stations on a communication link). A message sent by an individual to himself is interpreted as *remembering*.

For a given joint strategy, β, every state x of the environment determines an array $((b_{i0t}))$ of decisions, called a joint decision. Every joint decision, together with a state of the environment, determines an outcome. Thus every β determines, indirectly, an act. Denote this mapping of strategies into acts by $\mathbf{F}$.

The *normal form* of the n-person decision problem is determined by

$$\mathscr{B}, A;$$

$$\mathbf{F}:\mathscr{B} \to A;$$

$$(\underset{1}{\precsim}, \ldots, \underset{n}{\precsim}).$$

The *extensive form* includes, in addition to the above, the descriptions of X, R, and the sets B_{ijt}, and the function that transforms (state-of-the-environment, joint decision) pairs into outcomes (the outcome function of Chapter 1).

If all of the preference orderings, $\underset{i}{\precsim}$, are identical, then we have the special case of a *team*. In this case, there is no ambiguity about the appropriate concept of optimality. Nevertheless, as we have seen, the relation between strategies and acts is in general more complicated than in the single-person case, and we have to deal with the phenomena of interaction, coordination, communication, and so forth.

The general situation is usually called a *game*.

In the theory of games, each member i is usually assumed to have preferences that can be scaled in terms of utility and subjective probability (as in Chapter 1). In this case, to each joint strategy $\beta = (\beta_1, \ldots, \beta_n)$ is associated a vector of expected utilities, say

$$\Omega(\beta) = [\Omega_1(\beta), \ldots, \Omega_n(\beta)],$$

where $\Omega_i(\beta)$ is the *expected* utility for member i of the distribution of outcomes determined by $\mathbf{F}(\beta)$ and his own subjective probability distribution. The *normal form* can then be compactly characterized by the set $\mathscr{B}$ of joint strategies, and the "payoff function" Ω.

3. Optimality, Equilibrium, Viability

If the n preference orderings, $\underset{i}{\precsim}$, are not identical, then one cannot order acts from the point of view of the organization in a way that does not contradict at least one of the individual orderings. Further, one cannot expect to find an act that is maximal for all individual orderings simultaneously.

From the point of view of any given (nonempty) subset I of the set N of members of the organization, one can at least define a *partial* ordering of acts, say $\precsim_I$, that does not conflict with the preferences of any individual in I, as follows:[1]

$\mathbf{a}' \precsim_I \mathbf{a}$ means that for every i in I, $\mathbf{a}' \precsim_i \mathbf{a}$. (In particular, $\precsim_{\{i\}}$ is identical to the complete ordering $\precsim_i$.) We shall also have occasion to use the following notation:

$$\mathbf{a}' \underset{I}{\sim} \mathbf{a} \text{ means that for every } i \text{ in } I, \mathbf{a}' \underset{i}{\sim} \mathbf{a};$$
$$\mathbf{a}' \underset{I}{\prec} \mathbf{a} \text{ (or equivalently } \mathbf{a} \underset{I}{\succ} \mathbf{a}') \text{ means that } \mathbf{a}' \underset{I}{\precsim} \mathbf{a} \text{ but not } \mathbf{a}' \underset{I}{\sim} \mathbf{a}.$$

Since every joint strategy in $\mathscr{B}$ determines an act, the several preference orderings of acts induce corresponding orderings of strategies, which we shall indicate by the same symbols $\precsim_i$, $\precsim_I$, and so forth.

Special interest attaches to $\precsim_N$. If an act is maximal with respect to $\precsim_N$, then no other act is strictly better from the point of view of some individual, without at the same time being strictly worse from the point of view of another individual (in other words, "a is maximal with respect to $\precsim_N$" means that there is no $\mathbf{a}'$ such that $\mathbf{a}' \underset{N}{\succ} \mathbf{a}$). Such a maximal act is often called *Pareto-optimal*. There will, of course, typically be many Pareto-optimal acts—if there are any at all—and two such acts will typically not be equivalent from the point of view of any one individual.

In view of the difficulty of defining *optimality* for the organization as a whole in terms of a single ordering of acts, attempts have been made to substitute some concept of *equilibrium* or *viability*. Roughly speaking, an act is an equilibrium if no one of some specified class of groups of individuals would have both the desire and the ability to change the act by means of a change in their own joint choice of strategies.

When contemplating a change in its joint strategy, a group of individuals should consider whether or not such a change would induce further changes by others. Two different concepts of equilibrium or viability have been studied, differing according to whether such further changes are, or are not taken account of.

By a *coalition* is meant a nonempty set of individuals (a nonempty subset of N). We shall say that a joint strategy β in $\mathscr{B}$ can be *upset* by a coalition I

1. Although this notation is not strictly unambiguous, it will always be clear from the context whether $\precsim$ refers to an individual or a group.

if, roughly speaking, the coalition can change β into a joint strategy that it prefers by changing only strategies of its own members. Formally, for any (joint) strategy β in $\mathcal{B}$ define $\mathcal{B}^I(\beta)$ to be the set of joint strategies that can be obtained by changing the individual strategies of members of the coalition I, that is, $\mathcal{B}^I(\beta)$ is the set of all β' in $\mathcal{B}$ such that

$$\beta'_j = \beta_j \text{ for } j \text{ not in } I.$$

A strategy β can be *upset* by a coalition I if there is a strategy β' in $\mathcal{B}^I(\beta)$ such that

(10.1) $$\beta' \underset{I}{\succ} \beta.$$

In particular, to say that β cannot be upset by N is equivalent to saying that β is Pareto-optimal. A joint strategy that cannot be upset by any one-member coalition is called a *Nash-equilibrium*; one that cannot be upset by *any* coalition is called a *strong equilibrium* (see Aumann 1967).

The definition of upsetting suggests, if only implicitly, the possibility of some kind of agreement among the members of the coalition: otherwise the achievement of a preferred coalition strategy would appear to be left to chance. This, in turn, would seem to require the existence of some means of communication among individuals, which are to be used in the process of choosing a joint strategy but are not explicitly described already in the specification of the message sets B_{ijt}.

Suppose that, during this (hypothetical) process of choosing a joint strategy, a particular strategy, say β, is under consideration, and suppose further that β can be upset by a coalition I', by a change to a strategy β'. It may be that β' itself can be upset by a coalition I'', by a change to a third strategy, say β'', such that

$$\beta'' \underset{i}{\succ} \beta$$

for one or more members i of I'. In this case, the process of *upsetting* could lead to an actual worsening of the positions of one or more members of the coalition I' that started the process. Hence, if such further upsetting is anticipated, the members of any coalition would be well advised to adopt a more conservative attitude toward a proposed change of joint strategy.

One such conservative attitude is expressed by the concept of *blocking*. We shall say that an act **a** can be *blocked* by a coalition I if the coalition I can guarantee itself something better, that is, if there is a joint strategy for the coalition such that, whatever the strategies adopted by the other members of the organization, the resulting act will be preferred to **a** by the coalition I. Formally, **a** can be blocked by I if there are individual strategies $\hat{\beta}_i$, i in I, such that any strategy β in $\mathcal{B}$ for which

$$\beta_i = \hat{\beta}_i, \ i \text{ in } I,$$

has the property,

(10.2) $\mathbf{F}(\beta) \underset{I}{\succ} \mathbf{a}.$

Let $\mathscr{I}$ be any collection of coalitions I. An act $\mathbf{a}$ will be called *viable with respect to $\mathscr{I}$* if there is no coalition in $\mathscr{I}$ that can block $\mathbf{a}$. Three special cases invite particular attention:

Case 1. $\mathscr{I}_1 \equiv \{N\}$. This is equivalent to the definition of Pareto-optimality.

Case 2. $\mathscr{I}_2 \equiv$ the collection of all one-member coalitions. This corresponds, in the case of blocking, to the Nash-equilibrium in the case of upsetting.

Case 3. $\mathscr{I}_3 \equiv$ the collection of all possible coalitions. The set of all acts that are viable with respect to $\mathscr{I}_3$ is called the *core*.

From the point of view of overall organizational efficiency, Pareto-optimality is a minimal requirement. On the other hand, no member of the organization can be expected to accept an act that can be blocked by him alone; hence viability with respect to $\mathscr{I}_2$ would also appear to be a minimal requirement. Unfortunately, these two requirements are not always mutually consistent.

An act in the core has the *strongest possible viability* against blocking, and in particular is Pareto-optimal. Hence the core, if it is not empty, seems to offer a good solution to the problem of optimal organizational decision.

In the definitions of upsetting and blocking given above, it might be objected that not all members of I necessarily have a positive incentive to adopt the *preferred* coalition strategy, since the definitions do not exclude the possibilities that, for some i in I, in (10.1)

$$\beta' \underset{i}{\sim} \beta,$$

or in (10.2)

$$\mathbf{F}(\beta) \underset{i}{\sim} \mathbf{a}.$$

Hence we might wish to consider the stricter group preference relation:

$$\mathbf{a}' \underset{I}{\gg} \mathbf{a} \text{ means that for every } i \text{ in } I, \mathbf{a}' \underset{i}{\succ} \mathbf{a}$$

(to be read "I strictly prefers $\mathbf{a}'$ to $\mathbf{a}$).

Correspondingly, we could define *strictly upset and strictly blocked* by replacing $\underset{I}{\succ}$ by $\underset{I}{\gg}$ in (10.1) and (10.2).

The definitions of upsetting and blocking implicitly express certain assumptions about anticipations on the part of one coalition, concerning whether or not further changes of joint strategy are to be made by other organization members. It has also been pointed out that the concept of a coalition strategy implies the existence of some communication among prospective coalition members. One can easily imagine that quite complicated assumptions about anticipations, and about the possibilities of coalition formation, might be appropriate for a given organizational context. Pursuing this train of thought would lead us away from the search for a simple and universal characterization of *rationality* in organizational behavior, and toward a proliferation of special theories with a large element of descriptive detail. At the present stage of development of the formal theory of organization, we must perhaps be satisfied with our more limited direction of research.[2]

---

2. For discussions of various solution concepts for n-person games see Nash 1951, Shapley 1953, Aumann and Maschler 1964, Harsanyi 1963, and 1966, and Aumann 1967.

References

Abelson, R. P., and M. J. Rosenberg. 1958. Symbolic psycho-logic: a model of attitudinal cognition. *Behavioral Science* 3:1–13.

Arrow, K. J. 1951. Alternative approaches to the theory of choice in risk-taking situations. *Econometrica* 19:404–37. Reprinted in Arrow 1971.

Arrow, K. J. 1953. Le rôle des valeurs boursières pour la répartition la meilleure des risques. *Econométrie*, pp. 41–48, Centre National de la Recherche Scientifique, Paris. Or see the translation: The role of securities in the optimal allocation of risk bearing. *Review of Economic Studies*, 1964, 31:91–96.

Arrow, K. J. 1963. *Social Choice and Individual Values*, 2d ed. Cowles Commission Monograph No. 12, Wiley, New York.

Arrow, K. J. 1971. *Essays in the Theory of Risk-Bearing*. Markham, Chicago.

Arrow, K. J., L. Hurwicz, and H. Uzawa. 1958. *Studies in Linear and Non-Linear Programming*. Stanford University Press, Stanford, Calif.

Arrow, K. J., S. Karlin, and H. Scarf. 1958. *Studies in the Mathematical Theory of Inventory and Production*. Stanford University Press, Stanford, Calif.

Aumann, R. J. 1967. A survey of cooperative games without side payments. In M. Shubik, ed. *Essays in Mathematical Economics, in Honor of Oskar Morgenstern.* Princeton University Press, Princeton, N.J.

Aumann, R. J. and M. Maschler 1964. The bargaining set for cooperative games. In M. Dresher, L. S. Shapley, and A. W. Tucker, eds. *Advances in Game Theory.* Princeton University Press, Princeton, N.J.

Bayes, Thomas. 1763. An essay towards solving a problem in the doctrine of chances. *The Philosophical Transactions* 53:370–418. Reprinted in *Biometrika*, 1958, 45:296–315.

Beckmann, M. J. 1958. Decision and team problems in airline reservations. *Econometrica* 26:134–45.

Bellman, R. 1961. *Adaptive Control Processes: A Guided Tour*. Princeton University Press, Princeton, N.J.

Blackwell, D. 1953. Equivalent comparisons of experiments. *Annals of Mathematical Statistics.* 24:265–72.

Blackwell, D., and M. A. Girshick. 1954. *Theory of Games and Statistical Decisions.* Wiley, New York.

Bruner, J. S., J. J. Goodnow, and G. A. Austin. 1956. *A Study of Thinking*. Wiley, New York.

Carnap, R. 1962. The aim of inductive logic. In E. Nagel, P. Suppes, and A. Tarski, eds. *Logic, Methodology and Philosophy of Science.* Stanford University Press, Stanford, Calif.

Cox, D. R., and W. L. Smith. 1961. *Queues.* Methuen Monograph, Wiley, New York.

Cyert, R. M., and J. G. March. 1963. *A Behavioral Theory of the Firm.* Prentice-Hall, Englewood Cliffs, N. J.

Dantzig, G. B. 1963. *Linear Programming and Extensions*, 2d printing with corrections, 1965. Princeton University Press, Princeton, N.J.

Debreu, G. 1959. *Theory of Value.* Cowles Foundation Monograph 17, Wiley, New York.

Debreu, G. 1960. Topological methods in cardinal utility. In K. J. Arrow, S. Karlin, and P. Suppes, eds. *Mathematical Methods in the Social Sciences.* Stanford Univsity Press, Stanford, Calif.

de Finetti, B. 1937. La prévision: ses lois logiques, ses sources subjectives. *Annales de l'Institut Henri Poincaré* 7:1–68. Or see the translation, Foresight: its logical laws, its subjective sources. In H. E. Kyburg, Jr., and H. E. Smokler, eds. *Studies in Subjective Probability*, 1964, Wiley, New York.

de Finetti, B. 1968. Probability: interpretations. *International Encyclopedia of the Social Sciences* 12:496–505. Crowell Collier and MacMillan, New York.

Drèze, J. 1960. Les probabilités "subjectives" ont-elles une signification objective? *Économie appliquée* 13:55–70.

Drèze, J. 1961. Fondements logiques de la probabilité subjective et de l'utilité. In *La Décision*, Colloques Internationaux de 1959, Centre National de la Recherche Scientifique, Paris.

Edwards, W., and A. Tversky, eds. 1967. *Decision Making: Selected Readings.* Penguin Books, Harmondsworth, England.

Feller, W. 1968. *An Introduction to Probability Theory and Its Applications*, Vol. 1, 3d ed., Wiley, New York.

Fishburn, P. C. 1968. Utility theory. *Management Science* 14:335–78.

Fishburn, P. C. 1970. *Utility Theory for Decision-Making.* Wiley, New York.

Fisher, C. 1962. Linear programming under uncertainty in an l_∞ space. *Office of Naval Research Technical Report* No. 7, Center for Research in Management Science, University of California, Berkeley.

Friedman, M., and L. J. Savage. 1948. The utility analysis of choices involving risk. *Journal of Political Economy* 56:279–304.

Good, I. J. 1952. Rational decisions. *Journal of the Royal Statistical Society* B-14:107–14.

Groves, T. L. 1970. Towards a theory of incentives in a team. *Workshop Series* 7010, Social Systems Research Institute, University of Wisconsin (mimeographed).

Halmos, P. 1950. *Measure Theory.* Van Nostrand, Princeton, N.J.

Halmos, P. 1958. *Finite-Dimensional Vector Spaces*, 2d ed. Van Nostrand, Princeton, N.J.

Harsanyi, J. C. 1963. A simplified bargaining model for the *n*-person cooperative game. *International Economic Review* 4:194–220.

Harsanyi, J. C. 1966. A general theory of rational behavior in game situations. *Econometrica* 34:613–34.

Herstein, I. N., and J. Milnor. 1953. An axiomatic approach to measurable utility. *Econometrica* 21:291–97.

Hicks, J. R. 1946. *Value and Capital*, 2d ed. Clarendon Press, Oxford.

Hitch, C. 1953. Sub-optimization in operations problems. *Operations Research* 1:87–99.

Knight, F. H. 1921. *Risk, Uncertainty, and Profit.* Houghton Mifflin, New York. Reissued 1964 by Kelley, New York.

Koopmans, T. C., ed. 1951. *Activity Analysis of Production and Allocation.* Cowles Foundation Monograph No. 13, Wiley, New York.

Koopmans, T. C. 1960. Stationary ordinal utility and impatience. *Econometrica* 28:287–309.

Luce, R. D. 1959. *Individual Choice Behavior: A Theoretical Analysis.* Wiley, New York.

Luce, R. D., and P. Suppes. 1965. Preference, utility, and subjective probability. In R. D. Luce, R. R. Bush, and E. Galanter, eds. *Handbook of Mathematical Psychology,* Vol. 3. Wiley, New York.

McCarthy, J. 1956. Measures of the value of information. *Proceedings of the National Academy of Sciences* 42:654–55.

McGuire, C. B. 1961. Some team models of a sales organization. *Management Science* 7:101–30.

March, J. G., and H. A. Simon, with the collaboration of H. Guetzkow. 1958. *Organizations.* Wiley, New York.

Markowitz, H. M. 1959. *Portfolio Selection.* Cowles Foundation Monograph No. 16, Wiley, New York.

Marschak, J. 1950. Rational behavior, uncertain prospects, and measurable utility. *Econometrica* 18:111–41.

Marschak, J. 1954. Towards an economic theory of organization and information. In R. M. Thrall, C. H. Coombs, and R. L. Davis, eds. *Decision Processes.* Wiley, New York.

Marschak, J. 1959. Efficient and viable organizational forms. In M. Haire, ed. *Modern Organization Theory.* Wiley, New York.

Marschak, J. 1960. Binary-choice constraints and random utility indicators. In K. J. Arrow, S. Karlin, and P. Suppes, eds. *Mathematical Methods in the Social Sciences.* Stanford University Press, Stanford, Calif.

Marschak, J. 1963. The payoff-relevant description of states and acts. *Econometrica* 31:719–25.

Marschak, J. 1968. Decision-making: economic aspects. *International Encyclopedia of the Social Sciences,* 4, 42–55. Crowell Collier and MacMillan, New York.

Marschak, J. 1970. The economic man's logic. M. Scott, W. Eltis, and J. N. Wolfe, eds. *Induction, Growth and Trade,* Clarendon Press, Oxford.

Marschak, J. 1971. Economics of information systems. *Journal of American Statistical Association* (forthcoming).

Marschak, J., and K. Miyasawa. 1968. Economic comparability of information systems. *International Economic Review* 9:137–74.

Marschak, T. A. 1959. Centralization and decentralization in economic organizations. *Econometrica* 27:399–430.

Marschak, T. A. 1968. Computation in organizations: comparison of price mechanisms and other adjustment processes. In K. Borch and J. Mossin, eds. *Risk and Uncertainty.* St. Martin's Press, New York.

Mood, A. M., and F. A. Graybill. 1963. *Introduction to the Theory of Statistics,* 2d ed. McGraw-Hill, New York.

Nash, J. F. 1951. Non-cooperative games. *Annals of Mathematics* 54:286–95.

Neyman, J., and E. S. Pearson. 1967. *Joint Statistical Papers* (collected papers originally published between 1928 and 1938). University of California Press, Berkeley.

Pratt, J. W. 1964. Risk aversion in the small and in the large. *Econometrica* 32:122–36.

Radner, R. 1959. The application of linear programming to team decision problems. *Management Science* 5:143–50.

Radner, R. 1962. Team decision problems. *Annals of Mathematical Statistics* 33:857–81.

Radner, R. 1964. Mathematical specifications of goals for decision problems. In M. W. Shelly and G. L. Bryan, eds. *Human Judgments and Optimality.* Wiley, New York.

Radner, R., 1968. Competitive equilibrium under uncertainty. *Econometrica,* 36:31–58.

Raiffa, H. 1968. *Decision Analysis: Introductory Lectures on Choices under Uncertainty.* Addison Wesley, Reading, Mass.

Ramsey, F. P. 1931. *The Foundations of Mathematics and Other Logical Essays.* Routledge and Kegan Paul, London. Also reprinted by Humanities Press, 1950, New York. The relevant essays were written in 1926 and 1928.

Robinson, E. A. 1959. *An Introduction to Infinitely Many Variates.* Griffin's Statistical Monographs and Courses, No. 6, ed. by M. A. Kendall, New York.

Savage, L. J. 1954. *The Foundations of Statistics.* Wiley, New York.

Shannon, C. E., and W. Weaver. 1949. *The Mathematical Theory of Communication.* University of Illinois Press, Urbana.

Shapley, L. S. 1953. A value for n-person games. In H. W. Kuhn and A. W. Tucker, eds. *Contributions to the Theory of Games,* Vol. 2, Princeton University Press, Princeton, N.J.

Simon, H. A. 1956. Dynamic programming under uncertainty with a quadratic criterion function. *Econometrica* 24:74–81.

Strotz, R., and H. Wold. 1960. A triptych on causal systems. *Econometrica* 28:417–63.

Theil, H. 1957. A note on certainty equivalence in dynamic planning. *Econometrica* 25:346–49.

von Neumann, J., and O. Morgenstern. 1943. *Theory of Games and Economic Behavior.* Princeton University Press, Princeton, N.J. (3d ed., 1953.)

Wald, A. 1950. *Statistical Decision Functions.* Wiley, New York.

Winkler, R. 1967. The assessment of prior distributions in Bayesian analysis. *Journal of the American Statistical Association* 62:776–800.

Index

Abelson, R. P., 11*n*, 334
Accuracy, 305. *See also* Error; Garbling
Act, 13–14, 328, 332. *See also* Anticipating
Action, 9; final *vs.* intermediate, 5, 231, 237, 299, 306; conceivable *vs.* feasible, 15, 91; constant, 20; with two outcomes, 33–37; bench-mark, 35–36; associated with prospect, 39; expected payoff of, 43–44; as sequence, 67, 295; real-valued, 98, 126, 157, 183; of team, 127, 267, 271; vector-valued, 157, 239, 247; inconsistency in team, 321. *See also* Act; Cospecialization; Decision; Preference
—obsolete, 318. *See also* Delay
—rule of. *See* Decision function
Adjustment: person-by-person, 156; of instruction error, 201–02, 288
Alternatives: ordering of, 10; independence of irrelevant, 10*n*
Anticipating other members' acts, 327, 333
Appeal, court of, 322
Arrow, K. J., 10*n*, 33*n*, 41*n*, 42, 177, 178*n*, 180, 334
Aumann, R. J., 331, 333*n*, 334
Austin, G. A., 11*n*, 334
Authority, 313

Bayes, Thomas, 33, 59, 62–63, 69, 80, 334
Beckmann, M., vii, 124, 334
Behavior. *See* Consistent
Beliefs, vii, 5; in teams, 123; in general organizations, 327. *See also* Independence; Probability, subjective
Bellman, R., 4, 334
Bench-mark. *See* Action; Event
Bets: as actions, 3, 16; preference, indifference between, 22–23, 32
Bewley, T., vii
Blackwell, D., 65–66, 271*n*, 334
Blocking. *See* Strategy
"Boss," 290. *See also* Command
Bratton, D., vii

Brownian motion, 238–39, 243–50, 257–58; special, 250, 264
Bruner, J. S., 11*n*, 334

Capacity: human, 4; as maximum output, 99, 106, 133*n*, 172; of network instrument, 305; of organizer, 321
Carnap, R., 3, 334
Caution, 148
Central agency, 187, 198, 201, 287–88
Centralization, 130–39 passim, 146–51, 161–66 passim, 193. *See also* Decentralization
Certainty, 71, 111; -equivalent, 112, 237, 240–42
Channel. *See* Communication
Chebyshev's inequality, 77
Choice, 3, 10; probability of, 11
Coalition, 330–31
Coarse, 61, 305. *See also* Fineness
Command, 281, 288–90; partial *vs.* complete, 284, 288, 312
Commodity, divisible, 9
Communication, 4, 5, 187, 267; beneficial in case of interaction, 101; one-way, two-way, 131; no, 187, 193–94; complete, 189–90, 205; partitioned, 196; in organizing, 327; within coalition, 331–32
—noiseless, noisy, 129, 283, 289, 297. *See also* Error; Garbling
Complementarity, 101, 113*n*, 148, 189*n*. *See also* Interaction; Substitutability
Compromise between decisions, 112
Computation, 187; delay, 236; as transformation, 267; as task in network, 288
Concave. *See* Payoff function; Risk aversion
Conference, 131; emergency, 217–23; standing *vs. ad hoc*, 313
Consequence(s), 12; ordering of, 327. *See also* Outcome(s)
Consistent (rational) behavior, 10, 33, 41, 45, 333

339

Cowles Foundation Monographs

Orders for Monograph 8 should be sent to Principia Press of Trinity University, 715 Stadium Drive, San Antonio, Texas.

Orders for Monograph 3 should be sent to the Cowles Foundation, Box 2125 Yale Station, New Haven, Conn. 06520.

Orders for Monographs 12, 13, 14, 16, 17, 21, and 22 should be sent to Yale University Press, 92A Yale Station, New Haven, Conn. 06520.

Orders for Monographs 15, 18, 19, and 20 should be sent to John Wiley & Sons, Inc., 605 Third Avenue, New York, N.Y. 10016.